The Constitutional Conduct Group (CCG) is a group of former civil servants of the All India Services who have, over the course of their career, been a part of both Union and State Governments. They are passionate about the many tenets of the Indian Constitution and believe in the impartiality, neutrality and sanctity of it. The CCG was formed in 2017 and currently has 176 members.

IN DEFENCE OF THE REPUBLIC

Upholding the Values at the Heart of India's Democracy

CONSTITUTIONAL CONDUCT GROUP

Edited by Deb Mukharji, Meena Gupta, Amitabha Pande and Sundar Burra

SPEAKING TIGER

SPEAKING TIGER BOOKS LLP
125A, Ground Floor, Shahpur Jat,
Near Asiad Village, New Delhi—110 049

First published by Speaking Tiger Books in 2024

ISBN: 978-93-5447-763-8

10 9 8 7 6 5 4 3 2 1

Typeset in Adobe Devanagari by Jojy Philip, New Delhi
Printed at Impressions Printing & Packaging Limited

Contents

ELECTION AND VOTING

FUNDAMENTAL RIGHTS AND FREEDOM OF SPEECH

Foreword

This is an unusual compendium, emanating as it does from a group of persons professionally trained both to be knowledgeable and discreet.

Throughout human history, groups of persons agreeing to live together found it necessary to have a point of governance to whose authority they submitted. Thus was created the institution of governance, variously named, and the body of individuals subscribing to its authority. The professed objective of both is fair play and justice as per known rules and procedures. Both are required to be trained in objectives and procedures.

Kautilya needed an advisor or councillor to be 'intelligent, persevering, dexterous, eloquent, energetic, bold, brave, able to endure adversities and firm in loyalty.' A modern-day selection board would readily endorse these and add discretion as an essential requirement given today's norms and ease of communications. Each signatory would have qualified these tests over a lifetime.

For all these reasons the disclaimer in the letter of 27 August 2022 is strongly worded: 'We have no affiliation with any political party and are, instead, committed to the values enshrined in the Constitution and the judicial process that is protected by it.' It is suggestive of an uncommon experience, an outrage, and wishes to convey it to the highest points of appeal politically and constitutionally. It ends with an eloquent and specific plea for a corrective.

One must hope the plea would be heeded.

—M. Hamid Ansari
Vice President of India (2007-2017)

Introduction

Since we came together in the summer of 2017, many questions have been raised about who we are as a group, what we represent, what were our objectives in coming together and why we write the letters that we do, what we expect to achieve and so on.

While some of us may have strong political convictions or leanings or sympathies, none of us is formally or informally associated with any party or any party affiliates. Talking of 'us' as a group is itself a little problematic because we are not set up as an organisation, as a society or an NGO or an association. It is not even a Facebook group or a web platform—the Constitutional Conduct Group is nothing more than a mailing group. We come from very diverse social and economic backgrounds, different age groups and different regions of the country. Only a few of us have worked together in the past, and while we are familiar with each other by reputation, many of us have never met each other. Our views on many public policy issues are very different, with some leaning towards state interventionism, especially in favour of the poor and marginalised sections, and some who have a more libertarian, anti-statist approach. On economic issues, differences of opinion are often stark.

Yet, despite our varied backgrounds and differences, in our perspectives we happened to come together because some of us thought that having served a major part of our lives in public service, it was important for us to collectively reflect on current developments in public affairs and catalyse a debate on these issues. We believed that our combined experience gave us insights which could make a qualitative contribution to this debate and that this was a useful way of engaging ourselves with public affairs as concerned and informed citizens. We found the environment becoming increasingly oppressive and felt that we had a duty to our conscience and the nation to speak up. Given the very eclectic character of the group, we felt it best to avoid giving it a formal organisational shape. Most of our interactions are through a group email identity called the 'Constitutional Conduct'.

Our early letter on the Kathua and Unnao rape cases had attracted considerable media attention. It is important to clarify that this letter was not just about rape or sexual crime or the vulnerability of women and children or the weaknesses in our criminal justice system. It was not just about the administration of law and order which we as former administrators well know is a State subject. It was not just about the crimes themselves, heinous and horrifying as they were. It was about the pathology of hate and division pursued by the present ruling establishment and the manner in which the body politic has been infected by them, leading to a culture of impunity. It is about the collapse of the values on which our Constitution is based, about the systematic destruction of institutions, about the climate of fear and intimidation and the propagation of a virulent form of hyper nationalism, especially a nationalism identified with a singular religious and cultural identity. In a similar vein, most of our letters even when focused on a particular event are, collectively a window on the larger malaise that prevails.

Our initial focus was on the agenda of hate and division that was being insidiously introduced by the ruling establishment into our political processes, our institutions and even our daily discourse. We could see how this was rapidly eroding the values on which our Republic is based. Over the past six years the CCG has highlighted egregious acts of omission and commission by the establishment covering diverse fields, the issues ranging from, and including, the politics of communal hate, corruption and misgovernance, protection of human rights and freedom of speech, the role of the media, failures of the legal system, electoral reform, conservation and sustainable development, and the rights of marginalised and oppressed communities. During this period nine conclaves have also been held on topics of immediate interest. The CCG participated in a multidisciplinary series of discussions on electoral reform and produced a book encapsulating the conclusions. The Group appointed a citizen's committee comprising eminent personalities to look into the Northeast Delhi riots of February 2020, and their findings were published in *Uncertain Justice: A Citizens Committee Report on the North East Delhi Violence 2020*.

We felt that it would be appropriate at this stage to publish a compendium of the CCG letters over the past six years. This would be a ready handbook of reference on some of the major issues which have engaged the attention of the nation for individuals, libraries and scholars for both today as well as the future. We believe that these chronicles of dissent could encourage many others to speak up.

We have invited a number of eminent activists, advocates, academicians, journalists and jurists to comment on some of the issues addressed in the letters collected in this book, and we remain grateful for their contributions. We would also like to express our gratitude to Shri Mohammad Hamid Ansari, former Vice President of India, for his foreword to this volume.

We thank Speaking Tiger Books for the readiness of their response to the book proposal and for taking it forward.

—Constitutional Conduct Group
March 2024

COMMUNAL HATE AND VIOLENCE

When Existence Itself Becomes a Conspiracy

APOORVANAND

I had been evading writing this article as I did not know if there was anything about today's India that has not been said before. It is common knowledge that India is now a majoritarian and totalitarian state; that it has, in nearly all its aspects, become a country hostile to Muslims and also Christians; that the institutions meant to safeguard the Constitution have decided to serve the cause of the Hindutva majoritarian politics and ideology and that the media has become the main instigator of hatred and violence against Muslims and Christians… One could go on and on. All this has been said, written, again and again. We know it to be true. And yet, even those of us who will not lie about this truth force ourselves to call India a secular and civilised country. Calling it by its true name embarrasses us.

The reality is ugly. Yes, India remains a democracy as governments are still formed through a process which involves voting by the people, who still have the freedom to make their choice from the scores of political parties that can still operate in the field of political competition. Theoretically, eligible people from any religion can stand for elections. Theoretically, they can also hope to be elected to any office in the government. Yet, India's Muslims know it well that in practice, for any of them to aspire to represent the state as its head is an absurd thought. A Hindu can be the Prime Minister in the UK where Hindus are only 1.7 per cent of the population and where—it must also be underlined—they are either first or second generation citizens of that country. Yet they can aspire to become ministers and lead the country. But in India, Muslims, who are nearly 15 per cent of the population and have lived here more than 1,000 years, cannot imagine being elected as the head of any government. Neither in the states, nor at the Centre. They cannot think of being given any important portfolio in the governments. A Muslim home minister or finance minister or education minister is unthinkable in India.

This disenfranchisement of Muslims is complete. In fact, Hindus are asked not to vote for the Congress party as it can lead to a Muslim being installed as the chief minister. And what could be a more horrible thing to happen to Hindus? This is what the voters of Gujarat were told by the Bharatiya Janata Party in 2017 during the assembly elections. The BJP leaders told their electorate that Ahmed Patel would become chief minister if the Congress Party was voted to power, and that this was the secret plan hatched by the Congress and the Pakistani Army. Similarly, the Assam Hindu electorate were warned that a non-BJP coalition winning the election would mean Badruddin Ajmal becoming the chief minister of the state.

Jammu and Kashmir was one state where Muslims headed the governments; where their political voice mattered. That had to be ended. That is why the state was degraded, broken into union territories. A delimitation exercise has also been done with an objective of turning Muslims into a marginal electoral force in the state. Other measures have also been taken to change the demography of Jammu, Kashmir and Ladakh which would decisively change the character of the former state.

Muslims know it and have accepted it as their fate in a 'secular' country like India. The BJP, ruling at the centre for the last 10 years and which heads or is part of the governments in 16 states, does not care if its governments do not have Muslim ministers or MLAs or MPs. It brazenly declares that it does not want their votes either. Himanta Biswa Sarma, the second-time chief minister of Assam and one of the star campaigners of the BJP, recently mocked Muslims by saying that he would welcome them as his voters only after they have reformed themselves and got rid of their backward practices. Until then, they should not entertain any hopes of him asking for their votes.

In democracies, political parties want all sections to vote for them so that the majority they form is representative of the society. They also make efforts to form their ministries in such a manner that they reflect the diversity of the society. Great care is taken to give place to all castes, even to those which have a minuscule presence. But the BJP makes it very clear to the Muslims that it is isolating them. It also tells Hindus by this act that Muslims are effectively out of the business of democracy and the majority is defined by Hindus alone.

Other political parties have been intimidated into silence. They want Muslim votes but expect the community to 'understand' their reluctance to be seen to be appealing to the community for votes or even addressing its concerns. They do not project any Muslim leader as their face and do not talk about any 'Muslim' issue in their manifestos or election speeches.

Thus, Muslims have been reduced to the status of second-class citizens. They can vote but they should never dream of representing the larger society they live in.

The absence of Muslims from the forums and processes of law-making makes it easier to pass anti-Muslim laws like the CAA which creates a path to attain Indian citizenship from which only Muslims are barred, and laws criminalising Triple Talaq or religious conversion or the union of Muslim men with Hindu women or cow slaughter. A government without Muslim representation can ban the selling of eggs and meat in the open in the name of maintaining hygiene, prohibit non-vegetarian food, including eggs, from the menu of midday meals in schools—even in a place like Lakshadweep where Muslims, a vast majority of whom are traditionally non-vegetarian, are more than 99 per cent of the population. De-recognition of Madrasas or taking over their control in the name of secularising or modernising them, neglecting and supressing Urdu, reducing or doing away with the schemes and scholarships aimed at encouraging Muslims to join higher education are other ways of marginalising Muslims in different spheres of life.

We have seen open threats being issued by the CM of Assam to Muslims that the land they own would be taken away as they are not indigenous. He has also prescribed restrictions on the selling and eating of meat within 5 km of Hindu religious places. He openly calls for boycotting Muslim traders by calling them outsiders and asks 'locals' not to buy from and trade with them. Recently he launched a fresh assault on Muslims by saying that they are illegal as their papers are forged and they would not be able to live in the state under the cover of these 'fake' papers any longer.

The humiliation of Muslims has become part of the social and political culture of India. One can see it on display even in the highest bodies like the Parliament. A member of Parliament from the ruling BJP openly abused a Muslim MP on the floor of the house. No action was taken against him. After all, Muslims must see that their leaders can be humiliated and insulted.

Add to all this the violence the Muslims face in their daily lives. They are assaulted not only by organised forces affiliated to the Rashtriya Swayamsevak Sangh (RSS), like the Bajrang Dal and the Vishwa Hindu Parishad, but also by random goons or members of organisations not directly connected to the RSS but which espouse the ideology of Hindutva. Decentralisation of violence against Muslims is a development of recent years. Even individuals feel empowered to attack Muslims and also Christians. They know that they will be protected by the lawmakers and agencies tasked with maintaining law and order. 'Lynching' has now become part of the lexicon of nearly all Indian languages. Muslims can be assaulted, can be killed by mobs on any pretext. Sometimes it is the suspicion of them carrying or keeping beef, or smuggling cows, or slaughtering cows, or refusing to chant 'Jai Shri Ram', a gentle greeting of the devout which the Hindutva gang has appropriated and corrupted, turning it into a Hindu supremacist slogan.

Hindu religious occasions are routinely used to intimidate and humiliate Muslims. Hindutva groups use these occasions to forcibly take out their 'religious' processions through Muslim dominated areas, raising provocative slogans and playing songs on their DJ systems which are full of abuses for Muslims or call for violence against them.

Muslims cannot protest. If they do, they have to pay a very heavy price. After the enactment of the CAA, which has been called discriminatory against Muslims by jurists the world over, Muslims took to the streets in Uttar Pradesh. Twenty-one of them were killed and the state refused even to acknowledge it. The CM of the state threatened that he would take revenge on the protesters. Hundreds were arrested. The state alleged that the protesters had destroyed public property and hence they would have to pay damages. Recovery notices were sent to scores of Muslims and banners with their names, address and photographs were put up across Lucknow.

Elsewhere in the country, young Muslim activists like Umar Khalid, Sharjeel Imam, Khalid Saifi, Gulfisha Fatima and others were put in jail for having dared to protest. They are facing serious charges under the dreaded anti-terror law, the UAPA. For making peaceful speeches in defence of citizens' fundamental rights, they have been languishing in jail for more than three years. The courts, which should uphold the right of citizens to protest peacefully and protect them from persecution, have repeatedly rejected their bail pleas. Other young students who joined protests asking for the repeal of the CAA are sent threats by the police.

The State has devised another novel way to attack Muslims. Bulldozers are being used rampantly by government authorities to demolish the houses and business establishments of Muslims across India. Courts refrain from intervening to stop this State vigilantism—or, to call it by its proper name, State terror. Bulldozers are now proudly displayed in the political rallies of the BJP. Even Hindu diaspora groups in the USA march with bulldozers to celebrate and encourage the violent subjugation of Muslims in India.

Big media aids this project of communal governments and their Hindutva family through an industrial-scale campaign of defamation and demonisation. It is not only defamation but an active hate campaign against Muslims, which has now become the main feature of the Indian public sphere. The most recent survey by the TRT says that 85 per cent of the anti-Muslim posts originate from India, USA and UK. India is far ahead of these countries in this hate drive against Muslims. After Israel launched its genocidal campaign against the Palestinian people in Gaza and the West Bank, the maximum number of anti-Palestinian posts supporting Israel originated from India. India has now become the main producer and exporter of anti-Muslim hatred.

During the COVID-19 pandemic, governments and the media in India launched a vicious hate campaign against Muslims by holding them responsible for spreading the virus. It led to physical attacks on Muslims and also their arrests. Their religious places were sealed, Muslim vegetable or fruit sellers were shunned.

And in normal times, the media keeps portraying Muslims as a threat to the Hindus and India. If they are born, it is demographic warfare to take over India, if they educate themselves and try to get to public positions, it is a conspiracy to infiltrate the state apparatus, if they fall in love with Hindus, it is a conspiracy to defile and destroy Hindu womanhood, if they buy land, it is a conspiracy to capture India. Everything Muslims do is suspicious.

The objective of this hate campaign is to alienate Hindus from Muslims. But it is also aimed at humiliating and shaming Muslims. An obscene social media campaign putting professional Muslim women on auction became very popular. It did not lead to any outrage in the political establishment or society. It is as if Muslims should gulp the filth hurled at them without any complaint.

Hate campaigns against Muslims enjoy the patronage of the police and administration. Open assemblies abusing Muslims and calling for their annihilation have become commonplace in India. The police are often indulgent towards individuals and groups that deliver such hate speeches and call for genocide. And the courts think that they do not pose a real threat to Muslims. In fact, a bench of the Delhi High Court opined that if such hate speech is made with a smile, it should not be treated as a crime. Courts also think that hate speech against a Muslim does not necessarily mean what it says, it is a tool to energise Hindus and mobilise them as voters and therefore should not be taken seriously.

Most Hindus, even so-called liberals, do not see this as clear proof that their co-religionists are bigoted, intolerant and temperamentally violent people. But Muslim voices are seen as necessarily sectarian and 'fundamentalist'. A Muslim is always 'kattar'; a Hindu can never be. Hardly any one seems to consider this hypocrisy outrageous and shameful.

Public spaces are being 'cleansed' of 'Muslimness'. Muslims offering Namaz in the most un-obstructive manner in schools, colleges or other public spaces have been attacked, penalised, even arrested. The Azan from mosques is sought to be criminalised and treated as a nuisance. Muslim women with Hijab are disallowed in educational institutions or other public places and even attacked physically.

In Delhi, Mazars of Sufi saints have been removed, in Uttarakhand, they are broken and demolished openly. Muslim sounding names of towns, cities, roads and localities are being replaced with 'Indian' names. Monuments bearing an Islamic stamp are sought to be 'Indianised'.

The Prime Minister and his party keep repeating that Muslims are intruders and Muslim rulers, including the Mughals and Tipu Sultan, were outsiders who had colonised India. School textbooks are being purged of Mughal presence. The Hindutva brigade wants to brainwash the young into believing that the Muslims have made no contribution to the life and culture of India.

In the realm of popular culture, Hindi cinema has taken a conscious anti-Muslim turn. Films are being produced with covert and not so covert themes which promote anti-Muslim sentiments. Muslims being portrayed as terrorists, murderers and anti-nationals is common.

A new genre of popular music is emerging in India which mocks, insults and humiliates Muslims. Such songs are played in nearly all

Hindu festivals and celebrations. Hindu religious celebrations now essentially involve demonisation of Muslims. This new anti-Muslim aesthetic is shaping the minds and sensibilities of Hindus.

Thus a culture is emerging in India which is defined by anti-Muslim hatred. Political power, the police and administration allow it to get entrenched and many a time they themselves play an active role in this. The courts ignore this agenda of bigotry and hate. Or they contribute to it by delivering judgements that have a seriously negative impact on the lives of India's Muslims. The instance of the site of Babri Masjid being given to the Hindu parties by the Supreme Court is a prime example of India's judiciary bowing to Hindu majoritarian sentiments. The top court agreed that the mosque was standing as a mosque for more than 500 years, that there was no proof that it was built on the ruins of a Hindu Temple, that there was no possibility of any proof that the mosque stood at the exact spot where the figure of Ram was born. The Court further accepted that in a criminal act some idols of Hindu deities were smuggled into the mosque in 1949, that the demolition of the mosque in 1992 was a criminal act as well. And yet, the site of the demolished mosque was given to those who had participated in these crimes! It was such a breathtaking exercise of judicial usurpation.

The top court has not stopped here. A local court in Varanasi allowed the Archaeological Survey of India (ASI) to conduct a 'scientific survey' of the Gyanvapi mosque in order to determine its alleged Hinduness. The 1991 law, passed by the Parliament, prohibiting any attempt which can lead to a change in the nature of a religious place (as it stood on 15 August 1947) was thus violated. Citing this law, the decision of the local court was challenged in the Supreme Court. The top court applied a convoluted logic to uphold the lower court's order: it ruled that the curiosity to know about the nature of any place can be entertained and satisfied as it does not lead to a change in the character of the place. It thus allowed the survey of the mosque, which in effect changed its status quo. Not only that, the top court sealed a portion of the mosque where a 'shivlinga' was allegedly found. This portion of the mosque is now out of bounds to Muslim devotees. So, the very act of survey has in fact changed the character of this religious place. The Supreme Court has thus created a new dispute which can lead to another violence like the Babri mosque demolition.

Encouraged by this decision of the Supreme Court, now attempts are being made to turn the Shahi Masjid of Mathura into a disputed site, and local courts seem complicit in this. We now see courts finding ways to undermine the Religious Places Act of 1991 and turn Muslim places of worship into 'disputed structures'.

So, Muslims cannot exist in India as distinct cultural entities. It is seen as contamination of Indianness. They cannot demand political representation. It is seen as divisive and communal. They cannot participate in the economic life of India. It is seen as a conspiracy to take over the country. They cannot love non-Muslims as it is again a design to pollute the pristine Hindu or Indian identity.

The very existence of Muslims has become a conspiracy.

I have not spoken about the violence that Christians are being subjected to in India. That would require whole new essay.

Politics of Communal Hate and Violence

ANJANA PRAKASH

'The ultimate weakness of violence is that it is a descending spiral, begetting the very thing it seeks to destroy. Instead of diminishing evil, it multiplies it. Through violence you may murder the liar, but you cannot murder the lie, nor establish the truth. Through violence you murder the hater, but you do not murder hate. In fact, violence merely increases hate...Returning violence for violence multiplies violence, adding deeper darkness to a night already devoid of stars. Darkness cannot drive out darkness; only light can do that. Hate cannot drive out hate; only love can do that.'

—Martin Luther King Jr

When we gave ourselves a written constitution after independence, we sincerely believed it was going to work for us. The Preamble encapsulated all that we had yearned for through the long years of our freedom struggle. The equality we strove for was finally ours to fashion; justice, which had eluded us, was in our hands; the ideal of a welfare state for *all*—which was the core of the freedom movement—was finally achievable. This was the enlightened vision guiding India's Constituent Assembly, and the expectation of the Constitution they gave us was both noble and legitimate. India as a modern democracy was the outcome of a general consensus arrived at without selfishness and without creating any 'other'. However, over seven decades after Independence, as the Indian State has chosen to recede behind a dark, opaque curtain to hold puppet shows, the original vision has been betrayed. The citizens can only look on in agony.

Although democracy's ideal is 'by the people, of the people, for the people', in reality, adult franchise allows one to participate in the process only during elections. Once one's candidate loses, one is completely shut out from the rule-making, rule-enforcing mechanism. Sadly, the winning party, after succeeding in establishing a government with an adequate number of candidates—even with an overall minority in the number of polls in its favour—assigns itself the role of the chief arbiter. In a first-past-the-post electoral system as we have in India, genuine democracy can thus survive only if the winning party—which forms the government—respects the vision and spirit of the Constitution, or if it is held in check by the judiciary and a number of other autonomous institutions. But when the government subverts the Constitution, and the institutions that should prevent this are compromised and weakened, all sorts of dehumanizing acts will be committed in the citizen's name, making a tragic mockery of our Constitutional democracy. The danger of this is greatest when the government actively pursues the project of majoritarianism. In India today, this has taken the form of the Hindus, who are 80 per cent of India's population, being manipulated and mobilized to keep the Hindu right wing in power in perpetuity.

The Bharatiya Janata Party (BJP), the political wing of the Hindutva family, mobilizes the Hindu majority by spreading lies to build resentment against Muslims and other minorities, and create an 'other'—an enemy figure to unite all Hindus in hatred. It is said that a lie told a hundred times does not make it the truth. But one must also admit that the same lie, repeated aggressively over and over again, effectively clogs the human brain and the truth is unable to reach it anymore. As a result, a vast majority of a State's citizens become clones of each other, mouthing similar views, cheering the same despicable characters, divorced from reality and inhabiting an imaginary world. Human beings stop behaving like humans—turning instead into robotic 'things' controlled by a manipulating group or individual. These 'things' are only capable of reactions on stimuli; their thoughts are such as no rational, kind or reasonable human being can have.

Meanwhile, the dispensation that controls these robotic citizens and leads them to commit violent acts, perpetuates the violence through inaction and biased application of the law, or by not enforcing the law at all and by rewarding the perpetrators of violence. Even when such official deviousness is blatantly exhibited, there is little that the public can do—because vast numbers have been brainwashed, and the rest are afraid.

~

One of the essential principles, and a common consensus, by which the young Indian Republic was able to overcome the bloody legacy of Partition was the firm choice made by the 'People of India' to not resort to violence, and to live and let live. At the time of Independence 'We, the People of India' had decided not to choose any religion as the official religion of the country. We chose to remain secular. Although at first Secularism was not expressly mentioned in the Constitution of India, it was a common understanding that fundamental features such as Secularism, Democracy and the Freedom of the Individual would always remain at the heart of our welfare state. With the passage of time, the need for the express mention of the word 'Secular' in the Constitution of India arose, and thus it was inserted in the Preamble to the Constitution through the 42nd Constitutional Amendment Act of 1976.

To see violence—gruesome killings and loot—to lose your friends and family every other day, to feel the animal urge to react likewise, and yet, to tell yourself, 'No, I'm better than this; I seek peace and prosperity for all, and it can only be achieved together'—this mighty strength of heart was behind the philosophy of Indian secularism that our founders placed at the heart of our Constitution even when the terrible self-inflicted wounds of Partition were still fresh. The 1976 Amendment re-iterated and strengthened this faith and pledge. And barring a few instances of mass violence, this philosophy had been observed, respected and even celebrated by the common Indian citizen. Today, however, the spirit of harmony is under siege.

Things have changed drastically in recent years. After 75 years of Independence, while the Central government announces the dawn of the *Amrit Kaal* (the Ambrosial Age), bigotry is rampant and there is widespread violence on the basis of religion and ethnicity in this country. There has been a massive surge in communal sentiment, which has coincided with the rise of the self-styled 'Hindu nationalist' BJP to power in the Centre in 2014, and subsequently in many other Indian states.

Since 2014, a push towards 'Ram Rajya'—which in the Hindutva philosophy is a synonym for a Hindu majoritarian State, or Hindu Rashtra—has incorporated the need to weed out those who may be deemed unfit to become the citizens of such a Rashtra. A report by *The London Story*, an online web portal deriving data from a vast network of independent journalists and news outlets, released a study of instances of communal violence across 331 cities in India between 2014 and 2020. A total of 1,137 cases were reported, which works out to around 190 cases per year, and over three cases per city. The report also indicated that the vast majority of these crimes occurred in the so-called 'Hindi belt' of the country—the northern and central plains where the BJP has a stronghold. The Muslim population as a percentage of the whole ranges from 7 per cent to 19 per cent in the states and union territories in this belt. And yet, the BJP, RSS, Bajrang Dal and other Hindutva outfits have managed to convince the majority of Hindus in the region of the Muslim 'threat'. They have been given the heady drug of hatred.

The theme for the 18th G20 Summit, successfully conducted in India in 2023, was '*Vasudhaiva Kutumbakam*'. It is a Sanskrit phrase which translates to mean that the entire world is one family. The ruling BJP and the Prime Minister spoke a great deal about the summit and its theme. And yet, the same party practises exactly the opposite of what it preaches. The leaders of this government may claim in international fora that to them all the world is their family, yet in their own country they spread communal hate against minorities.

Part of the plan is to polarize society along religious lines and keep things constantly on the boil. Even while Hindus are communalized and radicalized, the Muslims and other minorities are baited and provoked, in order to manufacture reasons, however flimsy, for majoritarian violence, followed by partisan police action in which only the minority communities would be targeted.

There are several recent incidents of communal violence in the country that illustrate this.

Violence in Nuh (Haryana)

On 31 July 2023, communal violence erupted in the Muslim-majority Nuh district of Haryana during the annual Brajmandal Dharmic Yatra of the Vishwa Hindu Parishad (VHP), a Hindutva organization. The clash between Hindus and Muslims of the district led to the deaths of six people, including two Home Guards. The attacks began when the procession, led by abusive Muslim baiters and men accused of killing Muslim men, was stopped in Nuh's Kheda Mod by a mob of local Muslims who pelted the yatris with stones.

In retaliation, the Haryana administration bulldozed over 1,200 homes and shops of Muslim residents of the area—without passing any demolition order and ignoring all the procedures and safeguards envisaged under the law of the land.

The Hon'ble Punjab and Haryana High Court took suo moto cognizance (*Court on its Own Motion v. State of Haryana [CWP-PIL-68-2023])* and halted the demolition drive.

Hate Crime in Palghar (Maharashtra)

A Railway Protection Force constable shot dead four people, including his senior colleague, on a running train near Palghar railway station in Maharashtra. The three passengers killed in the incident were from the Muslim community. The accused was heard ranting against Muslims. The murders were supported and justified by thousands of sympathisers on social media, who, as they did so, also posted slogans against Pakistan and in support of BJP leaders.

Hate and Slander in Parliament

In an unprecedented incident in the temple of the democracy—the Lok Sabha—a Muslim Member of Parliament (MP), Kunwar Danish Ali of the Bahujan Samaj Party (BSP) was called a '*bhadwa, katwa, Mullah aatankwadi*' (a circumcised pimp and Muslim terrorist) by Ramesh Biduri, an MP of the ruling BJP. No legal action was taken against Biduri either by the speaker of the Lok Sabha (himself a member of the BJP) or by the party itself. In fact, Biduri's outrageous conduct was defended and justified by one of his partymen, also an MP.

Violence in Jamshedpur (Jharkhand)

Communal violence erupted in the Shastri Nagar area of Jamshedpur on 8 April 2023 after a Ram Navami flag was allegedly found with pieces of meat on it, near a temple. According to the local residents, stones were also thrown at the temple during a temple-committee meeting. Later, heavy stone pelting took place from both sides.

The Jharkhand police arrested 55 people who were involved in inciting the riot, including a local BJP leader, Abhay Singh. But Singh and the other accused of the majority community, despite their history of hate speech and communal incitement, were soon granted bail. It was argued that bail was granted since none of the appellants had been apprehended at the scene of the violence, and the role of the accused and the other 'unknown persons' was too 'general and omnibus'. The court also added that it could not be ascertained who the aggressor was between the two communities.

Manipur Violence

In May 2023, violence broke out in the Churachandpur district of Manipur following a protest by the Christian Kuki tribal groups against the demands of the Hindu Meiteis to be given official tribal status as well. The Kukis were protesting that granting tribal status to the majority Meitei community would strengthen the influence of this powerful and socially, culturally and economically dominant community. This would allow them to purchase land in Kuki areas and settle there.

The violence that followed the Kuki protests and the Meitei retaliation led to the loss of more than 150 lives, and the displacement of around 50,000 people. About two months after the violence began, a video showing two women being paraded naked and subjected to sexual violence went viral on social media and in the press. There was national and international outrage, and it was only then that the Prime Minister of India made a feeble and qualified statement about the violence against women—after two months of silence—and the Supreme Court took cognizance of the same.

Subsequently, in the case of *Dinganglung Gangmei v. Mutum Churamani Meetei and Ors. (S.L.P. [Civil] Diary No. 19206/2023)*, a three-Judge bench, comprising the Chief Justice DY Chandrachud, Justice JB Pardiwala and Justice Manoj Mishra, issued clarifications and directions to ensure the welfare of the affected individuals and the restoration of stability in the region.

~

The situation today in the world's largest democracy appears grim. The frequency of localized communal violence is rising across India, and the cultural discourse that supports and even glorifies such violence is spreading through the streets and mohallas and in the hearts of the majority at an alarming rate. It seems to be taking us to a point of no return. The philosophy of equality, fraternity and secularism upon which our nation was founded has been obscured by a smog of hatred.

However, a refreshing breeze and some rain is all it takes for the smog to dissipate.

We, the people of India, need that breeze and rain.

In his *Postscript on the Societies of Control*, Gilles Deleuze has written, 'There is no need to fear or hope, but only to look for new weapons.' Despite precautions and preventive measures—our

Constitution being a shining example—the pestilence of hatred has survived and found new ways to grow. But, the battle is never lost. We need a fresh analysis in the context of the contemporary economic and social order, and devise newer strategies to safeguard our democracy and humanity in the present climate of hate. In this, the vision of our Constitution will be our strength and our guiding light.

Letters and Statements

OPEN STATEMENT: GROWING INFLUENCE OF RELIGION IN STATE AND SOCIETY

8 February 2024

As a group of former civil servants deeply committed to the Constitution of India and its morality, we issue this open statement to express our deep disquiet about the manner in which the Indian state was closely associated with the consecration ceremony of the Shri Ram Temple in Ayodhya on 22 January 2024.

Religion is a private matter according to India's constitutional arrangements. All persons, including public officials, are free to follow their religious beliefs. However, it is imperative for public officials to be mindful to carefully separate their religious beliefs and practices from their official duties. This is especially important for a person holding the high constitutional office of Prime Minister, as the leader not just of people of one religious identity but of all people of India of diverse religious beliefs.

This separation between personal religious belief and practice and official duties was breached on 22 January 2024 when, in the presence of the Prime Minister, the statue of Shri Ram was installed and consecrated in the Ram Temple in Ayodhya. The event brings to our mind the advice given by India's first Prime Minister Jawaharlal Nehru to President Rajendra Prasad at the inauguration of the reconstructed Somnath Temple in Gujarat at a juncture when the wounds of Partition were still healing in the subcontinent: 'This is not merely visiting a temple, which can certainly be done by you or anyone else, but rather participating in a significant function which unfortunately has some implications.'

In the present case, the consecration of the idol of Shri Ram was undertaken at a site where, while granting the right to construct the temple at the site, the Supreme Court had clearly observed in its judgment of 9 November 2019:

> 'The exclusion of the Muslims from worship and possession took place on the intervening night between 22/23 December 1949 when the mosque was desecrated by the installation of Hindu idols. The ouster of the Muslims on that occasion was not through any lawful authority but through an act which was calculated to deprive them of their place of worship. After the proceedings under Section 145 of CrPC 1898 were initiated and a receiver was appointed following the attachment of the inner courtyard, worship of the Hindu idols was permitted. During the pendency of the suits, the entire structure of the mosque was brought down in a calculated act of destroying a place of public worship. The Muslims have been wrongly deprived of a mosque which had been constructed well over 450 years ago.'

Despite its above observations, the Supreme Court permitted the construction of the temple by a trust set up under Section 6 of the Acquisition of Certain Area at Ayodhya Act 1993. Given the troubled history of the last three decades, it would have been in the fitness of things if the consecration of the temple had been undertaken by heads of the Hindu religious faith rather than by a constitutional functionary, which goes against the basic credo of secularism enshrined in the Preamble to the Constitution of India.

Of even greater concern to us are the developments in the last month before and after the consecration of the temple. In the Prime Minister's speech at Ayodhya on 22 January 2024, he affirmed that the Ram temple construction reflected Indian society's maturity. Further, he stated that the consecration was an occasion of not merely triumph but humility too. However, the incidents at Mira Road in

Maharashtra and some other places in the country have witnessed a wholly unnecessary show of triumphalism by certain elements from the Hindu community leading to reactions from elements from the Muslim community. At times like these, it behoves the majority community to show restraint and maintain dignity, especially when a fractious issue has finally reached resolution. On the contrary, the efforts over the past few days to raise fresh issues concerning the religious faith of the two communities—the Gyanvapi mosque at Varanasi, the Krishna Janmabhoomi at Mathura, the conduct of the Shahjahan Urs at the Taj Mahal and the Haji Malang dargah at Kalyan (Maharashtra)—are unnecessary irritants to social peace and harmony at a time when so many more important issues confront the nation. Nor have matters been helped by the unnecessary haste shown by the authorities in Delhi in demolishing the Mehrauli dargah and madrasa and raising the issue of the removal of the Sunehri Bagh Masjid in the heart of New Delhi ostensibly on grounds of streamlining traffic flow. Surely, government agencies should have a sense of propriety to know when to bring up contentious issues.

As a multicultural society which has absorbed people from so many other lands over millennia, it ill behoves us as a nation for its citizens to adopt a narrow, xenophobic approach towards those who have different religious beliefs or belong to other ethnic communities. India's status in the world since 1947 has been, to a considerable extent, founded on its ability to successfully run a country of so many diverse groups and faiths on democratic principles. It is the primary responsibility of the Union Government and the state governments to maintain an equal distance from all religions, inculcate in their citizens the principle of fraternity enjoined by the Preamble to the Constitution of India and apply strictly the rule of law in ensuring that all citizens conduct their day-to-day affairs as laid down by the Constitution of India and the laws thereunder.

SATYAMEVA JAYATE

Constitutional Conduct Group (65 signatories)

OPEN STATEMENT ON MANIPUR: MANIPUR NEEDS THE HEALING TOUCH

6 August 2023

The Constitutional Conduct Group, a group of former civil servants firmly committed to the Constitution of India, and not affiliated to any political party, notes with the greatest concern the total breakdown of the rule of law and constitutional values in the state of Manipur since early May 2023. What started as a protest by the Kuki-Zo community against the decision of the Manipur High Court, directing the state government to recommend to the Government of India the grant of Scheduled Tribe status to the majority Meitei community, has since snowballed into a dangerous, internecine ethnic conflict that threatens not just to tear apart the social fabric of Manipur but calls into question the very spirit of harmony and fraternity that is the foundation of India's 'unity in diversity'.

We wish to strongly highlight the dereliction of their fundamental duty by the Manipur state government and the state police in protecting the life and property of their citizens. This has created the conditions for a complete breakdown of law and order, with a deliberately orchestrated and targeted carnage that has included large scale arson, lynching, collective rape, vandalism, looting, mob violence and obstruction of central security forces from carrying out their duties, followed by armed attacks and retaliation by both communities.

These atrocities have taken place under a double-edged internet ban, lifted only partially on July 25, that has prevented their horror and scale from coming out earlier, while also providing grist to rumour-mongering and spread of fake news. This total failure of the state has allowed the raiding of police armouries by perpetrators of the violence, reportedly resulting in around 4,500 weapons of varying sophistication and an estimated 5 lakh rounds of ammunition being looted, which is continuing even to the present day. Such looting is unimaginable and without precedent anywhere in India.What lends credence to the charge of the Chief Minister, Mr. N. Biren Singh, being partisan in his approach to tackling the tragedy is his demonisation and targeting of one community as 'illegal migrants', 'poppy cultivators', 'encroachers', 'narco-terrorists' and 'terrorists'. These 'dog whistles', which tend to smear an entire community, have served to excite the passions of the majority community to which the Chief Minister belongs. A high constitutional functionary, like the Chief Minister, is expected to restore the rule of law and take steps to cool inflamed passions, rather than stoke them further. The failure to take strong action against militant organisations of the Meitei community, the Arambai Tenggol and the Meitei Leepun, which openly issue threats of 'annihilation' and 'blowing up' of the tribal Kuki-Zo minority, or the Coordinating Committee on Manipur Integrity (COCOMI), which advocates a 'Manipuri national war against Chin-Kuki narco-terrorism' and the arming of civilians, only seems to confirm fears about the partisan approach of the state administration; the same applies to the approach of the law enforcement authorities of Manipur state to the aggressive actions of the Meira Paibis,* which include their preventing the army from apprehending those engaged in violent activities.

What causes us even deeper anguish, as former civil servants who have dealt with surcharged law and order situations in the course of our careers, has been the largely passive role that the union government has played in this entire imbroglio. What was required at the very onset of the violence in May 2023 was the imposition of President's Rule, given the abject failure of the state government to function in accordance with the provisions of the Constitution. However, instead of invoking Article 356 of

---

* Meira Paibi (Women torch bearers) is a women's social movement in Manipur. Referred to as the 'guardians of civil society', it derives its name from the flaming torches which the women carry while marching through city streets, often at night. They do so both as a patrol, and in protest, seeking redress against human rights violations committed by paramilitary and armed forces units against the innocent.

the Constitution to impose President's Rule, a Security Adviser to the state and a new Director General of Police from the cadre of a neighbouring state were appointed, and a Unified Command constituted, all reporting to the Government of Manipur, headed by the Chief Minister.

Apart from the visit to Manipur by the Union Home Minister end May-early June 2023, when he met with different sections of society, there has been no active political involvement of the centre in establishing peace between the opposing communities.

The union government also lost a golden opportunity to involve the opposition parties in trying to arrive at a political solution to the problem. Political expediency has won out: we are witness to the spectacle of a non-functioning parliament at a time of crisis, with the Prime Minister making no statement in Parliament on the Manipur crisis, which would enable the initiation of a dialogue on the issue.

We are even more appalled at the approach of the Union Government to the ghastly events of the stripping and parading naked of two women, the alleged gang rape of one of them and the murder of two male members, all of the same family, on May 4. While expressing his outrage over the incident, outside Parliament rather than on the floor of either House, the Prime Minister seemed to draw an equivalence between this incident in Manipur and other incidents in states like Rajasthan and Chhattisgarh, though the incidents are not at all comparable. There was no explanation of how his government and the Manipur state government were blissfully unaware of this heinous incident despite the filing of an FIR over two months ago.

We would like to bring to the Union Government's notice that the May 4 incident (along with other such similar incidents of sexual violence against women during the last three months in Manipur) represent the disgraceful phenomenon of Conflict Related Sexual Violence. The intent of the perpetrators of this violence and their instigators is to use women's bodies for signalling dominance. Failure to nip such perverted tendencies in the bud can lead to escalation in conflict and make reconciliation difficult.

While the Union Home Minister, during his visit to Manipur, announced the setting up of a panel headed by a retired High Court judge to investigate the reasons for the violence and to identify those behind the violence, this will not suffice to heal the wounds that have been caused by the ongoing violence and the severe trust deficit between the two communities, as well as the lack of confidence of the minority Kuki community in the impartial conduct of the state government and its police force. The nonpartisan and positive role played by the army, the Assam Rifles and central paramilitary forces, which has been appreciated, indicates that there is need to continue with the deployment of these forces in the buffer zones between the two communities, to forestall offensive attacks.

The immediate priority is to provide a healing touch to the affected persons of both communities. The lethargic relief measures taken by the state government have been very inadequate. Effective relief and rehabilitation measures as well as adequate compensation need to be provided to all affected individuals/families to enable them to rebuild their lives. These should include: (i) providing suitable shelters to the affected, either in public buildings or in requisitioned private premises, with proper hygiene and security, for as long as a return to their homes is not feasible; (ii) providing free food supplies for those in the relief camps and free PDS rations for internally displaced people residing elsewhere; (iii) starting the Mahatma Gandhi National Rural Employment Guarantee Act (MNREGA) works that could provide income to those affected; (iv) providing childcare, health, trauma care and education services that would meet the needs of those in the relief camps, especially mothers and children, including newborns; (v) in the medium term, providing assistance for rebuilding damaged houses and other public premises.

The underlying causes of the ongoing mayhem in Manipur need to be objectively identified and addressed within the bounds of constitutional parameters. Unsubstantiated charges and dangerous brinkmanship by all parties, and grave disruptions of the social fabric of Manipur, as well as sustained violence, could resonate and spill over not only into neighbouring states but also across international borders, where ethnic bonds exist. This would be a recipe for unimaginable strife which will not leave the rest of India unscathed.

We, therefore, urge the Government of India to take the following actions at the earliest:

1. Impose President's Rule in Manipur and appoint, as Advisers to the Governor, experienced former administrators and police officers who have knowledge of the region and can empathetically interact with the local populace. Every effort should be made to restore the trust of all sections of the citizenry in the local administration.
2. Provide relief and rehabilitation measures as well as compensation to affected individuals/families in a nonpartisan manner, with the aim of bringing back normalcy at the earliest.
3. Take severe punitive action against individuals and groups intent on fomenting unrest, including bringing to justice all the instigators and perpetrators of incidents of violence since the beginning of May, firmly checking hate speech, rounding up looted arms and ammunition and putting an end to offensive attacks against other communities. The message needs to firmly go out that no attempt by any non-state organisation to take the law into its hands will be tolerated.

We earnestly entreat the Government of India as well as other stakeholders not to let issues of prestige and political expediency inform actions, when the imperatives of both internal peace and external security warrant mature responses. We must all realise that if India loses, no one wins.

SATYAMEVA JAYATE

Constitutional Conduct Group (113 signatories)

OPEN LETTER TO THE CHIEF SECRETARY AND DIRECTOR GENERAL OF POLICE, GOVT. OF UTTARAKHAND: REQUEST FOR IMMEDIATE ACTION ON THE COMMUNAL SITUATION IN THE STATE

12 June 2023

Shri S.S. Sandhu, Chief Secretary, Govt. of Uttarakhand;
Shri Ashok Kumar, Director General of Police, Govt. of Uttarakhand

Dear Sirs,

We are a group of former civil servants of the All India and Central Services who have worked in the Central and State Governments during our careers. As a group, we have no affiliation with any political party but believe in impartiality and neutrality and share a commitment to the Constitution of India.

We write today to express our deep concern at the developing situation in Uttarakhand, particularly in Uttarkashi and Tehri Garhwal districts. We wish to draw, in particular, your attention to the fact that threats have been made regarding a mahapanchayat proposed to be held on 15 June 2023 in the town of Purola and a rally and 'chakka jam' programme on 20 June 2023 at Tehri, both explicitly associated with calls to expel Muslims from these areas. We call upon you to ensure that no such criminal, communal or intimidatory programme is permitted to take place on these dates or otherwise, and that the state police and administration functions as per the Constitution, the law, and the multiple directions of the Supreme Court to act against hate speech and mob violence.

We note that these programmes come in the wake of a communal campaign in the region, including bazaar bandh calls in over twelve towns and rallies and hate speech against Muslims, that has already led to forty-two Muslim families reportedly fleeing the town of Purola on May 28 and to Muslim shopkeepers vacating their premises in Purola, Badkot and possibly other locations. On the basis of available reports in the media, we cannot avoid the conclusion that this ongoing campaign is a criminal enterprise explicitly aimed at threatening our fellow citizens.

We note, in particular, that as per a report in the Hindustan Times on 5 June 2023, posters were put up in Purola on Muslim-owned shops demanding that their owners vacate before the mahapanchayat on 15 June. Amar Ujala subsequently reported on 11 June 2023 that a planning meeting for such a mahapanchayat has been held in Purola (and that a number of figures at the forefront of the anti-minority campaign attended this meeting). We also note that on 9 June 2023, Hindustan reported that the Vishwa Hindu Parishad had sent a letter to the Tehri District Magistrate saying that an 'ultimatum' has been given to all members of the Muslim community to leave the Jaunpur valley and in particular the towns of Nainbagh, Jakhar, Nagtibba, Thatyur, Saklana, Damta, Purola, Barkot and Uttarkashi, and that if this ultimatum is not complied with, these organisations will jam roads and hold protests in Tehri on 20 June 2023.

It is a mystery to us as to why, despite information being available in the public domain, the criminal campaign against minority communities underway since 26 May 2023 has seen no action whatsoever being taken by the administration beyond the registration of a case against 'unknown persons' after posters were put up. We wish to draw your attention to the fact that in April 2022, a similar mahapanchayat was planned in Haridwar, until the Hon'ble Supreme Court explicitly directed that the Chief Secretary of the state would be held responsible for any hate speech at this gathering after which the administration ensured the gathering did not take place, indicating that it was aware of what was likely to happen. We also wish to draw your attention to the fact that on 30 May 2023 twenty-three Supreme Court lawyers wrote to the Governor of Uttarakhand, pointing out that the state is in contempt of court and in particular of the 21.10.2022 order of the Court in *Shaheen Abdullah v. Union of India (WP(C) 940/2022)*, wherein the states of Uttarakhand, Himachal Pradesh and Delhi were specifically directed to 'ensure that immediately as and when any speech or any action takes place which attracts offences such as Sections 153A, 153B and 295A and 505 of the IPC etc., suo moto action will be taken to register cases even if no complaint is forthcoming and proceed against the offenders in accordance with law.' Yet till date nothing has been done.

We finally note that this intimidation campaign is being justified on the grounds of so-called 'love jihad' and that the Chief Minister of the state has been repeatedly making public statements claiming that 'land jihad' and 'love jihad' will not be tolerated in the state, notwithstanding that it is against both the law and our Constitution to target entire communities on the basis of supposed wrongdoing by individuals. We also note that the state government has been claiming that hundreds of religious shrines, the vast majority of them mazars, have been demolished in the last two months.

Uttarakhand is a state known for its social peace and harmony. Hence, we call upon you to act immediately, and in particular to:

1. Ensure that no communal, intimidatory, hate focused or other programme is permitted to be held on 15 June, 20 June, or any other date in the state of Uttarakhand.
2. Ensure that any person, whatever her/his political affiliation, who instigates or indulges in violence, harassment, or intimidation of any other person on the basis of their religious identity is prosecuted to the fullest extent of the law.
3. Ensure the full implementation in Uttarakhand of the 2018 judgment of the Hon'ble Supreme Court in *Tehseen Poonawalla v. Union of India and Ors* for prevention of hate speech and mob violence.
4. Direct the provision of security and compensation to any person or community who has been forced to flee from any area due to their religious identity.

We urge you to initiate action on the above on an urgent basis.

SATYAMEVA JAYATE

Yours faithfully,

Constitutional Conduct Group (52 signatories)

OPEN LETTER TO THE HON'BLE PRIME MINISTER OF INDIA: HARASSMENT OF THE CHRISTIAN COMMUNITY

4 March 2023

Honourable Prime Minister Shri Narendra Modiji,
We are a group of former civil servants of the All India and Central Services who have worked in the Central and State Governments during our careers. As a group, we have no affiliation with any political party but believe in impartiality, neutrality and share a commitment to the Constitution of India.

We write to you today because we are deeply perturbed by the continued harassment, through speech and criminal action, of minority groups in the country by persons associated with your government, your party, organisations connected to it, and by mischief makers from amongst the public. While we are concerned about the hate crimes and speeches against all minorities, we write to you today about the steadily increasing ugly words and actions against a small religious minority, the Christians. Our Constitution clearly spells out that all citizens, irrespective of religion, are equal and have equal rights, but we are compelled to protest to you against the increasing incidents of outright discrimination against Christians occurring in recent times.

Christians constitute but 2.3 per cent of India's population, and this percentage has remained more or less the same since the census of 1951. Yet, in the minds of some, this minuscule number poses a threat to the 80 per cent of the population that is Hindu! The principal allegation against Christians is one of forcible conversions, and because of this accusation, they have been subjected to attacks—verbal, physical, and psychological, against both their persons and against their institutions. It is an unfortunate but inescapable fact that there are elements amongst us who may feel that the denigration of others enhances themselves. It is an acknowledged fact that the role of Christians towards building our nation has been immense. The participation and leadership of Christians in the civil services as well as in the armed forces stands testimony to the community's national commitment.

This apart, Christians in India have been particularly active on three fronts, viz. education, health and social reform, carrying these to remote and inaccessible areas and to the most-deprived sections, the Dalits and tribal peoples. The beneficiaries have been from all faiths. Values which have been identified with Christianity, such as discipline, sacrifice and service have been the hallmark of Christian institutions. During the recent pandemic more than one thousand Christian-run hospitals were readily offered up for the treatment of patients. Not a single Christian institution—whether education or health related, restricts its benefits to Christians alone. Thirty percent of India's nurses are Christians.

Christians have consistently punched above their weight in every field. But today they are being accused of using these very institutions and services as instruments for conversion; and even of resorting to forcible conversion. One has to ask—if such large-scale conversions are happening, why has the percentage of Christians remained static over so many decades?

Notwithstanding this, in recent years the Christian community has been the victim of physical violence. It is troubling that violence against Christians in different parts of the country has persisted and has increased in recent years. Jesuit priest, Father Stan Swamy, for no fault of his except that he was closely working with the Adivasis, Dalits and other underprivileged people of Jharkhand, was virtually driven to his death by no less than the State. Churches and homes of tribal and Dalit Christians have been destroyed, graveyards vandalised, educational and health institutions have been attacked and prayer gatherings have been terrorised. These attacks have happened primarily in Chhattisgarh, Assam, UP, Madhya Pradesh, Odisha, Karnataka, Gujarat, and Maharashtra. According to the United Christian Forum, the attacks on Christians increased from 279 in 2020 to 505 in 2021 and to 511 in 2022 (up till October).

Some of these recent attacks have been particularly distressing. In August 2022, under the influence of Hindu extremist groups, more than a thousand tribal Christians were banished from their villages in Narayanpur and Kondagaon in Chhattisgarh because they refused to be converted to the Hindu faith. Again, on January 2, 2023, a mob of fifty people barged into a church in Chhattisgarh's Narayanpur district and vandalised it, attacking even the SP and other police officers who tried to control the trouble. Among the people arrested for this mayhem is a BJP leader. In January 2023, again, a group of forty goondas pledging allegiance to a Hindutva outfit, accused the teachers of a Catholic school travelling from Gujarat to Belagavi of trying to convert people to Christianity. And only a few days ago, at a 'dharma sansad' at Jantar Mantar in New Delhi, a sadhu shrilly exhorted the audience to slaughter Muslims and Christians. Ignoring all this, persons spewing hatred against Christians have been appointed to high office, even to the judiciary!

Our country has been home to Christianity since the first century CE, long before its introduction in many countries that are today predominantly Christian. Yet Christians today, and in fact, all minorities, are being made to feel strangers in their own country, and guilty about following their own faiths, because of some vocal extremists operating with impunity and at times even with the tacit approval of political or law enforcement authorities.

It is the duty of the State to safeguard the secular character of our country, to protect every citizen, and ensure enjoyment of his or her fundamental rights, regardless of religion. But it is doing little to protect religious minorities. As Prime Minister of our country, and all of its people including Muslims, Christians and other religious minorities, and as a leading member of the BJP, we ask you to speak out against these outrageous acts, and to ensure that the police and other officials prevent such incidents from recurring. Christians, today, and, all other minorities, need to be reassured that they are no less citizens of India than their Hindu brethren.

Hate speech has serious consequences. And the arc is swinging visibly from anti-Muslim to anti-Christian, not in one gory riot but in a series of provocations like church vandalism, defiling of statues, beating up worshippers, bogey of conversions, and public calls for genocide from the nation's capital. These together with the various anti-conversion laws intimidate and create a climate of fear among Christians and marginalise them. This may not be the case in the north-east, with its well-organised Christian communities, but exhibits itself repeatedly in the rest of the country to achieve partisan political gains.

All violence can be stopped immediately with just a word from the top leaders of the BJP, the Union Government and of each state government. As former civil servants, we also know that silence will beget only more violence. Christians, like all Indians now, need to be assured of equal and unbiased treatment by the executive and before the law. It is imperative that you, Mr Prime Minister, give them this reassurance.

SATYAMEVA JAYATE

Yours faithfully,

Constitutional Conduct Group (93 signatories)

OPEN LETTER: DEMAND FOR ACTION ON HATE SPEECH BY LOK SABHA MP PRAGYA THAKUR

7 January 2023

We are a group of former officers of the All India and Central Services who have worked with the Central and State Governments in the course of our careers. As members of the Constitutional Conduct Group, we believe in impartiality, neutrality and commitment to the Indian Constitution and in safeguarding its values.

It has been reported in the media that, on 25 December, 2022, while addressing a gathering of the Hindu Jagarana Vedike's South

Region annual convention in Shivamogga, Karnataka, Lok Sabha Member of Parliament (MP) Pragya Thakur, also known as Sadhvi Pragya, exhorted the crowd to guard their women against men of other communities. She urged them to keep their vegetable knives sharp so these could be used as weapons against those who allegedly kill Hindus; these knives could also be used to cut off the heads of those indulging in 'love jihad', if such an opportunity presented itself. Such action would be construed to be in self-defence, she said, a right which every individual has. She was clearly telling her Hindu audience that they had to be afraid of attacks from non-Hindus, and though the word 'Muslim' does not seem to have been specifically used, the context and the use of the term 'love jihad' leaves no doubt that it was the Muslim community that she was targeting. It is also possible that she was sending out a warning against Christians and other non-Hindu communities as well. Though Sadhvi Pragya Thakur appears to have cleverly chosen her words to avoid criminal charges being made against her, the disguise is only a thin one. She is obviously fomenting hate against non-Hindu communities, and advocating violence against them.

By her incendiary words, Pragya Thakur has not only committed several offences under the Indian Penal Code, she has also violated the oath taken by her as Member of Parliament to uphold the Constitution of India, which is premised upon the rights to life and liberty, secularism, equality and fraternity. A group of civil society organisations (the Campaign Against Hate Speech, Bahutva Karnataka, All India Lawyers Association for Justice and People's Union for Civil Liberties—Karnataka) has recently circulated a petition addressed to the Honourable Speaker of the Lok Sabha to disqualify Pragya Thakur from being a Member of Parliament because of her recent communal utterances at Shivamogga. We, in the Constitutional Conduct Group, also strongly believe that stern action should be taken against her as per the rules of the Lok Sabha. By her incendiary hate speech and her repeated acts of propagating hate, she has forfeited the ethical right to be a Member of Parliament.

As a society, we seem to have become inured to hate speech against minorities. A daily dose of venom is spewed, in the print, visual and social media against different non-Hindu communities, primarily against Muslims, and more lately against Christians as well. Often, these verbal attacks are accompanied by physical violence, assaults on their places of worship, anti-conversion legislation, hurdles placed in the way of inter-faith marriages, denial of livelihoods and a myriad other actions to lower their status in society. A compliant media and systematic distortion of history by people in positions of authority feed this frenzy of communal hate. Regulatory institutions are compromised through inducement or intimidation and oversight institutions of democracy have been suborned.

In this very charged environment, it is the judiciary that has from time to time passed orders which have helped to partly stymie the flood of hate and reclaim the republic. We would like to quote extracts from two Supreme Court pronouncements in particular, *Pravasi Bhalai Sangathan v. Union of India*, 2014 and the more recent statements of October 2022 by Justices KM Joseph and Hrishikesh Roy:

> Hate speech is an effort to marginalise individuals based on their membership in a group. Using expression that exposes the group to hatred, hate speech seeks to delegitimise group members in the eyes of the majority, reducing their social standing and acceptance within society. Hate speech, therefore, rises beyond causing distress to individual group members. It can have a societal impact. Hate speech lays the groundwork for later, broad attacks on vulnerable people that can range from discrimination, to ostracism, segregation, deportation, violence and, in the most extreme cases, to genocide. (2014)
>
> The Constitution envisages Bharat as a secular nation, and fraternity assuring the dignity of the individual and unity and the integrity of the country is the guiding principle enshrined in the Preamble... We feel that this court is charged with the duty to protect these fundamental rights and also protect and

preserve the constitutional values and the secular, democratic character of the nation and in particular the rule of law. (2022)

This latter order goes on to direct some of the respondents, viz. the governments of the NCT of Delhi, Uttarakhand and Uttar Pradesh that whenever any speech or any action takes place which attracts offences such as those under Sections 153A 153B, 295A and 505 of the IPC suo motu action will be taken even if no complaint is forthcoming and proceed against offenders in accordance with law any hesitation to act in accordance with this direction will be viewed as contempt. (All the sections of the IPC mentioned above have to do with offences in places of worship and against people belonging to religious and other groups.)

It is commendable that the police in Shivamogga have not been taken in by Sadhvi Pragya's attempt to disguise her speech as being about self-defence and have registered one or more FIRs against her under various sections of the Indian Penal Code. We hope they will speedily move to file a charge sheet in the court.

As a group committed to the rule of law, democracy and the checks and balances inherent in the Constitution, we are heartened by such action and by the judiciary's efforts to protect the India envisaged in the Constitution. We believe that not merely the judiciary, but every other relevant institution, should take action to protect the Constitution. A particular responsibility devolves on the Houses of Parliament which make laws for the country. Surely its members cannot be permitted to violate the principles of the Constitution? We therefore urge the Honourable Speaker of the Lok Sabha to take immediate action to refer the matter to the Committee of Ethics of the Lok Sabha for such action as may be deemed appropriate. The very fact that an FIR has been registered by the police against the Member of Parliament for inciting hatred should be ground enough to take action.

SATYAMEVA JAYATE

Constitutional Conduct Group (103 signatories)

OPEN LETTER TO THE HON'BLE CHIEF JUSTICE OF INDIA REGARDING THE BILKIS BANO CASE

27 August 2022

To
The Hon'ble Chief Justice of India Supreme Court of India,
New Delhi

Sir,
We, a group of former members of the All India and Central Services who have come together as the Constitutional Conduct Group, have worked in different capacities with the State and Central governments. We have no affiliation with any political party and are, instead, committed to the values enshrined in the Constitution and the judicial process that is protected by it.

Like the overwhelming majority of people in our country, we are aghast at what happened in Gujarat a few days ago, on the 75th anniversary of India's Independence. The premature release, by the Government of Gujarat, of 11 men convicted and jailed in the ghastly case of gang rape of the young and pregnant Bilkis Bano and two others and the murder of her family members in the riots that took place in Gujarat in 2002 has outraged the nation. We write to you because we are deeply distressed by this decision of the Government of Gujarat and because we believe that it is only the Supreme Court which has the prime jurisdiction, and hence the responsibility, to rectify this horrendously wrong decision.

The story of Bilkis Bano is, as you know, a story of immense courage and persistence. A five-month pregnant, then 19-year-old Bilkis, fled, along with her family and others, their village in Dahod district on 28 February 2002, when around 60 Muslim homes were torched; they hid in the fields outside Chhapparwad village where armed men attacked them. Bilkis, her mother and three other women were raped and her three-year old daughter's head was smashed. Later eight persons were found dead and six were missing. Bilkis, naked and unconscious, an old man, and a three-year-old survived; her own daughter did not. It is a remarkable story of courage that this battered and bruised young woman, hiding from her tormentors, managed to seek justice from the courts.

So influential were the persons accused of this ghastly crime and so politically fraught was the issue that not only had the case to be investigated by the Central Bureau of Investigation (CBI) instead of by the Gujarat police, but it also had to be transferred from Gujarat to a special CBI court in Mumbai, to ensure a fair trial, because of the death threats received by Bilkis Bano. In January 2008, the special CBI court in Mumbai sentenced 11 accused to life imprisonment on the charge of gang rape and murder of seven members of Bilkis Bano's family. The case was a rare one because not only were the rapists and murderers punished, but so, too, were the policemen and doctors who tried to tamper with and erase the evidence to protect the accused and cover up the crime.

After serving 15 years in jail, one of the accused, Radheshyam Shah, approached the Supreme Court with a plea for his premature release. The Gujarat High Court which had earlier been approached for this purpose had dismissed his plea while observing that the 'appropriate government' to decide the case was that of Maharashtra and not Gujarat. Shah then filed a plea in the Supreme Court.

On 13 May 2022, the Supreme Court passed an order in *Radheshyam Bhagwandas Shah @ Lala Vakil v. State of Gujarat* that, since the crime was committed in Gujarat, the state of Gujarat was the appropriate government to examine Shah's application. Surely, going by the past history of the case and the collusion of the state officials with the perpetrators of the crime that was apparent, this case should have been dealt with differently! We have learnt that there is a judicial precedent in the Constitution Bench judgement of 2 December 2015 (*Union of India v. V Sriharan alias Murugan*), which holds that the appropriate government to decide the issue shall be the state government where the conviction took place, which in this case would be the state of Maharashtra. We consider it unfortunate that the Constitution Bench precedent laid down in V Sriharan's case was not followed in the Radheshyam Shah judgement of 13 May 2022.

The Supreme Court, on Radheshyam Shah's plea, also directed that the application for premature release be considered by the Gujarat government within two months, and in terms of its policy dated 9 July 1992. We are puzzled about why the Supreme Court saw the matter as so urgent that a decision had to be taken within two months, as also by the Supreme Court ordering that the case should be examined as per Gujarat's 1992 remission policy and not its current one. While it may be the practice, as held by the Supreme Court in its judgment of 22 March 2010 in *State of Haryana & Ors v. Jagdish*, to examine a remission proposal on the basis of the policy existing at the time of conviction, surely the Supreme Court could not be unaware of the major changes in the punishment for rape and murder and the policy for remission which were made much more severe in 2014 after the Nirbhaya case? Can persons who committed rape and murder in 2002 be less liable than persons who rape and murder at the present time?

The Gujarat government duly considered the application for remission on the basis of their remission policy of 1992 and not only cut short the sentence of Radheshyam Shah who had filed the petition, and set him free, but also 10 other persons who had been convicted of the same crime and sentenced with Radheshyam Shah. It is our view that in doing so the Gujarat government committed several errors: (1) According to Section 435 of the Code of Criminal Procedure (CrPC), where a case has been investigated by the CBI, clearance of the Union Government has to be taken before giving remission in sentence. We are unaware whether such permission was taken, but it does not seem that it was; (2) According to Section 432(2) of the CrPC , the opinion of the presiding Judge of the court that passed the order of conviction has to be taken before granting such remission. The Government of India, while writing to the State governments in February 2013, quoted the Supreme Court order which inter alia stated 'Before actually exercising the power of remission under Section 432 of the CrPC the appropriate Government must obtain the opinion (with reasons) of the presiding judge of the convicting or confirming Court. Remission can, therefore, be given only on a case-by-case basis and not in a wholesale manner.' It appears that the view of the presiding judge of the CBI court was not taken; (3) In a case like this where the victim, her family and witnesses braved death threats and threats of physical harm in fighting the case and shifted residence repeatedly for safety, it was obligatory for the Gujarat government to ascertain how such a release would impact their lives. This was not done even though the victim and her supporters have often stated that they were threatened with violence by the convicts (who were liberally granted parole while in jail) as well as by the families and friends of the convicts. Bilkis has reportedly changed homes some 20 times over these years, because of threats to her life. With the celebrated release of the convicts from jail, the trauma, suffering and vulnerability to harm for Bilkis will be significantly heightened; (4) It is also shocking that five out of ten members of the Advisory Committee, which sanctioned the early release, belong to the Bharatiya Janata Party, while the remaining are ex-officio members. This raises the important question of the impartiality and independence of the decision, and vitiates both the process and its outcome.

In view of these glaring deviations from established law, departure from government policy and propriety, and the chilling impact that this release will have, not just on Bilkis Bano and her family and supporters, but also on the safety of all women in India, especially those who belong to minority and vulnerable communities, we urge you to rescind the order of remission passed by the Gujarat government and send the 11 persons convicted of gang rape and murder back to jail to serve out their life sentence.

SATYAMEVA JAYATE

Yours faithfully,

Constitutional Conduct Group (134 signatories)

OPEN LETTER TO THE HON'BLE CHIEF JUSTICE OF INDIA REGARDING RECENT ACTS OF STATE VIOLENCE IN UTTAR PRADESH

20 June 2022

To
The Hon'ble Chief Justice of India, Supreme Court of India,
New Delhi

Dear Chief Justice of India,
We, the members of the Constitutional Conduct Group comprising former civil servants, have read the appeal sent to you on June 14, 2022 by a select group of former judges of the Supreme Court and the High Courts and leading advocates, requesting you to take suo-motu cognisance of the recent acts in Uttar Pradesh of illegal detention, bulldozing of residences and police violence on protesters and those in police custody following protests against certain objectionable remarks made by BJP spokespersons.

We fully support this plea and urge your immediate intervention. We believe that unless the judiciary at the highest level steps in to intervene, swiftly, firmly and decisively, the entire edifice of constitutional governance that has been so carefully and meticulously constructed over the last seventy two years, is likely to collapse.

We are aware that since this appeal for suo-motu cognisance of the shocking incidents in Uttar Pradesh was made to you, a writ petition against the demolition of allegedly unauthorized constructions has been filed by the Jamiat Ulama-i-Hind before the bench of Justices Bopanna and Vikram Nath and that after the preliminary hearing, the response of the State Government has been sought and a hearing will take place next week. While the legality or otherwise of the arbitrary, motivated and wanton destruction of the properties of alleged protesters, all of whom belong to the minority community, is being considered by this bench, and hopefully this will prevent further precipitate and highhanded action by the State

Government as far as demolitions are concerned, we believe that the issues raised by former judges and other lawyers are much wider and relate to the complete subversion of state policy for vicious, ideological ends.

The demolition drive and the abuse of municipal and civic laws for political ends is just one element of a larger policy for converting the administrative and police apparatus into an instrument of brutal majoritarian repression. There are explicit directions to invoke the National Security Act 1980 and the Uttar Pradesh Gangsters and Anti-Social Activities (Prevention) Act 1986, to brutally quell any protest. The policy has the sanction of the highest levels of the Government and while local level officials and police personnel are certainly answerable for arbitrary use of power, the real culpability lies at the highest levels of the political executive. It is this corruption of the edifice of constitutional governance which requires the Supreme Court to step in and stem the rot.

As former civil servants who have spent several decades in the service of the Constitution, we are particularly alarmed that the threat we currently face is completely unprecedented. It is no longer just a case of 'excesses' of the police and the administration at the local level which can be brought under check by higher levels of administration and political authority, it is the fact that the very idea of the Rule of Law, of 'due process', of being treated as 'innocent until proven guilty' is being turned upside down. What we have seen in Prayagraj, in Kanpur, in Saharanpur and many other towns which have a sizeable Muslim population, follows a pattern and is politically directed. What is even more alarming is that the idea of 'bulldozer justice', of inflicting brutal punishment on citizens who dare to protest lawfully or criticise the Government or express dissent by using ostensibly legal instruments, is now becoming the norm rather than the exception across many Indian States. There is a sense of impunity and the arrogance of majoritarian power which seems to be driving this disregard for constitutional values and principles.

We believe that the immediacy of the threat is critical and we join hands with the former judges and the advocates who have petitioned you, in urging you to take cognisance of the situation and intervene appropriately.

SATYAMEVA JAYATE

Yours faithfully,

Constitutional Conduct Group (90 signatories)

LETTER TO THE PRIME MINISTER—CALL FOR END TO POLITICS OF HATE

26 April 2022

Dear Prime Minister,

We are witnessing a frenzy of hate filled destruction in the country where at the sacrificial altar are not just Muslims and members of the other minority communities but the Constitution itself. As former civil servants, it is not normally our wont to express ourselves in such extreme terms, but the relentless pace at which the constitutional edifice created by our founding fathers is being destroyed compels us to speak out and express our anger and anguish.

The escalation of hate violence against the minority communities, particularly Muslims, in the last few years and months across several States—Assam, Delhi, Gujarat, Haryana, Karnataka, Madhya Pradesh, Uttar Pradesh and Uttarakhand, all states in which the Bharatiya Janata Party (BJP) is in power, barring Delhi (where the Union Government controls the police)—has acquired a frightening new dimension. It is no longer just the politics of an assertive Hindutva identity, nor the attempt to keep the communal cauldron on the boil—all that has been going for decades and in the last few years had become a part of the new normal. What is alarming now is the subordination of the fundamental principles of our Constitution and of the rule of law to the forces of majoritarianism, in which the state appears to be fully complicit.

The hate and malevolence directed against Muslims seems to have embedded itself deep in the recesses of the structures, institutions and processes of governance in the states in which the BJP is in power. The administration of law, instead of being an instrument for maintaining peace and harmony, has become the means by which the minorities can be kept in a state of perpetual fear. Their constitutional right to practice their own faith, follow their own customs, dress code and personal laws and exercise their own food choices, is threatened not merely by letting vigilante mobs inflict violence on them with impunity but, by twisting the law itself, to circumscribe their freedom of choice and make it convenient for a prejudiced, communal executive to make colourable use of state power. State power is thus used not only to facilitate vigilante violence targeted against a community but to make ostensibly legal means available to the administration (e.g., anti-conversion laws, laws proscribing consumption of beef, encroachment removal, prescription of uniform codes in educational institutions) to strike fear in the community, deprive them of their livelihoods and make it evident to them that they have to accept their status as inferior citizens who have to subordinate themselves to majoritarian political power and majoritarian social and cultural norms. The likelihood of our becoming a country that systematically makes sections of its own citizens—minorities, Dalits, the poor and the marginalised—targets of hate and knowingly deprives them of their fundamental rights is now, more than ever, frighteningly real.

While we are not aware if the current spurt in communal frenzy is coordinated and directed by the political leadership, it is evident that the administration at the state and local levels provides a facilitating environment for mischievous lumpen groups to operate without fear. Such facilitation and support is not limited to that offered by the local police and other administrative officials; it appears to have the tacit approval of the highest political levels in the State and Central

Governments, which provide the enabling policy and institutional environment for local level tyranny. While the actual commission of violence may be outsourced to fringe groups, there is little doubt as to how the ground for their operations is made fertile, how each of them follows a master script and shares a common 'tool kit' and how the propaganda machinery of a party as well as the state is made available to them to defend their actions.

What distinguishes the incidents that are taking place now from earlier communal conflagrations is not merely that a master design is being unveiled to prepare the grounds for a Hindu Rashtra, but that the constitutional and legal framework designed to prevent such a development from taking place is itself being twisted and perverted to make it an instrument of majoritarian tyranny. No wonder then that the bulldozer has now become the new metaphor for the exercise of political and administrative power, literally and figuratively. The edifice built around the ideas of 'due process' and 'rule of law' stands demolished. As the Jahangirpuri incident shows, even the orders of the highest court of the land appear to be treated with scant respect by the executive.

Prime Minister, we, the members of the Constitutional Conduct Group—all of us are former civil servants who have spent decades in the service of the Constitution—believe that the threat we are facing is unprecedented and at stake is not just constitutional morality and conduct; it is that the unique syncretic social fabric, which is our greatest civilizational inheritance and which our Constitution is so meticulously designed to conserve, is likely to be torn apart. Your silence, in the face of this enormous societal threat, is deafening.

We appeal to your conscience, taking heart from your promise of Sabka Saath, Sabka Vikas, Sabka Vishwas. It is our fond hope that in this year of 'Azadi Ka Amrit Mahotsav', rising above partisan considerations, you will call for an end to the politics of hate that governments under your party's control are so assiduously practising. The idea of India that our founding fathers had envisioned and fought for needs a climate of fraternity and communal harmony to thrive. Hate will engender hate, rendering the environment too noxious for the idea to survive.

SATYAMEVA JAYATE

Yours sincerely,

Constitutional Conduct Group (108 signatories)

OPEN LETTER TO CORPORATES: POLICY ON ADVERTISING ON MEDIA CHANNELS

31 October 2020

We are a group of former officers of the All India and Central Services who have worked with the Central and State Governments in different capacities. We have come together as a group known as the Constitutional Conduct Group (CCG). This group does not support any political party but believes in impartiality, neutrality and commitment to the Constitution of India.

In the normal course, when we observe a flagrant violation of the principles embodied in the Constitution, we write letters or make open statements pointing this out to the concerned governments and to constitutional/statutory bodies. However, upholding the principles of the Constitution is not a function of governments alone. All of us, as individual citizens as well as members of various organisations in the country—social, political, professional or business—have a duty to uphold the values enshrined in the Constitution and to follow these principles both in our work as well as in our personal lives. Unfortunately, in recent times, we see growing discord and distrust among the people of the country and a steady erosion of democratic values with long term consequences for everyone.

Today, we are addressing this open letter not to the government but to an equally important segment of society, viz. the various companies, business houses and corporates in the country. These entities, responsible for wealth creation in the country, have not, we believe, been doing their bit in upholding the rights and freedoms spelt out in the Constitution. Sadly, an impression has gained ground that these bodies have preferred to look the other way even as a rising tide of hatred and divisiveness threatens the very foundations of our society. Many well-established corporates have shown no hesitation in advertising their products on media channels which have made it a practice to ramp up their viewership by spewing hatred, creating divisions on the basis of religion and caste, manufacturing false narratives and making criminals out of law-abiding people. It is possible that these corporates have not given sufficient thought to how their acts have unwittingly strengthened the forces which divide the nation through deliberate false propaganda.

Our Constitution, as we know, guarantees fundamental rights to each and every one of its citizens. Article 15 of the Constitution prohibits discrimination on the grounds of religion, race, caste, sex and place of birth. It is a matter of concern for all of us that several media channels have gone against this fundamental right on a regular basis and yet receive advertisements from many companies. Channels which communalise the spread of COVID-19, allege that the UPSC has allowed Muslims to 'infiltrate' the higher civil services and dub sensitive advertisements about communal harmony as 'Love Jihad' are unfortunately patronised by many corporates. Corporates often go by apparently doubtful TRP numbers to decide their policy for advertisements. It is certainly time to look beyond such technical considerations.

Advertising on channels which spread divisiveness is bad not only on moral grounds but bad for business as well. As several economists and social scientists have pointed out, investments tend to wither when there is unrest. And that is, unquestionably, what has been happening in India. India's investment as a percentage of the nominal GDP has declined from 41.2 per cent in September 2011 to 21.4 per cent in June 2020. Many other growth parameters have been on a downward spiral too. Distrust, fear and uncertainty hurt not just the fabric of society but business as well.

In the midst of this gloom, a few corporates stand out like shining beacons: they have taken a stand against advertising on media channels which foment hatred and disharmony. We commend them for their initiative and courage. We also fervently hope that other corporates will follow their example. To all companies, business houses and corporate bodies we would like to say: let not any of your actions, even inadvertently, help forces that create discord and ill-will amongst our people. This country and its people deserve better. It is time to show, through both substantive and symbolic acts, that we uphold the principles of our Constitution and are committed to the peace and prosperity of all our citizens.

SATYAMEVA JAYATE

Constitutional Conduct Group (95 signatories)

AN OPEN LETTER SEEKING INVESTIGATION INTO THE MALICIOUS CAMPAIGN OF CALUMNY AGAINST SOLDIERS OF THE MUSLIM FAITH IN THE INDIAN ARMED FORCES

21 October 2020

We are a group of former civil servants of the All India and Central Services, who have worked for decades with Central and State Governments in the course of our careers. As a group, we have no affiliation with any political party but believe in the credo of impartiality, neutrality and commitment to the Indian Constitution. We continue to uphold the oath of allegiance to our Constitution we took when we entered service.

We are deeply disturbed to note the malicious campaign of calumny against soldiers of the Muslim faith in the armed forces of India which has caused distinguished Veterans of our armed forces to petition the Hon'ble President of India, who is also the Supreme

Commander of our armed forces, seeking redress. The contents of the letter have been widely publicized.*

The letter from the Veterans points out that there was no such Muslim regiment in the first place. It forcefully establishes that the charges of dereliction of duty or disloyalty laid against Muslim troops in false social media posts, which have been named, have no basis whatsoever. We support the requests of the Veterans, namely:

1. Investigate the antecedents of individuals who have made 'Muslim Regiment' post.
2. Identify and charge individuals who have made the post, for anti-national activities.
3. Issue warning to Facebook and Twitter who have enabled these posts.
4. Issue instructions to all state governments that generation of such false and seditious messages in social media should be acted upon with alacrity.

While assaults against the dignity of our Muslim citizens, as indeed physical assaults, are becoming commonplace, this particular theme which casts doubts on the loyalty of Muslim soldiers has wider implications which could have serious repercussions on our security and on fields of battle. At a time, particularly, when India is facing grave external threats, attempts to divide the armed forces could well be termed acts of treason.

We, the undersigned, would therefore urge that our armed forces as also the Government of India take cognisance of these fake news and issue suitable statements to negate the efforts to sully the image of our forces and our country. As the Veterans have significantly

---

* 'Hundreds of Armed Forces Veterans Write to President on "Muslim Regiment" Fake News', *The Wire*, 14 October 2020 (https://thewire.in/communalism/muslim-regiment-armed-forces-veterans-open-letter-president; Accessed March 2024)

pointed out, 'the public assumes that it is the truth, especially when there is no official action against the perpetrators.'

We further demand that appropriate investigative agencies be urgently tasked to thoroughly investigate and determine whether elements that have been pursuing a hate-cum-polarising agenda in the country are deliberately propagating this fake news with a view to causing divisions in our armed forces, weakening our national resolve and security.

SATYAMEVA JAYATE

Constitutional Conduct Group (91 signatories)

OPEN LETTER TO THE CHIEF MINISTER OF UTTAR PRADESH: BLATANT VIOLATIONS OF THE RULE OF LAW

3 October 2020

Dear Chief Minister,

Just when we thought that nothing could numb our consciences and brains further, the handling of the Hathras incident by the Uttar Pradesh administration has shown that, as a nation, we are plumbing the depths of depravity and callousness in governance. A young Dalit woman is brutally violated. Almost three weeks after the incident, the police are yet to confirm the crime of rape and are still spinning theories around it, although the video of what amounts to her dying declaration seems to confirm it. Her neck was lacerated, her spinal column was broken and there were cuts on her tongue. Instead of promptly admitting her to a hospital with advanced facilities for dealing with trauma, she was allowed to languish in the Jawaharlal Nehru Medical College and Hospital, Aligarh. She was moved to Delhi only two weeks after the incident, that too on the request of her family, a case of too little, too late. What followed was an even greater travesty of justice and basic human values. After her death, her body was despatched post haste to her village and cremated in the dead of night by policemen. Being a person attached to a persuasion of the Hindu faith, you would be well aware that Hindu customs require the nearest kin to offer agni to the mortal remains. Both the sacred traditions and the family's pleas that they would perform the cremation in the morning were ignored. To add insult to injury, a policeman is reported to have told the bereaved family that they were also to blame and the District Magistrate has apparently been captured on video making veiled threats to the family that they should be careful about their statements to the media, because the officials would be around even after the media departs.

It is being touted in the media that the Prime Minister has asked you to 'fast track' this case to secure an early conviction. With our experience as erstwhile administrators in different departments of the Central and state governments, our group of former civil servants had, in the past, highlighted the brazen violations of the rule of law in the Unnao rape case and in the murder of the police inspector in Bulandshahr. We note with concern that, even after two years, the ghastly murder of a brother officer has not stirred the UP police and your administration to bring the case to closure. In these circumstances, we may be forgiven for viewing UP's fast track justice system with scepticism.

We are, in fact, concerned with the novel interpretations of fast track justice in the state governed by you. In recent days, we have seen two instances where alleged criminals have met their deaths while being transported by the police to Uttar Pradesh. Even if they were guilty of the offences listed against them, they were entitled, under the Constitution of India and the laws of the land, to a fair trial. Denial of this right amounts to violation of Article 21 of the Constitution. Your administration has also initiated draconian measures against anti-CAA protesters, including detention and levy of punitive fines. You seem to believe in combining the roles of judge and executioner, as evidenced in a recent interview where you advocated the philosophy of 'an eye for an eye.' Equally reprehensible, some months ago, you ordered the withdrawal of cases registered against you in the past. Politicians never tire of saying 'the law must take its course'. Why depart from this article of faith for your party and government?

The Hathras district administration feels it can flout human sentiments at will, apart from rapidly disposing of evidence in cases of offences against the body. All those complicit in these violations of law and tradition must be punished. While it is in the order of things that you have suspended the Superintendent of Police, there are adequate grounds for immediate suspension of the District Magistrate as well; we insist that departmental proceedings against them be started at the earliest. Action under Section 4 of The Scheduled Castes and Scheduled Tribes (Prevention of Atrocities) Act, 1989 must be initiated against all those officers and men of the district police and the executive magistracy who have wilfully neglected the duties enjoined on them under this Act. We also note with regret that the Chief Secretary and the Director General of Police have failed abjectly in exercising control over a highly compromised administration. We urge them to live up to the proud traditions of the Indian Administrative Service and the Indian Police Service, in whom the people of this country still repose faith. The meek surrender of the Uttar Pradesh bureaucracy and police, especially its All India Services, to political diktat has shamed all of us who deem it a badge of honour to belong to these services.

But, ultimately, all responsibility rests with you as the Chief Executive of the state. Your actions over the past three and a half years give us little reason to believe that your actions are motivated by respect for the rule of law. We urge you to conduct your administration in accordance with the letter and spirit of the Constitution of India, to which you have sworn allegiance when you assumed office. In the present instance, we hope you will deliver justice to the victim and her family, without fear or favour, despite the efforts of specific upper caste groups to interfere with the course of justice. We also hope you will ensure that officers of your administration implement the rule of law in a just and fair manner.

SATYAMEVA JAYATE

Yours sincerely,

Constitutional Conduct Group (92 signatories)

LETTER SEEKING ACTION AGAINST SUDARSHAN TV FOR ITS MALICIOUS CAMPAIGN TO PROMOTE HATRED AND DIVISIVENESS IN SOCIETY

1 September 2020

Honourable Home Minister of India,
Honourable Minister for Information and Broadcasting, India,
Chairman, National Human Rights Commission,
Chairman, Minorities Commission Chairman, Union Public Service Commission,
Chairman, News Broadcasting Standards Authority, Honourable Lt Governor, Delhi,
Honourable Chief Minister, Delhi,
Secretary, Ministry of Home Affairs, Govt of India,
Secretary, Ministry of Information & Broadcasting, Govt. of India,
The Commissioner of Police, Delhi,

We are a group of former civil servants belonging to the All India and Central Services who have worked with the Central Government as well as different State Governments of India. As a group, we have no affiliation with any political party but believe in being neutral, impartial and committed to the Constitution of India.

We are raising, through this letter, an urgent issue regarding the proposed telecast of a communally charged, divisive and sensational series by Sudarshan News TV channel. This series claims to be an expose of a conspiracy in the recruitment process that has resulted in a sudden increase in the number of Muslim officers selected for the two most prestigious services in the country, the IAS and the IPS. Jamia Millia Islamia has been singled out in this context. We understand that the Delhi High Court has granted an interim stay on the telecast. However, we feel stronger legal and administrative action is warranted.

It is completely perverse to allege that there is a conspiracy to infiltrate Muslim officers into the services, or to use terms like UPSC Jihad or Civil Services Jihad in this connection. These communal and irresponsible statements amount to hate speech and are defamatory of an entire community.

The telecast of the programme, if allowed, will have the following effects:

- It will generate hatred towards the largest minority community in the country, viz. Muslims, without having any basis in fact. The country is already smouldering with hate speech against Muslims, including allegations of Corona Jihad and Love Jihad, which various courts have found to be false. This telecast will add further fuel to that fire.
- It will tar the impeccable reputation of the Union Public Service Commission (UPSC), the premier organisation for civil service recruitment, by claiming that it is biased in its recruitment processes. UPSC's recruitment processes are widely recognised as being entirely fair, above board and without any bias towards any language, region, religious or other community. The UPSC is one of the few institutions in the country which still enjoys an unblemished reputation for integrity and has enormous credibility both with the government and with the people of India. The telecast will destroy people's faith in this highly regarded institution.
- It will spread a false belief about a disproportionate increase in the number of Muslims being selected for government services, especially for the IAS and IPS. A recent report in *The*

Indian Express said that 'Muslims make up 3.46 per cent of the country's 8,417 IAS and IPS officers. Of 292 Muslim officers, 160 are among the 5,862 who had been selected through the Civil Services examinations conducted by the UPSC, while the remaining 132 are among 2,555 who were promoted to the IAS or IPS from the state civil services on the basis of seniority and performance, which is also assessed by the UPSC.' It should be noted that this 3.46 per cent is far short of the percentage of Muslims in the population, which is 14.2 per cent. Over the last forty years, the number of Muslim candidates has been going up and down. In fact, there have been years when not a single Muslim candidate was selected in the IAS, and, therefore, allegations such as these are totally unfounded. Such a telecast may also persuade other caste, linguistic and regional groups to look at their rate of success in the civil services examination, an examination which should be, and is, based on merit. In the process, the credibility of UPSC will be compromised.

- It will malign the reputation of Jamia Millia Islamia, which has recently been rated as the top central university in India. Jamia Millia Islamia has, in fact, been fulfilling a major social obligation to the country by offering free coaching services to disadvantaged candidates (Muslims, SCs, STs and women) to help them succeed in the UPSC examinations. The telecast will discourage Jamia Millia Islamia and others like them from offering services to socially disadvantaged groups.

The use of terms like 'UPSC Jihad' and 'Civil Services Jihad' are an attempt to divide the civil administration of the country along religious lines and undermines the excellent contributions made by administrators across the board to the development of India.

In a case filed before the High Court of Delhi a few days ago, the petitioners have urged that offences have been committed under 'Sections 153A(1) Promoting enmity between different groups on grounds of religion, race, place of birth, residence, language, etc., and doing acts prejudicial to maintenance of harmony, 153B(1) Imputations, assertions prejudicial to national-integration, 295A Deliberate and malicious acts, intended to outrage religious feelings of any class by insulting its religion or religious beliefs, and Section 499 Defamation, of the Indian Penal Code.' These alleged offences need to be investigated thoroughly.

In a recent judgement on the same matter, the Supreme Court, while not granting a stay on the telecast of the programme, has stated 'We note that under statutory provisions, competent authorities are vested with powers to ensure compliance with law, including provisions of the criminal law intended to ensure social harmony and the peaceful co-existence of all communities.'

We, therefore, urge the Union Home Ministry, the Lieutenant-Governor of Delhi, the Chief Minister, Delhi and the Commissioner of Police, Delhi to order the lodging of FIRs under the relevant legal provisions. We also request the Ministry of Information and Broadcasting and the News Broadcasting Standards Authority of India to investigate whether or not the show would run afoul of the Cable Television Networks (Regulation) Act, read with the Cable Television Networks Rules 1994, and the Code of Ethics and Broadcasting Standards and take suitable action. The National Human Rights Commission, the Minorities Commission, and the Union Public Service Commission are also requested to take notice of this vicious hate campaign to malign a particular religion and community through the propagation of slanted news that will not stand scrutiny by any objective criterion.

SATYAMEVA JAYATE

Constitutional Conduct Group (91 signatories)

AN OPEN LETTER TO MARK ZUCKERBERG, CEO, FACEBOOK

24 August 2020

We are a group of former civil servants of India belonging to the All India and Central Services, who have worked, in the course of our careers, with the Central Government as well as different State Governments of India. As a group, we have no affiliation with any political party but believe in being neutral, impartial and committed to the Indian Constitution. We have, in the past, written to the government and government institutions whenever we felt that the democratic rights of Indian citizens were being violated. We have not, so far, written to any non-Indian body. We are writing to you now, in a departure from our usual practice, because certain actions (or the absence of certain actions) by Facebook in their operations in India have thrown into danger some of the fundamental rights of the people of India. Our attention has been drawn to this by an article in *The Wall Street Journal* (WSJ) dated 14 August 2020.

Most democratic countries assure their citizens of several basic rights and freedoms. Both the United States, the country of which you are a citizen, and India, do the same.

Democratic rights can be adversely affected by hate speech, as you very well know. Which is why Facebook has made it part of its policy not to allow hate speech. Facebook defines hate speech as a direct attack on people for characteristics such as 'race, ethnicity, national origin, disability, religious affiliation, caste, sexual orientation, sex, gender identity and serious disease.' Given this clear definition in your own policy, we are surprised that Facebook did not take action against some clear and serial offenders in India—persons like T Raja Singh and a few others—for their derogatory comments against people belonging to a different religion, accusing Muslims of spreading COVID-19, indulging in 'love jehad' and various other misdemeanours. What is striking about Facebook's leniency towards these persons is that all of them happen to be members of the political party in power. That Facebook did consider the posts to be offensive is apparent from the fact that these posts were deleted on 17 August, after the *WSJ* wrote to Facebook seeking its comments. We are dismayed to learn, again from the *WSJ* article, that the Public Policy Head of Facebook India consciously opposed applying Facebook's hate speech rules to members of the ruling Bharatiya Janata Party (BJP) because doing so would adversely affect the company's business prospects in India.

Mr Zuckerberg, you surely cannot be unaware that religious unrest has become a serious problem in India. The recently passed Citizenship Amendment Act (CAA), coupled with the proposed National Registry of Citizens (NRC), threatens to take away the citizenship of hundreds of thousands of Muslims and other minorities in India and put them in detention centres. You cannot also be ignorant of the communal riots that took place in Delhi in February 2020, in which 53 persons were killed, two-thirds of them Muslims. Several cases of lynching and torture, primarily of Muslims and Dalits (oppressed castes and groups), have also occurred in India in recent years. The majority of these are related to 'cow vigilantism', i.e. religious extremists resorting to violence in apparent efforts to protect cows from being illegally slaughtered. Many of these crimes have been instigated through hate speech spread through various communication channels, such as Facebook, WhatsApp, and Twitter. Despite being aware of this, Facebook has failed to implement its own policy of discouraging hate speech in India, or has implemented it in a clearly partisan manner. That this seems to have been done to protect Facebook's commercial interests is even more reprehensible. We note that such behaviour on Facebook's part has become a subject of debate in other countries as well. Commercial interests at the cost of human lives? If these are the crass calculations Facebook indulges in, it is no surprise that the calculus of hate is spreading like a virus in many parts of the world. To blame the algorithms of artificial intelligence is both to evade corporate responsibility and to deny the human agency involved in the framing of those very algorithms.

We are writing to you in the expectation that you will make serious efforts to audit the implementation of Facebook's hate speech policy in India and, while such an audit is under way, ensure that the present Public Policy Head of Facebook, India, is not in a position to influence the investigations. We also fervently hope that in future, you will not let your company's business prospects stand in the way of implementing your own policy against hate speech and posts which can lead to hate crimes. This is a sure way of demonizing minorities and inflicting violence upon them while undermining the democratic and secular basis of the Indian Constitution.

Yours sincerely,
Constitutional Conduct Group (54 signatories)

AYODHYA LETTER: ON 27 YEARS OF BABRI MASJID DEMOLITION

6 December 2019

We, a collective of retired civil servants deeply committed to the values and guarantees of the Indian Constitution, share with our fellow Indians our extreme grief and deep concern about where India stands today, 27 years after the demolition of the Babri Masjid in Ayodhya on 6 December 1992.

We recall that 6 December is also the anniversary of the day on which the man who led the creation of one of the finest constitutions in the world, Dr Bhimrao Ambedkar, left this world. The battle for the land on which the medieval mosque in Ayodhya stood was at its core a battle for the defence of the highest values of this constitution.

This was not simply a title dispute over a tiny piece of land in a dusty small town. It was not even a contest between a medieval mosque, now razed, with a grand temple, still imagined. It was a dispute about what kind of country this is and will be in the future, to who does it belong, and on what terms must people of different identities and beliefs live together in this vast and teeming land.

We feel intense anguish because 27 years after the mosque was demolished, those who were responsible for this crime which tore India apart and led to the highest levels of communal bloodletting after the Partition riots, have still not been punished, even though the Supreme Court directed that this criminal case be heard on a day-to-day basis. Instead, many of those who led and participated in this assault not just on a mosque but on India's constitutional morality, have held some of the highest offices in this country.

We worry also that the recent judgment of the Supreme Court of India in effect rewards this grave crime. It also creates a false and illusory notion that a verdict favouring those who claim to speak for the majority community can result in peace and reconciliation and everyone should move on, injustice notwithstanding.

In this deeply troubling moment in the journey of this country which we love, we contest resolutely the message that it seems to convey to India's religious minorities that their claim to this country and its democratic institutions is subordinate to anyone. We would like to recall the famous dictum 'Freedom is the outcome of the tranquillity of peace and peace emanates from justice.' Freedom and justice are the soul of our constitution.

This is a time when every Indian should recall Mahatma Gandhi's last fast, two weeks before he was assassinated. One of his three demands was that the mosques and dargahs in Delhi in which Hindu idols had been inserted should be returned respectfully to the Muslims. Hinduism, he said, would be emptied for him of meaning if a single place of worship of another faith was desecrated in the name of the Hindu faith.

We who sign this letter to the Indian people include a Jain, Hindus, Muslims, Christians, Sikhs, atheists and agnostics. We are together convinced that true religion never teaches violence and hate of another. Therefore, on 6 December, we first express our collective agony and atonement that a place of worship was pulled down with such hate. We also pledge that we will not allow our great Constitution to be emptied of its soul.

SATYAMEVA JAYATE
Constitutional Conduct Group (46 signatories)

OPEN STATEMENT BY FORMER CIVIL SERVANTS— CHARGESHEETED TERROR ACCUSED AS PARTY CANDIDATE

24 April 2019

Our group of former civil servants of the All India and Central Services has no affiliation with any political party and is firmly committed to the Constitution of India. We write to express our disbelief and dismay at the candidature of Pragya Thakur for the Bhopal Lok Sabha seat. This decision could have been dismissed as yet another example of political expediency but for the enthusiastic endorsement by no less a person than the Prime Minister of India, who has termed her candidature as a symbol of our civilisational heritage.

As if it were not enough to nominate a person who is undergoing trial for acts of terror (the Malegaon Bomb Blast Case), Pragya Thakur, who is out on bail on medical grounds, has used the political platform she has been provided not just to propound her brand of bigotry, but also to insult the memory of Shri Hemant Karkare, the IPS officer who laid down his life in the fight against terror. For Ms Thakur, Shri Karkare died not because he sacrificed his own life defending ours, but because she had put a curse on him for daring to investigate her and, through his meticulous investigations, successfully charging her for terrorist crimes. In her worldview, anyone who has the audacity to investigate a self-styled 'Hindu' religious leader in a 'Hindu' country earns divine wrath and therefore would naturally be destroyed.

As former civil servants, we are not normally wont to give voice to our feelings. However, this dishonouring of a former colleague, an officer known for his professionalism, has come as the ultimate shock and saddened us beyond words. The country needs to honour the sacrifice of Shri Karkare and not allow deviant individuals to denigrate him and his memory. Every officer who has served with or supervised the work of Shri Karkare has testified that he was a person of impeccable integrity and an inspiration to all who came in touch with him.

But this statement is not just about Shri Karkare. It is also about the atmosphere of hate and divisiveness that characterises not just this electoral campaign but seems to be percolating through society as a whole. The candidature of Pragya Thakur is not a symbol of our civilisational heritage. Our heritage is not that of acts of terrorism. It is not of majoritarianism but of celebrating our diversity. It is of tolerance, fraternity and of the unifying spirit of the Constitution of India.

To this end, we appeal to the Prime Minister of India to unequivocally condemn, through actions and statements, the existence of terror in any form. He cannot escape the irony of his party seeking votes in the name of fighting terrorism and at the same time endorsing the candidature of a person accused of terror crimes. Martyrdom cannot be selectively appropriated or given up for the pursuit of political ambition.

To institutions like the Election Commission and the Judiciary, we would like to point out that their efforts to contain the politics of divisiveness and of hate have had little impact so far. It is necessary to be far more proactive to stamp out this aberration. Inaction will only exacerbate the situation.

We, who came together to use our pooled experience in the service of the Constitution and to further the values enshrined therein, call upon our fellow citizens to join us in:

- Condemning unequivocally, the statement of Pragya Thakur;
- Demanding that the BJP withdraw her candidature;

- Reminding the Prime Minister of his oath to uphold Constitutional values and appealing to him to take the lead in putting an end to the climate of fear and intimidation and communal viciousness that seems to be permeating the entire electoral process.

We appeal to our fellow citizens to come together and use our collective might to ensure that the India that was dreamt of by Mahatma Gandhi—an India engaged in a ceaseless quest for truth and nonviolence—and the India that the founding fathers of our Constitution conceived of, remains intact and rises to its full potential.

We also appeal to our fellow citizens to reject the pervading atmosphere of hate and divisiveness. Every citizen of India, irrespective of caste, creed or religion, belongs to this country. Let us celebrate our unity in diversity and recall that, together, we have given unto ourselves this Constitution.

SATYAMEVA JAYATE

Constitutional Conduct Group (71 signatories)

OPEN LETTER FROM FORMER CIVIL SERVANTS: MURDER OF POLICE OFFICER IN BULANDSHAHR DISTRICT, UTTAR PRADESH

18 December 2018

We are a group of retired civil servants from the All India and Central Services who, having spent long years in the service of the Constitution of India, have come together to express ourselves on issues of governance and public policy that have a bearing on constitutional principles, conduct and ethics. Since June 2017, when we first came together, we have spoken out on several occasions when we felt that constitutional values were under threat and that it was incumbent on us to voice our concerns publicly. As a group we have no affiliations with any political party nor do we subscribe to any ideology other than the values enshrined in the Constitution.

It is a measure of the rapid erosion of constitutional values that we, as a group, have felt a compelling need to speak out as many as nine times in the last eighteen months. The pace of erosion has been frightening and with each slip we seem to sink further into a lawless abyss.

The mob violence in Bulandshahr in Uttar Pradesh (UP), on 3 December 2018, instigated and engineered with malicious intent, which led to the cold blooded murder of a police officer brave enough to step forward single-handedly to pacify the mob, marks the most dangerous turn yet in the direction taken by the politics of hate in recent times. It shows that in India's most populous state, Uttar Pradesh, fundamental principles of governance, of constitutional ethics and of humane social conduct stand perverted. The Chief Minister of the state acts as a high priest of the agenda of bigotry and majoritarian supremacy—an agenda which now seems to take precedence over everything else.

Why is this incident such a frightening indicator of the complete collapse of constitutional values? This is not the first instance of a situation intentionally created to foment communal tension. The history of UP is replete with such instances. This is not the first time that a policeman has been killed by a frenzied mob. This is also not the first time that the politics of cow protection has been used as a means of isolating and cornering the Muslim community and deepening the social divide.

All this we have seen before but, so far, we had the confidence that whenever a political party actually forms a Government it keeps its partisan political agenda at bay and begins to exercise power with a sense of responsibility so as to gain wider political acceptability. The Bulandshahr episode, which follows a succession of events aimed at isolating and intimidating Muslim communities in UP, shows that, under Yogi Adityanath, that confidence is misplaced and that hooliganism and thuggery have been mainstreamed into governance not just to intimidate minorities but to teach a lesson to anyone, including police personnel and others in the administration, who dare to be evenhanded in their approach to minority communities.

While it may be premature to come to conclusions about the murder of Inspector Subodh Kumar Singh before the investigations are over, there is no doubt that there was nothing spontaneous about the violence that led to his killing, nor is there any doubt as to who the political elements were that aided and abetted the violence. This was a deliberate attempt to display majoritarian muscle and send a message to the Muslim communities living in the region that they have to live in fear, accept their subordinate status and conform to the cultural diktats of the majority community.

Inspector Subodh Kumar Singh's reputation of being independent and even-handed and his refusal to act in haste on the complaint of illegal cow slaughter that allegedly took place under his watch, was obviously seen as defiance of the majoritarian will. The local BJP and Sangh Parivar elements had already complained about his anti-Hindu conduct and sought his transfer. He was an impediment to their communal plans and had to go. Much as the Chief Minister may try to mislead by calling it an accident, this was murder with intent. It was murder most foul.

As horrifying as the brazen, daylight murder of a courageous police officer is the response of the administration to the event. The Chief Minister refuses to acknowledge the gravity of the incident and its communal intent, condemn the perpetrators of violence or direct the police to take action against them but instead asks them to focus attention on those responsible for illegal cow slaughter. The police authorities themselves draw an equivalence between the killing of a police officer and the illegal slaughter of cows and claim that unless both crimes are investigated together it will not be possible to come to any conclusions about the violence of the mob and the murder of a colleague.

Ample video graphed evidence exists to show that those engaged in violence and their leaders, as well as those who egged them on, are allowed to roam scot-free while, at the same time, alleged cow killers, against whom not a shred of evidence exists, are taken into custody, just because they are Muslims. Three of the main accused in the mob violence leading to the death of the police officer flaunt their affiliations to the Sangh Parivar and one of them openly declares that the slain police officer was corrupt, friendly with Muslims and anti-Hindu, implying thereby that he deserved his fate.

World over, in any civilized society, the killing of a policeman is a more serious offence than any other crime, because it represents an assault on the very basis of that civilisation. It brooks no tolerance and even the most fractious of social and political groups come together to ensure that the perpetrators of such a crime are given exemplary punishment so that no one ever dares to attack the authority of law. In UP on the other hand we are witness to the entire administration, presided over by a Chief Minister who flaunts his bigotry as his badge of identity, preparing the ground not for bringing the perpetrators to book but for protecting them as defenders of faith and culture. This is the Rule of Lawlessness.

Our colleagues in service, in the Police and the Civil Administration appear, with honourable exceptions, to have capitulated readily to this perverted political order. They seem to have forgotten that their primary allegiance is to the Constitution and the Rule of Law, and that their constitutional status provides them an armour of such extraordinary strength that, had they taken steps to check the growing menace of the Hindutva brigade, they could certainly have prevented the outbreak of violence. Instead they not only allowed these hooligans to grow in confidence and gather political strength, they helped them gain impunity in their lawless actions. Even now if they—the Chief Secretary, the Director General of Police, the Home Secretary, the District Magistrate and the district police authorities—stand together to uncover the insidious political agenda, identify its masterminds and bring the hooligans involved in the violence to book, they stand a chance to redeem their pledge to the Constitution and live up to the expectations that citizens have of the higher civil services.

Our Prime Minister, who is so voluble in his election campaigns and who never tires of telling us of how the Constitution of India is the only holy book he worships, maintains stony silence even as he sees a Chief Minister handpicked by him treat that same Constitution with sheer contempt. It is evident that, for the Sangh Parivar, constitutional morality is of no value and is necessarily subordinate to the ideals of majoritarian supremacy.

Never before in recent history has the politics of hate, division and exclusion been so dominant and the poisonous ideology which informs it penetrated so deep into the body politic. Never before has hate been directed with such calculated intent against minority communities, hate which is nursed, aided and abetted by those in power. Violence has been given social and political sanction and perpetrators of violence have been treated with kid gloves while victims have been punished and harassed.

This is a critical moment and we cannot take it lying down anymore. We call upon all citizens to unite in a crusade against the politics of hate and division—a politics which aims to destroy the fundamental principles on which our Republic is founded. We ask all citizens to whom constitutional values matter to join us in reasserting our sovereignty as citizens to:

- Demand the resignation of the Chief Minister for his failure to abide by the Constitution to which he has sworn his allegiance. We know that this can happen, if together, we build a groundswell of public opinion by which we hold him accountable for his conduct and compel him to resign.
- Remind the Chief Secretary, the Director General of Police, the Home Secretary, and all other members of the higher civil services concerned, of their constitutional duty to fearlessly implement the Rule of Law rather than the perverse dictates of their political masters.

- Request the High Court at Allahabad to take suo motu cognisance of this incident and order a judicial enquiry supervised by them to uncover the true facts, expose the political collusion, fix responsibility and recommend action.
- Work towards a citizen-led national campaign against the politics of hate and violence—in particular, the structural violence directed against Muslims, Adivasis, Dalits and women—violence which finds sustenance in the structures of political power.
- Salute Inspector Subodh Kumar Singh for his bravery in standing up for constitutional values and refusing to yield to political pressure even at the cost of his life and for setting an example to his children and the younger generation that values matter more than career success. We also acknowledge and applaud the dignity with which his family has faced this crisis and their quiet resolve to uphold the principles for which Subodh Kumar Singh sacrificed his life. His martyrdom will not be in vain.

SATYAMEVA JAYATE

Constitutional Conduct Group (83 signatories)

PUBLIC STATEMENT ON A UNION MINISTER'S ACTIONS

9 July 2018

Our group of retired civil servants has, over the past year, drawn the attention of the powers that be, particularly the Government of India, to the promotion of an environment that encourages violence, in both word and deed. Apart from reckless utterances at election times aimed at fostering a feeling of hate and enmity in the majority community about the 'other', a number of other specific instances have highlighted the horrifying apathy, if not implicit support, of various governments, at the central and state levels, to vigilante violence directed against individuals of specific communities. But what has been even more mind-numbing has been the open challenge to the rule of law by those entrusted with its protection.

The latest happening at Hazaribagh has been especially shattering for our group, coming as it did from a member of the Union Council of Ministers. Those convicted of the brutal lynching last year at Ramgarh (Jharkhand) are entitled to the due process of law, including getting bail pending a decision of the High Court on their conviction. It was, however, most unseemly of the Union Minister of State for Civil Aviation, Shri Jayant Sinha, to felicitate the convicts as though they were some revolutionaries in a freedom struggle. His subsequent feeble justifications on social media do not hold water. If he genuinely felt that the law should take its course, prudence (if not humanity) dictated that he should have been circumspect in his actions. We strongly condemn his action, which amounts to showing contempt for the rule of law and the Constitution of India, which he is duty bound to uphold. The latest episode comes on the heels of repeated incidents which highlight the contempt which representatives of the ruling party and their followers have for the rule of law.

Whether it is the act of a Union Minister draping the body of an accused rioter in the national tricolour, the instigation by ruling party ministers of Jammu and Kashmir in the Kathua rape case or the efforts to subvert due process of law in the brutal Rajsamand murder case, all such cases only indicate a majoritarian mindset that believes it is entitled to use the law to meet its own narrow ends. The larger and chilling message that Shri Sinha's action sends out is that there is a license to kill minorities and that those who are accused of such crimes will be enthusiastically supported financially, legally and politically.

In the past, when there were protests against partisan support for such revolting actions, the Central Government conveniently used the fig leaf of constitutional separation of powers to argue that the locus standi lay with the concerned states, despite most of these states being ruled by the same party which was in power at the Centre. Now that a Union Minister has openly questioned a criminal case where his own party government in the state had, admirably in our opinion, prosecuted and brought to justice the accused, we would like to know what stand the Government of India proposes to take.

We demand the immediate resignation/removal of Shri Jayant Sinha from the Union Council of Ministers and an apology to the people of India from the party he represents for brazenly sympathizing with those convicted of murder. We also urge our colleagues in the civil services to firmly adhere to the rule of law and not be intimidated by the actions of powerful and influential groups which seek to spread the poison of disharmony and enmity in our multicultural society.

SATYAMEVA JAYATE
Constitutional Conduct Group (50 signatories)

LETTER TO THE PRIME MINISTER: CONCERNS REGARDING DECLINING SECULAR, DEMOCRATIC AND LIBERAL VALUES

15 April 2018

Shri Narendra Modi
Honourable Prime Minister of India

Honourable Prime Minister,
We are a group of retired civil servants who came together last year to express our concern at the decline in the secular, democratic, and liberal values enshrined in our constitution. We did so to join other voices of protest against the frightening climate of hate, fear and viciousness that the ruling establishment had insidiously induced. We spoke then as we do now: as citizens who have no affiliations with any political party nor adherence to any political ideology other than the values enshrined in our Constitution.

We had hoped that as someone sworn to upholding the Constitution, the Government that you head and the party to which you belong would wake up to this alarming decline, take the lead in stemming the rot and reassure everyone, especially the minorities and vulnerable sections of society that they need not fear for their life and liberty. This hope has been destroyed. Instead, the unspeakable horror of the Kathua and the Unnao incidents shows that the Government has failed in performing the most basic of the responsibilities given to it by the people. We, in turn, have failed as a nation which took pride in its ethical, spiritual and cultural heritage and as a society which treasured its civilisational values of tolerance, compassion and fellow feeling. By giving sustenance to the brutality of one human being against another in the name of Hindus we have failed as human beings.

The bestiality and the barbarity involved in the rape and murder of an eight-year-old child shows the depths of depravity that we have sunk into. In post-Independence India, this is our darkest hour and we find the response of our Government, the leaders of our political parties, inadequate and feeble. At this juncture, we see no light at the end of the tunnel and we hang our heads in shame. Our sense of shame is all the more acute because some of our younger colleagues who are still in service, especially those working in the districts and are required by law to care for and protect the weak and the vulnerable, also seem to have failed in their duty.

Prime Minister, we write to you not just to express our collective sense of shame and not just to give voice to our anguish or lament and mourn the death of our civilisational values—but to express our rage. Rage over the agenda of division and hate your party and its innumerable, often untraceable offshoots that spring up from time to time, have insidiously introduced into the grammar of our politics, our social and cultural life and even our daily discourse. It is that which provides the social sanction and legitimacy for the incidents in Kathua and Unnao.

In Kathua, it is the culture of majoritarian belligerence and aggression promoted by the Sangh Parivar which emboldened rabid communal elements to pursue their perverse agenda. They knew that their behaviour would be endorsed by the politically powerful and those who have made their careers by polarising Hindus and Muslims across a sectarian divide. In Unnao in UP, it is the reliance on the worst kinds of patriarchal feudal Mafia Dons to capture votes and political power that gives such persons the freedom to rape and murder and extort as a way of asserting their own personal power. But even more reprehensible than such abuse of power, it is the response of the state government in hounding the victim of rape and her family instead of the alleged perpetrator that shows how perverted governance practices have become. That the Government of UP finally acted only when it was compelled to do so by the High Court, shows its hypocrisy and the half-heartedness of its intent.

In both cases, Prime Minister, it is your party which is in power. Given your supremacy within the party and the centralised control you and your Party President exercise, you more than anyone else have to be held responsible for this terrifying state of affairs. Instead of owning up and making reparations however, you had until yesterday chosen to remain silent, breaking your silence only when public outrage both in India and internationally reached a point when you could no longer ignore it.

And even then, while you have condemned the act and expressed a sense of shame, you have not condemned the communal pathology behind the act nor shown the resolve to change the social, political and administrative conditions under which such communal hate is bred. We have had enough of these belated remonstrations and promises to bring justice when the communal cauldron is forever kept boiling by forces nested within the Sangh Parivar.

Prime Minister, these two incidents are not just ordinary crimes where, with the passage of time, the wounds inflicted on our social fabric, on our body politic and the moral fibre of our society will heal and it will soon be business as usual. This is a moment of existential crisis, a turning point—the way the Government responds now will determine whether we as a nation and as a republic have the capacity to overcome the crisis of constitutional values, of governance and the ethical order within which we function. And to this end we call upon you to do the following:

- Reach out to the families of the victims in Unnao and Kathua and seek their forgiveness on behalf of all of;
- Fast-track the prosecution of the perpetrators in the Kathua case and request for a Court-directed SIT in the Unnao case, without further ado;
- In the memory of these innocent children and all other victims of hate crime, renew a pledge to offer special protection to Muslims, to Dalits, to members of other minority communities, to women and children so that they need not fear for their life and liberty and any threat to these will be extinguished with the full force of State;
- Take steps to remove from Government anyone who has been associated with hate crimes and hate;
- Call for an All Party Meeting to deliberate on ways in which the phenomenon of hate crime can be tackled socially and politically.

It is possible that even this may be too little too late but it will restore some sense of order and give hope that the free fall into anarchy can be arrested. We live in hope.

Yours faithfully,
Constitutional Conduct Group (49 signatories)

OPEN LETTER REGARDING VIOLENCE AND DISCRIMINATION AGAINST MINORITIES IN INDIA

28 January 2018

We, retired civil servants belonging to different Services and batches, wish to register our deep concern at the continuing incidents of mindless violence in the country, especially those targeting the minorities, and the lackadaisical response of the law enforcement machinery to these attacks.

The killing of Mohammed Afrazul, a migrant worker from West Bengal in Rajsamand, Rajasthan, on the 25th Anniversary of the demolition of the Babri Masjid has deeply shaken each of us. The recording of the brutal act on video and the circulation of the justification for the killing over the internet cuts at the roots of an inclusive and pluralistic society drawing its inspiration from the teachings of Buddha, Mahavira, Ashoka, Akbar, the Sikh Gurus, Hindu Sages and Gandhi. The violent incidents in Udaipur in support of the alleged killer are a pointer to how deep the sectarian poison has spread among the population of this country.

In the last nine months, we have seen the death of Pehlu Khan on 3 April after he was attacked by a crowd of so called Gau Rakshaks near Behror, Alwar, on 1 April. The killers named by him have not been arrested so far. However, seven others have been arrested and subsequently let off on bail.

The second killing on 16 June of Zafar Khan was in the name of Swachh Bharat Abhiyan. The Municipal Chairman and other Safai Karmacharis in Pratapgarh reportedly beat him to death while he was opposing the naming and shaming process for making Pratapgarh open and defecation-free. There is no arrest so far with the police claiming that Zafar Khan died of a heart attack.

The third killing in June 2017, was that of 16-year-old Junaid Khan on a train, returning after Eid shopping in Delhi, following a dispute over seats on the train when following abuses and insults he was stabbed and thrown out of the train at Asoti station, where he bled to death.

Following an outcry against this incident both within and outside India, the Prime Minister made a statement that 'killing people in the name of "Gau bhakti" is unacceptable'. He repeated this once again a day before the Parliamentary session started on 15 July 2017, at an All India Meeting of the BJP, where he placed the onus on taking stringent action in these cases on the state governments. However, the killings continue without any check.

The fourth killing happened on 27 August 2017, when Anwar Hussain and Hafizul Sheikh, both 19 years of age, who were transporting cattle purchased from Dhupguri in West Bengal to Tufangunj in Cooch Behar. As they got lost on the way, a mob accosted them in the early hours and when they could not pay the 50,000 rupees demanded of them, beat them both to death. Though three persons were arrested for the lynching, efforts to identify others in the mob have not produced any result so far.

The fifth killing happened on 10 November 2017, when Umair Khan and his friends transporting cows were fired on by so called Gau Rakshaks in Govindgarh Tehsil in Alwar district. Umair Khan was killed and his body was carried to the railway track in an attempt to destroy all evidence. Of the seven killers only two were arrested. However, two of the victims, Tahir and Jawed, were placed behind bars.

The Indian Express of 25 December quotes a BJP MLA from Rajasthan—Gyan Dev Ahuja of Ramgarh—who said that 'if one engages in cow smuggling or slaughters a cow, he will be killed.' Such language is an open incitement to violence, acts of which are slowly poisoning the body politic and examples of which are listed above. Such words and actions have no place in a civilized society and fly in the face of established jurisprudence. Vigilantism is let loose upon a hapless group with all its tragic consequences.

Apart from the murders, we are deeply concerned to see the acceleration of a process of ghettoisation through organised resistance to sale of properties to Muslims, or refusal by owners to have them as tenants. A recent case reported in the media relates to prevention of a Muslim buyer to take possession of a house in the Maliwara locality of Meerut that he had paid for. The daily indignities that the Muslims face in this and many other ways is bound to lead to an atmosphere of resentment in that religious community that will further vitiate an already poisoned environment. The 'love jihad' campaigns of right-wing Hindu groups are again symptomatic of the efforts by extremist elements of the majority religion to interfere in the basic constitutional rights of citizens to enter into marriage with a partner of their choice.

In the past few weeks in December, we are witness to increasing targeting of Christians around the observation of Christmas. On 15 December, police detained groups singing carols in Satna. When a group of priests went to make enquiries, they were also reportedly detained by the police. In Uttar Pradesh, the Hindu Jagran Manch warned Christian schools in Aligarh against observing Christmas. In Rajasthan, members of the Vishwa Hindu Parishad allegedly stormed a Christmas function on the grounds that this was an attempt at forced conversion.

We seek now and without delay a clear response from the Hon'ble Prime Minister and his government on these issues, along with immediate and firm action against the perpetrators of such hate crimes against minorities in this country by the respective law enforcement authorities.

These recent incidents undermine our Constitutional values and weaken the rule of law to create a new normal in society. Our existing laws provide adequate protection if they are implemented with the necessary will and determination. Legal protection alone however is not a solution when the communal virus has already spread far and wide in the society. It is essential for each of us as individuals to reflect on the repercussions of a situation where the present trends could threaten the peace and cohesion that is a fundamental pre-requisite for our growth and development. And for all of us, most of all for those who belong to the majority community, to go beyond mere reflection, to stand us, oppose and publicly condemn the communalisation of our society and our country.

SATYAMEVA JAYATE

Constitutional Conduct Group (67 signatories)

AN OPEN LETTER ON INCREASED RELIGIOUS INTOLERANCE

10 June 2017

We are a group of retired officers of All India and Central Services of different batches, who have worked with the Central and State Governments in the course of our careers. We should make it clear that as a group, we have no affiliation with any political party but believe in the credo of impartiality, neutrality and commitment to the Indian Constitution. A sense of deep disquiet at what has been happening in India has prompted us to write this open letter to chronicle our reservations and misgivings about recent developments in the body politic. What has gone wrong?

It appears as if there is a growing climate of religious intolerance that is aimed primarily at Muslims. In Uttar Pradesh, in the run-up to the elections, an odious and frankly communal comparison was made between the relative number of burial grounds and cremation grounds. The question was also asked as to whether electricity was being supplied equally to different communities during their religious festivals. All this without any basis in fact or evidence. The banning of slaughterhouses targets the minorities and affects their livelihoods as well. Such intolerance breeds violence in a communally charged atmosphere—even to the extent of a local leader in UP provoking an attack upon the residence of a Superintendent of Police, whose family was terrorised.

Vigilantism has become widespread. An Aklaq is killed on the basis of a suspicion that the meat he has is beef and a Pehlu Khan is lynched while transporting to his place two cows he had bought and for which he had the necessary papers. Nomadic shepherds are attacked in Jammu and Kashmir on some suspicion as they practice their age-old occupation of moving from one place to another along with their cattle and belongings. Gau Rakshaks function with impunity and seem to be doing so with the tacit complicity or active encouragement of State machinery. Punitive action against the perpetrators of violence does not take place promptly but cruelly, the victims have FIRs registered against them. The behaviour of vigilantes—who act as if they are prosecutor, judge and executioner rolled into one—flies in the face of law and jurisprudence. These actions undermine the rule of law and the Indian Constitution since only the State—through its various organs and institutions—has the power to enforce the law.

Vigilantism has become popular as 'anti-Romeo' squads threaten young couples who go out together, hold hands and are perhaps in love with each other. A thinly veiled effort to prevent a Hindu-Muslim relationship or marriage, there is no justification in law to harass these couples, particularly when there is no complaint from the woman of being ill-treated.

Student groups and faculty members on campuses like Hyderabad and JNU, who raise troubling questions about equality, social justice and freedom are subject to attack by the administration, with a supportive government to back them. In Jodhpur, a planned lecture by a renowned academic was cancelled under pressure and the faculty that organised the event subjected to disciplinary action. What happened in Jodhpur has happened at other institutions as well. Argumentation and discussion about different perspectives—the life-blood not only of institutions of learning but of democracy itself—are being throttled.

Disagreement and dissent are considered seditious and anti-national. Such attitudes have a chilling impact on free speech and thought.

Several reputed NGOs and civil society organisations are being charged with violating the provisions of the FCRA and the Income Tax Act. While we agree that genuine violators should be identified and penalised, we note with dismay that several of the targeted groups are those who have taken stands against government policies, expressed dissent or supported communities in cases against the State.

We are also seeing an ugly trend of trolling, threats and online intimidation of activists, journalists, writers and intellectuals who disagree with the dominant ideology. How does this square with free speech?

There is a growing hyper-nationalism that reduces any critique to a binary: if you are not with the government, you are anti-national. Those in authority should not be questioned—that is the clear message.

In the face of a rising authoritarianism and majoritarianism, which do not allow for reasoned debate, discussion and dissent, we appeal to all public authorities, public institutions and Constitutional bodies to take heed of these disturbing trends and take corrective action. We have to reclaim and defend the spirit of the Constitution of India, as envisaged by the founding fathers.

SATYAMEVA JAYATE

Constitutional Conduct Group (65 signatories)

ELECTION AND VOTING

Electoral Reforms

ANJALI BHARDWAJ

Credible elections, though not sufficient, remain a necessary condition for any polity to be considered democratic. Even as the Prime Minister hails India as the 'Mother of Democracy', there are growing concerns about several aspects of our electoral system which are eroding public trust in elections and threatening the foundations of our constitutional democracy.

Ensuring the purity of the electoral process requires multiple reforms—a basket of measures, which includes: removing the influence of money power in elections, ensuring transparency in the functioning of political parties and in the electoral process, and having an independent and impartial regulator.

Transparency in the functioning of political parties

In India, where most people vote for parties rather than individual candidates and the constitutional framework allows political parties decisive control over voting by their legislators, an enlightened, or even a functional, democracy requires that people have information about the working of political parties. People should know, for instance, where parties are getting their funds from and what criteria they are following while taking policy decisions, supporting or opposing bills in Parliament, or while selecting candidates for various elections. There can be little information that is more critical for ensuring that people elect the party that is closest to their aspirations.

Unfortunately, the political system in India has traditionally been hostile to the idea of transparency. In 2013, a full bench of the Central Information Commission (CIC) declared six national political parties 'public authorities' under the Right to Information (RTI) Act, 2005. Parties were required to appoint Public Information Officers and submit themselves to provisions of the transparency law. So strong was the resolve of parties to shield themselves from public scrutiny, that immediately a bill was introduced in Parliament to amend the RTI law to exclude political parties from the ambit of the legislation. The bill enjoyed near unanimous support of the political parties across the spectrum. It was only due to strident public opposition that the amendments were first referred to a Parliamentary committee and finally not pursued. Nevertheless, following the policy of what can only be termed 'uncivil disobedience', without obtaining a stay on the Commission's order from any Court, parties have steadfastly refused to comply with the directive of the CIC. The matter is hanging fire in the Supreme Court.

Addressing the malaise of money power and secret electoral bonds

In the 1957 *Jayantilal Ranchhoddas Koticha v. Tata Iron and Steel Co Ltd* judgment, where a proposal by the Tata Iron and Steel Company to make contributions to political parties was being adjudicated, Justice M.C. Chagla noted, '...it is difficult to accept the position that the integrity of the voter and of the representative is safeguarded if large industrial concerns are permitted to contribute to political funds... It is a danger which may grow apace, and which may ultimately overwhelm and even throttle democracy in the country.'

Nearly seven decades later, problems emanating from the influence of money power in elections are widely recognised. Political financing in India has evolved—from political parties mobilising funds primarily through memberships and small contributions to corporate funding of parties becoming the norm over time. This has paved the way for quid pro quo, with corporates making large contributions to parties to advance their own interests.

The existing pattern of electoral funding in the country compromises the integrity of democracy in multiple ways—it raises the entry barriers to politics; excludes honest candidates and parties; leads to big money controlling the State; distorts policy making into wasteful, inefficient and anti-democratic directions and exacerbates polarisation. These are not trivial costs for any democracy. Though there is a limit on expenditure by candidates during elections in India, there are no limits for party expenses. Big parties usually spend more money per constituency than the limits of individual candidates.

Party financing has become the fountainhead of corruption in India, bringing with it the malaise of black money. A factor that abetted large cash donations and use of black money in political party funding was the provision in the Income Tax Act exempting political parties from disclosing sources of donations of less than Rs 20,000. In 2010–11, just six national parties had a combined declared income of Rs 700 crore and a whopping 90 per cent were reported as having been received in denominations smaller than Rs 20,000 thus doing away with the requirement to disclose the source of donation. Most of these 'anonymous' donations were large cash donations made by industrialists and corporates, which were 'broken down' and shown as multiple small donations.

A clear imperative, therefore, was to remove any scope or loopholes allowing anonymous funding to parties, to ensure every donation is diligently documented and reported to the people of India to enable them to scrutinise and blow the whistle on instances of quid pro quo. When the BJP government announced the launch of a new instrument of political party funding to ostensibly ensure greater transparency and eliminate black money from the system, it was hoped that the issue of anonymous financing would be squarely dealt with. However, using the Money Bill route to bypass the Rajya Sabha, the government brought regressive amendments to the Income Tax Act, Companies Act, RBI Act and the Representation of the People Act, to introduce electoral bonds which allowed donors to anonymously donate unlimited amounts of funds to political parties.

Under the Electoral Bond Scheme of 2018, an electoral bond (EB), issued in the nature of a promissory note, can be bought by any Indian citizen or company incorporated in India. The scheme allows parties to receive these bonds without the public, the Election Commission or even the Income Tax department knowing the identity of donors. It has legitimised opacity and opened the floodgates for anonymous donations to parties, dealing a severe blow to voters' right to know. People's ability to track donations by big businesses and expose quid pro quo have been severely undermined.

Responses to the RTI applications reveal that the government was forewarned of the grave dangers associated with electoral bonds. Copies of communication between the Reserve Bank of India (RBI) and the Finance Ministry obtained under the RTI Act show that the RBI warned that bonds would violate the principle and spirit of the Prevention of Money Laundering Act (PMLA), as the original buyer need not be the actual contributor to the political party. While the person buying the bearer bond will need to fulfil the Know Your Customer (KYC) requirements, the identity of the intervening entities will be unknown. The then RBI Governor, Urjit Patel, flagged serious concerns about the Electoral Bonds Scheme on the grounds that it could easily be misused for money laundering, forgery and counterfeiting.

Further, the Election Commission of India, expressing its opposition to amendments made to laws for enabling introduction of electoral bonds, contended that they will have an adverse impact on transparency in political party financing and would make it impossible for the ECI to ascertain whether donations received were in compliance with the statutory framework governing political parties. The ECI also raised concerns that amendments to the Companies Act, which removed the cap imposed on companies to contribute no more than 7.5 per cent of the average net profits in the preceding three financial years, would open up the possibility of shell companies being set up with the sole purpose of making donations to political parties.

These objections were particularly alarming given the amendments that were made to the Foreign Contribution (Regulation) Act, which enabled Indian subsidiaries of foreign companies to make donations to political parties. Electoral bonds, therefore allowed anonymous financing by even foreign entities opening Indian elections to the influence of foreign interests. In effect, they enabled the setting up of fly-by-night operators only for the funnelling of funds to political parties with no legitimate businesses or profits to show.

The rationale given by the government for introducing electoral bonds was to allow donors to use legitimate funds to support political parties by protecting them against the wrath of rival parties, especially the party in power. In reality, however, bonds create an asymmetry of information in favour of the ruling party. As bonds are issued only through the State Bank of India, it would not be difficult for the party in power to access information about the identity of purchasers and details of bonds sold to them, and match those to deposits in political party accounts. It is no surprise, therefore, that the lion's share of donations through bonds have been cornered by the ruling BJP.

Along with the slew of amendments in 2017, another change that was made to the Income Tax Act was to fix the limit for cash donations at Rs 2,000, to ostensibly curb the use of black money. However, this has done little to address the problem as all that is required to bypass this rule is to show larger donations as parcels of less than Rs, 2,000 each, to enjoy the shield of anonymity. Rather than addressing the malaise of anonymous funding of parties through cash, electoral bonds have made even funds through banking channels anonymous.

Bonds of more than Rs 13,500 crore have been sold so far (till October 2023) and have resulted in consolidating the role of big money in electoral politics. A constitution bench of the Supreme Court finally heard the batch of petitions challenging the electoral bonds, and on 2 November 2023 reserved its judgment. It is hoped that the Court will strike down this so called 'reform', which lends itself to use by special interest groups, corporate lobbyists and foreign entities to acquire a stranglehold on the electoral process and governance at the expense of citizens.

Reforming the EVM/VVPAT voting system

Over the last few years, there have been serious concerns regarding the country's electoral process due to questions around the EVM/VVPAT voting system. Though the voting mechanism has evolved from being only the EVM (Electronic Voting Machine) to now the EVM+VVPAT (Voter-Verifiable Paper Trail) system, experts have pointed out that it does not comply with the essential 'Democracy Principles'—that each voter should be able to verify that her vote is cast-as-intended, recorded-as-cast and counted-as-recorded. The VVPAT has been reduced to the level of a 'bioscope' which shows up a tiny 'paper slip' for seven seconds which then vanishes and is not counted. Multiple petitions to the Supreme Court, seeking counting of VVPAT slips prior to declaration of results, have not borne fruit thus far—the Court has merely increased the random checking of VVPAT slips from one EVM to five EVMs in every Assembly segment/constituency. This counting is also not done prior to the declaration of results.

The Citizens' Commission on Elections, headed by a former Judge of the Supreme Court of India, consulted national and international experts on the vexatious issue of the EVM/VVPAT voting, and concluded that it does not provide provable guarantees against hacking, tampering and spurious vote injections and that the existing VVPAT system does not allow the voter to verify the slip before the vote is cast. The Commission has recommended that to ensure the integrity of voting and counting, the VVPAT system should be re-calibrated to be fully voter-verifiable. The VVPAT slips must be printed in such a manner that they can be preserved for a minimum of five years and a voter should be able to get the VVPAT slip in her hand and cast it in a chip-free ballot box for the vote to be valid. These slips should be fully counted for all constituencies before the results are declared and the results of the counting of VVPAT slips should be cross verified with the electronic tallies of the EVMs for every constituency before the results are declared. In case of any mismatch, the counting of the VVPAT slips should be treated as the final result. Petitions to the ECI, urging the regulator to act on these recommendations, have fallen on deaf ears thus far.

Ensuring transparency in Electoral Rolls

Accurate electoral rolls are critical for ensuring free and fair elections that reflect the will of the people. In several recent elections, there have been reports of sizeable arbitrary deletions of voters' names, calling into question the integrity of the Electoral Rolls based on which elections were conducted. In August 2023, taking cognisance of such concerns, the Supreme Court directed that the ECI must follow proper procedures prior to deletion of any name from the voters list and that a prior notice must be issued to every voter whose name is proposed to be deleted. This is critical to ensure that no voter is left behind and people are not removed from the list based solely on automated processes.

To empower citizens to engage in ensuring the integrity of electoral rolls and monitor implementation of the August 2023 Supreme Court directions, it is imperative that voters' lists be made available in the public domain. Democracies routinely ensure public disclosure of voters' lists with names, addresses and other data to enable public scrutiny and prevent electoral fraud. Though electoral rolls are public documents in India, due to several recent changes made by the ECI it has become increasingly difficult for people to access them and carry out public verifications. The electoral rolls are published on the ECI website as image PDFs only, which cannot be searched or exported to programs like Excel to enable people's monitoring. The lists are available only for a single booth at a time, making it extremely cumbersome to access and collate electoral rolls for even a constituency-wise verification exercise. Further, there are apprehensions that following the enactment of the Digital Personal Data Protection Act in 2023, there may be a push to remove all publicly available personal information, including the information contained in the electoral rolls.

Voters' lists must be made available on the ECI website in a searchable database. In addition, they must be publicly displayed in the most accessible manner at the booth level for those who do not have access to the internet. Citizens should be able to verify not just their own information, but also check for arbitrary deletions or addition of bogus names and duplicates in the rolls.

Independent and impartial regulator

The Election Commission of India (ECI) is responsible under Article 324 of the Constitution for the superintendence, direction and control of elections to Parliament and State Legislatures. It is vested with plenary powers to hold free and fair elections.

The conduct of the ECI in recent years has raised serious concerns. The report of the Citizens' Commission on Elections documents several instances where the ECI either failed to act, or responded inadequately, in cases involving allegations of violations of the Model Code of Conduct by the ruling party and its leaders. For instance, in the run up to the 2019 general elections, a television channel—'NaMo TV'—carrying Prime Minister Modi's rallies and other promotional material of the BJP, started broadcasting on several DTH and cable TV platforms as a free-to-air service. Despite complaints being lodged, it continued to be on air throughout the period of elections and mysteriously went off air a day after voting ended in all states. The ECI's action in the face of such an egregious violation was restricted to merely seeking a clarification from the

Information and Broadcast ministry. No directions were given to pull NaMo TV off air.

The clean chits given by the ECI to members of the ruling party during the 2019 Lok Sabha elections caused significant internal strife in the ECI. The refusal to record the dissenting views of an election commissioner, who disagreed with the clean chits, forced him to seek recusal from the ECI meetings.

Concerns have also been expressed about the ECI's conduct with respect to the announcement of dates of elections—with allegations being made about Commission delaying the announcement of election dates to suit the ruling party at the Centre, sharing the dates with individuals close to the ruling party prior to announcement, and even withdrawing the dates announced to suit the ruling party.

Such incidents led to a clamour for reforms in the ECI, and an intervention in the Supreme Court resulted in a landmark judgment regarding the process of selection of the Chief and Election Commissioners. In March 2023, a constitution bench of the apex court ruled against the system of the Central government making these selections. To ensure that the ECI is free from executive interference and its independence is sufficiently protected, the Court recommended that till the Parliament legislates on the issue, a committee comprising the PM, Leader of Opposition in Lok Sabha, and the Chief Justice of India will make the selections. In a blatant move, going against the very basis of the Supreme Court judgment, the government brought a bill which seeks to replace the CJI with a Union Minister on the collegium. The bill, which is currently pending in Parliament, also proposes to downgrade the status of the Election Commissioners, which would adversely impact their autonomy.

~

There is little incentive for political parties and leaders to be more transparent and put curbs on their own arbitrary actions and functioning. In several crucial matters involving reforms, the judiciary has also been found wanting. Even in cases where the courts have intervened, there is the looming threat of the gains being reversed through the legislative route. Eternal vigilance and a sustained nationwide people's movement are the only way to course-correct and herald in the electoral reforms needed to ensure the sanctity of the election process and save our democracy.

Letters and Statements

OPEN LETTER TO THE ELECTION COMMISSION OF INDIA

9 March 2024

Shri Rajiv Kumar,
Chief Election Commissioner,
Shri Arun Goel,
Election Commissioner,

Dear Shri Rajiv Kumar and Shri Arun Goel,

We are a group of former civil servants of the All India and Central Services who have worked in the Central and State Governments during our careers. As a group, we have no affiliation with any political party but believe in impartiality, neutrality and commitment to the Constitution of India.

We are writing to you with reference to the extraordinary request of the State Bank of India (SBI) to the Supreme Court of India (SCI) to extend the time to submit information regarding electoral bonds till 30 June 2024, by which time the elections to Parliament would be over. We note with dismay that it took SBI seventeen days to inform the Court on 4 March that they are not in a position to collate the data by 6 March. For India's largest bank with 48 crore accounts and boasting high levels of digitisation, a pathetic excuse has been proffered that records were kept manually and hence the extension sought. Thomas Franco, former General Secretary of the All India Banking Officers Confederation, has pointed out that SBI had asked the Government of India by a letter of June 2018 for a sum of more than Rs 60 lakhs for development of IT systems for the electoral bond scheme. In the same piece, Franco has also published an RTI reply that gives, in just a period of six days, details of bonds sold over six years. Subhash Chandra Garg, Finance Secretary at the time of finalisation of the scheme (and a defender of it), has said in interviews that it should not take more than ten minutes to get the information sought. He also makes the important point that the SCI has not asked for details linking the purchase of bonds with the political parties to whom they have been given; so, the demand for time is wholly unjustified.

While striking down the scheme of electoral bonds as unconstitutional, the SCI had flagged both the right to information of the citizens of India to know about funding of political parties and how there would be no level playing field if one party got undue financial advantage. The SBI's denying this information and indicating that it would not be available before the general elections seems to indicate that the SBI is shielding the Government in power from any criticism that there was a quid pro quo between the bonds and favours given to some firms or raids/intimidation to pressurise the corporates to fall in line. The media portals *Newslaundry* and *The News Minute* have already published material linking thirty corporates and their purchase of bonds worth about Rs 335 crore in the previous five years to the blatant misuse of enforcement agencies to make these corporates fall in line.

We would like to reference the letter of 6 March 2024, written by EAS Sarma, a former Secretary to the Government of India, in which he has requested the ECI not only to freeze any unspent funds of political parties from the scheme but also not to publish the schedule of elections till the SBI gives the information ordered by the SCI. We note that the term of the present Lok Sabha is up to 16 June 2024, and to complete the election in time, the ECI could announce the schedule by 27 March, or even earlier. The SBI should give the electoral bonds data much before the announcement of the elections. This is an opportunity for the ECI to reclaim its reputation and its integrity by using its powers under Article 324 of the Constitution. As Shri Sarma has suggested, it should direct the SBI to immediately release the information. The ECI should also make it clear that it will not announce the schedule for the 2024 general elections till the SBI furnishes this information. If the ECI remains quiescent, it will not live up to its Constitutional mandate of respecting the right to information of Indian voters and of holding free and fair elections on a level playing field. That would be a death blow for democracy in India as we know it.

SATYAMEVA JAYATE

Yours faithfully,

Constitutional Conduct Group (79 signatories)

OPEN LETTER TO THE ELECTION COMMISSION OF INDIA

19 August 2023

Dear Chief Election Commissioner and Election Commissioners,

We are a group of former civil servants of the All India and Central Services who have worked with the Central and State Governments in the course of our careers. As members of the Constitutional Conduct Group, we are firmly committed to the Constitution of India and are not affiliated to any political party.

We have had written and face to face meetings with the Election Commission of India (ECI) over the past five years. Our communications with the ECI have focused on specific electoral areas calling for remedial action relating to the abuse of money and muscle power, the misuse of print and electronic media, the egregious violations of the Model Code of Conduct by the blatant resort to slanderous and hateful speech, the defects in the process of registration of voters and the opacity as regards the recording and counting of votes during the actual election process. Our group had also taken the initiative to constitute a Citizens' Commission on Elections: two published volumes of its recommendations have been sent to you earlier. As former colleagues of yours, we note with regret that you have not deemed it necessary to interact with us to discuss our suggestions.

We are now at a juncture where, in the next one year, general elections are due for the Lok Sabha as well as for a number of Legislative Assemblies of states. A host of issues, relating to money and muscle power, media and manipulation, the registration of voters and machine management, still await satisfactory resolution to ensure that the election process is carried out in a free and fair manner.

The Union Government rushed through the issuance of electoral bonds in the Lok Sabha as a money bill in 2018. Electoral funding is now totally opaque and open to wholesale corruption. With no information on the contributors to the election chests of different political parties, the doors are wide open for favours being doled out to preferred parties by governments in power, leading to concentration of wealth in a few hands and the complete distortion of economic policy. These bonds give the party handling the reins of governance greater access to funds, which, in the absence of publicly available audit reports, can be used for purposes inimical to the democratic process, such as inducing wholesale defections after elections (increasingly witnessed in recent years). The ECI is focused only on the misuse of money power during elections, ignoring the larger problem of the suborning of the choice of voters in the interregnum between elections. The issue is attaining serious dimensions with the instances of toppling of governments in Karnataka, Madhya Pradesh and Maharashtra in recent years. After some initial reservations about electoral bonds, the ECI has made no efforts to raise this critical issue in the Supreme Court.

Alongside the abuse of money power is the misuse of muscle power. Muscle power has now assumed new forms. Just before elections and at times when legislators are sought to be persuaded to change their party loyalties, the services of law enforcement agencies are selectively utilised to bring pressure to bear on political opponents. The unedifying spectacle of Nationalist Congress Party legislators in Maharashtra switching loyalties and being rewarded with ministerial posts, barely days after being castigated publicly by the Prime Minister for corruption, reflects the depths to which our politics has sunk.

What is very troubling are the unabashed efforts to arouse the sectarian sentiments of voters by appealing to religious and ethnic loyalties. The ECI has been found wanting on this score over the past few years. Our group had raised this issue during the Lok Sabha elections of 2019, when no action was taken on divisive religious rhetoric at election rallies in Wardha and Nanded in Maharashtra. The pattern has continued since, with the latest instance being the open call by the Prime Minister to the voters of Karnataka to chant a religious invocation—'Jai Bajrang Bali'—while casting their votes. The ECI, despite being approached on this matter, took no cognisance.

In spite of clear guidelines issued by the ECI, the media slant towards the Bharatiya Janata Party is clearly visible during the election process. During the recent Karnataka legislative assembly elections, an inordinate amount of time was given by many electronic news channels to the roadshows of the Prime Minister. The silent period of 48 hours before the polling process is completed has also been cleverly exploited by skilful use of the ubiquitous range of modern-day media systems. The very purpose of maintaining a level playing field in respect of media exposure of the election activities of persons belonging to different political parties is defeated in such cases. Our group had pointed out, in a letter to the Hon'ble President of India sent before the 2019 Lok Sabha elections, that the operation of NAMO TV constituted a clear breach of the Model Code of Conduct. In this instance, too, the ECI took no action whatsoever.

The process of registration of voters is still far from satisfactory. Names of genuine voters are often found to be missing from the electoral rolls, while names of those no longer residents at specific locations are still on the rolls, providing scope for bogus voting. A social audit involving voters should be carried out in all assembly constituencies in advance of elections. This would facilitate verification of voter information as well as deletion of names of bogus voters and duplicate entries. After display of booth wise voters' lists for, say, fifteen days, a day should be fixed when voters are invited to a location to examine the electoral rolls and hear the name-wise reading out of the rolls. This exercise would be carried out by the booth level officer in the presence of Panchayat/Municipal officials and representatives of political parties and civil society organisations who choose to be present. The ECI should also ensure that Electoral Registration Officers scrupulously follow its instructions that due process of law is followed in case of any proposed deletion and all voters are served with notices and given an opportunity of hearing before the proposed deletion of their names.

It would seem that the ECI, after introducing VVPAT machines with much fanfare nearly a decade ago, is lukewarm about using these as a manual check on the accuracy of the EVM count. The initial decision of the ECI to verify the VVPAT count in one polling booth per assembly constituency lacked any sound statistical base. The 2019 Supreme Court decision to verify five VVPATs in each assembly constituency is equally statistically unsound. More importantly, the ECI has not introduced any transparency in the VVPAT count. In no election, starting with the 2019 Lok Sabha elections, have the comparative EVM and VVPAT counts of the sample polling booths in assembly constituencies been made available in the public domain. In fact, in the 2019 Lok Sabha elections, counting of the VVPAT slips and matching them with the EVM counts for the corresponding polling stations was not done before the results were publicly declared. As pointed out by the Lok Sabha Committee on Government Assurances, the ECI is, four years after the last Lok Sabha general elections, yet to provide an explanation for discrepancies between the EVM and VVPAT counts in the five assembly constituencies in each parliamentary constituency where VVPAT counts were undertaken as per the directions of the Supreme Court.

For a credible voting process that commands the confidence of voters, the voter should be reasonably confident that her/his vote has been correctly recorded as cast and correctly counted as recorded. Forms 17A and 17C should be tallied and publicly disclosed at the end of polling on the polling day itself and tallied with the counts of VVPAT printouts. We recommend that all VVPAT slips be counted for every assembly constituency, both in Lok Sabha and Assembly elections. The EVM counting and 100 per cent VVPAT slip counting should be taken up simultaneously in every assembly constituency to arrive at the result as expeditiously as possible. Where the EVM count and the VVPAT count yield different results as to who is elected, the VVPAT count (as a manual, verifiable count) should be the basis for declaring the election result.

With the paramount objectives of instilling confidence in the voter and ensuring that, in accordance with the vast powers vested in it under Article 324 of the Constitution of India, its writ runs in any election, the ECI must take the following actions at the earliest:

(i) Move the Supreme Court for an early hearing of the Electoral Bonds case, to bring about transparency in election funding.

(ii) Initiate a dialogue with representatives of political parties to facilitate the amendment of Article 102 of the Constitution of India to disqualify MPs/MLAs, who defect after being elected on the ticket of a particular political party, from contesting any election for a period of six years from the date of defection.

(iii) Strengthen provisions of the Model Code of Conduct to bar all sectarian, divisive communal propaganda/statements that are likely to influence the voting process and initiate severe action against offenders, including even prohibition from contesting polls for a specified period of time.

(iv) With new forms of media coming into play, evolve norms to ensure fair play and even access to all forms of media—print, electronic and social.

(v) Carry out social audit of electoral rolls as indicated above.

(vi) Develop a robust cross-verification system of EVMs through systematic VVPAT use, as detailed above.

You are the inheritors of a rich tradition of conducting free and fair elections that has withstood the test of time over seventy years. We urge you to continue the legacy of your eminent predecessors in maintaining the sanctity of the electoral process and safeguarding democracy.

SATYAMEVA JAYATE

Constitutional Conduct Group (89 signatories)

OPEN STATEMENT LINKING VOTER ID AND AADHAAR—A DANGEROUS MOVE

29 December 2021

We are a group of former civil servants of the All India and Central Services who have worked with the Central and State Governments in the course of our careers. As a group, we have no affiliation with any political party but believe in impartiality, neutrality and commitment to the Constitution of India.

We are issuing this open statement to voice our grave apprehensions regarding the provision in the recently enacted Election Laws (Amendment) Act, 2021 to link the Electoral Photo Identity Card (EPIC-Voter ID) issued by the Election Commission of India (ECI) with the Aadhaar card issued by the Unique Identification Authority of India (UIDAI), an agency of the Government of India.

The ECI is mandated by Article 324 of the Constitution of India with the superintendence, direction and control of elections to parliament, the state legislatures and the offices of the President and Vice President of India. Accurate electoral rolls and the Voter IDs issued by the ECI ensure free and fair elections that reflect the will of the people of India. The requirement of Aadhaar verification, even if voluntary, from a prospective or registered voter implies the superimposition of a government-issued identity card for identity and address verification that could seriously undermine the independence and integrity of the ECI and cast doubts on the fairness of the entire electoral process.

There are six reasons (listed below) why the move to require Aadhaar verification for Voter IDs is defective, bad in law, in bad faith and liable to potential misuse by the state:

1. The Voter ID is issued on the basis of citizenship while the Aadhaar card is issued on the basis of identity, without proof of citizenship being required. Section 9 of the Aadhaar Act, 2016 is clear that Aadhaar may not be used as proof of address, age, gender, citizenship or relationship. Even if it is argued that Voter IDs may be wrongly issued to non-citizens, the verification by Aadhaar in no way solves this vexing problem; in fact, it is quite likely that even non-citizens may be registered as voters if Aadhaar is used as the only proof.
2. Unlike Aadhaar enrolments, which need only production of existing documents, Voter IDs are based on physical verification and 'house visits' by a Block Level Officer. The Voter ID is certified by the Electoral Registration Officer while there is no certification of the Aadhaar by the UIDAI. It cannot be ruled out that, with the linkage of Aadhaar numbers to Voter IDs, and in the absence of physical verification by the election authorities, efforts may be made to manipulate electoral rolls by getting persons registered as voters in constituencies where they do not reside.
3. The recent legislation which inserted sub-sections (4), (5) and (6) in Section 23 of the Representation of the People Act,

1950 (RPA-1950) and clauses (hhha) and (hhhb) in Section 28(2) of the RPA-1950 makes it evident that the Government of India is dissembling when it states that linking the Aadhaar number to the Voter ID is voluntary. These new insertions, in effect, make it mandatory for a voter to furnish her/his Aadhaar details or risk disenfranchisement. The new sub-section 6 of Section 23 is especially revealing in its intentions. It states 'No application for inclusion of name in the electoral roll shall be denied and no entries in the electoral roll shall be deleted for inability of an individual to furnish or intimate Aadhaar number due to such sufficient cause as may be prescribed;' (emphasis added). The possible mischief that this wording can give rise to is made amply clear by the subsequent clauses in the Amendment Act which permit the government to prescribe, under its rule-making powers, the process for intimation of Aadhaar numbers by voters. Rules made by the government require no parliamentary approval. A rule can, therefore, easily be introduced making the furnishing of Aadhaar numbers a prerequisite for voter enrolment. The scope for large-scale deletion of names from the electoral rolls can then become a distinct possibility, given that many existing voters may not (or may choose not to) furnish their Aadhaar details to the Electoral Registration Officer. There is also the likelihood that the UIDAI's powers to omit or deactivate Aadhaar numbers under Section 23 (g) of the Aadhaar Act could lead to widespread deletions from the electoral rolls.

4. The experience to date in attempting to clean up data base registries of other government programmes like MGNREGA and PDS, using the Aadhaar data base, has been discouraging: names of thousands of beneficiaries have been arbitrarily deleted from systems without any notice, resulting in mass disentitlement.
5. Linking Aadhaar numbers to Voter IDs will open the floodgates for illegal profiling and targeting of voters,

especially in the run-up to elections, when the Model Code of Conduct is not in place. It is instructive to learn from the recent experience of Andhra Pradesh and Telangana, where software residing in the State Resident Data Hub (SRDH) of the state governments and maintained by a private company was used by the governments to provide information on duplicate voters to the Chief Electoral Officers of the states, a clear violation of electoral laws.

6. There is a distinct possibility that Voter IDs linked to Aadhaar cards and thence to mobile phones could be linked to social media. This social media can be linked to algorithms that are in turn linked to user interests/views. Without a robust Data Protection law and accompanying regulatory mechanisms in place, voter profiling, selective exclusion and targeted campaigns are all possible. The 2016 presidential campaign in the USA brought to light the Cambridge Analytica scandal. Justice B.N. Srikrishna, former Judge of the Supreme Court, who chaired the expert committee that drafted the Data Protection Bill categorically condemned the linkage of Voter IDs with Aadhaar as 'the most dangerous situation'. His graphic warning was that 'instead of having a Cambridge Analytica you'll have a Delhi Analytica, a Mumbai Analytica, a Calcutta Analytica…!'

It has already been shown at point no. 3 in the preceding paragraph that the wording of the amendments introduced in the RPA-1950 gives ample scope to mandatorily enforce the linkage of Aadhaar with Voter IDs. Even if one were to presume the good intentions of the government in not bringing in delegated legislation to enforce the linkage, we are familiar with the manner in which the public was literally coerced to link their bank accounts with their Aadhaar numbers, despite the apparent 'voluntary' nature of executive directions and the specific orders of the Supreme Court. In fact, many government departments and private bodies today routinely ask for Aadhaar numbers for provision of services, in clear violation of Supreme Court orders, which specified the use of Aadhaar-based identification for government welfare schemes funded from the Consolidated Fund of India. Those who wish to avail of these services are compelled to disclose their Aadhaar numbers. Matters have come to a pass where Aadhaar numbers are required even for cremation or burial purposes.

It is unfortunate enough that the Government of India has, without any effective parliamentary oversight or discussion, brought in this crucial legislation that could have a major impact on electoral outcomes. It is even more unfortunate that the ECI has seen fit to promote a move which has the capacity to restrict its independence and integrity in the conduct of elections. What is now called for is strong judicial intervention to nip this highly dangerous move in the bud.

SATYAMEVA JAYATE

Constitutional Conduct Group (104 signatories)

OPEN LETTER TO THE ELECTION COMMISSION OF INDIA: URGENT NEED FOR UPDATED, ACCURATE ELECTORAL ROLLS

2 September 2021

To

Shri Sushil Chandra

Chief Election Commissioner

Dear Shri Chandra,

Our group of former civil servants is nonpartisan and believes firmly in the Constitution of India. We have had a number of opportunities to interact with your predecessors in the Election Commission of India (ECI) over the past four years on issues relating to the impartiality and integrity of the electoral process, which is the bedrock of our democracy.

As part of our duty as responsible citizens of India, we had constituted the Citizens' Commission on Elections (CCE), which brought out its reports in two volumes earlier this year (Report of the Citizens' Commission on Elections—Vol. I* and Report of the Citizens' Commission on Elections—Vol. II†). While a number of critical issues pertaining to the conduct of elections have been brought out in these two reports, our present letter focuses on the integrity and accuracy of the electoral rolls, including special care to include vulnerable populations, which alone guarantee the citizen of India her/his precious and basic right to vote. Vol. II of the CCE report highlights the following aspects:

(i) the persistence of the exclusion of vulnerable and disadvantaged groups, such as persons from religious and caste minority communities, women, Dalits, Adivasis (especially Particularly Vulnerable Tribal Groups or PVTGs), trans-people, the urban homeless, persons with disabilities and persons with mental health issues, from the electoral rolls;

(ii) failure of the Electoral Registration Officers (EROs) to ensure the full and verifiable enrolment of persons from all such categories;

(iii) discrepancies in the registration process wherein, even if a person is provided with an EPIC, there is no guarantee that her/his name will figure in the relevant electoral roll;

(iv) problems in voting for categories like circular migrant labour and those whose physical condition (due to age and disability) inhibit their travel to polling stations to vote.

* For further information, see: https://constitutionalconduct.files.wordpress.com/2021/04/citizens-commission-on-elections-vol.-i.pdf

† For further information, see: https://constitutionalconduct.files.wordpress.com/2021/04/citizens-commission-on-elections-vol.ii_.pdf

In view of the above infirmities in the electoral registration process, we suggest the following remedial measures for your urgent consideration:

1. Ensuring registration of all eligible voters

It must be impressed upon EROs that it is their paramount duty to ensure that all eligible voters are included in the electoral rolls. If certain populations are excluded from electoral rolls because of their social and economic disadvantage, this amounts to their disenfranchisement and the denial to them of their most fundamental right in a democracy, namely to cast their vote during general, state, municipal and panchayat elections. Due care should be taken by the EROs to scrupulously attend to claims and objections from citizens for inclusion, deletion and corrections to voter records. While the central and state election staff must do all that it takes to undertake a thorough exercise to include all names, we urge that the electoral registration (ER) machinery in the districts and municipal areas also enlist the active support and cooperation of NGOs and civil society groups who can bring to the notice of the ER machinery the names of those not enrolled. Political parties registered in the respective constituencies could also be requested, indeed encouraged and facilitated, to bring to the notice of the ERO such excluded names, which can then be verified by the ER machinery. It is essential that the ECI appoints senior civil servants from outside the state/UT where such exercise is under way as Special Observers to oversee the electoral registration process to ensure accuracy and objectivity.

In particular, we wish to stress the need for the ECI to make special rules for the urban homeless and put in place special measures for differently abled persons. The normal procedures for registration and verification that apply before a name is included in the electoral lists create virtually unsurpassable barriers for the urban homeless. Typically, homeless women and men have no documents that prove their identity or address. For these groups (members of which have no homes), special rules that permit either self-verification, or verification by any individual whose name exists in the electoral lists, are needed. Since they have no fixed address, we propose that the address of the nearest homeless shelter where they sleep at night, or the address of an NGO that works with homeless populations in the city, should suffice for purposes of the electoral list.

Any information that is publicly required to be made available to people about the election processes etc. must be available in accessible formats. Information necessary to enable a person to exercise her franchise in a legal and informed way must be made accessible to all, especially people who communicate differently. There should be detailed awareness drives and some proactive measures (with civil society assistance) to get vulnerable populations, including persons with disabilities, to exercise their right to vote.

2. Foolproof mechanism for verification by voter of inclusion of name in relevant part of electoral roll

There have been far too many instances in recent years of voters reaching polling stations on voting day and finding their names missing from the electoral rolls, most often because of deletion/transposition of names without notice to voters. The insistence of the ECI on publishing the electoral rolls as image PDF files online makes prior verification of a voter's name an arduous task, requiring scrolling through many pages to locate her/his name. There is also evidence to show discrepancies between the NVSP data and the electoral rolls. Unless a simple process for verification of voter names by electoral roll part is developed (as outlined in point no. 5 of this letter), this problem will continue to trouble voters.

3. Deletion of duplicate names, shifted/dead voters

To check bogus voting, concerted efforts need to be made to systematically weed out names of those voters who have relocated elsewhere or are no more, especially given the migration and mortality trends in the COVID-19 pandemic period. The electoral rolls are also replete with duplicate entries. Assistance should be taken, as mentioned earlier, of civil society groups and political parties to weed out names. With regard to duplicate entries, metaphones and fuzzy-matching approaches can be employed to identify similar voter-name and relative-name sets. Thereafter, photographs of voters within these sets can be compared using image comparison software. There is need to improve the data entry software, with built-in warnings when duplicate entries are being made and verification by the ERO where such warnings are ignored by lower staff.

4. Using Aadhaar to validate Voter IDs constitutes a gross violation of the citizen's right to privacy

The Aadhaar ID is meant to be used for specific purposes, such as disbursal of benefits. The EPIC-Voter ID is given to voters by a constitutional authority (the ECI) and forms the basis of the electoral roll, whereas the Aadhaar ID is a government sponsored identity. Linking the Voter ID and the Aadhaar number appears to be clearly unconstitutional, apart from not being provided for in the Aadhaar Act (the 2017 judgment of the Supreme Court in *Puttaswamy v. Union of India* is relevant here) or in the Representation of the People Acts, 1950 and 1951. Those whose Aadhaar fails on authentication due to biometric change (as in those of advanced age), technology failure or any other reason are excluded whenever authentication is required. This has been the unfortunate experience of ration card holders in different parts of the country. The Telangana CEO reported in September 2018 that 2.2 million people were excluded from the electoral rolls after Aadhaar based 'verification' was carried out in 2015, thus depriving them of the right to vote in the general elections to the Telangana legislative assembly. Enrolment and continuance of names on the electoral rolls is based on the integrity of the electoral database. The risk of the electoral database being compromised will be far higher if it is linked to the Aadhaar database, which is not under the control of the ECI and can be tampered with by an outside body. The Cambridge Analytica episode, highlighted in 2018, brings out the dangers of influencing voters by targeting messages to them based on their psychometric profiles. It is very likely that the linkage of Aadhaar numbers to Voter IDs would allow the targeted manipulation of the beneficiaries of subsidies, benefits and services. We strongly oppose any move to link Aadhaar numbers with Voter IDs.

5. Ensuring error-free, verifiable electoral rolls

Three aspects must guide the preparation of electoral rolls: (a) processes for inclusion of all voters, irrespective of whether they apply or not; (b) avoiding exclusion through correct processing of all applications for inclusion and ensuring no spurious deletions; (c) ensuring no duplicate/false entries.

These require careful process design at community levels and defining standards of data processing and data organisation that will enable local communities to publicly audit and verify all additions and deletions from electoral rolls.

We recommend maintaining of electoral records on online Public Bulletin Boards, enabling both complete transparency and public verifiability of all decisions regarding enrolments, updations and deletions. Two such public bulletin boards should be maintained by the ECI for each assembly constituency with updation as and when changes occur:

(i) A self-contained bulletin board of the entire electoral roll, which will be the official master electoral roll correct up to the time of the last update. The list of valid voters on any date can be publicly determined from this bulletin board.

(ii) A bulletin board of transaction records, which enables every voter given a receipt for application for enrolment, updation or deletion to search for the application process status on this bulletin board. A detailed exposition on these Bulletin Boards may be viewed in Vol. II of the CCE Report (link given in paragraph 2 of this letter).

We reiterate our complete opposition to the linking of Aadhaar numbers and Voter IDs which, in our opinion, constitute a gross violation of the right to privacy of the individual while also allowing executive manipulation of access to beneficiaries to influence election outcomes.

We had earlier sent the ECI copies of both the volumes of our Report for examination and comment but have not heard from you so far. The links to the two volumes are given in the body of this letter. We urge you to respond to our concerns and take remedial actions as suggested in the two volumes. The matter assumes urgency in view of the upcoming general elections to state assemblies in 2022.

Our representatives are available for any discussion with the ECI on the issues involved.

SATYAMEVA JAYATE

Yours sincerely,

Constitutional Conduct Group (100 signatories)

STATEMENT ON SIMULTANEOUS ELECTIONS TO PARLIAMENT AND STATE ASSEMBLIES

8 December 2020

The Constitutional Conduct Group (CCG) is a group of former civil servants from the All India and Central Services and is non-partisan and apolitical in nature. Many of its members have conducted, managed and supervised elections to Parliament and State Assemblies during their time in government service.

We have noted Prime Minister Narendra Modi's call for simultaneous elections to Parliament and State Assemblies saying that it is 'not only a subject of debate but a necessity for India.' The main reason given is to avoid frequent suspension of development programs and welfare activities due to the repeated imposition of the Model Code of Conduct by the Election Commission of India.

The additional reasons given are to avoid huge expenditure in conducting frequent elections and to reduce the influence of black money, caste, religion and communal issues in elections.

Proponents of this suggestion argue thus: 'Getting out of the "permanent election mode" will be a structural change in mind-set that could potentially provide the much-needed space to governments to focus on governance and long-term transformational measures without worrying about impending elections.' Supporting this contention, some quote the American example of simultaneous elections for all electoral offices from President downwards.

We are of the view that these arguments lack sincerity and are being used only to divert attention from the many flaws in our electoral laws and practices, including those relating to safeguards in the use of EVMs and to the use of post-election defections to gain power. To the Prime Minister's rhetorical question, 'Why should the country waste so much money?' the response would be that money is being spent on a number of items other than elections as well, e.g. purchasing aircraft for the President and Prime Minister's exclusive travel, building massive Parliament and Secretariat buildings in Delhi's Central Vista and many others.

It is well known that 'simultaneous elections' is what India started with in 1951 and continued with up to 1967, during which period the Lok Sabha and State Legislative Assembly elections were held together without much fanfare. It was after this period that the cycle of synchronised elections got disrupted, primarily because many state governments (as well as governments at the Centre) could not complete their term of five years. Restoring status quo ante to synchronise elections to the State Legislatures and Parliament would present major constitutional hurdles, apart from huge logistics, security, and manpower issues being involved.

The 'One-Nation-One-Election' proposal, as envisaged, has little regard for the fact that in a federal democracy, once the respective domains of each unit of democracy—small or big—have been constitutionally demarcated and defined, that unit functions autonomously within its domain. The interests, the priorities, the mores and the conventions of each unit are its own and are not subordinate to those of the Union, except where the Constitution itself so mandates. The term of the Legislative Assembly of a state has nothing to do with the term of the Lok Sabha and depends primarily on the way electoral politics plays out within that state.

Holding of simultaneous elections is a political agenda of a state aiming at a unitary polity, in which the Centre is conflated with 'national' and the states treated as its subordinates, with their individual political fortunes deferring to those of the Centre. This is an assault on the fundamental principle of federalism in which each unit of democracy and governance is expected to function with relative autonomy and take its own decisions, whether it is the timing of elections, the framing of its laws and/or formulating its own policies in respect of subjects in the State List/Concurrent List.

What is worrying is not just the disregard for the federal character of the country, which is implicit in the 'One-Nation-One-Election' idea, but the barely concealed contempt for electoral democracy itself. The dangerous assumption here is that the need to periodically seek the mandate of the people is an unnecessary burden which comes in the way of efficiency. Governance, here, is viewed as something superior to and outside the practice of democracy and as the preserve of the administrative and political executive which controls it. The implication is that the people, the voters, have nothing to do with it, a totally unacceptable principle in a democracy.

India is a Union of States and the administrative convenience of the Central Government or the Election Commission of India cannot dictate the political processes of a state. Doing so could decimate whatever is left of the federal nature of the country and alter the basic structure of the Constitution as laid down by the Supreme Court in the Kesavananda Bharati (1973) and the S.R. Bommai (1994) cases.

At the same time, it is common knowledge that there are serious flaws in the current electoral processes and practices, with many electoral reforms being urgently needed. The flaws include the use of money and muscle power in elections, the increasing participation of criminal elements in the election process as candidates, the faulty preparation of electoral rolls, the lackadaisical implementation of the Model Code of Conduct and addressing the mounting concerns on the integrity of EVM voting and VVPAT counting, as well as on the opaque electoral bonds system. We are of the considered view that it is electoral reforms that are the need of the hour today and not the idea of 'One-Nation-One-Election', which, if implemented, will be destructive of our federal structure. If the Government of India sincerely wish to improve the operation of the electoral system in India, it should work in tandem with all political parties (and in consultation with the Election Commission of India) to initiate reforms to improve the fairness and transparency of the election process.

SATYAMEVA JAYATE

Constitutional Conduct Group (90 signatories)

REMINDER LETTER ON SERIOUS IRREGULARITIES IN CONDUCT OF LOK SABHA GENERAL ELECTIONS 2019

19 November 2019

Shri Sunil Arora, Chief Election Commissioner,
Shri Ashok Lavasa, Election Commissioner,
Shri Sushil Chandra, Election Commissioner,
Election Commission of India,
Nirvachan Sadan,
New Delhi, India

Copied to: Chief Electoral Officers of all States and Union Territories

Subject:- Your Silence on Issues Raised with Regards to Serious Irregularities in the Conduct of Lok Sabha General Elections, 2019

Ref:- Our letter dated 2 July 2019 and reminders dated 20 July 2019 and 10 August 2019

Please refer to the letter dated 2 July 2019 on the above subject of addressed to you by 64 former civil servants and endorsed by 83 veterans of the defense services, academics, and other concerned citizens. Subsequent reminders have been sent as indicated above.

Your failure to respond to any of the points raised in the letter and reminders, or to even acknowledge their receipt, leads us to wonder whether we will ever receive a response. The issues raised are critical for the well-being and proper functioning of our democratic republic. Our group has been in touch with your predecessor, Shri O.P. Rawat, on a number of issues related to the conduct of elections. As a group of former civil servants, many of whom have been associated with election processes over the past six decades, we consider it our duty to work with the Election Commission of India (ECI) to address the doubts that have arisen in the public mind about the impartiality and fairness of our electoral processes.

Many of these questions would have been avoided if the ECI, currently under your stewardship, had accepted the principle of agent transparency vis-à-vis its principal, which, in this case, is the people of India. So, disclosure should be the rule rather than the exception. All information relating to the conduct of elections should be open to the public except where specifically needing to be exempted. Even when disclosure of some information is exempted, the criteria for keeping it confidential must be made public and transparent.

We do not believe that there is any justification for the ECI not displaying on its website:

(i) the Parliament Constituency-wise, Assembly segment-wise, and polling station-wise figures of (a) votes polled in EVMs [i.e. other than postal ballots] and (b) votes as counted in EVMs. Ideally, there should be no discrepancies between the two sets of figures.

(ii) details of the 5 polling stations chosen as 'samples' for each Assembly segment, and the polling station-wise figures of (a) EVM electronic count and (b) VVPAT manual count. Ideally, there should be no discrepancies between these two sets of figures also.

But there have been extensive media reports about large-scale discrepancies in respect of both (i) and (ii) above. While we are aware that media reports may not always be correct, the ECI has failed the test of transparency by not disclosing the above sets of its figures on its website, thereby paving the way for an adverse presumption being drawn in this matter.

In the interests of transparency and electoral integrity, we call upon the ECI to:

- immediately display on its website, the figures indicated in (i) and (ii) above;
- disclose the 'decision rules', if any, of the ECI about manual counting in the event of discrepancies of either type occurring;
- disclose if there were any occasions to apply these decision rules during the recently concluded Parliamentary Elections.

Even while our letter of 2 July 2019 was waiting for some kind of a response from you, various media reports have appeared, suggesting that:

a) unauthorised private engineers had access to the EVM and VVPAT machines in the General Elections, 2019;
b) Bharat Electronics Limited (BEL) and Electronics Corporation of India Ltd (ECIL) have refused to provide information in response to RTI queries on EVMs and VVPATs even after having collected the fees for the same, though we understand that now the RTI first appellate authority has directed the ECIL to provide the information while the BEL first appellate authority for RTI has directed them to transfer the queries

relating to the number of EVMs and VVPATs deployed for the 2019 Lok Sabha elections to the ECI.

Clearly, the issues relating to the EVM and VVPAT machines are yet to be resolved satisfactorily, and the ECI, under your stewardships, needs to put this controversy to rest. Recent reports also seem to suggest that a programme installed in the VVPAT can access VVPAT memories and alter the input to the Control Unit, thereby manipulating the people's mandate. To set at rest doubts in the public mind, we suggest a social audit of the functioning of the EVM and VVPAT machines used in the recent Lok Sabha General Elections. Social audits are an accepted tool in all democracies and, even in our country, we have used them to monitor the functioning of various social sector programmes. We are ready to work with you in the organisation and conduct of such a social audit.

To conduct such a Social Audit, we propose as follows:

1. Access to the entire electoral records, including EVM and VVPAT machines used in 20 select Lok Sabha Constituencies (representing merely 3.6 per cent of the total Lok Sabha constituencies), in the recently concluded General Elections, 2019, be provided to a Social Audit Group, comprising three representatives each of civil society representatives (which will include members of our group of former civil servants) and the ECI.
2. The twenty Lok Sabha Constituencies will be selected by the Social Audit Group and the same will be intimated to the ECI for making the records/machines available.
3. The ECI will release these records, EVM and VVPAT machines under whatever supervisory arrangement it considers necessary to ensure that while the auditors have full access, these records are not tampered with in any way during the audit. The only rider would be that these arrangements would not in any way fetter the ability of the Social Audit

Group to examine the records and machines in any way the Group considers necessary.

4. To test the integrity and security system of the EVM and VVPAT machines, the Social Audit Group will, in consultation with the ECI, have the freedom to appoint an independent third-party team of IT experts from India or from abroad, if necessary, who have the experience of conducting hackathons. There would be no restrictions on the hackers—they would be free to check the hardware, the software, and also the programmes embedded in the chips of all these machines to determine whether the EVM/VVPAT machines are capable of being manipulated either before, during or after each step of the electoral process.
5. All the EVM and VVPAT machines used for the hackathon would be disabled for future use under the joint supervision of the Social Audit Group and ECI, to ensure that none of these is ever used again in any future election.

We are sending copies of this letter to the Chief Electoral Officers of all States and Union Territories, to keep them apprised of our proposal. Furthermore, as many of the electoral records, EVM and VVPAT machines are lying in the immediate custody of various state government agencies, they too are custodians of public property.

We look forward to an early response from you. A delegation from our group is willing and keen to meet you at a mutually convenient time to discuss the further modalities of the Social Audit.

Yours faithfully,
Constitutional Conduct Group (45 signatories)

LETTER TO THE ELECTION COMMISSION OF INDIA: SERIOUS IRREGULARITIES IN THE CONDUCT OF GENERAL ELECTIONS, 2019

2 July 2019

Shri Sunil Arora, Chief Election Commissioner,
Shri Ashok Lavasa, Election Commissioner,
Shri Sushil Chandra, Election Commissioner,
Election Commission of India,
Nirvachan Sadan, New Delhi, India

Subject:- Serious Irregularities in the Conduct of General Elections, 2019

Sirs,
We are a group of former civil servants that takes up, from time to time, matters of exceptional national interest, seeking to remind our cherished democratic institutions of their responsibility to uphold the lofty ideals of the Constitution. We write to you today to draw your attention to the several very troubling and still unexplained issues pertaining to the conduct of the General Elections, 2019, by the Election Commission of India (ECI).

From time to time, the media has reported on various irregularities in the conduct of the 2019 General Elections. While we accept that not every media report is accurate or true, the ECI's non-rebuttal of an untrue or inaccurate story leaves the public to draw its own conclusion: that the ECI has no valid explanation to. The mere dismissal of the allegations as baseless, without an explanation as to why they should be so considered, is unsatisfactory. As the custodian of the most precious commodity in a democracy—the people's mandate—it is your duty to be transparent, and accountable to the Constitution and the people of India.

The 2019 General Elections appear to have been one of the least free and fair elections that the country has had in the past three decades or so. In the past, despite the efforts of criminal elements, musclemen, and unscrupulous politicians, the persons who graced the ECI did their best to ensure that elections were conducted as freely and fairly as possible. In these General Elections, however, an impression has gathered ground that our democratic process is being subverted and undermined by the very constitutional authority empowered to safeguard its sanctity. It was rare in the past for any serious doubts to be raised about the impartiality, integrity and competence of the ECI. Unfortunately, the same cannot be said about the present ECI and the way it has conducted the General Elections of 2019. So blatant have been the acts of omission and commission by the ECI that even former Elections Commissioners and CECs have been compelled, albeit reluctantly, to question the decisions of their successors in office.

The bias of the Election Commission towards one particular party became evident from the date of announcement of the elections. The announcements of the 2004, 2009 and 2014 Lok Sabha Elections were made by the ECI on 29 February, 1 March and 5 March respectively of those years. The announcements of the State Assembly elections, due in April-May, also used to be made between 1 March and 5 March. But this convention was not followed for the 2019 Lok Sabha Election and the announcement was delayed, without any explanation or justification, till 10 March. This led to the reasonable doubt that the ECI deliberately delayed the announcement to enable Prime Minister Narendra Modi to complete the inauguration blitz of a slew of projects (157 of them) that he had scheduled between 8 February and 9 March. Instead of the government adjusting the dates of its inaugural functions to the ECI's (well known) schedule for announcement of elections, we have here a case of the ECI adjusting itself to the government's schedule, thereby raising questions about its independence and impartiality.

The election schedule raised many questions. It was the longest election in the country's history, and gave room for suspicion that it had openly and unabashedly favoured the ruling party at the Centre. There was no apparent rationale to the number of polling days fixed for different states. In states like Tamil Nadu (39 seats), Kerala (20), Andhra Pradesh (25) and Telangana (17) where the BJP is weak and had no likelihood of winning, the polling was held in a single phase. In states with comparable or fewer Lok Sabha constituencies such as Karnataka (28), Madhya Pradesh (29), Rajasthan (25) and Odisha (21), where the BJP faced tough competition or was likely to gain ground, the polling was scheduled in multiple phases, possibly to give the Prime Minister more time for campaigning. The polling for the Varanasi constituency from where the Prime Minister contested was conveniently slotted in the last phase of polling on 19 May 2019.

Several reports were published in the media of large scale voter exclusion, with some reports suggesting that voters from certain minority groups were the most affected. While we do not believe that these charges were necessarily true, it was incumbent upon the ECI to investigate them and respond. Many voters who had exercised their mandates in earlier elections found their names missing. The ECI's failure to effectively answer these allegations further tarnished its reputation.

The blatant flouting of the Model Code of Conduct (MCC) by many candidates, in particular the making of hate speeches and communally loaded statements by candidates, primarily of the BJP, was, initially, blithely ignored by the ECI on the plea that it had no powers to take action. For example, Mr Amit Shah was reported to have said that illegal immigrants would be thrown into the Bay of Bengal, a statement which clearly invited action under the Indian Penal Code (IPC) and the Representation of People Act. Only when pulled up by the Supreme Court did the ECI suddenly discover its powers, even then exercising them selectively on the small fry and ignoring the more egregious cases of violation by the Prime Minister and the BJP. Even the strongest action that it took, viz. the curtailing of the campaigning in the last phase in West Bengal, was done in a manner so that the PM's campaign could be completed before the ban came into effect. Its partisanship confirmed, the approach of the ECI further emboldened the Prime Minister, Mr Amit Shah and other party representatives.

The Prime Minister's blatant misuse of the Pulwama and Balakot issues to whip up nationalistic, or more correctly, jingoistic fervour and channel it in favour of the BJP was another shocking violation of the MCC. The Election Commission strangely did not even issue a show cause notice to the PM for these repeated violations though the incidents were reported by the State Election Commissioners and there was a divide within the ECI itself on whether or not there was a breach of the MCC. The ECI ignored the difference of opinion and merely dismissed the incidents. The dissenting opinions of Commissioner Ashok Lavasa should have been published as is done in the case of the judiciary. In our opinion, Article 19 of the Constitution and the citizens' right to information have been undermined.

The bias of the ECI was glaringly apparent in the case relating to Mr Mohammed Mohsin, the IAS officer who was sent to Odisha as a special election representative. Mr Mohsin was suspended for checking the PM's helicopter for any non-permissible cargo. According to the ECI, the official had not acted in conformity with the ECI's instructions of not checking SPG's protected persons. Constitutional obligations were trumped by administrative instructions. It was pointed out, even at that time, that similar checks had been carried out on the helicopters of the Odisha CM Mr Naveen Patnaik and the then Petroleum Minister Mr Dharmendra Pradhan, with no objections from the dignitaries concerned. However, the ECI could not and did not explain its double standards.

A serious matter in which the ECI exonerated the government of wrongdoing was the misuse of official resources. The Niti Aayog had officially written to the various UTs and some districts in the country to provide local information about the area since the PM was likely to visit these places. This was done so that the information could be used in the Prime Minister's election campaigns. Even though this was a blatant violation of the MCC, the ECI merely dismissed the complaint. Why did the ECI treat the MCC in such a cavalier fashion and apply it in so obviously discriminatory a manner? Action was also called for under the Representation of People Act.

The refusal of the ECI to take note of the many media violations—particularly by the ruling party—caused a great deal of concern to the public. The most blatant violation of this was the opening of a new channel called NaMo TV which continuously telecast speeches and events about Prime Minister Narendra Modi. NaMo TV had, strangely, neither obtained permission from the Information and Broadcasting Ministry to go on air nor had it complied with the many regulations necessary to start a new channel. Even though the ECI ordered the channel to be closed, NaMo TV continued to telecast almost until the end of the elections. Procrastination, silence and inaction characterised ECI's responses in so many matters. There were other violations as well: a programme anchored by the actor Akshay Kumar centred on the PM's unofficial persona, which was telecast by several TV channels while the elections were underway, giving the PM's campaign an undue edge over those of others; the media attention given to the PM's meditation in a cave in Kedarnath, even while the last phase of the polling was going on was another such instance. As far as we are aware, none of these expenses have been added to the PM's electoral expenses.

In terms of transparency of electoral funding, this election was the most opaque ever, both because of the widespread use of electoral bonds, and also because of the enormous amounts of cash, gold and drugs, amounting to Rs 3,456 crores, which were seized during the polls. While the ECI acted strongly in the matter of the seizure of cash in Tamil Nadu, cancelling the polling in one Parliamentary constituency, it has not acted as strongly in others. Though Rs 1.8 crore was recovered from the Arunachal CM's convoy, there is no information of what action was taken by the ECI on this clear violation of rule and norm. Where, one might ask, was the level playing field?

The use of Electronic Voting Machines (EVMs) for polling has been a subject of much controversy. Despite the ECI's repeated statements that the EVMs used in India are tamper-proof, doubts on that score have persisted, particularly because the ECI has not been transparent in its responses to various reports. There were widespread reports of a mismatch in the number of EVMs manufactured by the two authorised PSUs and those in the inventory of the ECI. According to one media report, responses to an RTI query have revealed that as many as 20 lakh EVMs that the manufacturers affirm having delivered to the ECI were apparently not in the ECI's possession. To queries about this huge discrepancy, the ECI's response has been a bland denial, leaving no one any the wiser. Complete facts and figures need to be revealed for public scrutiny.

People's confidence in the EVMs would have been greater if the ECI had been more cooperative about using the Voter Verifiable Paper Audit Trail (VVPATs) in a manner that would confirm the results of the EVMs, but from the beginning the ECI was extremely reluctant to match the number of votes recorded in EVMs with the votes in the VVPAT machines on any significant scale, despite representations by different groups, including political parties. The ECI stated that tallying the votes of 50 per cent of the VVPATs with the EVMs would take about 6 days (even though it is a well-known fact that in the past 100 per cent of paper ballots were counted in 12-18 hours). The ECI insisted that the purpose of verification would be served if such tallying was done in only one EVM per Assembly constituency. On the insistence of the Supreme Court, the ECI agreed to increase this number to five EVMs per constituency The ECI's refusal to listen to, and accept, globally adopted statistical tools to determine the number of VVPATs that need to be counted to rule out any errors, or to lay down the steps that would have to be taken in case of a mismatch between the EVM and VVPAT counts, has left a cloud of confusion in the mind of the citizens.

Between the last day of polling and Counting Day, there were several reports of unexplained movement of EVMs to and from the strong rooms in various states. These movements have not been satisfactorily explained, and the ECI's bland denial, without explaining exactly which EVMs were being transported, and why, does not inspire trust.

The request by a large number of parties to tally the EVM and VVPAT votes at the beginning of Counting Day was also turned down by the ECI without any specific reason. This was a simple request and would have satisfied many of the political candidates. In fact, at every stage the ECI has refused to accommodate any request that could bolster the confidence of the electorate that the elections were conducted freely and fairly. Matching of five VVPATs as mandated by the SC was relegated to the end of the counting process—so that few would remain to watch the outcome. The result of this exercise is not quite clear from the media reports. It appears, though, that the mismatch between the number of votes cast, the numbers recorded by the EVMs, and as reported in the VVPATs has been quite numerous—some media reports put the number at affecting more than 370 Lok Sabha Constituencies.

Reports about the mismatch in the EVM, VVPAT and votes cast numbers are being explained away as being insignificant, since in almost all the cases, the victory margin (almost invariably of candidates put up by the BJP or its allies) is far greater than the discrepancy. During the paper ballot days, discrepancies in counting used to be ignored if they were too small to make a difference to the final But that logic does not apply to VVPAT-based audit of EVMs. Here, even a small discrepancy between the EVM count and the VVPAT in the chosen sample of EVMs, and a small discrepancy between the EVM count and the votes polled in a polling booth as reported by the Presiding Officer in Form 17C at the end of the poling day are very serious matters and are symptomatic of a greater malaise. While the Returning Officers and even Counting Agents may be taking it lightly due to deficiency in their understanding of an appropriate statistical sample, surely the ECI knows better. Accepting this argument is akin to an accountant saying that in a balance sheet of crores, an un-reconciled few hundred rupees do not matter, and the accounts should be accepted. When we are using electronic systems, even a discrepancy of one vote throws the entire election into doubt.

A well-known academic recently wrote, '...we can only raise questions on the basis of scattered information available to us. It is not our job as citizens to offer proof of wrong-doing of the highest institutions of the land, when these institutions function in so opaque a manner. It is our job to raise questions about visible anomalies. It is the responsibility of the Election Commission to explain the anomalies.'

Our Election Commission used to be the envy of the entire world, including developed countries, for its ability to conduct free and fair elections despite the huge logistical challenges and the hundreds of millions of voters. It is indeed, saddening to witness the process of the demise of that. If it continues, it is bound to strike at the very heart of that founding document the people of India proudly gave themselves—the Constitution of India—and the democratic ethos that is the very basis of the Indian Republic.

Viewed in totality, there is no doubt that the mandate of 2019 has been thrown into serious doubt. The concerns raised are too central to the well-being of our democracy for the ECI to leave unexplained. In the interests of ensuring that this never happens again, the ECI needs to pro-actively issue public clarifications in respect of each of these reported irregularities, and put in place steps to prevent such incidents from occurring in future. This is essential to restore the people's faith in our electoral process.

Yours sincerely,

Constitutional Conduct Group (64 signatories)

LETTER TO HON'BLE PRESIDENT OF INDIA: WEAK-KNEED RESPONSE OF THE ELECTION COMMISSION OF INDIA TO VIOLATIONS OF THE MODEL CODE OF CONDUCT

8 April 2019

To
The Honourable President of India
Rashtrapati Bhavan, New Delhi Copies to:
Chief Election Commissioner, Election Commission of India
Election Commissioners, Election Commission of India

Respected Rashtrapatiji,
We are a group of former civil servants of the All India and Central Services who have come together to use our pooled experience of decades of service to the Constitution of India to protect and further the values enshrined in it. As a group, we have no affiliations with any political party. Many in our group have, over the past six decades, been involved with the conduct and supervision of elections in India.

We write to express our deep anguish that the Election Commission of India (ECI), which has had a long and honourable record of holding free and fair elections despite the enormous challenges of scale and complexity, is suffering from a crisis of credibility today. The ECI's independence, fairness, impartiality and efficiency are perceived to be compromised today, thereby endangering the integrity of the electoral process which is the very foundation of Indian democracy. We are distressed to note the misuse, abuse and blatant disregard of the Model Code of Conduct (MCC) by the ruling party at the Centre, and the ECI's pusillanimity in coming down with a heavy hand on these violations. We would like to bring to your attention a number of glaring instances:

1. The Prime Minister made a public announcement on 27 March 2019 about the successful launch of India's first anti-satellite weapon (ASAT), which made India the fourth nation in the world with anti-satellite missile capabilities. While the

timing of the exercise is questionable, even more questionable is the fact that the announcement of the launch was made with much fanfare by the Prime Minister when propriety demanded that it should have been left to the officials of the Defence Research and Development Organisation (DRDO) at a time when the MCC was operative. The country was facing no immediate security threat that required the Prime Minister, who is an election candidate himself, to make a public announcement. On the purely technical ground that the announcement was not made on the public broadcasting service, the ECI held that there had been no violation of the MCC. We feel, however, that parading the achievements of a government in this manner after the announcement of elections is tantamount to a serious breach of propriety and amounts to giving unfair publicity to the party presently in government and that the ECI's decision does not stand up to the standards of impartiality expected of it.

2. Our group addressed a letter to the Chief Election Commissioner (which was also made public) on 26 March 2019, requesting the ECI to issue directions to withhold the release of all biopics and documentaries on any political personages through any media mechanism until the conclusion of the electoral process. While the ECI is still to respond to our letter, we understand from media reports that a biopic on the present Prime Minister is slated for release on 11 April 2019, on the day of commencement of the polling process. This, in our opinion, represents a backdoor effort to garner free publicity for a political person (and his party). In the event that this biopic is released even while the election process is ongoing, we contend that the entire expenses on the production, distribution and publicity of the biopic should be debited to the election expenses of Shri Narendra Modi.
3. The same principle should also be applied to the 10-part web series *Modi: A Common Man's Journey*, the first five episodes

of which are out on the streaming platform Eros Now, with the ECI again doing nothing but going through the motions of calling for details.

4. The ECI has been acting with the same lethargy in respect of the NaMo TV channel launched on 31 March 2019, which, without any formal approval of the Ministry of Information and Broadcasting, is propagating the image and views of Shri Narendra Modi. The DTH service provider Tata Sky initially called it a 'Hindi news service channel' and later back-tracked and called it a 'special service' not requiring any licence. The brazen violation of democratic norms may be seen from the fact that the channel has been added to all subscribers' accounts 'as a launch offer' with 'no option to delete the individual channel.'
5. While the ECI has passed orders transferring three top police officers and the Chief Secretary in Andhra Pradesh and four top police officers in West Bengal, we find it curious that no such steps have been taken in Tamil Nadu, where the present Director General of Police (DGP) is reportedly under investigation by the Central Bureau of Investigation in the Gutkha scam case and there have been repeated appeals by the Opposition parties in Tamil Nadu seeking his removal from that post. He is also on extension beyond the normal date of his superannuation and, as per ECI norms, such officers should not be assigned election duties. Even more significantly, the same officer had been ordered by the ECI to be transferred during the 2016 Tamil Nadu Assembly elections. It is unfortunate that different yardsticks have been applied in the cases of the former Commissioner of Police, Kolkata and the DGP, Tamil Nadu.
6. The Governor of Rajasthan, Shri Kalyan Singh, has made certain statements that virtually amount to canvassing for a specific political party. The ECI has also apparently apprised your office that the MCC has been violated in the instant case.

Since this amounts to a grave misdemeanour, which impacts the sanctity of the Constitution of India, we request you to either remove Shri Kalyan Singh from the post of Governor or direct him to submit his resignation forthwith.

7. The Chief Minister of Uttar Pradesh, Yogi Adityanath, had, at a recent public election meeting, referred to the armed forces as the army of Shri Narendra Modi. A similar statement has been made at another election meeting by Shri Mukhtar Abbas Naqvi, a senior BJP functionary. Such irresponsible statements by a very high constitutional functionary and a political party official not only constitute an insult to your position as the Supreme Commander of the Defence Forces of India, but also amount to a deliberate attempt to mislead the general public, apart from damaging the tradition of the armed forces as apolitical formations. Strongest action is required from the ECI to nip such cavalier statements in the bud, but the ECI has contented itself in the present case with a mild reprimand to the UP CM. We certainly hope and pray that such mild responses do not embolden others to violate the MCC and weaken the institutions that support our democracy.
8. We also note with consternation the departure from all civilised norms in the speeches being delivered by political personages, both those holding high constitutional positions and others. In particular, we would like to draw attention to a speech by Shri Narendra Modi at Wardha, Maharashtra on 1 April 2019 where, to quote the news channel *News18*, he allegedly said 'The Congress insulted Hindus. People have decided to punish it in the election. Leaders of that party are now scared of contesting from constituencies dominated by the majority population. That is why they are forced to take refuge in places where the majority is a minority.' He has made a similar statement at an election rally in Nanded, Maharashtra on 6 April 2019. Such divisive speeches, with

clear innuendoes, constitute a violation of one of the first requirements stipulated in the MCC: '*No party or candidate shall indulge in any activity which may aggravate existing differences or create mutual hatred or cause tension between different castes and communities, religious or linguistic.*' It is incumbent on the ECI to keep a close watch on all such activities and make it clear to all political parties, candidates and their workers that any such efforts to exploit communal or other divisions in society will attract the strongest action. We understand from media reports that the ECI has sought a report from the Chief Electoral Officer, Maharashtra. We hope that appropriate strict action will be taken to discourage all such incendiary speeches.

9. In our open letter dated 24 February 2019, our group detailed our proposal to the ECI for the proper implementation of VVPAT-based audits of EVMs in the forthcoming elections. The ECI made an astonishing submission before the Supreme Court that if manual counting of VVPAT slips of 50 per cent of EVMs is done (as prayed for in a joint PIL by 21 Opposition Parties), the election results would be delayed by six days when everyone is aware that, even in the days of paper ballots, the counting used to get over within 8 to 15 hours and the results were declared either the same day or the next day. The ECI had constituted an Experts Committee to make recommendations on VVPAT-based audit. This was a simple matter which required only two or three sittings of the Expert Committee and could have been finalised in less than a month. The first meeting of the Expert Committee was held on 4 October 2018. The next meeting of the Expert Committee was mysteriously delayed by five months and it was held without inviting the members who expressed dissenting views in the first meeting! The ECI's obdurate conduct and its reluctance to undertake a proper VVPAT audit when its present sample size fails to detect a 'defective EVM' (i.e. a malfunctioning or manipulated

EVM) 99 per cent of the time raise serious questions about its motives for doing so.

Hon'ble Rashtrapatiji, we are deeply concerned about the weak-kneed conduct of the ECI, which has reduced the credibility of this constitutional body to an all-time low. Any erosion in the people's confidence in the fairness of the ECI has very grave consequences for the future of our democracy and we hope that the gravity of the situation will be appreciated by the ECI. We appeal through you, Hon'ble Rashtrapatiji, to the ECI to conduct itself in a manner where its independence, fairness, impartiality and efficiency are not questioned and to firmly exercise the extensive mandate given to it under Article 324 of the Constitution of India to ensure that the Indian voter is able to exercise her/his franchise without fear or favour.

Yours faithfully,
Constitutional Conduct Group (66 signatories)

LETTER TO CHIEF ELECTION COMMISSIONER—RELEASE OF BIOPICS WHEN THE MODEL CODE OF CONDUCT IS IN PLACE

26 March 2019

To
Shri Sunil Arora,
Chief Election Commissioner, Election Commission of India,
New Delhi

Copied to:
1. Shri Ashok Lavasa, Election Commissioner
2. Shri Sushil Chandra, Election Commissioner

Dear Shri Arora,
Our group of former civil servants of the All India and Central Services have interacted with the Election Commission from time

to time on issues of public interest. We are now writing to you to draw your attention to a potential threat to the correct applicability of the Model Code of Conduct (MCC).

There are media reports that a biopic on our Prime Minister, Shri Narendra Modi, is being readied for release. The release was set for 12 April 2019, then, unexpectedly, it was brought forward to 5 April 2019. You will appreciate that such a film would create enormous electoral mileage for the Prime Minister and the party in power. It is, therefore, necessary to examine whether the release of this biopic after the announcement of elections and the coming into force of the MCC is consonant with the principles of a free and fair election. The same principle would apply to any similar biopic on any other candidate in the forthcoming elections, since news reports mention a biopic on the president of the Indian National Congress, Shri Rahul Gandhi (though there is no mention of the date of release).

We deeply appreciate your efforts to get social media platforms to adopt a code of conduct for their activities and responsibilities during the election process. In our view, the same principles apply to the process of film certification and release during an ongoing election process. It is specially required, under the MCC, that 'the party in power whether at the Centre or in the State or States concerned, shall ensure that no cause is given for any complaint that it has used its official position for the purposes of its election campaign.' It cannot be said that the Information and Broadcasting Ministry has no role in this, given that the Central Board of Film Certification falls under its jurisdiction.

When even appointments to the Boards of Public Sector Undertakings are not permitted under the MCC, open advocacy of the role of the Prime Minister (or of any other candidate) in biopics or documentaries focused on them amount, in our view, to propaganda in favour of individuals belonging to particular political parties at a time when the MCC is in force.

When expenditures on behalf of a candidate even without his/her formal permission are deemed to be counted as part of the expenses incurred by the candidate, a view also needs to be taken whether the expenditures on the production of such biopics or documentaries and their distribution/publicity should be added to the expenses incurred by the candidate directly.

We are of the view that there is no urgency for the release of such biopics or documentaries at this juncture, except to garner publicity for political personages and the political parties they represent. We, therefore, request the ECI to issue directions to withhold their release in cinema theatres or as home videos or on the Web (via YouTube, Netflix, Hotstar or similar channels) or via social media (Facebook, Twitter or any other) till the date when the MCC ceases to operate, i.e., on a date after 23 May 2019.

In a catena of judgments both before and after *Association for Democratic Reforms v. Union of India' (2001)*, the Supreme Court has ruled that Article 324 of the Constitution of India operates in areas 'left unoccupied by legislation' and the expressions 'superintendence, direction and control' as well as 'conduct of all elections' in Article 324 are the 'broadest of terms'. Therefore, 'the Commission can cope with a situation where the field is unoccupied by issuing necessary orders'. In other words, the ECI's power under Article 324 is to be construed liberally and given its widest possible meaning.

Thus, the ECI is fully competent to tackle the situation where biopics or documentaries on candidates are released during the middle of the election process by suitably amending the MCC or issuing such other directions as are deemed appropriate. We are confident that the ECI will uphold the highest constitutional principles in this regard.

With all good wishes for the successful conduct of the forthcoming elections.

Yours sincerely,
Constitutional Conduct Group (47 signatories)

OPEN LETTER ON THE PROPER IMPLEMENTATION OF VVPAT-BASED AUDIT OF EVMS

24 February 2019

We are a group of former civil servants of the All India and Central Services who have worked for decades with the Central and State Governments during our careers. We wish to make it clear that, as a group, we have no affiliation with any political party but believe in impartiality, neutrality and commitment to the Constitution of India. With our collective experience of conducting and supervising elections from the local body to the parliamentary level, we wish to suggest what needs to be done to make the actual process of voting and counting as free as possible from suspicions of Electronic Voting Machine (EVM) malfunction and manipulation.

It is common knowledge that EVMs are 'black boxes' in which it is impossible for voters to verify whether their votes have been recorded and counted correctly, and in which miscounts due to EVM malfunction or manipulation are undetectable and unchallengeable. Hence, there is an imperative need for an additional verifiable physical record of every vote cast, in the form of 'voter verified paper audit trail' (VVPAT). It allows for a partial or total recount independent of the EVM's electronic count and helps detect counting mistakes and frauds that would otherwise go undetected. In 2013, the Supreme Court passed an order mandating the use of EVMs with VVPAT units, and the Election Commission of India (ECI) has been deploying VVPAT units in Assembly Elections from 2017 onwards.

If VVPAT is to have any real security or accuracy value, it should form the basis of a proper audit plan. This entails tallying the electronic count as per the EVMs with the manual count as per the VVPAT slips for a 'statistically significant' sample size of EVMs chosen at random from a suitably defined 'population' of EVMs. Equally important is a clear 'decision rule' about what should be done in the event of a 'defective EVM' turning up in the sample. A 'defective EVM' is one in which the EVM count does not tally with the VVPAT count due to either EVM malfunction or manipulation. But the audit plan that the ECI has followed in recent elections suffers from the following serious shortcomings:

First, the ECI has prescribed a statistically incorrect sample size of just 'one polling station [i.e. 1 EVM] per Assembly Constituency' uniformly for all Assembly Constituencies and all states. It has not taken into account the fact that the number of EVMs in an Assembly Constituency varies widely across states from about 20 to about 300, and in a state from 589 (for Sikkim) to 23,672 (for Chhattisgarh which is the median state) to nearly 1,50,000 (for Uttar Pradesh). We are of the view that a uniform sample size for widely varying finite population sizes does not conform to fundamental principles of statistical sampling theory.

Second, the ECI has not made public as to how it arrived at its sample size nor has it specified the population to which this sample size relates. The latter is important because the sample size is dependent upon how the population is defined. If we assume that one percent of the EVMs are defective, the probability that the ECI's present sample size will fail to detect at least one defective EVM is 99 per cent if 'EVMs deployed in an Assembly Constituency' are defined as the population; 94 per cent if 'EVMs deployed in a Parliamentary Constituency' are defined as the population; and varies from about 2 per cent (UP) to 40 per cent (Chhattisgarh) to 71 per cent (Sikkim) if 'EVMs deployed in a state as a whole' are defined as the population. Such high margins of error are unacceptable in a democracy.

Third, the ECI has been vague about its 'decision rule' in the event of one or more defective EVMs turning up in the chosen sample.

Fourth, the ECI has not been transparent about the results of its VVPAT-based audit of EVMs for the various Assembly Elections held in 2017 and 2018 and the details are not available on its website.

In short, the ECI's audit plan is unable to detect outcome-altering miscounts due to EVM malfunction or manipulation, which defeats the very purpose of introducing VVPATs. Spending hundreds of crores of rupees on procurement of VVPAT units makes little sense if their utilisation for audit purposes is reduced to an exercise in tokenism.

Our group has been engaged over the past nine months in discussions with the ECI on issues relating to the proper VVPAT-based audit of EVMs. In our letter dated 10 December 2018 to the Chief Election Commissioner, we had sought clarifications from the ECI about certain pointed queries regarding the sample size and the decision rules. We had requested that in the interest of ensuring public confidence and the cooperation of political parties, it would be in the fitness of things if the clear reasons for adoption of a particular sample size and the decision rule for counting of VVPAT paper ballots are placed in the public domain, including on the ECI website. But there has been no action on this front.

The lack of transparency in VVPAT-based audit of EVMs has fuelled various conspiracy theories about 'mass rigging of EVMs'. There have been unacceptable demands for reversion to paper ballots. But the real issue today is not about 'EVMs versus Paper Ballots'; rather it is about 'EVMs with perfunctory VVPAT audit versus EVMs with proper VVPAT audit'.

Any electronic equipment is inherently subject to random malfunction. By its own admission, the ECI keeps about 20-25 per cent of EVMs and VVPAT units in reserve to replace those which malfunction on the polling day within a few hours of the commencement of the poll. There is every likelihood that a certain percentage of EVMs may again malfunction randomly during the long interval of 15-30 days between the date of polling and the date of counting. Perhaps this explains the occasionally noticed random discrepancies between the polling station-wise figures of voter turnout and the votes as counted in EVMs. The argument that some Presiding Officers 'forgot' to initialise the EVM count to zero at the end of the mock poll demonstration before the regular polling commences does not explain why there are positive as well as negative discrepancies.

As regards EVM manipulation, we wish to state that though it is highly improbable, this low probability can increase significantly with insider collusion. While the ECI has put in place a security protocol and various administrative safeguards that look impressive on paper, vulnerabilities do exist. Large-scale rigging of EVMs may not be possible or necessary because potential attackers need to target only select EVMs to tip the balance in a few marginal, closely fought constituencies. What is worrisome is that without a credible VVPAT-based audit of EVMs, the fraud may be undetectable and may be carried on with impunity.

We, therefore, appeal to the ECI to go in for a statistically correct sample size that can detect at least one defective EVM with 99.9 per cent reliability, in a suitably defined population, by adopting the hypergeometric probability distribution model. In something as important as ensuring the integrity of the election process—a process which in any case takes about 2-3 months from the date of announcement to the date of counting—a delay of a few hours or even a day in the manual counting of VVPAT slips of a larger (statistically correct) sample size of EVMs should not matter at all.

We also appeal to the ECI to adopt the following 'decision rules'. Full manual counting of VVPAT slips should be done (1) for all the remaining EVMs of the defined population if the sample throws up one or more defective EVMs, (2) for closely contested constituencies where the margin of victory is below 2 per cent of the votes cast or 1000 votes, whichever is less, even if no defective EVM turns up in the sample, and (3) for those polling stations where the discrepancy between the votes polled in EVMs and votes as counted in EVMs is more than 2 per cent.

We request the ECI to implement these suggestions in the Lok Sabha elections due in April-May 2019. Though the counting process may take a little longer, the confidence of the voters and political parties in the electoral process will be reinforced. The ECI has a long and honourable record of holding free and fair elections. It is in the spirit of supporting it in maintaining these high standards that we write this open letter.

SATYAMEV JAYATE

Constitutional Conduct Group (73 signatories)

ELECTORAL INTEGRITY—ENSURING RELIABILITY OF EVMS AND VVPAT AND HAND COUNTING OF LARGE PERCENTAGE OF PAPER SLIPS—REPRESENTATION THEREOF

4 July 2018

Mr O.P. Rawat, Chief Election Commissioner,
Mr Sunil Arora, Election Commissioner
Mr Ashok Lavasa, Election Commissioner
Election Commission of India, Nirvachan Sadan,
Ashoka Road, New Delhi—110001

Subject: Electoral integrity—ensuring reliability of EVMs and VVPAT and hand counting of large percentage of paper slips—representation thereof

Dear Sirs,
We are a group of retired civil servants and Armed Forces veterans who interact, discuss and deliberate on important issues of public concern and as found necessary take it up with concerned authorities. We found it necessary to take up this important issue of electoral integrity with the Election Commission. Hence this Memorandum.

You, Sirs, more than anyone else in our polity, would know that elections are synonymous with democracy and are meant to translate the consent of the citizens into governmental authority. To achieve this, elections should be held in strict conformity with democracy principles. These principles as we understand are:

a) In view of the 'public rationale of elections', the process should be transparent in a manner that the general public can be satisfied that their vote is correctly recorded and counted;
b) All essential steps in the elections should be subject to public scrutiny/examinability;
c) Ordinary citizens should be able to check the essential steps in the election process without special expert knowledge and
d) There should be verifiability in the counting of votes and ascertainment of the results reliably without special knowledge.

Electronic Voting Machines (EVMs) that are being presently used to conduct elections may be devices of technological excellence. But the question is—do they comply with the above 'Democracy Principles'?

There are broadly 5 types of voting systems in use around the world:

(i) Paper Ballots—Vote recorded on paper and counted by hand.
(ii) Direct Recording EVM—Vote recorded in memory. Counted electronically.
(iii) Direct Recording EVMs with Voter Verified Paper Audit Trail (VVPAT). Vote recorded in memory and printed on paper. Counting done electronically and by hand facilitating verification/auditing BEFORE declaring result.
(iv) Machine-readable Paper Ballots that are scanned and electronically counted using Optical Mark Recognition (OMR) technology.
(v) Internet-based Voting or Online Voting. Most vulnerable, not suited.

India abandoned (i) and adopted (ii) and now in the process of implementing (iii). Of these only ballot papers fully conform to democracy principles.

The Federal Constitutional Court of Germany in a landmark judgment in March, 2009 held the use of EVMs unconstitutional if they do not comply with 'Democracy Principles'. The Court ruled that in view of the 'public rationale of elections', the process should be transparent in a manner that the general public can be satisfied that their vote is correctly recorded and counted. The standard the Court set for this purpose was that there should be a provision whereby 'the votes are recorded and counted in another way besides electronic storage' and there is 'retraceability' of the election result independently of the electronic count.

In Civil Appeal No. 9093 of 2013 and WP (C) No. 406 of 2012 on 8.10.2013, the Supreme Court of India passed an order mandating the use of voter verified paper audit trail along with EVMs and directed the Election Commission of India (ECI) to implement the VVPAT system in a phased manner. The Supreme Court observed: 'From the materials placed by both the sides, we are satisfied that the 'paper trail' is an indispensable requirement of free and fair elections. The confidence of the voters in the EVMs can be achieved only with the introduction of the 'paper trail'. EVMs with VVPAT system ensure the accuracy of the voting system. With an intent to have fullest transparency in the system and to restore the confidence of the voters, it is necessary to set up EVMs with VVPAT system because vote is nothing but an act of expression which has immense importance in democratic system'.

The Supreme Court has repeatedly stressed that principles of democracy are a part of the basic structure of the Constitution of India. Replacement of paperless EVMs with VVPAT EVMs is imperative for the following reasons:

a) To impart confidence in citizens that their vote will be recorded and counted accurately.
b) To allow for a recount.
c) To provide a backup in cases of loss of votes due to malfunction.

d) To test—through a sizable random selection of machines—whether the paper result is the same as the electronic result.

It is our studied belief that the legitimacy of the electoral process in India, and, as a consequence, of democracy itself today faces a grave threat. This is because the system of using EVMs has not only been repeatedly shown to be riddled with glitches, but also because insufficient steps have been taken thus far to allay these concerns. We also note with concern the spate of VVPAT malfunction in the recent byelections—as high as 20.82 per cent in Kairana, 19.22 per cent in Bhandara-Gondia and 13.16 per cent in Palghar byelections against the EC norm of 5 per cent which itself is too high.

In fact, the ECI has delegated a number of crucial functions regarding the conduct of elections—like manufacturing, checking and maintenance of EVMs—to the EVM manufacturers and other agencies over which it has little or no administrative control. Even the most critical manufacturing of semiconductor chips and embedding them is outsourced to foreign companies. The Election Commission lacks the technical capability necessary for exercising effective technical control on these activities and operations. In order to ensure the integrity of the electronic voting system, the ECI must take immediate steps to assume greater administrative and technical control over the 2 EVMs manufacturers and related agencies in so far as the manufacturing, checking and maintenance of EVMs are concerned.

In our considered opinion, there is scope for 'insider frauds' at three stages:

(i) At the EVMs manufacturing stage.

(ii) At the district level, during the non-election period, when the EVMs are stored in archaic godowns in multiple locations with inadequate security systems.

(iii) At the stage of 'first level checks' prior to an election when the EVMs are serviced by 'authorised technicians' from BEL and ECIL.

Although, pursuant to the 8 October 2013 order of the Supreme Court, the EC has confirmed that all EVMs will be accompanied with VVPAT for the upcoming 2019 general elections, it is seen, as explained in your letter of 13 February 2018, the chief electoral officers in all States and Union Territories have been directed to mandatorily verify VVPAT paper slips in only one randomly selected polling station in each assembly constituency. This defeats the very object of installing VVPATs in all EVMs which would be rendered nugatory tantamounting to non-implementation of the Supreme Court Order.

The main purpose behind the introduction of VVPATs is to bring in accuracy, verifiability and transparency in the casting and counting of votes. With the presence of VVPATs, voters can verify if their vote has been cast to the right candidate. Needless to say, it is only when the paper slips as verified by the voters are counted that the true purpose behind the introduction of VVPATs is served. Without counting of VVPAT paper slips in a significant percentage of polling stations in each assembly constituency, the objectives of verifiability and transparency in the democratic process would remain unrealised.

The direction to hand-count VVPAT slips in just 'one polling station per Assembly Constituency' works out to 0.4 per cent of EVMs on an average. This is nothing but an exercise in tokenism. This would defeat the very purpose of introducing VVPAT and, what's more, would also be fraught with all the risks of conducting elections with paperless EVMs. In the rush to declare results and the winners, the Election Commission cannot turn a blind eye to the possibilities of wrong totaling due to EVM malfunction or EVM tampering. Surely, in something as important as ensuring the integrity of the election process, a delay of a few hours or even a couple of days shouldn't matter at all, more so when the entire election process, from the date of announcement to the date of counting, lasts for 2-3 months. Cost and time, we submit, cannot be considerations when the integrity of the entire electoral process is at stake.

Sample of 'one polling station per Assembly Constituency' is statistically unsound in terms of size. Also, because the various polling stations in the constituency are not similar the sample drawn may not be truly representative of the constituency as a whole. There is an imperative need for stratified sampling with a random sample of one or more polling stations drawn from each of the following 'strata': urban (middle/upper class); urban (poor/slums); semi-urban; rural; Dalits/minorities; remote hilly/desert/forest areas; those with very heavy voter turnout (> 80 per cent); with moderate voter turnout (50 per cent to 80 per cent); with low voter turnout (<50 per cent); those about which a large number of complaints received etc.

We, therefore, suggest that VVPAT slips must be simultaneously counted for a sample size of at least 25 per cent of the polling stations in an Assembly Constituency with the samples drawn randomly from the different strata and verified with the electronic count. This random selection of booths should be done in consultation with the candidates or their authorised representatives. If any variation is found then the entire VVPAT slips in the constituency should be counted and tallied with the electronic count before declaring the result. We believe this is a direction that can be issued by the Commission immediately for the 2018 State Assembly elections for testing and refining so that it can be fully implemented in the forthcoming 2019 general elections to Parliament? This alone would ensure greater standard of verifiability and integrity in the electoral process.

An accurate recording of the democratic will of the electorate, to the satisfaction of the electorate, is indispensable to the democratic process. The exercise of the right to vote must take place in a manner that is in consonance with the highest principles of integrity and fairness as enshrined in the Constitution of India. Our suggestions, if implemented, will help instil in the electoral process greater transparency and fairness. We believe it is imperative that the EC implements our suggestions in order to ensure the sustenance of the principles of republican democracy that stand at the bedrock of the Constitution of India.

As it is, not everyone is convinced of the fairness of the EVMs. This has caused deep doubts and apprehensions among the political parties and voting public about the reliability and integrity of electronic voting and therefore its compliance with democracy principles. The ECI introduced VVPAT mandated by the SC could bring about some compliance of these principles. And this is possible only if total (100 per cent) reliability of the EVMs and VVPATs is ensured and large percentage of paper slips hand-counted and cross-verified before declaring results. Former CECs have also suggested this course of action.

The Constitution of India (Article 324) mandates the ECI with the superintendence, direction, control and the conduct of all elections. What we are seeking is well within the powers of the ECI and therefore immediately doable. In the event, we urge the Commission to expeditiously issue the directions requested for in the interest of Electoral Integrity which is the bulwark of Democracy.

Yours faithfully,
Constitutional Conduct Group (57 signatories)

FUNDAMENTAL RIGHTS AND FREEDOM OF SPEECH

A Reasoned Engagement with Free Speech and Expression

PAMELA PHILIPOSE

'The ultimate tragedy is not the oppression and cruelty by the bad people but the silence over that by the good people.' Every one of the letters written by the CCG is a reminder of this observation made by Martin Luther King.

Here were retired civil servants, numbering a hundred or thereabouts, who did not keep silent in the face of rising tyranny. They came together driven by the need to resist through their words and collective wisdom what they saw as an 'alarming decline in the secular, democratic, and liberal values enshrined in our Constitution'. At a crucial moment in India's history, when civil rights and liberties were steadily declining in a climate of coercion, surveillance and fear under the Narendra Modi government, this group asserted their right to free speech, even as a great number of their compatriots chose to keep their counsel or, worse, justify the actions of those in power.

The letters are valuable because they reflect decades of experience and understanding garnered by one-time guardians of the country's administrative apparatus. But what makes them invaluable is the unambiguous and fearless manner in which they critiqued the ruling establishment. They anticipated the profound democratic backsliding that this country, which projects itself as the world's oldest democracy, experienced in the decade of Modi rule.

A major trope that emerged from these letters written over a period of six years was the primacy of freedom of speech. Article 19(I)(a), which lays down that 'all citizens shall have the right to freedom of speech and expression', was perceived by a member of the Constituent Assembly as the 'charter of our liberties' and 'probably the most important article in the whole Draft Constitution'.[1] It was not a singular construct. A plethora of other freedoms, including the right to dissent, the right to form associations, the right of free assembly, and the right to a free media, is attached to it. This has been recognised and reiterated in innumerable judicial verdicts. The *Shreya Singhal v. Union of India* judgment, to take one instance, dwelt upon the 'foundational importance of free speech in a pluralist democracy', and recognised it as a guarantee that 'allowed advocacy of repugnant or even revolutionary views, and only permitted the State to penalise speech that constituted 'incitement to violence'.[2] The CCG drew on the more expansive understanding of Article 19(I)(a).

A striking characteristic of the Modi regime, as its dictatorial character began to assert itself, was its ruthless suppression of dissent. Nothing reflected this more than the rash of arrests of sixteen human rights defenders in the Bhima Koregaon cases, starting from mid-June 2018 onwards. While many in the country may have been shocked by these arbitrary detentions made under draconian laws, there were few willing to express their outrage in public. In sharp contrast, a CCG letter, appearing six weeks after the first arrests, spoke out loud and clear.[3] It characterised the use of the Unlawful Activities (Prevention) Act (UAPA) against the detainees, as 'the most brazen display yet of coercive authority by the State'.

Such displays of 'coercive authority' were to intensify as time wore on. UAPA emerged as the legislation of choice used by the authorities to crush dissent. In 2019, it was amended to allow individuals to be framed as terrorists (rather than groups which was the case earlier), without proper judicial due process or even the necessary evidence to convict them. A range of people, arbitrarily framed as 'anti-Indian' by the State, were made to come under its ambit.

That early letter was distinctive for three prescient observations. One, it earmarked the modus operandi resorted to by the government:

those accused were framed as enemies of the State by having vague allegations and outright fabrications made out against them.

Two, it pointed to the hypocrisy of treating so-called Maoist sympathisers as dangerous terrorists, while allowing murderous sympathisers of the Bajrang Dal or Sanatan Sanstha or Hindu Mahasabha a free hand. This was a pattern that kept recurring. During the violence in northeast Delhi of February 2020, while JNU and Jamia students were arrested for coming out in support of those protesting the newly enacted Citizenship Amendment Act (CAA), BJP politicians like Kapil Mishra and Anurag Thakur, who openly and publicly raised murderous and communal slogans, attracted little police attention.

Three, the letter emphatically underlined how a climate of fear was created to ensure that those disturbed by the direction in which the country was headed were deterred from articulating and acting on their misgivings. The term 'Urban Naxals', newly minted by a prominent propagandist close to the ruling establishment, was promoted for just this purpose and it continued to be used in the days ahead, sometimes by the Prime Minister himself.

The Bhima Koregaon arrests were followed by innumerable others, with the police even resorting to doctoring evidence to incarcerate a range of individuals which included university students on the threshold of a bright future. A case in point was the video of a speech delivered by former civil servant, Harsh Mander, during the fraught days following the passage of the CAA in December 2019. The video had been edited to make it appear that Mander was inciting violence when in reality he was advocating resistance through Gandhian non-violence.[4] Such maliciousness on the part of the coercive apparatus of the State disturbed the CCG greatly: 'Police establishments across the country [are] appearing to have become proxies for the respective ruling parties.' It was a trend, they feared, that would lead to India emerging as a 'police state'.[5]

Another institution crucial to the functioning of democracy—the media—also drew the CCG's attention. The First Press Commission, set up in heady days of Independence, had laid down a rule of thumb for media freedom. The Constitutional guarantee of freedom of expression, it said, 'should be understood as meaning freedom to hold opinions, to receive and to impart information...without interference from any public authority.'[6] It went on to say that the 'tender plant of democracy' can only flourish in 'an atmosphere of the free interchange of views and ideas which one not only has a moral right but a moral duty to express.' Yet, seventy years later, in that season of death, when the COVID-19 pandemic raged, press freedom too came under grave threat. Journalists across India faced FIRs, dismissals and jail terms for reporting on the mishandling of the health crisis by State authorities. The CCG expressed alarm over these developments and spoke for many when it iterated that 'All Indians must unite in defence of the Rule of Law and Article 19, the repository of the democratic right to freedom of speech and to dissent.'[7]

Aspects of media functioning had also become extremely worrisome, including the widespread emergence of television channels aligned to the ruling party, devoted to peddling disinformation to stir up popular emotions and foment communal anger. Sudarshan News TV channel, headed, controlled and anchored by Suresh Chavhanke, a notorious peddler of hate speech, came up with a series labelled 'UPSC Jihad', which alleged that there was a 'sudden rise of Muslim officers'[8] in the IAS and IPS as a result of a supposed recruitment scam perpetrated by the Union Public Service Commission (UPSC). It must be remembered that the word 'jihad' had by now become code for Muslim aggression and conquest and was being freely linked to any issue of contemporary concern to demonise the entire community.

In its detailed repudiation of the programme at a time when it had come to the notice of the court, the CCG pointed to several very serious consequences that would ensue should such a skewed programme be allowed to be broadcast. Apart from the negative social impacts of such vicious hate speech, it highlighted how the reputation of an institution like the UPSC, widely recognised to being fair, could be irreparably tarnished. The CCG went on to dismantle the false claim being made that there has been a disproportionate rise in the number of Muslims coming into the Civil Services when the data in fact indicate the contrary reality.

The rapid and largely unregulated changes in the media landscape combined with rising communalisation of the social and political sphere, required just such careful scrutiny. During the early months of the pandemic in 2020, there were consistent attempts to scapegoat the Muslim community as being responsible for the spread of COVID-19. Major news channels and even newspapers were conduits of such disinformation, but what was also obvious was the manner in which social media platforms were being instrumentalised for such ends. Facebook, which had around 300 million Indian users at this time, was a major offender. A CCG letter addressed to its CEO, Mark Zuckerberg,[9] demanded to know why, despite Facebook's own definition of hate speech as a 'direct attack against people...on the basis of what we call protected characteristics: race, ethnicity, national origin, disability, religious affiliation, caste, sexual orientation, sex, gender identity and serious disease', the platform did nothing about removing offensive posts. The letter also politely pointed out to Facebook's hypocrisy in rushing to take action only after a investigation by *The Wall Street Journal*—'Facebook's Hate-Speech Rules Collide With Indian Politics'—called out Facebook's pronounced bias towards the BJP. The CCG letter also underlined how the Public Policy Head of Facebook India had 'consciously opposed applying Facebook's hate speech rules to members of the ruling Bharatiya Janata Party because doing so would adversely affect the company's business prospects in India.'

A little over two months after this letter came out, Facebook India's Public Policy Head, Ankhi Das, resigned. The attention paid to this issue by US and civil society groups at home had clearly played a role in this development. It was yet another instance of the moral authority of prominent citizens speaking out on issues of public importance.

A distinctive feature of the CCG's stances on the media was their insistence on the need to use the Constitution as the ultimate reference point. One letter came as a reminder to advertisers that by seeking to sell their products through the agency of media channels that actively promoted communal hate and prejudice, they were in violation of Article 15 of the Constitution that prohibits discrimination on the grounds of religion, race, caste, sex and place of birth. 'To all companies, business houses and corporate bodies we would like to say: let not any of your actions, even inadvertently, help forces that create discord and ill-will amongst our people.'[10]

At the heart of the CCG's argument was the existential threat facing the foundational values of the Republic under the relentless assault of an 'arrogant, majoritarian state'.[11] The crisis demanded urgent responses from civil society, which the CCG defined as a 'diverse mass of formal and informal groups occupying the vast democratic space outside government and business.' Such a definition drew on Jurgen Habermas' formulation of the public sphere as a space from which concerned citizens may confront and critique the State. According to this formulation, a stronger democracy makes for a more sturdy civil society, and vice versa. The problem today, as the CCG emphasised, is that civil society itself has come to be framed as an enemy of the country by the ruling establishment. Its voice is being systematically choked; those who speak for it are jailed; and rules and orders are formulated in order to weaken its institutions.

That these were not mere conjectures was confirmed when the National Security Adviser of the country, Ajit Doval, argued in a public speech of November 2021 that 'The new frontiers of war, what you call the fourth-generation warfare, is the civil society.' According to the Doval formulation, civil society can be subverted, suborned, divided and manipulated 'to hurt the interests of a nation'. In response the CCG letter pointed out that the term 'fourth-generation warfare' is normally understood to refer to terror groups and insurgents. By resorting to such a pejorative framing, one of the Modi government's highest functionaries was deliberately casting aspersions on a section of citizens who, far from working to undermine the Republic, were engaged in extending the social and economic rights of various categories of vulnerable Indians.

With the passing years, an elaborate policy architecture designed to ring-fence civil society organisations has come into view. The Government's instrument of choice in order to achieve this has been Foreign Contribution Regulation Act under which nonprofits in India seeking financial assistance from foreign sources required GOI certification. By mid-2023, there were innumerable instances of well-known and respected civil society organisations, some with a history of having worked in the country since the post-independence era, being denied such permission, leading to a severe curtailment, or even suspension, of their activities. In a letter to the Union Home Minister, the CCG pulled no punches.[12] It pointed out how a hugely problematic law was being systematically exploited to harass voluntary organisations. Advocating a drastic overhaul of the FCRA, it urged the Government to 'cease needless harassment of organisations serving the people of India, especially its most marginalised and disadvantaged sections.'

Instrumentalising problematic laws was only half the problem; enacting and steamrolling them through Parliament was the other. Much like the discriminatory Citizenship (Amendment) Act, which was passed in Parliament without public discussion or House debate, a set of three farm laws were barrelled through when the country was facing the COVID-19 crisis. It gave rise to what was perhaps the most serious challenge the Modi Government had to ever face, leading to farmers from Punjab and across India staging protests at Delhi's doors for 15 months. The CCG endorsed these protests over two letters written in the space of a few weeks because it perceived the great injustice being done to this crucial section of society. Not only was severe police repression unleashed on them, they were stigmatised as terrorists and traitors: 'The approach of the Government of India towards the farmers' protest has been an adversarial and confrontationist one from the very beginning, treating the apolitical farmers like an irresponsible opposition to be derided, demonised and defeated.'[13]

It is a measure of the strong moral arguments made by a range of voices across the country, as indeed the resolute resistance of the farmers that a government which had never conceded to the demands of those it accused of being 'anti-India', was forced to withdraw the controversial farm legislations in December 2021.

In the Preface to his book, *The Idea of Justice*, Amartya Sen argues that democracy 'must also be seen more generally in terms of the capacity to enrich reasoned engagement through enhancing informational availability and the feasibility of interactive discussions.'[14] Each of the CCG letters is an attempt at reasoned engagement with some of the most critical issues of the day against a backdrop of growing political authoritarianism. For that reason alone, it must be seen as a uniquely democratic undertaking.

NOTES

1. Sukumar Muralidharan, *Freedom, Civility, Commerce: Contemporary Media and the Public*, Three Essays Collective, 2018, p. 122.
2. Bhatia, Gautam, *The Transformative Constitution A Radical Biography in Nine Acts*, HarperCollins India, New Delhi: 2021, p. 251.
3. CCG, 'Open Letter: Arrests of Activists', August 30, 2018.
4. CCG, 'In defence of Harsh Mander: An Open Letter to the media', March 22, 2020.
5. CCG, 'Letter to the Attorney General for India regarding the Mohammed Zubair Case', July 15, 2022.
6. *Report of the Press Commission: Part 1*, Government of India Press, Delhi: 1954, p. 517.
7. CCG, 'Assault on the Rule of Law, Free Speech and Right to Dissent', July 4, 2020.
8. CCG, 'Letter Seeking Action against Sudarshan TV for its Malicious Campaign to Promote Hatred andDivisiveness in Society', September 1, 2020.

9. CCG, 'An Open Letter to Mark Zuckerberg, CEO, Facebook', August 24, 2020.
10. CCG, 'Open Letter to Corporates: Policy on Advertising on Media Channels', October 31, 2020.
11. CCG, 'Civil Society: Enemy Of The State?', November 28, 2021.
12. CCG, 'Open Letter To Union Home Minister – Harassment Of Voluntary Organisations Under Fcra', July 4, 2023.
13. CCG, 'Open Statement in Support of Farmers', February 5, 2021.
14. Amartya Sen, *The Idea of Justice, Allen Lane*, London: 2009, p. xiii.

Human Rights

MADAN LOKUR

Human rights are being curtailed through the application of stringent laws and their unsustainable interpretation. Unfortunately, the courts are not actively protecting the fundamental rights of citizens. In the long term, the consequences can be disastrous.

Consider personal liberty, the most valuable and basic human right, and the law on sedition. The sedition law is stringent, no doubt, carrying the possibility of imprisonment for life. On a plain interpretation, the law punishes a person who excites disaffection towards the government established by law. Disaffection has been given an inclusive definition and it includes disloyalty and all feelings of enmity. How do you define disloyalty or feelings of enmity towards the government? To somewhat temper the vagueness of the law, disaffection has also been given an exclusionary definition, and therefore it is not disapprobation of government measures, administrative or other action, but it must excite hatred, contempt or disaffection.

Gandhiji called sedition 'perhaps the prince among the political sections of the Indian Penal Code designed to suppress the liberty of the citizen.' However, a government that chooses to suppress the liberty of a citizen can have a field day in interpreting the law on sedition and, I am afraid, this is precisely what transpired a few years ago, until the Supreme Court put an interim halt to it, resulting in more severe, though unintended consequences. The police interpreted sedition a couple of years ago to jail a teenager for shouting '*Pakistan zindabad*'. How was she exciting disaffection towards the government? But she was in jail for 110 days, with the Sessions Judge refusing bail to her. She was eventually granted default bail by a Magistrate because the police failed to file a charge sheet within 90 days.[1] I believe both the Judge and the Magistrate abdicated their judicial responsibility. The Sessions Judge for not appreciating the plain language of the law and the Magistrate for not appreciating that default bail is automatic after 90 days. So much for personal liberty.

Again, a few years ago, a young anti-climate change activist was whisked away to Delhi from Bengaluru and jailed for sedition for putting up a toolkit shared by Greta Thunberg on her social media platform during the farmers agitation near Delhi. The agitating farmers, the ostensible cause of the toolkit, were not charged with sedition, but the activist was. The Sessions Judge who eventually granted her bail is reported to have said that not an iota of evidence was brought to his notice linking her with any violence.[2] These are two shocking instances, but I could go on and on. Several others have been victims of the strange interpretation of the law on sedition. The obvious reason being to silence them and have a chilling effect on others.

A research study published sometime in 2021 reveals that between 2014 and 2020, as many as 559 cases of sedition were filed against 2,293 known accused persons and 6,535 unknown accused persons. The study further found that the accused were most likely to spend about 50 days in jail before being granted bail by the Trial Court and about 200 days in jail before being granted bail by the High Court.[3]

I believe in many instances, the judiciary failed to safeguard the fundamental right of citizens to personal liberty as well as their freedom of speech and expression when it was needed. The Supreme Court did, later, 'suspend' operation of the sedition law, one of the reasons being that the government was re-examining the law.[4] Unfortunately, the re-examination has resulted in a more stringent law, without the word 'sedition' being used in the Bharatiya Nyaya Sanhita Bill, 2023.

Equally worrisome, the 'suspension' order has unintentionally resulted in enabling the government to misuse the Unlawful Activities (Prevention) Act, 1967 (UAPA) to quell dissent. The definition of 'unlawful activity' in the UAPA includes causing or intending to cause disaffection against India—not the government, but India. It's not difficult for any hyperactive police to accuse a person, without an 'iota of evidence' of causing disaffection against India by branding them anti-national (or even terrorists).[5] In such a case, the provision for 'default bail' kicks in after 180 days. The Supreme Court obviously did not visualise that by suspending the law on sedition it would be opening the doors to a different abuse of the law.

If it can get worse, it will. The National Security Act, a draconian law, has been used to incarcerate a person who disputed recovery of land revenue. The Supreme Court described the preventive detention as shocking and unsustainable. It is a clear case of non-application of mind by all authorities concerned.[6] Shocking and unsustainable, yes; but non-application of mind, I doubt it. An order of preventive detention is made by the Central Government or the State Government, as the case may be. The order is passed by a senior officer empowered for this purpose. That senior officer passes an order of preventive detention on being subjectively satisfied that a case for preventive detention is made out. The decision is conscious and is made with full application of mind. A senior officer cannot afford not to apply his or her mind to detain a person and deprive the hapless person of his or her liberty. Under this law, there is no provision for bail and usually a person has no chance of coming out of detention until the order is set aside by a constitutional court. Simply put—the power is draconian and is now being roundly abused.[7]

The solution? The time has come, I earnestly believe, for the courts to hold the government authorities accountable for their acts of omission or commission. Deprivation of personal liberty is a major event in the life of any person and the authorities should not be allowed to get away with arresting a person only because they have the power to do so. The courts must step in in every case and exercise their judicial power. Our constitutional courts must continue to act as a sentinel on the *qui vive* particularly in matters of personal liberty. This can be done by removing the armour of immunity and suitably punishing an officer who jails a person for the most trivial of reasons and also compensating the victim of the whims and fancies of the authorities. Why do I say so? Try and imagine having to spend a few days or weeks in jail for absolutely no rhyme or reason, and only because some person in authority thinks you should be jailed.

In addition to introducing accountability, the judiciary needs to be far more liberal in matters of grant of bail and recognising the rights of under-trials. Remember Stan Swamy, a patient of Parkinson's? He was denied a straw and sipper and had to approach a court for this.[8] Think about it—should such a matter have ever come to court? Was any action taken against the jailor who refused the straw and sipper? Was any action taken against the investigating officer who instructed the prosecution lawyer to oppose the request? Was any action taken against the judge who gave 20 days to the prosecution to file a reply? Under-trial prisoners who are medically unwell or disabled, fight for bail and unfortunately are unsuccessful or put to severe restrictions. Again, there are several such cases. It seems that some key players in the criminal justice system have lost feelings of humanity and compassion. Do we not need a change here?

The occasional failure of the judiciary to dispense justice in crunch issues and side with the establishment rather than the citizen has resulted in an I-don't-care attitude regarding orders and directions of the courts, including the Supreme Court. This is dangerous.

Consider the government's assault on the freedom of speech and expression. Apart from journalists punished for their writings and generally doing their work, common citizens are adversely impacted by a variety of measures. For example, unreasonable restrictions have been put in place on access to the internet. The Supreme Court laid down the law, in rather restrictive terms, on internet shutdowns.[9] But, in clear violation of the law, access to the internet was recently unavailable in Manipur for several weeks and earlier, in Kashmir. Internet shutdowns, for prolonged periods, have had an adverse impact on healthcare and access to medicines; the studies of students have been affected; there has been untold economic loss and social services have also been badly affected.[10] There are no known benefits of an internet shutdown. Contrast this with no internet shutdown in war-torn Gaza, except for a recent blackout for about 36 hours.[11] One of the causes for the shutdown is said to be the intense bombardment in Gaza by the Israel Defence Forces.[12] We have regular shutdowns at the drop of a hat.

Journalists, whose job it is to write and report, are facing an assault on their freedom of speech and expression. A recent study on press freedom shows a declining trend with our country slipping in rank from 142 in 2020 to 161 in 2023 out of 180 countries across the world. Select individuals are targeted as exemplars. The case of senior journalist Vinod Dua, accused of sedition is too well known, but it took the Supreme Court to grant relief to him.[13] Mohammad Zubair has been in the crosshairs for quite some time now and will, I expect, continue to be so.[14] Again, I could go on and on.

Contrast this with mild action or inaction in respect of those indulging in hate speech, sometimes publicly.[15] Virulent hate speeches have been given by some leaders and some have even given a call for genocide. No coercive action has been taken against them. The Supreme Court has taken a strict view of hate speech and a direction given to take *suo motu* action against hate mongers, but the I-don't-care attitude persists.[16] The courts are helpless and so are we.

Another fundamental right—the right to protest peacefully has been virtually emasculated. A Nirbhaya style protest at the India Gate lawns, a Shaheen Bagh sit-in or a massive farmers' protest is now an impossibility. Permission is now required from the police, in some instances, to stage a peaceful protest. Gradually the law enforcement authorities are beginning to decide which cause to allow, the number of protestors and the location for protesting. A perfectly valid and justified protest by champion wrestlers at Jantar Mantar, protesting incidents of sexual harassment was violently broken up by the police and to make matter worse, the wrestlers were accused of rioting.[17]

What next? The courts, particularly the Supreme Court is considered the last bastion, the hope of the people that their fundamental rights will be protected and preserved. There was a time, not so long ago, when the Supreme Court was proudly referred to as the People's Court. Not so today; it is now perceived to be more pro-executive and less pro-citizen, particularly in matters pertaining to personal liberty. It is worth recalling the words of Lord Denning, a celebrated judge who referred to the practice in English courts and said that 'liberty is so precious that whenever one of the King's judges takes his seat, there is one application which by long tradition has priority over all others. Counsel has but to say, "My Lord, I have an application which concerns the liberty of the subject" and forthwith the judge will put all other matters aside and hear it. It may be an application for a writ of habeas corpus, or an application for bail, but, whatever form it takes, it is heard first.' Can our courts learn from this?

NOTES

1. 'After 110 Days in Jail for Saying "Pakistan Zindabad," 19-Year-Old Activist Gets "Default Bail"', *The Wire*, 11 June, 2020 (https://thewire.in/rights/amulya-leona-bail-bengaluru; Accessed March 2024)
2. 'Sedition in India: Case of Disha Ravi and many others over the decades', *Times Now News*, 26 February, 2021 (https://www.timesnownews.com/india/article/sedition-in-india-case-of-disha-ravi-and-many-others-over-the-decades/725421; Accessed March 2024)

3. *A Decade of Darkness: The Story of Sedition in India*, Article 14 (https://sedition.article-14.com/; Accessed March 2024)
4. 'Supreme Court puts sedition law on hold: 5 key points', *The Times of India*, 11 May 2022 (https://timesofindia.indiatimes.com/india/supreme-court-puts-sedition-law-on-hold-5-key-points/articleshow/91486383.cms; Accessed March 2024)
5. 'Why UAPA is a threat to media freedom in India', *Frontline, The Hindu*, 6 October, 2023 (https://frontline.thehindu.com/columns/uapa-media-freedom-newsclick-china-terrorism-modi-government/article67388663.ece; Accessed march 2024)
6. 'Shocking and unsustainable: Supreme Court on NSA detention of Samajwadi Party's Yusuf Malik in revenue case', Bar and Bench, 14 April, 2023 (https://www.barandbench.com/news/litigation/supreme-court-uttar-pradesh-nsa-detain-sp-leader-revenue-case#:~:text=The%20Supreme%20Court%20recently%20took%20exception%20to%20the,%5BYusuf%20Malik%20v.%20Union%20of%20India%20and%20ors%5D; Accessed March 2024)
7. 'In Uttar Pradesh, more than half of NSA arrests this year were for cow slaughter', *The Indian Express*, 11 September, 2020 (https://indianexpress.com/article/india/in-uttar-pradesh-more-than-half-of-nsa-arrests-this-year-were-for-cow-slaughter-6591315/; Accessed March 2024)
8. 'For 20 Days, Stan Swamy, 83, Has Been Asking For A Straw And Sipper', *NDTV*, 26 November, 2020 (https://www.ndtv.com/india-news/stan-swamys-wait-for-a-straw-and-sipper-extended-not-till-december-2330570; Accessed March 2024)
9. *Bhasin v. Union of India*, Global Freedom of Expression, Columbia University (https://globalfreedomofexpression.columbia.edu/cases/bhasin-v-union-of-india/; Accessed March 2024)
10. 'How Internet Shutdowns Wreak Havoc in India', *Time*, 15 August, 2023 (https://time.com/6304719/india-internet-shutdowns-manipur/; Accessed March 2024)
11. 'Internet access in Gaza partially restored after blackout', *TechCrunch*, 31 October, 2023 (https://techcrunch.com/2023/10/30/internet-access-in-gaza-partially-restored-after-blackout/; Accessed March 2024
12. 'Gaza's disappearing internet, visualized', *CNN*, 13 October, 2023

(https://edition.cnn.com/2023/10/13/middleeast/gaza-internet-outage-map-visuals-dg/index.html; Accessed March 2024)

13. 'SC Quashes Sedition Case Against Vinod Dua, Says Every Journalist Entitled to Protection', *The Wire*, 3 June, 2021 (https://thewire.in/law/supreme-court-quash-vinod-dua-sedition-case; Accessed March 2024)
14. 'Alt News co-founder and Journalist Mohammad Zubair arrested in Delhi for "hurting religious sentiments"', *The Economic Times*, 27 June, 2022 (https://economictimes.indiatimes.com/news/india/alt-news-co-founder-and-journalist-mohammad-zubair-arrested-in-delhi/articleshow/92497721.cms; Accessed March 2024)
15. 'Haridwar Dharma Sansad: 2 more booked in hate speech case', *India Today*, 1 January 2022 (https://www.indiatoday.in/india/story/haridwar-dharma-sansad-hate-speech-fir-1894929-2022-01-01; Accessed March 2024)
16. 'Supreme Court calls hate speech "complete menace", cautions Centre, states', *The Hindustan Times*, 14 January, 2023 (https://www.hindustantimes.com/india-news/supreme-court-calls-hate-speech-complete-menace-cautions-centre-states-101673636542025.html; Accessed March 2024)
17. 'Police Case Against Wrestlers After They Tried To March To New Parliament', *NDTV*, 28 May, 2023 (https://www.ndtv.com/india-news/police-case-filed-against-protesting-wrestlers-after-they-tried-to-march-to-new-parliament-today-4074296; Accessed March 2024)

Freedom of Expression and the Media

AAKAR PATEL

India has taken an unnatural trajectory after 2014 that has deeply affected its economy and its social fabric.

On the side of the economy it has fallen behind Bangladesh in per capita GDP for the first time. In current US dollars, India's per person GDP is $2,277, while Bangladesh's is $2,503. In 2014, India was at $1,573 and Bangladesh was at $1,118. These are World Bank figures that are provided by the national governments and there is no dispute over them. This slipping of growth has been accompanied by joblessness being above 6 per cent since 2018 and a labour force participation rate that is the worst in South Asia. Again, this is government data and not disputed. The Periodic Labour Force Survey for 2022-23 tells us that the number of people 'employed' as unpaid household labour has gone up in the last six years by 3 crore.

Today, and for the next five years to come, 60 per cent of India's population is dependent on six kilos of free grain and dal per month, a total of 80 crore people (more than the population of Europe) showing the distress levels. On the side of the social fabric we are passing through a term defined by Muslim exclusion from politics. A deliberate exclusion imposed by the largest political party which has no Union Minister or MP from India's largest minority community.

With this, the party has legislated laws at the Centre and state levels, specifically targeting Muslims. On citizenship, criminalising Muslim divorce, inter-faith marriage, possession of beef and forcible ghettoisation. In Kashmir, the only part of South Asia today to not have democratic representation, the situation has become frozen. The popular political endorsement of this record means that this trajectory on both the side of the economy and the social fabric will continue unless there is resistance from society and a pressure to change course.

This resistance has been slow in coming, as all who have lived through the period know, the question is why. Let us examine this through the media and its role since 2014. First, before we jump into the details, we must try to frame the issue properly and outline what the problem is. The Indian State exerts control over media in two ways. The Union government is the largest advertiser in South Asia. This money is handed out discretionarily and ruling parties withhold or hand out to reward and punish media groups and outlets. Second, the state controls licensing and can use it as a stick or carrot. This extends to wider infrastructure and other projects which large media houses are invested in. To give one example, and a recent one, on 21 August 2022, it was announced that Gautam Adani was purchasing the *Dainik Bhaskar* group's thermal power assets for Rs 7,017 crore. *Dainik Bhaskar* is the second largest newspaper in India.

Now while power was always exerted by the Union government against the media, including during the infamous Emergency, it has never been done so nakedly. And the media has never been as supine, and often as enthusiastically supportive, of the government. This is why it has been as if one were living in two realities. The first that is reflected by the numbers on the economy, on joblessness, the large gashes that have been torn in the social fabric and the total opacity on national security. The second is the bizarre, almost celebratory, manner in which the media has reported the period. Here we try to understand why this has happened.

In a study published at the end of 2020, political scientist Christophe Jaffrelot and data analyst Vihang Jumle examined the Republic TV's content. They wrote: 'We studied all prime-time debates held since the channel was launched in May 2017, until April 2020, when we began the study—1,779 in all. Our conclusion was clear: Republic TV's debates have been consistently biased in favour of the Modi government and its policies, as well as the ideology of the BJP. What's worse, these debates have rarely featured some of the most pressing issues that impact Indians, such as the state of the economy, education or health. Instead, they have consisted mostly of attacks against the Opposition as well as any groups or persons that oppose the ruling government's ideology. Some figures are staggering, if unsurprising. Nearly fifty per cent of Republic TV's political debates criticised the Opposition, but it has not conducted even one debate that we could classify as being in the Opposition's favour.'

It used to be the case that the government mouthpieces in India were the State-run channels. Whichever party was in power, one remembers the Opposition of a few decades ago complaining that it was not given enough representation on Doordarshan. During the tenure of Hamid Ansari as Vice President, Rajya Sabha TV (which was under the control of the Vice President, as chairperson of the Rajya Sabha) used to have open debates. In fact, these debates were more open than the privately owned channels. That freedom for Rajya Sabha TV has now, of course, gone. But State-run media is not required in India any longer when it is the free press that is doing the propaganda and the disinformation. State-owned stations are not needed in a nation where most of the private ones have become shills for the government and more particularly for Modi personally. They seem to revel (perhaps the word is wallow) in the swamp of anti-minority hate.

To understand this shift towards majoritarianism in the media in India (obvious to anyone who has watched its news channels become deranged, a process which has accelerated after 2014), it may be instructive to look first at the background. If there is such a thing as a national media in India, it is the English newspapers and English news television channels ecosystem. The so-called regional language media, even if large by readership, is restricted mostly to a single state, such as the newspapers of Kerala, Gujarat, Tamil Nadu, Odisha, Bengal, Punjab, Karnataka and Andhra Pradesh. Hindi has a much bigger audience than English in terms of numbers, but it is geographically narrower. English alone can claim to reach all states, especially all the urban spaces. The paradox is that English media is less expressive of its audience's sentiments than the regional language media for the following reasons.

Firstly, English newspapers address a more disparate audience than, say, a Gujarati or Tamil newspaper does. The geographical spread, the levels of exposure, the varieties of educational background and professions, the levels of cultural and political interests are much wider in the all-India readership of the English newspaper than any other medium. And, naturally, English communicates in a highly globalised vocabulary. This makes it difficult for the English newspaper to be as eloquent idiomatically as a regional language paper.

Secondly, English newspapers come from a longer tradition than most regional newspapers in India, with only very few exceptions like *Bombay Samachar*, a Gujarati newspaper which is 200 years old. English newspapers had a precedent in British-run media in India, and for decades after Independence continued or tried to continue this tradition. This made our English newspapers less Indian in tone. Meaning they were more reserved and more formal. Assistant editors, inexperienced individuals often from elite institutions and sometimes even from Oxbridge, were put in charge of or wrote on these organs' opinion pages.

Thirdly, because English newspapers attracted a disproportionately large part of advertising revenue, the content had to be such that it did not put off the elite and, in fact, catered to them. This elite had global exposure and did not see themselves as identifying purely with nativism. For these reasons, English newspapers have always been edited socially to the left of the reader, meaning that on many issues the English newspaper editor in India was more liberal than her reader. Certainly, on social issues, this was the case. There were exceptions to this but they were so few that they could be singled out as being very different. Girilal Jain, editor of *The Times of India*, who supported the campaign against the Babri Masjid, was the most striking of these. In our time, it is the columnist Swapan Dasgupta. These individuals ploughed lonely furrows in the English press, till the arrival of Modi.

The acceptability and legitimacy of Hindutva, meaning an explicitly anti-Muslim majoritarianism, is recent in English media. This is a different position from what has historically been the case in the regional media. The local language had idiomatic connect with the reader and was more expressive. These papers, and particularly ones in the north, were also edited closer to the reader, meaning they were less liberal and more aligned to the conservatism of the broad readership. To illustrate this, let us look at a study done on the media in 2002 after the riots in Gujarat. After the violence, the Editors Guild of India sent three of its members to do a fact-finding mission report on the role of the media in the violence. I was one of the three along with Dileep Padgaonkar and B.G. Verghese, both senior newspaper editors. Our findings were published and released on 3 May 2002. This was perhaps the first time that many who read and viewed their news mainly in English saw what all of India began to see later with respect to reporting on Muslims. We interviewed Modi, all the major owner-editors of newspapers, bureaucrats, Vishwa Hindu Parishad (VHP) and RSS leaders, businessmen and members of civil society between 31 March and 6 April. The report concluded that 'the role of sections of the Gujarati media, especially the *Gujarat Samachar* and more notably, *Sandesh* [the state's largest and second largest newspapers], was provocative, irresponsible and blatantly violative of all accepted norms of media ethics. This cannot be lightly passed over.' Here is some of what the fact-finding report found: Falgun Patel, owner-editor of *Sandesh*, said the English media had sided 'out and out' with the Muslims, but the Gujarat papers were 'pro-Hindu'. He said Hindus were not temperamentally prone to starting riots, but this time Hindu anger, irrespective of class, was inflamed by the incident at Godhra. Even Hindu women felt '*Theek hai, salon ko maaro*' (Good, kill the scoundrels). He asked of Muslims: 'Can a 20 per cent minority take the majority for a ride? There has to be a limit.' He said that Muslims had thought that they could get away with anything, but when Modi took office a clear message had gone out to them. When the Guild members asked Patel how collective punishment was justified, he said the idea was 'to pressurise ordinary Muslims to put pressure on Muslim goons to behave'. After the way 'these Muslims' had behaved, *'Hinduism ke naam per hum kuch bhi karenge'* (We can also do anything in the name of Hinduism). The Guild report said: 'An article in *Gujarat Samachar* had implied that former Congress MP Ehsan Jafri, who was brutally slain, "got what he deserved". Queried on this, the owner-editor, Bahubali Shah, said he stood by what the paper had written.' *Sandesh's* Patel dismissed Jafri's murder saying that he had a 'bad record'. The Guild report said that the Gujarat government press notes reflected similar language: 'The phraseology most often used for the Godhra incident was "inhuman genocide", "inhuman carnage" or "massacre" while the subsequent riots were invariably described as "disturbances", and occasionally as "violent disturbances/incidents".' One paper, *Madhyantar*, carried an eight-column commentary on its front page headlined: 'Muslims will have to prove that they are full Indians!' (*Mussalmanon-e puravo aapvo padshe ke te kharekhar Hindustani che!*). This may appear shocking to the reader even today, but it is not recent or new. This was how large parts of the regional media had always operated. What Modi has done is to align almost all national media with the sentiment that the media in Gujarat had shown against Muslims. Modi has legitimised and given credibility to Hindutva, which expresses itself essentially in anti-minority terms. This has made it easier for the media to broadcast their material through its filter.

The English media, which with its more diverse, more national audience, was structurally not prone to being extreme, succumbed. The decline of print and the dominance of television news made this easier: it is easier to communicate emotion and anger through visuals and sound rather than through the written word. The regional media has shifted farther away from inclusion and is comfortable with its coverage of a Hindutva-minded Union and what it is doing to Indian society. The interesting thing is to examine the ease with which this has happened. One reason is economic. The media space in India is funded primarily by advertising. The reader or viewer pays very little by way of subscription and our newspapers are the cheapest in the world. *The New York Times* and *The Guardian* cost the equivalent of Rs 100 or more per copy for about the same amount of newsprint material that goes into a copy of *The Times of India* or *The Hindustan Times*, which charge their readers only Rs 5 or less (of which one-third goes to the distributor and vendor). Even in Pakistan, Sri Lanka and Bangladesh, newspapers cost three or four times more than papers in India. How is it then possible for Indian newspapers to exist and be profitable? Advertising, of course, which is by far the largest source of revenue for media companies. And the largest advertiser in India is the Union government through its Directorate of Audio Visual Publicity (DAVP). In the year ending of March 2017, the Modi government spent nearly Rs 1,300 crore on advertising and publicity, of which Rs 468 crore went to newspapers. This was down from Rs 508 crore the year before, though DAVP's budget went up by 8 per cent. Television and digital had got the rest. To put the sum in context, it is more than what is spent on advertising by all of India's telecom companies put together. When you see the 'Swachh Bharat' and 'PM Garib Kalyan Yojana' ads on TV and in newspapers, this is paid for by taxpayer money, but it gives the government extraordinary leverage and control over the media. When the COVID-19 crisis broke and it was apparent that government revenues would be squeezed, Sonia Gandhi wrote to Modi suggesting that government advertising be put on hold. She was saying this both for economic and political reasons. She knows a lot about what that spending on media means to Modi. She pointed out that the government currently spends an average of Rs 1,250 crore per year (not including an equal or greater amount spent by PSUs and government companies), and that this amount could instead be used to alleviate the social and economic impact of COVID-19.

There is, therefore, a total of Rs 2,500 crore a year that Modi can give at his discretion to the media. It should not surprise us, therefore, that India's media has been unable to perform its essential function in the Modi years. Severely hit by demonetisation and the national lockdown, the media not only stopped short of criticising Modi, it was in fact obliged to turn to him to save it. The share of print (newspapers and magazines) in the overall advertising pie across sectors is shrinking. In 2019, for the first time in history, digital advertising overtook print in India, and by a lot. Digital got 27 per cent of advertising money spent in India, while print got 22 per cent. Television remained number one at 43 per cent, but both TV and print shrank further in 2020, and conceded share to digital. The COVID crisis accelerated this process and newspapers are now going bust. They cannot afford, therefore, to antagonise their largest advertiser—Modi. This is why readers may have noticed that many newspapers have attempted to bring in 'balance' on their opinion pages by adding writers who promote the government or the Hindutva perspective. After the lockdown had cut circulation and advertising numbers in half, the Indian Newspaper Society wrote to Modi asking for a 'stimulus package' to save India's print media. The proprietors wanted the government to: increase the spend on newspapers by 200 per cent, pay its old dues, increase the rate DAVP paid them by 50 per cent, remove the customs duty on newsprint and give them a two-year tax holiday. The industry had lost around Rs 12,500 crore in the eight months after the lockdown. The same newspapers which had to report on the Modi government and were expected to be critical of it were going to Modi, cap in hand, asking to be saved. It should not surprise us that the media is now called 'Godi' (a word meaning to be in the lap of, and of course, rhyming with Modi), because he is their patron and can do them damage. It is true that this power has been in the hands of all governments of the recent past as Union advertising spends have gone up. But under Modi, the Union has used the advertising carrot also as a stick. Advertising money was denied to those publications which fell foul of the government for a variety of reasons including being 'disrespectful', and for reasons of 'inaccurate news reports'. Modi actually brought the newspapers to heel. India has more cable news channels than any other nation. In 2021, India had 178 functioning news channels. Tata Sky lists 143 of them (51 Hindi, 12 English, 8 Kannada, 7 Bengali, 8 Marathi, 15 Telugu, 14 Tamil, 9 Gujarati, 6 Odiya, 8 Malayalam, 5 Punjabi). All of these must kowtow or face punishment because Modi is eager and willing to inflict it. Even the granting of a licence to broadcast depends on the approval of the government. It is withheld for those who are seen as not being pliant. Raghav Bahl, who set up Network 18 and is one of the most respected names in television news globally, for years did not receive a licence to set up a TV channel. It was kept pending by the Modi government till Bahl folded up his TV operation in April 2020. After years of resistance to pressure and cases from enforcement agencies of the Union government, Prannoy and Radhika Roy sold NDTV to Gautam Adani in late 2022. There appears to be no space for dissent.

This may help explain why media has shifted so effortlessly in television to become overtly majoritarian with no internal resistance. There is another reason why media has become more majoritarian and this is a result of technology and the understanding of what the consumer wants and is comfortable with. The newspaper is a product created afresh every day, but its feedback loop is quite slow. Meaning that it is not easy for the editor to tell what the sentiment or mood of the reader is. One objective way is through the sale of copies. Say, a particular banner headline on Tuesday results in an increase over the number of copies sold on Monday. That would indicate that the reader is more interested in the content of that Tuesday story. However, the majority of newspaper sales is through subscription (home delivery). The sample size of retail sales through stands or vendors, where the headline actually matters because it is on display before the purchase is made, is low. A longer-term way in which an editor can judge the mood and sentiment is through skewing the newspaper towards a particular ideology. Meaning, load the stories with opinion passing off as reportage (like TV news does). This may show results over the course of a few months or so. The growth in readership (usually measured annually by an industry body in a sort of census) or circulation will then indicate what the public mood is. Naturally, such an experiment could also backfire and readers might leave, because they prefer their papers non-ideological. Also, keep in mind the earlier point made about English newspapers being structurally less able to shed their centrism. For these reasons, the feedback loop received by the newspaper editor is slow and it is not easy for her to change. This is not however the same for television news.

TV news is measured through something called television rating points, commonly called TRPs. The measuring agency sets up a few thousand devices connected to set-top boxes in homes across the country. These record what was watched and when. The aggregated data is then extrapolated for the country and there is a rating that shows how many people are likely to have watched something. This rating is made public weekly and so the feedback loop is much shorter. The TV news producer will have a good idea of whether story A, which was broadcast on Monday, was viewed more than story B on Tuesday. The content can then be sharpened and focused. Material that doesn't appear to interest the viewer can be discarded and only that which 'sells' retained. The danger, from the journalistic point of view, is that the content becomes skewed away from material that might be important but is serious and not entertaining. However, the benefit of more viewers is material from the revenue point of view—higher TRPs result in more advertising. For this reason, TV journalists are better judges of mood and sentiment than newspaper journalists, on the issues that they choose to cover. We can also conclude from this, with some dismay, that the bilious anti-Muslim material that is regularly produced and often concocted by Indian television is broadcast because it meets with viewer approval. A third reason why TV has shifted—less important than the previous two, but as visible—is the success of its most shrill voices in the important time band of 8-11 p.m., which is when most advertising revenue comes in. The rest of the day doesn't really matter. In this space, Republic's Arnab Goswami is the main figure in 'national' (i.e., English) news. He has imitators, but they are not as good as he is at what he does, and what he does is to run down the Opposition and attack Muslims and Pakistan. With this basic formula and plenty of theatrics, he has the highest ratings along with Times Now.

Let us see how these channels function to understand why it is that their content appears to many as so removed from reality. On 19 June 2020, NDTV correspondent Arvind Gunasekar tweeted the text of a note the government had given to journalists as 'talking points' after an all-party meeting on the Chinese intrusion. This was the meeting in which Modi claimed that there had been no intrusion by China. Gunasekar said: 'This was circulated to media from [the] PMO as "Govt Sources" even when the meeting was underway. Whoever has drafted this, didn't know that Naveen Patnaik didn't attend the all-party meeting convened by PM Modi while Pinaki Misra represented BJD.' The talking points that the Modi government wanted the media to focus on in their headlines included:

India stands solidly behind the PM. Most leaders express their confidence in the way Modi Government has handled the situation.

Congress efforts to create wedges trashed by KCR, Naveen, Sikkim Kranti Morcha. The channels obeyed the instructions. The primetime debate for Times Now a few hours later was headlined: 'All parties unite behind India but Sonia Gandhi won't slam China?' The next night it was: 'Congress disarmed our braves first and now supports "tukde" ethos?' and 'PM Modi's strong message over India-China LAC standoff decoded'. Republic TV's main debates by Goswami on 19 June were headlined: 'Unarmed with fact, Congress insults army'; 'Is there a "special relation" between Congress and China?' and 'People's movement against China gets bigger'. The next day's debates were: 'PM sends a powerful message to the nation on LAC' and 'Cong traitor caught: "Break India" forces reveal their agenda'. Not all channels followed the Prime Minister's office's (PMO's) line. NDTV India's Ravish Kumar's debate was headlined, '*Desh ke liye jaan dene wale jawanon ko shhradhanjali*' (Tribute to India's martyrs). The next day it was, '*Pulwama ke samay jaisi parampara jari reh sakti thi*' (Pulwama's tradition could have been continued)—a reference to how differently the State had treated the 20 men killed by China against the 40 killed by a bomb in Pulwama in February 2019, whose coffins were received by Modi personally. A few days later, the *Indian Journalism Review* published another note that the PMO had circulated to channels, instructing them on what to focus on. The note read: 'Modi Effect loud and clear. Taming expansionist China is a herculean task but the right strategies and actions can yield to [*sic*] outstanding results. China hasn't pulled back. China has been pushed back, by a united nation led by a leader who led from the front.'

And there was more:

'Chinese had come to expect that India would be soft going by past precedent. However, within days, they got to know they're dealing with New India of Narendra Modi. PM has made it clear that this is an India that knows to embrace friends as well as to embargo adversaries. By taking decisive military, economic and strategic moves, PM Modi has pushed back China. On China, PM Modi was clear since day 1—India's sovereignty will not be negotiable. All options on the table were exercised. PM Modi's visit to Leh seems to be the final nail in the coffin. It showed the world India will fight and overcome any challenge to its strategic interests. His speech to the army personnel has boosted the morale of the forces, who are more than ready to deliver a severe blow to any expansionist eyes. In the past, people have seen how in Doklam also PM Modi showed remarkable patience and strength. Even in case of the talks on One Belt, One Road initiative, PM Modi stood his ground and did not even send any representation worth talking about. This when other nations send high ranking representatives for the talks. The notion of economic infallibility of China has received a tight slap with the PM's clarion call of Aatmanirbhar Bharat. Etcetera.'

Times Now responded with debates headlined: 'PM Modi punishes "Expansionist" China, doubters put to shame?'; 'China admits it was "pushed back", will army doubters surrender?'; 'China admits push back but Lobby continues to lie?' And Republic with: 'Prime Minister leads from the front'; 'PM Modi's strong leadership pushes back China'; 'Ladakh reality check: Galwan victory a slap in Lobby's face'. Note the alignment, including the specific use of phrases Modi wants promoted—'expansionist' China, China 'pushed back', PM 'led from the front', and even 'slap'. In essence, the two largest English news channels in India speak in Modi's voice. They are told what to carry each night by Modi and his office, and they do so, with enthusiasm. It is instructive to examine what this is. What follows is the full list of the subjects on which the two channels had primetime debates over three months, from the beginning of May 2020 to the end of July. This was a period in which between 7 June and 27 June, the price of petrol/diesel was hiked every single day for 21 days. On 16 June India announced that it had lost 20 soldiers, who were bludgeoned to death in hand to hand combat with the Chinese in Ladakh. On 14 June, Bollywood actor Sushant Singh Rajput killed himself. Daily COVID infections rose from 2,300 cases on 1 May to over 57,000 daily cases on 31 July. It was also a period in which it was announced that India would have its first economic recession in forty years. In such a period what were these channels broadcasting every night? Headlines on Times Now like: 'Congress accuses NDA of exploiting migrants for train fares. Is Party faking fear?'; 'Rahul Gandhi lauds pictures of "Azad": Sacrifice of braves insulted?'; 'Handwara martyrs avenged. Dreaded terrorist killed but backers attack our braves?'; 'PoK on India weather map. Safest in PM Modi's hands?'; 'India united to fight pandemic but Lutyens spreads "Communal virus"?'; 'PM-CMs crucial meet to put lifeline back on track but why Opposition red flags?'; 'PM Modi's motto to power self-reliance but Congress sees "No real relief"?'; and on Republic like: 'Congress and Lobby politicise Aurangabad tragedy'; 'Rahul Gandhi aide to Nirav Modi's rescue?'; 'Congress in trillion-dollar controversy'; 'Are states blocking migrant movement?'; 'Mystery over Congress' China strategy'; 'Congress plays petty namecalling over 20 lakh crore package'; 'India leads global fight to expose China'; 'Migrants need trains, not lies and propaganda—Congress dumps migrants'; 'Proof demolishes Congress' "1000 buses" claim'; 'Priyanka Gandhi's bus sham falls apart, Congress loses plot'.

In addition to this abject surrender, the reality is that India's media also needs a watchdog to ensure that the government does not abuse press freedom. India has one of the worst records of any democratic nation on this front. Journalists are regularly killed (six in 2018 alone), assaulted and arrested and jailed without charge, often in preventive detention. Reporters Sans Frontiers (RSF) says that 'ever since the general elections of 2019, won overwhelmingly by Modi's BJP, pressure on the media to toe the Hindu nationalist government's line has increased'. The RSF says that 'those who espouse Hindutva, the ideology that gave rise to Hindu nationalism, are trying to purge all manifestations of "anti-national" thought from the national debate. The coordinated hate campaigns waged on social networks against journalists who dare to speak or write about subjects that annoy Hindutva followers are alarming and include calls for the journalists concerned to be murdered. The campaigns are particularly virulent when the targets are women. Criminal prosecutions are meanwhile often used to gag journalists critical of the authorities, with some prosecutors invoking Section 124a of the penal code, under which "sedition" is punishable by life imprisonment.'

The feedback loop that tells news organisations that violent anti-minority rhetoric is popular is even shorter for social media, and is close to instantaneous. What is popular, what is 'trending' and what tends to be circulated and 'go viral' is public information. This has advantages and the most obvious of these are the democratisation of media, with every individual having the ability to reach the world. There is also transparency, in the sense that everyone knows what is popular and therefore, at least to some extent, relevant. Social media is one of the great developments of our society in that respect. The danger is also manifest. It is that as a society we discard what is boring and serious in favour of what is entertaining or emotive. The boring and serious material might be more important in the longer term and, in fact, even vital, but it gets discounted because we have 'voted' in some fashion for what is currently popular and 'viral'. In societies where the basics are sorted, meaning that everyone has access to food, shelter, education, healthcare and rule of law, it may be less important for the serious material to be thus demoted. There is no need to discuss food, shelter, education, healthcare and rule of law if it is already available for the most part. In societies where these conditions are not prevalent, such as India and our neighbourhood, it becomes dangerous for us to be distracted endlessly. The question is what can be done about this. The answer is nothing. The democratisation of social media carries with it the understanding that its users will be responsible. For this reason it is less regulated than print or television media, if indeed it has any regulation at all. On Twitter, the government has aggressively sought to silence dissent. Of the total global legal demands on Twitter, 96 per cent came from only five countries: Japan, Russia, South Korea, Turkey and India. Between July 2013 and July 2014, the Manmohan Singh government sent Twitter 13 legal demands for removal of content. In the first six months of 2020, the Modi government sent Twitter 2,772 legal demands for removal of content or blocking accounts. Between July and December 2021 this doubled to 4,000 legal demands.

For this reason, while it is true that some space exists for individuals to express themselves on social media, that space is closing, just as it has pretty much fully in the mainstream media. India will have to figure out how to exit this period of economic distress and social division without the asset of a free and independent and conscientious media. And it is difficult to see how this is going to happen soon. This is a dismal view of the near future, but it is the only realistic one.

Letters and Statements

OPEN LETTER TO UNION HOME MINISTER—HARASSMENT OF VOLUNTARY ORGANISATIONS UNDER FCRA

4 July 2023

Dear Home Minister,

We are a group of former civil servants of the All India and Central Services who have worked with the Central and State Governments in the course of our careers. Our group has no affiliation with any political party, and we, as its members, believe in impartiality, neutrality and commitment to the Constitution of India.

We write today to express our concern over what appears to us to be the very negative approach of the Government of India in renewal of FCRA licences of nonprofits engaged in different sectors in India. Newspaper reports indicate that the FCRA registrations of nearly 5,933 NGOs lapsed as of 1 January 2022. While there are undoubtedly cases where NGOs have not applied in time for renewal, the denial of renewal to a number of internationally reputed NGOs occasions cause for concern.

In the recent past, FCRA licences of four well-known nonprofits—Commonwealth Human Rights Initiative (CHRI); Oxfam India; Centre for Policy Research (CPR); and Centre for Equity Studies (CES)—have been cancelled or suspended. These are all institutions whose activities are aimed at addressing the problems of the most marginalised sections of Indian society. Rights to food, work, wages, health and shelter and the right to lead a dignified life based on the fundamental rights guaranteed under the Constitution of India feature prominently in the work of these organisations.

Oxfam has been working in India since 1951 and has been involved in a number of humanitarian and development activities over the past seventy years in various parts of India. CHRI activities range from advocacy of the right to information of citizens to prison and police reforms and promoting media freedom and the right to free expression. CPR is a prominent public policy think tank, with distinguished former civil servants and corporate professionals on its Governing Board. CES, set up in 2001, aims to influence public policy and law for sustainable long term solutions towards the rights and care of underprivileged sections of society.

The cancellation/suspension of the FCRA licences of these organisations and the initiation of punitive action by various law enforcement agencies of the Government of India is an outcome of the highly flawed provisions of the FCRA. It seems as though, using the FCRA, the Government of India seeks to deter civil society organisations from seeking funding from foreign sources, although such access to foreign funds, through other legally sanctioned means is freely available to the private sector, digital and print media and political parties.

Section 3 of the FCRA virtually prohibits the free expression of opinion by anyone associated with an NGO obtaining foreign contributions. Section 5 gives sweeping powers to the Government of India to declare any organisation as 'of a political nature', thereby rendering it ineligible to receive foreign contributions. The scope of Section 7 of the FCRA has been narrowed down, by its 2020 amendment, to prohibit transfer of foreign contributions from one FCRA-registered party to another. Section 12 uses broad terms like 'sovereignty and integrity of India' and 'public interest' to give the government full discretion to decide whether to permit foreign contributions to any organisation/person.

All these restrictive and vaguely worded clauses in the FCRA have been used to act against organisations that take an independent view on economic, social and political issues, which may not be to the liking of the government. Thus, columns by persons like

Harsh Mander and his associates, relating to their professional areas of competence, have been deemed to be violative of Section 3. The provisions of Section 7 have been broadly interpreted to exclude even collaboration between CES and other non-FCRA organisations in the joint publication of reports. Payments received by Harsh Mander and his associates for specified outputs (and not for articles written by them) have been deemed to violate Sections 3, 8 and 12(4)(vi) of the FCRA. The Central Bureau of investigation has reportedly alleged violation of Sections 8 and 12(4) of the FCRA in payments made by Oxfam India to CPR. Detailed clarifications from all four organisations to queries by the Ministry of Home Affairs have elicited no meaningful response from your Ministry.

The Government of India should clarify how nonprofit organisations can access foreign contributions if every moment is spent in complying with restrictive legislative provisions. Every expression of difference of opinion or dissent cannot be construed as violating the integrity and sovereignty of the country or as being against public interest. The actions of your Ministry and the various law enforcement agencies give rise to a strong suspicion that independent assessments of or perspectives about socio-economic indicators of the country are not welcome. It ill behoves a government professing adherence to democratic ideals to be intolerant of criticism of its policies and encourage its agencies to adopt intimidatory practices, such as searches, seizures, inquisitorial questioning and information leaks to the media aimed at damaging the reputation of these organisations in the minds of the public. These organisations are helmed by persons with an impeccable and rich record in public life.

Rather than facilitating socio-economic initiatives by civil society organisations, the hobbling of the operations of major nonprofits and entangling them in tortuous, long-drawn legal battles will lead to a drastic reduction in the involvement of such organisations in catalysing community involvement in socio-economic development. The Government of India stands to lose

valuable inputs it can obtain in planning policy initiatives if it fails to develop a healthy interaction with field-level and public policy nonprofit institutions.

The relentless harassment of voluntary organisations amounts to cutting off one's nose to spite one's face. For what these organisations are doing is to supplement the government's efforts in crucial areas of health, education, employment, human rights, conservation of nature etc. They work in areas where the government's own reach is limited or ineffective. The government should view them as partners and not as adversaries. Most importantly, these organisations work at the lowest levels of our society, with mostly marginalised groups who have fallen through the cracks in the government's own welfare schemes, and have no safety net to take care of them. Deliberate denial of even this modicum of assistance or advocacy to them does not do credit to a government whose rallying cry is 'sabka saath, sabka vikas, sabka vishwas'.

As former civil servants closely associated during our careers with development processes at different levels of government, we would urge you to adopt a cooperative rather than an adversarial relationship with these essential components of any civilized society. The FCRA need to be drastically overhauled to make it a facilitating rather than restrictive piece of legislation. We hope your government will take steps in this direction and direct agencies under your control to cease needless harassment of organisations serving the people of India, especially its most marginalised and disadvantaged sections.

SATYAMEVA JAYATE

Yours faithfully,

Constitutional Conduct Group (86 signatories)

LETTER TO THE ATTORNEY GENERAL FOR INDIA REGARDING THE MOHAMMED ZUBAIR CASE

15 July 2022

To
The Attorney General for India

Dear Attorney General,
We, a group of former civil servants of the All India and Central Services, who have come together as the Constitutional Conduct Group and are committed to the values enshrined in the Indian Constitution, are deeply disturbed by recent events which strike at the very root of fundamental freedoms enshrined in the Indian Constitutions to its citizens.

We specifically refer to the continued detention and deprivation of personal civil liberties of Mohammed Zubair on charges that would not stand the barest of legal scrutiny. You would have read the comprehensive article written on this case by none other than Justice Madan B Lokur, retired judge of the Supreme Court, which clearly spells out the wrong application of law by the police as well as the judiciary. A copy of the article is attached for your perusal.

We have been watching with dismay the cynical overzealousness of not just the law enforcement agencies but also the law officers under you to manufacture cases day after day to deliberately deprive individuals, identified as inconvenient by the Government, of their basic freedoms. As votaries of the Constitutional precept of equality before the law, it is deeply disturbing to see the patently discriminatory treatment meted out as between a Nupur Sharma and a Mohammed Zubair. Such selective application of law flies in the face of justice as we understand it.

No doubt, we need not remind you of your bounden duty to uphold and protect the Constitution and the personal liberties of its citizens from arbitrary and illegal action. We note that you, personally, have an unblemished and outstanding record of over

half a century and therefore we have high expectations that you will step in against such flagrant violations of the law on the part of law enforcement agencies as well as subordinate courts. We call upon you to advise the government to issue a directive to the police authorities to stop any further witch hunt against citizens exercising their right to free speech and ensure that no baseless cases are filed in the future as also to instruct government advocates not to routinely oppose applications for bail. The Supreme Court in a recent ruling has stated that indiscriminately arresting people and putting them in jail is making India a 'police state'. We are at a loss to understand why the Solicitor General takes it upon himself to appear in all kinds of cases even to oppose bail.

As the highest law officer of this land, having earned the respect of so many across the legal and political fraternities as also the discerning public, we feel you have an obligation to rectify the situation. If this moral imperative is left unheeded, we fear that there will be disastrous consequences for the country. We do hope that you will act swiftly to provide our people the freedom that our democracy is expected to sustain.

We intend to release this letter to the media after a period of 24 hours.*

SATYAMEVA JAYATE

Yours faithfully,

Constitutional Conduct Group (72 signatories)

---

* Enclosed with this letter was the article: Madan B. Lokur, 'As Zubair Is Hounded by Deliberate Chicanery and Legal Malafides, Is UAPA Next?', *The Wire*, 9 July 2022, (https://thewire.in/law/zubair-legal-malafide-uapa; Accessed March 2024)

OPEN STATEMENT ON THE SUPREME COURT ORDER IN THE ZAKIA JAFRI CASE

6 July 2022

The recent three-judge verdict in the *Zakia Ahsan Jafri v. State of Gujarat (SLP Crl. No. 7899-90/2015)*, decided on 24.06.2022 has, to say the least, left citizens totally disturbed and dismayed. We, a group of former civil servants of the All India and Central Services who have come together as the Constitutional Conduct Group and are committed to the values enshrined in the Constitution, are deeply anguished by some of the contents of that judgement and the arrests that have followed in its wake.

It is not just the dismissal of the appeal that has surprised people—an appeal may, after all, be allowed or dismissed by an appellate court; it is the gratuitous comments that the bench has pronounced on the appellants and the counsel and the supporters of the appellants. In the most astonishing comment, the Supreme Court has lauded the officials of the Special Investigation Team who have defended the State and has excoriated the appellants who have challenged the findings of the SIT. The Supreme Court says in Paragraph 88:

> 'While parting, we express our appreciation for the indefatigable work done by the team of SIT officials in the challenging circumstances they had to face and yet, we find that they have come out with flying colours unscathed. At the end of the day, it appears to us that a coalesced effort of the disgruntled officials of the State of Gujarat along with others was to create sensation by making revelations which were false to their own knowledge. The falsity of their claims had been fully exposed by the SIT after a thorough investigation. Intriguingly, the present proceedings have been pursued for last 16 years (from submission of complaint dated 8.6.2006 running into 67 pages and then by filing protest petition dated 15.4.2013 running into 514 pages) including with the audacity to question the integrity

of every functionary involved in the process of exposing the devious stratagem adopted (to borrow the submission of learned counsel for the SIT), to keep the pot boiling, obviously, for ulterior design. As a matter of fact, all those involved in such abuse of process, need to be in the dock and proceeded with in accordance with law.'

'Need to be in the dock...'!! Has the Supreme Court now decided that appellants before it and their counsel should be proceeded against merely for being assiduous and persistent in their appeal? What about the NHRC reports and the report of amicus curiae, Raju Ramachandran, which had stated that investigation was required to probe the role of then Chief Minister Narendra Modi? These were weighty grounds to question the view taken by the SIT and therefore, they would confer sufficient heft to a petition that sought to challenge the SIT's findings. Moreover, the Supreme Court's own earlier observations clearly mention the laxity of the state government officials. On April 12, 2004, a bench of Justices Doraiswamy Raju and Arijit Pasayat while ordering a retrial in the Vadodara Best Bakery case, said:

'Those who are responsible for protecting life and properties and ensuring that inestigation is fair and proper seem to have shown no real anxiety. Large number of people had lost their lives. Whether the accused persons were really assailants or not could have been established by a fair and impartial investigation. The modern day 'Neros' were looking elsewhere when Best Bakery and innocent children and helpless women were burning, and were probably deliberating how the perpetrators of the crime can be saved or protected. Law and justice become flies in the hands of these wanton boys.'

It went on to say:

'One gets a feeling that the justice delivery system was being taken for a ride and literally allowed to be abused, misused and mutilated by subterfuge. The investigation appears to be

perfunctory and anything but impartial without any definite object of finding out the truth and bringing to book those who were responsible for the crime. The public prosecutor appears to have acted more as a defence counsel than one whose duty was to present the truth before the Court. The Court in turn appeared to be a silent spectator, mute to the manipulations and preferred to be indifferent to sacrilege being committed to justice. The role of the State Government also leaves much to be desired.'

The implications of the Zakia Jafri judgement are extremely serious. It has overturned a core precept that, we believe, ought to guide an apex court established under a liberal democratic Constitution: to safeguard the basic right to life and liberty against questionable actions of the state. The Court has come out with a doctrine which enjoins the state to arrest and prosecute persons who dare to question the findings of investigating agencies, if the Court decides that these findings are beyond reproach.

Our distress mirrors the horror and anguish that the words used by the Supreme Court, and the events that have occurred in the aftermath of this judgement, have evoked amongst respected individuals and organisations wedded to upholding human rights and the democratic values that underlie our Constitution. The directions contained in the order of the Court have been characterised in words never known to have been used before in the case of judgements delivered by the Supreme Court. The immediate action of the state in arresting human rights lawyer Teesta Setalvad and former DGP, RB Sreekumar, as well as filing a fresh case against Sanjiv Bhatt, who is already in prison, clearly occurred because the Supreme Court told the State government authorities to put those who 'kept the pot boiling' 'in the dock', though these persons were neither the appellants nor the accused in the case.

Constitutional lawyer and legal scholar Gautam Bhatia tweeted: 'Indian SC's contribution to global jurisprudence is to decide an individual vs State case by telling the State to arrest the individual. A remarkable constitutional innovation.' Amnesty International

India observed that 'Detention of prominent human rights activist @TeestaSetalvad by the Indian authorities is a direct reprisal against those who dare to question their human rights record. It sends a chilling message to the civil society and further shrinks the space for dissent in the country'. A group of 300 lawyers and activists have, in a letter to the Chief Justice of India, said 'This sequence of events has sent a chilling message for the practice of law in the courts and for the rule of law in the country. It appears that a petitioner or a witness, who diligently pursues a cause in the courts, runs a risk of being put in the dock if the court deems the cause as devoid of merits.' We also endorse the statement made in support of Teesta Setalvad, R.B. Sreekumar and other human rights defenders by concerned citizens of the world in the alliance named Solidarity for the Prisoners of Conscience in India.

Here are some fundamental questions: Can the constitutional right to approach courts be treated in so cavalier and revengeful a fashion that the persons seeking justice are put behind bars? Shall we henceforth presume that natural justice can be given the go-by as a cardinal principle of our jurisprudence and people condemned without being heard?

We would urge the Supreme Court Justices to suo motu review their order and withdraw the observations contained in Para 88. We would also request them to adopt the course of action advocated by a distinguished former member of their fraternity, Justice Madan Lokur. He has said that the court would do well to issue a clarification to the effect that it was not their intention that Teesta Setalvad should face arrest and at the same time order her unconditional release. Every day of silence lowers the prestige of the Court and raises questions about its determination to uphold a core precept of the Constitution: safeguarding the basic right to life and liberty against questionable actions of the state.

SATYAMEVA JAYATE

Constitutional Conduct Group (92 signatories)

SUBMISSION TO THE BHIMA KOREGAON COMMISSION*

5 June 2022

This submission intends to express deep concern over the nature of the investigation in the Bhima Koregaon case, especially the way the sixteen activists, lawyers and academics accused of an apparent Maoist conspiracy have been arrested and treated.

The context of the Bhima Koregaon violence is inextricably linked to conflicting accounts of history. Dr Ambedkar inaugurated an annual celebration of the Battle of Bhima Koregaon in 1927 as a victory over caste oppressors. This is contested by Hindutva sources, who insist Ambedkar would never have supported the celebration (Chari and Satheesh, 2018, Scroll). Some accounts further say that Govind Gaikwad, of the Mahar community, defied orders in the late 1600s to put together the body and conduct last rites for Sambhaji Maharaj, killed by Aurangzeb. To honour this story, Dalits who come to celebrate the battle victory on 1 January visit the samadhis of Sambhaji and Gaikwad at Vadhu Budruk as a detour.

Hindutva groups contest this history, claiming that a Maratha, and not a Dalit Mahar, conducted Sambhaji's last rites. This has led to friction over the inscriptions on the official board outside the samadhi. Ambedkarite groups claim the board has been changed in recent years to reflect the Maratha version (Chari and Satheesh, 2018, Scroll).

On 27 December, Hindutva activist Milind Ekbote received a call from Vadhu Budruk villagers about a scuffle breaking out between Dharmaveer Maharaj Smruti Samiti members and Dalit residents because the former's members were encouraging caste Hindus to boycott 1 January as a 'black day' (Shantha, 2018, *The Wire*). On 28

---

* This note was submitted by the CCG to the Bhima-Koregaon Commission appointed by the Government of Maharashtra, comprising Justice JN Patel, former Chief Justice of the Calcutta High Court, and Mr Sumit Mullick, former Chief Information Commissioner for Maharashtra. It is being released publicly for the first time here.

December a board mentioning Gaikwad was put up at Sambhaji's samadhi which 'Hindutvadis' took down along with tearing down the roof of Gaikwad's samadhi the following day. A few Dalits of the village registered a police complaint, despite the police initially refusing to file it, with 49 people named in the FIR. Though the complainant mentioned Ekbote's name in the complaint, the police did not include it in the FIR (Punwani, 3 February 2022, Rediff).

On 31 December 2017, Dalits from Maharashtra (mostly Mahars) gathered in Shaniwar Wada in Pune to commemorate the event through an Elgar Parishad. This was led by two retired lawyers, one being a retired Supreme Court judge. During this meeting, the government was criticised and they challenged the ruling party's 'homogenizing Hindutva'. The next day (1 January 2018), Dalits congregating to nearby Bhima Koregaon were beaten and pelted with stones by upper-caste Hindu nationalists bearing saffron flags, and one of the latter died. Property was smashed and burned, with buildings and cars set aflame (Deb, Guardian; Jaffrelot, 2021, 400).

Multiple fact-finding teams which gathered accounts in the following months concluded that Hindutva groups were responsible for the violence. RPI(A) leader Siddharth Dhende, deputy mayor of Pune, led an independent fact-finding committee in January 2018 which compiled a report of the events at Bhima Koregaon. It concluded that two leaders of Hindutva organisations—Sambhaji Bhide and Milind Ekbote—played important roles in inciting tensions in and beyond Vadhu Budruk (Chari and Satheesh, 2018, Scroll). Justice Chandra Kumar's fact-finding report, first reported upon in September 2018, concluded that there was 'collusion between rioters and police' in allowing a procession from the Vadhu Budruk area to the victory pillar at Bhima Koregaon. The report also said that in the three-four days before 1 January, social media was rife with messages on behalf of Bhide and Ekbote to observe a bandh from 1 January, and hotels were warned not to welcome visitors. Stones that had been stored in advance were pelted at visitors on the day (Shantha, 2018, *The Wire*). Rashtra Seva Dal's report from

January 2018 claimed that Ekbote-led organisation, Hindu Aaghadi, had been holding public meetings for three weeks and warning people that those assembling on 1 January were anti-national. There are clear indications that violence was premeditated (Rashtra Seva Dal, Fact-Finding Report, January 2018).

Dalit activist and eyewitness Anita Salve filed a police complaint against two men who were then booked on 2 January 2018, the first being Bhide, an activist who was associated with the RSS. The second was Ekbote, a former BJP corporator. They were accused of inciting the violence by making hate speeches a week earlier. Ekbote was now booked for conspiracy charges, rioting, unlawful assembly and attempt to murder. Another case was lodged against them in Aurangabad. Both cases were transferred to Shikrapur police in Pune district (Banerjee, 2018, The Hindu). Despite reports of his role in instigating the violence, in February 2018, the Supreme Court addressed the Maharashtra Police for not doing enough to arrest Ekbote, seeking a status report from the investigating officer. A bench of J Kurien Joseph and J Mohan M Shantanagoudar asked the police if they should hold the investigation instead, since the police had made no attempt to arrest him despite the order and his availability (21 February 2018, Indian Express). Ekbote briefly went to jail, but the police began to look for other accused parties when a disciple of Sambhaji Bhide, Tushar Damgade, filed a complaint against others.

Bhide had a formidable following in Western Maharashtra, as well as strong political connections with the ruling party and opposition. Ekbote filed an affidavit saying he was not in Bhima Koregaon that day, while Bhide said he was in another district (Banerjee, 2018, The Hindu; Chari and Satheesh, 2018, Scroll). Testimonies before the Commission have shown that the violence was started by mobs holding saffron flags, who stoned the Dalits going towards Bhima Koregaon. Witnesses like Manisha Khotkar, ex-policeman Tukaram Gavare and Tanaji Sable recounted their stories of the atmosphere of fear, violence and intimidation they faced from crowds with

saffron flags (Mahamulkar, 8 September 2018, *The Times of India*; Punwani, 7 September 2018, *Rediff*; Modak, 6 September 2018, *The Indian Express*). They also show that the violence was linked to the fight in Vadhu Budruk a few days earlier, over the samadhi of Govind Gaikwad ((Mahamulkar, 8 September 2018, *The Times of India*; Ganayapatye, 8 September 2018, *Mumbai Mirror*). The 16 intellectuals arrested in the Bhima Koregaon case had nothing to do with either of these events.

In September 2021, Pune rural police filed a charge sheet against 41 people excluding Bhide, saying they could find no evidence against him. Yet Pimpri police filed a case against him, under the SC/ST Atrocities Act and various IPC charges including attempt to murder. As of May 2022, the Pune rural police reported that the case against Bhide has been dropped due to lack of evidence. The Chief Minister in 2018, Devendra Fadnavis, also granted Bhide a clean chit in the state assembly just one day after protestors at Azad Maidan demanded his arrest (Punwani, 8 February 2022, Rediff).

The failure to properly investigate Ekbote and Bhide's role coincided with a major shift in the investigation. This took place during the time that the Forum for Integrated National Security—an RSS-affiliated Pune-based think tank—alleged a 'Maoist conspiracy'. Their report from March 2018 blamed the distortion and falsification of history, specifically the Bhima Koregaon battle, as the reason for the riots and violence. It included Ekbote's letter to the district collector, which said the history of the battle is baseless and defamatory to Marathas and it outlined attacks on non-Dalits and non-Dalit property. In this vein, the report claimed that the Elgar Parishad had Maoist links and mentioned Sudhir Dhawale, calling him a 'key organiser' of the Elgar Parishad (Koregaon Bhima Report, FINS).

During this period, the Pune police began arresting the new accused in the Bhima Koregaon violence in a pan-India investigation, putting aside the main accused, Bhide and Ekbote. An FIR lodged by Pune businessman and Bhide disciple Tushar

Damgude, which the police filed as a first information report in January 2018, claimed that leftist activists instigated the January 1 Bhima Koregaon violence through Maoist links and the Elgar Parishad of the previous day. They were presented as 'Urban Naxals. These 'urban Naxals' were alleged to be a front for underground Maoist groups and were accused of inciting Dalits to rise up against the government. This new angle was presented to the media and the country as the 'Bhima Koregaon conspiracy' ((Deb, The Guardian; Shantha, 2022, *The Wire*).

Acting on Damgude's report, the Pune police carried out raids in several cities in April 2018, a month after the FINS report. Laptops and gadgets of the organisers of the Elgar Parishad were seized, but at the same time, raids also targeted activists and intellectuals who had nothing to do with the event (Shantha, 2022, *The Wire*). Those arrested were activists, with careers characterised by fighting for the rights of exploited and marginalised communities across the country. Of those arrested on 6 June 2018, Surendra Gadling is a lawyer, Shoma Sen a retired English professor, Sudhir Dhawale a publisher and poet, and Mahesh Raut and Rona Wilson human rights activists. Two months later they arrested 'poet-activist' Varavara Rao, lawyer and trade unionist Sudha Bhardwaj, and activists and authors/columnists Arun Ferreira and Varun Gonsalves. Then in April 2020 Anand Teltumbde, professor and writer, and Gautam Navlakha, member of People's Union for Democratic Rights. Associate professor at Delhi University Hany Babu and Jesuit priest and Jharkhand tribal rights activist Stan Swamy were also arrested. Anti-caste activists and singers of cultural group Kabir Kala Manch were arrested in April 2020: Sagar Gorkhe, Jyoti Jagtap, and Ramesh Gaichore. Only Dhawale and Sen were actually present at the Elgar Parishad event. All of them have been charged under provisions of anti-terror law Unlawful Activities (Prevention) Act and the Indian Penal Code (Shantha, 2022, *The Wire*).

All of those arrested were accused of a conspiracy to overthrow the government and assassinate the Prime Minister on the basis of

letters recovered from the computers of two of the arrestees. While searching the houses of the accused, Maharashtra police listed unbanned books as evidence against them, and commented on their socio-political ideas and attitudes. For example, in the house of Varavara Rao's daughter and son-in-law, they asked why they have books on Mao and Marx, books published in China, and photos of Ambedkar and Phule but no photos of gods. They asked his daughter why she follows no traditions like wearing sindoor despite being a Brahmin (Jaffrelot, 2021, 403).

Throughout the process of their arrests and incarceration, the rights of the accused were continuously violated in a blatant manner. While committing these violations, the Pune police often flouted the judiciary. In March 2018, the investigating officer, Shivaji Pawar, asked the judicial magistrate first class, Pune, for a search warrant saying that the accused possessed documents linking them to the Bhima Koregaon case. He claimed they would not cooperate if sent notices under section 91 of CrPC but he never actually sent the notice. The court denied this request, saying it cannot be assumed that the accused would not cooperate. Despite this, the Pune police raided residences of the accused and seized all kinds of items. They raided Hyderabad and Delhi residences without warrants too (Goyal, 2021, Newslaundry). The law mandates that when a house is raided and material seized, residents of good public standing from the same locality must be witnesses. But the police brought along witnesses from Pune. The material confiscated must be submitted to a local court, but the police did not do so for the possessions of Wilson, Gadling and Dhawale. The Information Technology Act of 2000 mandates that the hash value of confiscated electronic evidence must be taken before it is sent for forensic analysis to protect against tampering. The hash value is unique and changes if a document or file is planted on the device. Yet the police did not provide hash values of equipment despite being accompanied by a cyber expert (Goyal, 2021, Newslaundry).

Furthermore, if police make arrests in areas beyond their jurisdiction, they are required to get a transit remand for the accused

from the local court. For Gadling, Sen, Swamy and Bhardwaj, they simply arrested and transported them without transit remands. When they took Gadling to an Amravati court (not the local court), the court refused to grant a transit remand yet they flew him to Pune anyway. The Supreme Court had granted Teltumbde protection from arrest for 4 weeks, but he was arrested anyway by the Pune police. A Pune sessions court accordingly declared his arrest illegal and ordered his release. In April 2020, Navlakha surrendered to the NIA and was lodged in Tihar jail, from where he made a bail application to the Delhi High Court. The day before his bail hearing, he was flown to Mumbai without the court's permission—the High Court reprimanded the Pune police for this to no avail (Goyal, 2021, Newslaundry). There seems to be no justifiable reason for this continuous disregard for the judiciary.

Other aspects of the law were disregarded in pursuit of the accused in the 'Bhima Koregaon conspiracy.' Arrest memos were not provided to the families of the accused. Police did not let the accused get lawyers when they were produced before a Pune court on 7 June 2018. The police chose a lawyer for them. Under the law, the police are required to give an explanation of the reasons for arrest to the accused in a language they can understand. Rao, Wilson, Navlakha, Bhardwaj and others were given documents in Marathi, which they cannot understand (Goyal, 2021, Newslaundry).

UAPA cases must be heard by a special court according to the law, if not available, then they may be heard by a regular court. For this case, the matter went to a sessions court despite Pune having a special NIA court. The law says a charge sheet must not be filed in a sessions court, but this is exactly what was done by the Pune police. Under the CrPC, the accused has a right to default bail if no charge sheet is filed within 60 days; under the UAPA this may extend to 180 days with sufficient cause. The Supreme Court had set aside an order of the Bombay High Court in June 2018 to release the accused on account of the Pune police illegally seeking another 90-day extension. The accused continued to remain incarcerated (American

Bar Association, Center for Human Rights Report). The Pune police was reprimanded by the Supreme Court for showing undue haste in procedures to extend the deadline for filing the charge sheet. When it wasn't filed after 90 days, the state's lawyer asked for another 90 on a Friday and the accused were told to appear in court the next day. They could not inform their lawyers at such short notice and protested against the prosecution's hurry. Regardless, the special hearing was held the next day on Sunday.

The day after the Shiv Sena-NCP-Congress government came to power in Maharashtra and decided to review the charge sheet against the accused, the Union Ministry of Home Affairs hurriedly handed over the investigation to the NIA. When a case is registered under UAPA, the state government has to inform the Central Government within 5 days and then the Central Government can decide whether the case should be given to the NIA in another 15 days. If the investigation is handed to police, it cannot just be reassigned. Yet the Home Ministry took this case away from the new government of Maharashtra. The NIA's supplementary charge sheet contains additional allegations like ISI connections and the threat of an 'urban revolution' (Goyal, 2021, Newslaundry). Gaichor and Gorkhe told a Mumbai sessions court that the NIA was pressurising them to make false statements saying that the accused were Naxalites. The court acknowledged they had been pressured but did not see the NIA's conduct as improper (Goyal, 2021, Newslaundry).

There have been multiple criminal charges against these individuals before, who believe that they have been targeted in an attempt to stop their work in struggling for marginalised communities in India (American Bar Association, Center for Human Rights Report). Historian Romila Thapar, along with other scholars, filed a petition against these arrests in August 2018. According to the petitioners, the Pune police had selectively released provocative but unverified allegations to selected media channels in order to create a negative image of the accused. They pointed out that the organisers of the Elgar Parishad denied receiving any funding from

the accused or any connection of the event with the letters allegedly attributed to Rona Wilson and others (Romila Thapar and Ors v the Union of India, 2018).

Two out of three judges of the bench refused to release the accused on bail, stating that the accused cannot be released simply because the petitioners 'under the guise of a public interest litigation' were friends of the 'so-called human rights activists'. Yet for the dissenting judge, Justice Chandrachud, the Bhima Koregaon case was 'an attempt by the state to muzzle dissent. Each of them is prosecuted for being a defender of persons subjected to human rights violations.' He wrote that the letters attributed to Comrade Prakash, known to be the pseudonym G.N. Saibaba, are ex-facie fabricated since the latter was in Nagpur jail at the time they were allegedly written. Justice Chandrachud also noted the violation of laws which rendered the search and seizure unlawful, such as using witnesses from Pune and failing to use transit remands (Romila Thapar and Ors v the Union of India, 2018).

Aside from these blatant violations of the law, reports from independent expert investigations point to the conclusion that the evidence against the accused activists was itself planted. The initial charges against the accused relied upon incriminating letters recovered from their electronic devices, especially Rona Wilson's laptop. According to the police, one letter was addressed to a Maoist militant and requested guns and ammunition while speaking of the need to assassinate the PM. At the request of Wilson's lawyers, Arsenal Consulting, a Massachusetts-based digital forensics firm, examined an electronic copy of Wilson's laptop. Their 2021 report revealed that an attacker had used malware to infiltrate the laptop before his arrest and deposited at least ten letters on it in a hidden folder, including the letter containing the alleged conspiracy. Three outside experts, at the request of Washington Post newspaper, reviewed the report and said its findings were valid. The report stated that in June 2016, Wilson received an email seemingly from a fellow activist, with a link that deployed NetWire, a commercially

available malicious software that enables hacking. His keystrokes, passwords and browsing activity were compromised, the letters were planted, and steps were erased. The letters were created on a newer version of Microsoft Word than the one Wilson possessed on his laptop. Arsenal Inc. said that it was 'one of the most serious cases' of tampering they had investigated, 'very organized', 'unique and deeply disturbing' and that there was a large timespan between when the laptop was first compromised and when the last letters were planted (Masih and Slater, 10 February 2021, *Washington Post*).

According to the report, Wilson was not the only victim of the unidentified attacker. His co-accused were targeted through the same IP addresses and servers over a period of 4 years. In July 2021, a new report showed how Gadling's computer also had evidence planted by a hacker, including a letter allegedly written by Sudha Bhardwaj to Maoist militants (Slater and Masi, 20 July 2021, Washington Post). California-based cybersecurity firm SentinelOne found that Wilson's laptop was targeted well before previously known, as early as 2013.

Amnesty Tech came to similar conclusions (*The Wire*, 12 February 2022).

Amnesty found that three of the people trying to help the activists were targeted in 2019 by NSO's Pegasus software, which is sold only to governments. The telephone numbers of eight of the accused appeared on a list of surveillance targets of clients of NSO group. Seventeen media partners, as part of the Pegasus Project, revealed the 1,000 names on the list in India.

Besides the accused, the numbers of their families, friends and lawyers are also on the list. It is unknown how many of these were actually selected for surveillance—forensic analysis of 22 of these numbers from India showed that at least 10 were infected with Pegasus spyware (Slater and Masih, 20 July 2021, Washington Post). Citizen Lab, a research group at the University of Toronto which specialises in studying Pegasus, said it found evidence that India has been a client of NSO. The Israeli reporter who helped

break the story confirmed that India bought Pegasus as a part of a two-billion-dollar deal in 2018 with Israel according to *The New York Times* (Bergmann and Mazzetti, 31 January 2022, *The New York Times*). A statement from India's Ministry of Electronics and Communication Technology said the allegation of government surveillance over certain individuals has no basis in truth. Bhardwaj's number was on the list, and Justice Chandrachud had expressed doubt about a letter allegedly written by her that contained words and phrases typical to Marathi, which she does not speak (*The Wire*, 12 February 2022).

The implications of these reports are grave and disturbing. Spying and surveillance may fall under the state's authority according to the Indian Telegraph Act of 1885, section 5. However, conditions must be met to obtain permission for this, for example, evidence of guilt of the accused, and proof that their conduct threatens the country's safety or public order. Moreover, there are time limitations on this authority and repeated review of permissions must take place. Yet despite this, planting evidence, spyware and hacking remain illegal (Ismat Ara, *The Wire*, 5 August 2021). The government's 2019 amendment to the UAPA allowed the state to designate individuals as terrorists (Jaffrelot, 2021, 400). Moreover, the Supreme Court's Watali judgment (2019) ruled that bail under Section 43 of the UAPA can be denied by relying on prosecution documents, even though they may be inadmissible as evidence during the actual trial, since a very strong suspicion was founded to justify the framing of the charge (*NIA v Zahoor Ahmad Shah Watali*, 2019). This matter thus warrants very serious investigation, in light of the fact that the case against the accused rests upon evidence which appears to have been planted through spyware and hacking.

Aside from the many violations of the rights of the accused, they have suffered further in jail. The health of three of the accused—Varavara Rao, Father Stan Swamy, and Hany Babu deteriorated in Taloja jail. They were granted medical care of quality only after their families moved the High Court. Taloja jail has three ayurvedic

doctors and no nursing staff. When Father Stan Swamy had a cough and fever, he was treated with antibiotics by the ayurvedic doctor leading to diarrhoea. Prisoners cannot get essential equipment from their families either. Swamy was denied a straw and sipper to drink, which he required due to his hand shaking from Parkinson's. He had to appeal to court, and it took two months to get the request approved. Swamy and Dhawale were denied COVID-19 vaccines for not being able to produce Aadhaar cards. Swamy had lost his card, while Dhawale's was submitted to state authorities during a previous arrest and never returned by them. Prison authorities refused to replace the broken spectacles of Surendra Gadling and the lost spectacles of highly myopic Gautam Navlakha. Hany Babu's eye infection deteriorated for 10 days until his eyeballs began to jut out, and finally after his family approached the media and Kerala Chief Minister Vijayan intervened, he was taken to the hospital (Goyal, 2021, Newslaundry).

Varavara Rao suffered UTIs and dementia in jail. Though healthy when arrested, his health began deteriorating in May 2021 and the police took him to JJ hospital, rushing him back to jail before his medical tests were completed. When his condition worsened, he was sent back to the hospital where his family found him soaked in urine and COVID-positive. At the intervention of the NHRC, he was sent to Nanavati hospital. The state sent him back to jail in August without informing his family or the court—another two-month legal battle followed, after which he was finally admitted back to Nanavati hospital. Gadling developed a heart issue in jail, and he was admitted in the hospital but not allowed to see his wife who sat outside his room and watched from afar. Despite being the state's responsibility, she bore the cost of his treatment. She requested his medical records and was denied. Swamy, who had spent over thirty years fighting for the Adivasi rights and challenging the state for indiscriminate arrests of young Adivasis, became very unwell in jail. He was denied medical bail multiple times and ultimately died in July 2021 (Goyal, 2021, Newslaundry).

There are further diabolical elements that exhibit unfair treatment of these activists in jail. Anand Teltumbde wrote an article in Caravan magazine on 10 March 2021. He was served a samajh patra after its publication, to which he responded. In the following months, the families of his co-accused in the Bhima Koregaon case realised that they were not receiving letters from their incarcerated family members on time. In-person meetings (and court appearances) had stopped due to the lockdown. The jail authorities were posting the letters weeks, even months, after they were written, despite the prisoners having paid for speedpost. Teltumbde and Gonsalves' wives submitted a petition to the Bombay High Court demanding that communication with prisoners is a statutory right, quoting Bombay Prison rules and previous Supreme Court judgments (Punwani, 5 July 2021, Rediff). Additionally, the Superintendent of Taloja jail moved an application in the trial court for the accused to be moved to another jail, saying they were using 'false complaints' to their families and lawyers in order to pressurise the jail (Punwani, 5 July 2021, Rediff). More recently, Navlakha's partner reports that he is no longer allowed phone calls since in-person meetings have resumed. She is elderly and cannot fly frequently to Mumbai, while he has been placed in the high-security barrack on Taloja jail with no fresh oxygen, sunlight, or area to walk besides the high-walled corridor (25 October 2021, *The Wire*).

According to the American Bar Association's Center for Human Rights, the legal treatment of the sixteen accused in the Bhima Koregaon case goes against India's international treaty obligations including obligations to protect freedom of expression, association, against arbitrary detention, and fair trial rights (American Bar Association, Center for Human Rights Report).

There are thus, overall, gravely serious concerns that the state has not demonstrated sufficient evidence to link these individuals to a threat to national security. Under the guise of a Maoist conspiracy, those reportedly responsible for the Bhima Koregaon violence have been absolved of blame while sixteen activists from across India

have been painted as the true perpetrators. Different independent cybersecurity experts and organisations have reported that the evidence against them was planted and thus the case against them rests on shaky foundations. Continuous violations of the rights of the accused, only a portion of which were mentioned above, add to these concerns. This prolonged incarceration without proof of guilt, and the ill-treatment borne by the accused, have cost Father Stan Swamy his life and multiple others their health. Meanwhile, under the UAPA, there remains no way to discuss the prosecution's evidence during bail pleas. The decision to incarcerate and deny bail to a group of leading scholars, activists, and lawyers from around the country indicates a deeper and pre-planned move to muzzle dissent.

Constitutional Conduct Group (86 signatories)

SOURCES

American Bar Association Center for Human Rights Report, *Preliminary Report: Arrest of Indian Attorneys and Activists in Apparent Retaliation for Human Rights Work*, October 2019.

Ara, Ismat, 'Pegasus Findings: Former Top Cops Call For Relook at Case Against Elgar Parishad 16', *The Wire*, 5 August 2021, (https://thewire.in/rights/pegasus-bhima-koregaon-police-officers; Accessed March 2024).

Banerjee, Shoumojit, 'Bhima Koregaon clashes: Court quashes bail plea of Milind Ekbote', *The Hindu*, 23 January 2018, (https://www.thehindu.com/news/national/other-states/bhima-koregaon-clashes-court-quashes-bail-plea-of-milind-ekbote/article22493545.ece; Accessed March 2024).

Bergmann, Ronan and Mazzetti, Mark, 'The Battle for the World's Most Powerful Cyberweapon.', *The New York Times*, 28 January 2022, (https://www.nytimes.com/2022/01/28/magazine/nso-group-israel-spyware.html; Accessed March 2024).

'Bhima Koregaon violence: Do your job, arrest accused, probe case, Supreme Court tells police', *The Indian Express*, 21 February 2018, (https://indianexpress.com/article/india/bhima-koregaon-violence-

do-your-job-arrest-accused-probe-case-supreme-court-tells-police-5072080/; Accessed March 2024).

Chari, Mridula, and Satish, Shone, 'Tensions over a 300-year-old history hold the key to Bhima Koregaon violence—not a Maoist plot', *Scroll.in*, 15 September 2018, (https://scroll.in/article/894403/tensions-over-300-year-old-history-hold-the-key-to- per cent20the-bhima-koregaon-violence-not-a-maoist-plot; Accessed March 2024).

Deb, Siddhartha, 'The unravelling of a conspiracy: were the 16 charged with plotting to assassinate the Indian Prime Minister framed?', *The Guardian*, 12 August 2021, (https://www.theguardian.com/world/2021/aug/12/bhima-koregaon-case-india-conspiracy-modi; Accessed March 2024).

Report On Koregaon – Bhima Riot on January 1, 2018, Forum for Integrated National Security (https://drive.google.com/file/d/1t7__LhglmbcC8-utAHQ0mCNGSmCma8NX/view; Accessed March 2024)

'Gautam Navlakha's Health Worsening in 'High-Security' Barrack, Not Being Allowed Calls, His Partner Says', *The Wire*, 25 October 2021, (https://thewire.in/rights/gautam-navlakhas-health-worsening-in-high-security-barrack-not-being-allowed-calls-his-partner-says; Accessed March 2024).

Ganapatye, Shruti, 'Bhima Koregaon hearing: Milind Ekbote's lawyer badgers witness about 1818 battle', *Mumbai Mirror*, 8 September 2018, (https://mumbaimirror.indiatimes.com/mumbai/crime/bhima-koregaon-hearing-milind-ekbotes-lawyer-badgers-witness-about-1818-battle/articleshow/65727168.cms?; Accessed March 2024).

Goyal, Prateek, 'Bhima Koregaon case: Three years of legal and rights violations', *Newslaundry*, 2 January 2021, (https://www.newslaundry.com/2021/01/02/bhima-koregaon-case-three-years-of-legal-and-rights-violations; Accessed march 2024).

Jaffrelot, Christophe, *Modi's India: Hindu Nationalism and the Rise of Ethnic Democracy*, Princeton University Press, New Jersey: 2021.

'Hindutva leader Sambhaji Bhide's name dropped from Bhima Koregaon case, say police', *Scroll.in*, 5 May 2022, (https://scroll.in/latest/1023280/hindutva-leader- per cent20sambhaji-bhides-name-dropped-from-bhima-koregaon-case-say-police; Accessed March 2024).

Indian Kanoon (https://indiankanoon.org/; Accessed March 2024).

Mahamulkar, Sujit, 'Police scolded us instead of saving us: Bhima riots

witness', *The Times of India,* 8 September 2018, (https://timesofindia.indiatimes.com/city/mumbai/police-scolded-us-instead-of-saving-us-bhima-riots-witness/articleshow/65727576.cms; Accessed March 2024).

Masih, Niha and Slater, Joanna, 'They were accused of trying to overthrow the Modi government. The evidence was planted, new report says.' *The Washington Post,* 10 February 2021, (https://www.washingtonpost.com/world/asia_pacific/india-bhima-koregaon-activists-jailed/2021/02/10/8087f172-61e0-11eb-a177-7765f29a9524_story.html; Accessed March 2024).

Masih, Niha and Slater, Joanna, 'Indian activists jailed on terrorism charges were on the list with surveillance targets.' *The Washington Post,* 20 July 2021, (https://www.washingtonpost.com/world/2021/07/20/indian-activists-surveillance/; Accessed March 2024).

Modak, Sadaf, 'Bhima koregaon violence: Judicial commission begins hearings', *The Indian Express,* 6 September 2018, (https://indianexpress.com/article/cities/mumbai/bhima-koregaon-violence-judicial-commission-begins-hearings-5342440/; Accessed March 2024).

NIA v. Zahoor Ahmad Shah Watali, 2019.

Punwani, Jyoti, 'Bhima Koregaon Hearing: 'I am here to ask for justice,' *Rediff,* 7 September 2018, (https://www.rediff.com/news/special/bhima-koregaon-hearing-i-am-here-to-ask-for-justice/20180907.htm; Accessed March 2024).

Punwani, Jyoti, 'Bhima Koregaon: Is Milind Ekbote Being Protected?' *Rediff,* 3 February 2022, (https://www.rediff.com/news/special/bhima-koregaon-is-milind-ekbote-being-protected/20220203.htm; Accessed March 2024).

Punwani, Jyoti, 'Bhima Koregaon: Outcome of a "Larger Conspiracy"?' *Rediff,* 5 October 2021, (https://www.rediff.com/news/special/bhima-koregaon-outcome-of-a-larger-conspiracy/20211005.htm; Accessed March 2024).

'What Really Happened In Bhima Koregaon—Fact Finding Report', *Countercurrents.org,* 15 January 2018, (https://countercurrents.org/2018/01/really-happened-bhima-koregaon-fact-finding-report/; Accessed March 2024).

Romila Thapar and Ors v. the Union of India, 2018, Indian Kanoon (https://indiankanoon.org/doc/52834611/; Accessed March 2024).

Shantha, Sukanya, 'A Reporter Saw the Bhima Koregaon Violence Coming. Now, He Fears For His Life.' *The Wire*, 18 September 2018, (https://thewire.in/caste/a-reporter-saw-the-bhima-koregaon-violence-coming-now-he-fears-for-his-life; Accessed March 2024).

Shantha, Sukanya, 'Bhima Koregaon Violence: Four Different Theories, but No Justice in Sight', *The Wire*, 1 January 2022, (https://thewire.in/rights/bhima-koregaon-violence-four-different-theories-but-no-justice-in-sight; Accessed March 2024).

Shantha, Sukanya, 'Independent Inquiry Slams Pune Police for 'Inaction' During Bhima Koregaon Violence', *The Wire*, 4 September 2018, (https://thewire.in/law/independent-inquiry-pune-police-inaction-bhima-koregaon-violence; Accessed March 2024).

OPEN LETTER TO CITIZENS OF INDIA

28 November 2021

CIVIL SOCIETY: ENEMY OF THE STATE?

Dear fellow citizens,

We are a group of former civil servants of the All India and Central Services who have worked with the Central and State Governments in the course of our careers. As a group, we have no affiliation with any political party but believe in impartiality, neutrality and commitment to the Constitution of India.

A disturbing trend in the direction of the country's governance has become discernible over the past few years. The foundational values of our republic and the cherished norms of governance, which we had taken as immutable, have been under the relentless assault of an arrogant, majoritarian state. The sacrosanct principles of secularism and human rights have come to acquire a pejorative sense. Civil society activists striving to defend these principles are subjected to arrest and indefinite detention under draconian laws that blot our statute book. The establishment does its best to discredit them as anti-national and foreign agents.

Civil society, a diverse mass of formal and informal groups pursuing their own interests, occupies the vast democratic space outside of government and business. As the locus of critique, contestation and negotiation, it is an important stakeholder in governance, as well as a force multiplier and partner in the project of meeting popular aspirations. But civil society is viewed through an adversarial prism today. Any entity, which dares to highlight deviations from the norms of Constitutional conduct, or question the arbitrary exercise of executive authority, runs the risk of being projected as a foreign agent and enemy of the people. At a systemic level, the financial viability of civil society organisations is being progressively undermined by tweaking the legal framework governing foreign contributions, deployment of corporate social responsibility funds and income tax exemptions.

Our anxiety with regard to the articulation of the state-civil society interface has been heightened in recent weeks by statements emanating from high dignitaries of the state. On the occasion of the Foundation Day of the National Human Rights Commission, its Chair, Justice (retd.) Arun Mishra, asserted that India's creditable record on human rights was being tarnished at the behest of international forces. The Prime Minister, on his part, discerned a political agenda in what he felt was selective perception of human rights violation in certain incidents, while overlooking certain others. And quite shockingly, General Bipin Rawat, Chief of Defence Staff, gave a fillip to the growing menace of vigilantism by endorsing the killing of persons believed to be terrorists by lynch mobs in Kashmir.

Taken together, these portents indicate a deliberate strategy to deny civil society the space and wherewithal for its operation. The contours of this strategy have now been revealed in the New Doval Doctrine propounded by the National Security Adviser (NSA).

Reviewing the passing out parade of IPS probationers at the National Police Academy in Hyderabad, Shri Ajit Doval proclaimed:

> 'The new frontiers of war, what you call the fourth-generation warfare, is the civil society. Wars have ceased to become an effective instrument for achieving political or military objectives. They are too expensive and unaffordable and, at the same time, there is uncertainty about their outcome. But it is the civil society that can be subverted, that can be suborned, that can be divided, that can be manipulated to hurt the interests of a nation. You are there to see that they stand fully protected.'

Instead of exhorting the IPS probationers to abide by the values enshrined in the Constitution to which they had sworn allegiance, the NSA stressed the primacy of the representatives of the people, and the laws framed by them.

It would be pertinent to recall here that the term 'fourth-generation warfare' is normally employed in relation to a conflict where the state is fighting non-state actors, such as terror groups and insurgents. Civil society now finds itself placed in this company. Earlier, the term 'Urban Naxal' was being used to denigrate individual human rights activists. Clearly, under the New Doval Doctrine, people like Father Stan Swamy would become the arch enemy of the Indian state and the prime concern and target of its security forces.

The NSA's clarion call for an onslaught on a demonised civil society is of a piece with the narrative of hate targeting defenders of Constitutional values and human rights that is regularly purveyed by the high and mighty in the establishment.

The defining traits of the current dispensation are hubris and an utter disregard of democratic norms. These were manifest in the steamrolling of a discriminatory Citizenship (Amendment) Act through Parliament, its linkage with the National Register of Citizens, and the ruthless suppression of the spontaneous protests that erupted in various parts of the country.

The same traits were in evidence in the enactment of a set of three farm laws without public debate, stakeholder consultations or endorsement by alliance partners, and the high-handed treatment

accorded to the agitated farmers encamped at the gates of Delhi. Their heroic resistance over fourteen months elicited the choicest of epithets from the establishment. Dubbed variously as 'Andolanjeevis' (professional agitators), 'Left-wing extremists' and 'Khalistanis', they were accused of working at the behest of 'Foreign Destructive Ideology', in a bizarre word-play with the acronym FDI referring to Foreign Direct Investment. Electoral compulsions might have led the Prime Minister to announce the decision to repeal the hated laws, but the damage done to the nation's polity and social fabric will be hard to repair.

Let us hope that the government will realise the pitfalls of demonising dissent and trying to suppress civil resistance by brute force. It is also hoped that the alumni of the National Police Academy, or indeed our security forces in general, will not be swayed by the NSA's rhetoric and remember that their primary duty is to uphold Constitutional values, which override the will of the political executive. Even the laws framed by the legislatures have to be tested on the touchstone of constitutionality and accepted by the people. If this fundamental principle is not accepted, we may turn to the well-known satirical poem 'The Solution', written in a different context by the famous German playwright Bertolt Brecht, which concludes with the following words:

Would it not be easier
In that case for the government
To dissolve the people
And elect another?

SATYAMEVA JAYATE
Constitutional Conduct Group (102 signatories)

OPEN LETTER TO CITIZENS OF INDIA: THE GOVERNMENT OF INDIA MUST REPLACE UAPA WITH LEGISLATION THAT FIGHTS TERRORISM WHILE SAFEGUARDING PERSONAL LIBERTIES

16 August 2021

Dear Citizens of India,

We are a group of retired officers of the All India and Central Services who have worked with the Central and State Governments in the course of our careers. As members of the Constitutional Conduct Group, we believe in impartiality, neutrality and commitment to the Indian Constitution and in safeguarding its values.

We are writing this in the matter of the Unlawful Activities (Prevention) Act (UAPA) that violates the Constitutional guarantees of citizens' fundamental rights. Though this law has been in existence in India's statute books for over five decades, the harsh amendments it has gone through in recent years has made it draconian, repressive, and amenable to gross misuse at the hands of ruling politicians and the police. Typical of such misuse are the cases of the three anti-CAA student protestors—Devangana Kalita, Natasha Narwal and Asif Iqbal Tanha—who were arrested under UAPA without any valid grounds but were recently granted bail by the Delhi High Court in a detailed and unprecedented order.

On 9 March 2021, the Union Minister of State for Home, Shri G. Kishan Reddy, in a written reply to the Lok Sabha, admitted to the uncommon overuse of the UAPA. He confirmed that 1,948 persons were arrested under the UAPA in 1,226 cases across the country in 2019, which showed a 72 per cent increase as compared to 2015. The following figures will show the increase in cases and arrests between 2015 and 2019—2015: 897 cases with 1,128 arrests; 2016: 922 cases with 999 arrests; 2017: 901 cases with 1,554 arrests; 2018: 1,182 cases with 1,421 arrests; 2019: 1,226 cases with 1,948 arrests

The highest number of arrests in the country was in 2019,

particularly in the states of Uttar Pradesh (498) Manipur (386), Tamil Nadu (308), Jammu and Kashmir (227) and Jharkhand (202).

Despite the large number of arrests under the UAPA, the number of prosecutions and convictions shows a steep decline. The Government of India has admitted that a mere 2.2 per cent of the cases registered between 2016 and 2019 resulted in conviction. We may conclude that the vast majority of the arrests under UAPA were made on specious grounds just to spread fear and muzzle dissent.

The UAPA has a chequered history. This legislation, first passed in 1967 on the recommendations of the National Integration Council to combat communalism, casteism, regionalism and linguistic chauvinism and to deal with associations engaged in secessionist activities, has changed colour over time and has now become a statute that has created new categories of offences and punishments.

The UAPA was not used extensively prior to the last decade as the Government of India had, meanwhile, enacted preventive detention laws such as the Maintenance of Internal Security Act (MISA-1971), the National Security Act (NSA-1980), the Terrorist And Disruptive Activities (Prevention) Act (TADA-1987) and The Prevention of Terrorism Act (POTA-2002). But after the 9/11 terror attack on the USA, the UN Security Council passed a resolution asking national governments to enact countrywide anti-terror laws. The Government of India complied by passing the UAPA Amendment Act, 2004, carrying stringent provisions to suppress terrorism.

However, the Government of India seriously departed from the principles of criminal jurisprudence and from the provisions of the Constitution when the UAPA (Amendment) Act, 2008 was codified after the 26/11 Mumbai terror attack. This was done during the tenure of the United Progressive Alliance (UPA) government. Successive UPA and NDA Union governments which have been or are in power are responsible for the extreme stringency of the UAPA. In 2008, the UPA government made bail provisions much more stringent, increased the pre-charge detention period from 90 days to 180 days and, most damagingly, placed the burden of proof on the accused.

In 2019, the NDA government further amended the UAPA to allow individuals, not merely organisations, to be designated terrorist. This amendment also gave unfettered and autocratic powers to the executive, in particular the National Investigation Agency (NIA), to enter any State and arrest any person. Though some voices of protest were raised when these amendments were made, most political parties supported the move. For the UPA members or any other party to act outraged now is, therefore, disingenuous.

The most shocking of the arrests under the UAPA have been of persons accused in the Bhima-Koregaon case. Several well regarded activists who have fought throughout their lives for the rights of tribal people and other oppressed groups have been arrested as terrorists and, even today, languish in jail. The names of those arrested are well known—Sudha Bhardwaj, Rona Wilson, Gautam Navlakha, Anand Teltumbde, Arun Ferreira and Varavara Rao, to name a few. And, of course, Father Stan Swamy—an 84 year old Jesuit priest—suffering from Parkinson's and other ailments, who was not granted bail despite repeated requests and eventually died while in custody.

Former judge of the Patna High Court, Justice Anjana Prakash, is on record stating that 66 per cent of the total number of persons booked under the UAPA were for conspiracy without any allegations of accompanying acts of violence. She also revealed that out of the total number of 386 cases being investigated by the NIA, 74 cases were for non-UAPA offences while 312 pertained to UAPA offences. She added that NIA has not been able to submit charge-sheets in 56 per cent of these cases, meaning that the accused in these cases still remain in custody. These figures definitely point to an unhealthy practice of 'governance by fear' which has no legitimate place in a democracy.

The law, as it stands today, has many flaws and loopholes making it amenable to large scale abuse and misuse by some politicians and overzealous policemen. Things have come to such a pass that at a recent webinar on 'Democracy, Dissent and Draconian Laws',

organised by the Campaign for Judicial Accountability and Reforms, four former Supreme Court judges—Justices Aftab Alam, Madan B Lokur, Gopala Gowda and Deepak Gupta—came down heavily on UAPA and sedition laws and the way they are being misused to suppress democratic dissent and curb fundamental rights. Justices Gopala Gowda and Deepak Gupta were of the view that since Section 43D(5) of the UAPA takes away the power of courts to grant bail and order a judicial review, the law is unconstitutional. All the former Supreme Court judges agreed that the UAPA should not remain in the statute book in its present form. We believe, like them, that such a draconian law has no place in a civilised society, particularly in a country claiming to be the world's largest democracy.

Participating in a session at the G-7 Summit in Cornwall, United Kingdom, held between 11 and 13 June 2021, Prime Minister Narendra Modi spoke of democracy and freedom being part of the Indian ethos. If the Prime Minister is true to his word, his government should heed the call of legal luminaries and the ordinary public, appreciate that the UAPA in its present form poses a serious threat to the freedom of our citizens and to democracy and, after consulting legal experts and taking into account the views of Parliament, enact fresh legislation to replace the UAPA which, while addressing concerns regarding terrorism, safeguards the right to liberty of those exercising their fundamental right of free expression as guaranteed by Article 19 of the Constitution of India.

SATYAMEVA JAYATE

Constitutional Conduct Group (108 signatories)

OPEN LETTER TO THE CHIEF MINISTER, UTTAR PRADESH: WITHDRAWAL OF ORDINANCE ON INTERFAITH MARRIAGE

29 December 2020

Mananiya Mukhya Mantriji,

It is with deep disapproval and concern that we, a group of former civil servants, seek to address your government on a matter of overriding importance for the continued unity of our nation. We should like to clarify at the start that we, as a group, have no political affiliation but share a commitment to the idea of India as defined in our Constitution.

Today we wish to share our anguish at the infamous Moradabad incident, and several similar incidents that have occurred at about the same time in your state. In the Moradabad incident, 22-year-old Rashid and his 25-year-old brother, Saleem, were arrested, to be released only two weeks later when Rashid's wife, Pinki, gave testimony that she had married him willingly, without any compulsion. Rashid and Pinki, who married in July 2020, well before the promulgation of any ordinance on the issue of interfaith marriage, were on their way to have their marriage registered on 5 December when they were accosted by alleged Bajrang Dal men, who accused Rashid of 'love jihad', and took them to the police. Saleem was with them at the time. While Rashid and Saleem were arrested, Pinki was sent to a shelter home. Pinki repeatedly told the media, the police and the court right then that she had married Rashid willingly and wanted to live with her husband's family. The vigilantes who had accosted them brought Pinki's family to the police station. What is inexcusable is that the police remained mute as the vigilantes harassed and interrogated the innocent couple. Pinki suffered a miscarriage, possibly as a result of the harassment. Rashid is reported to have said, 'I told the Bajrang Dal men my wife is pregnant, but they hurled abuses at us. They dragged us to a police station and called my in-laws. We were then locked up and sent to a quarantine centre. I wasn't able to meet my wife.' (Rehman

and Sinha, *The Indian Express*, 20 December 2020). Does this not amount to effective murder of an unborn child and is the police force of your state, by their inaction, not complicit in this?

Regrettably this is only one of a series of heinous atrocities committed by your administration against young Indians across Uttar Pradesh (UP), Indians who are simply seeking to live their lives as free citizens of a free country. These atrocities, regardless of the indignation of all Indians devoted to the rule of law, continue unabated. The anti-conversion ordinance of your state is being used as a stick to victimise especially those Indian men who are Muslim and women who dare to exercise their freedom of choice. While the various High Courts, including the Allahabad High Court, have ruled unequivocally that choosing one's life partner is a fundamental right guaranteed under the Constitution, the state of UP is blithely undermining that very Constitution. The vigilantes are acting as a power unto themselves in intimidating innocent Indian citizens. It has become painfully evident that, in recent years, UP state, once known as the cradle of the Ganga-Jamuna civilisation, has become the epicentre of the politics of hate, division and bigotry, and that the institutions of governance are now steeped in communal poison. What is worse is that your law enforcement machinery, with the active backing of your government, is playing a role reminiscent of the secret police in authoritarian regimes. You can pose no greater threat to the nation than by turning its own citizens against one another, a conflict that can only serve the country's enemies. As Chanakya taught us, a crafty politician must sow dissension amongst rivals. Here you are sowing dissensions among our own people.

We, therefore, demand that the illegal ordinance be withdrawn forthwith and those Indians that have suffered from its unconstitutional enforcement be suitably compensated. The policemen who were responsible for allowing this must be called to account under the law, suitably investigated at a senior level of the magistracy and if found to have facilitated the death of the unborn infant, be put to trial under the IPC. Moreover, the entire police force

of Uttar Pradesh needs to be trained without delay in respecting the rights of all citizens; and the politicians of UP, including yourself, need to re-educate yourselves about the provisions of the Constitution which you and other lawmakers have sworn to uphold. While our past communications to you give us little reason to expect that your government will take corrective action to uphold the rule of law, we do hope this letter will contribute to mobilising informed public opinion against these developments and that the Courts will take notice and intervene to stem the rot.

SATYAMEVA JAYATE

Constitutional Conduct Group (104 signatories)

STATEMENT OF THE CONSTITUTIONAL CONDUCT GROUP: ASSAULT ON THE RULE OF LAW, FREE SPEECH AND RIGHT TO DISSENT

4 July 2020

This statement by our group of former civil servants arises from our deep concern at the assault on the Rule of Law in India and on its citizens' rights to free speech and dissent, basic elements of any democracy. The whole constitutional edifice is dependent on the Rule of Law, which implies the subjection of all the organs and instrumentalities of the state to the law and the absence of arbitrary power. The rights to Freedom of Speech and Expression, Freedom of Assembly and the like, guaranteed by Article 19 of the Constitution, are a corrective to the plight of the poor and the disadvantaged across the axes of income, gender, religion, caste and community. To uphold the rule of law and enforce the rights to freedoms, the judiciary must be the vigilant sentinel guarding the values of constitutional propriety.

Scholars like Nobel Laureate Amartya Sen have established that the elimination of famine, a colonial legacy in India, came from

the clamour of the media, the legislatures and the courts as also concerns of political parties seeking re-election. Public Interest Litigation has given voice to the suppressed on issues like bonded labour, child labour and the illiterate without work or food finding resonance in the corridors of power. Article 19 of the Constitution of India guaranteeing freedom of speech is the key in this struggle.

The rampant erosion of the rule of law in evidence today militates against the actualisation of the freedom of speech which is the cornerstone of democratic functioning. The gulf between the Rule of Law rhetoric and reality is getting wider and wider. The police establishments across the country appear to have become proxies for the respective ruling parties. Independent experts like Special Rapporteurs and members of the Working Group on Arbitrary Detentions associated with the United Nations, in referring to the arrest of eleven activists, including Kafeel Khan, Safoora Zargar, Akhil Gogoi and Sharjeel Imam, say succinctly: 'These defenders, many of them students, appear to have been arrested simply because they exercised their right to denounce and protest against the CAA (Citizenship Amendment Act), and their arrest seems clearly designed to send a chilling message to India's vibrant civil society that criticism of government policies will not be tolerated.' Journalists like Gauri Lankesh, a free-spirited journalist writing in Kannada, have been murdered, shot in cold blood allegedly by right-wing groups.

According to the Press Freedom Index of Reporters without Borders, India stands at 142 out of 180 countries in 2020, falling six places since 2015. Flagrant misuse of draconian laws of sedition and the Unauthorized Activities (Prevention) Act (UAPA) has led to the arrest of journalists, intellectuals, university students, film-makers, human rights activists and popular figures who dared criticise the present regime. When, as happened in Karnataka, in consequence of a school play critical of the CAA a primary school teacher and the mother of a student are charged with sedition and two young children aged 9 and 10 are questioned by police over many days, this becomes a theatre of the absurd.

Any criticism of government is considered 'anti-national' and invites punitive wrath. The law of sedition, itself a colonial relic, is resorted to by a succession of governments, but its application has sharply increased. From 2016 to 2018, 332 persons were arrested under this law but only seven convicted, exposing the absence of evidence and exercise of vendetta. The online portal *Scroll.in* reported that more than '10,000 Adivasis in Jharkhand have been accused of sedition and disturbing public order' in connection with the Pathalgadi movement.

In the case of UAPA, court proceedings drag on while detention continues. In the celebrated Bhima-Koregaon case several of India's finest social and human rights activists like Sudha Bharadwaj, Shoma Sen and Gautam Navlakha and public intellectuals like Anand Teltumbde languish in prison under the malevolent label of 'urban Maoists', which consigns such exemplars of civic life to the reviled category of 'anti-national'. Attacks on students of Jawaharlal Nehru University and Jamia Milia Islamia recently choked the rights of students and faculty to voice their criticism of the existing state of affairs, including the CAA.

The Corona-virus pandemic has been an excuse for curbing freedom of speech across states. A report of the Rights and Risks Analysis Group has it that 55 journalists were singled out for writing on the mishandling of the COVID situation: threats, FIRs, assaults and arrests were amongst the intimidatory tactics used. Though the largest number was in UP, such cases also took place in states with governments of different political parties. Dhaval Patel in Gujarat and Rahul Zori in Maharashtra, with FIRs filed against them, and Major Singh Panjabi being beaten up in Punjab by the police are examples. Earlier in the year, one Dr Indranil Khan in Kolkata was interrogated, threatened with arrest and had his phone and SIM card confiscated for commenting online of deficiencies in the supply of PPE to doctors and nurses working with Corona patients. In a rare defence of the freedom of speech, the Kolkata High Court in his case said: 'Freedom of speech and expression which is granted under

Article 19 of the Constitution of India has to be scrupulously upheld by the state. If an expression of opinion brings the government into disrepute, it cannot defend this allegation by intimidation of the person expressing the opinion by subjecting him to prolonged interrogation, threatening arrest, seizing his mobile phone and SIM card and so on.'

When Siddharth Varadarajan, founding Editor of *The Wire*, faced criminal charges for reporting that the UP Chief Minister attended a religious event after the lockdown was announced, more than 4,600 signatories protested, amongst them eminent academics, a retired Supreme Court Judge, a former National Security Adviser, a former Chief of Naval Staff and well-known persons connected with the arts. 'A medical emergency should not serve as the pretext for the imposition of a de facto political emergency,' they wrote.

The detentions in Kashmir of hundreds of political activists and the suspension of communications for several months after the revocation of its special status is a blot on India's democracy, with Kashmir described by the International Press Institute as amongst the 'world's most repressive spots for the press.' In many parts of India, Section 144 is imposed for extended periods of time to prohibit the assembly of people despite the Supreme Court ruling that such curbs be restricted to emergencies.

Finally, the investigations into the riots in northeast Delhi have betrayed an institutional bias against the minority community. Dr M.A. Anwar, the proprietor of Hind Hospital in New Mustafabad, whose prompt action in providing help to injured people during the targeted violence in Northeast Delhi in late February 2020 was praised by many, including the Delhi High Court, is now named in a charge-sheet filed in a murder case and for instigating local people against the government on the issue of CAA-NRC. The UAPA has been used against activists who opposed the CAA through peaceful protest. People like Harsh Mander and Yogendra Yadav have been named in charge sheets even though they are not amongst the accused. Harsh Mander's speech, which called for peace, was made

in December 2019, weeks before the outbreak of any violence. Yet there are rumours of his intended arrest which, were it to occur now, would make a travesty of the law. Meanwhile, Kapil Mishra and Anurag Thakur, BJP leader and Minister respectively, who had openly called for violence, widely projected in the media, which followed almost immediately thereafter, face no action.

All Indians must unite in defence of the Rule of Law and Article 19, the repository of the democratic right to freedom of speech and to dissent.

SATYAMEVA JAYATE
Constitutional Conduct Group (99 signatories)

LETTER TO THE MEDIA: STOP THE VILIFICATION OF HARSH MANDER

11 June 2020

Dear friends in the media,
On 22 March 2020, 95 retired civil servants belonging to the Constitutional Conduct Group wrote an Open Letter 'In defence of Harsh Mander: An Open Letter to the media' regarding the mischaracterisation of his speech at Jamia Millia Islamia on 16 December 2019. In the letter, we had said: '...Harsh Mander, as a public-spirited citizen of India, had filed a petition before the Honourable Supreme Court in connection with the registering of FIRs against certain political leaders for using hate speech and inciting violence that resulted in the deaths of more than 50 people in Delhi.' Instead of responding to those specific allegations, the Solicitor General of India alleged that Harsh had both incited violence and been contemptuous of the Supreme Court (SC) in that speech.

In our letter, we had pointed out how a selectively edited video was used in the affidavit of the Deputy Commissioner of Police filed

before the SC. We argued that if the full video had been presented, it would have proved that neither had he incited violence nor had he been contemptuous of the SC. Citing excerpts from the speech, we said that it had to be read in context, in sequence and in full to appreciate its true exhortations. The following extract makes clear his philosophy: 'We have learnt from Gandhiji how to respond to violence and injustice. We will fight with non-violence. Anyone who instigates you toward violence or hatred, they are not your friends.' Regarding the allegation that he was contemptuous of the SC, it is clear that it is baseless because all he did was to say: 'Which is the place in which this fight will eventually be decided? That is in our hearts, in my heart, in your heart, we have to give a response—if they want to fill our hearts with hate, if we respond with hate, hatred will become deeper.'*

We have learnt that the Delhi Police has filed a chargesheet† in the Chand Bagh Ankit Sharma murder case. The early paras indicate the continued position of the Delhi police, claiming that his Jamia speech on 16 December was a hate speech instigating people to violence and against the SC. They write that he used a facade of peace but it was a hate speech! The other two charged with hate speech here are Sharjeel and Azad. This indicates the story that they are trying to build up for the larger conspiracy. It is likely that they will become co-accused in this way in many or all the riot cases, in addition to the conspiracy case.

We are writing to you to please consider whether you can bring to the notice of the general public the continued misrepresentation and mischaracterisation of his speech at Jamia Millia on 16 December 2019, and the possible misuse of law against a champion of non-

* 'Harsh Mander addressing students at Jamia Millia Islamia', *Karwan e Mohabbat*, 16 December 2019, YouTube (https://www.youtube.com/watch?v=yXS2MvqXNsM; Accessed March 2024)

† Chargesheet for the Ankit Sharma murder case (https://constitutionalconduct.files.wordpress.com/2020/06/charge-sheet-65.20-dayalpur-corrected.pdf; Accessed March 2024)

violence and believer in the rule of law. In the meanwhile, those political leaders who publicly used hate speech and incited violence roam free with impunity.

SATYAMEVA JAYATE

Yours sincerely,

Constitutional Conduct Group (94 signatures)

IN DEFENCE OF HARSH MANDER: AN OPEN LETTER TO THE MEDIA*

22 March 2020

We are a group of retired civil servants belonging to the All India and Central Services from all over India. As a group, we do not subscribe to any particular political ideology but rather, focus upon issues that have a bearing upon the Indian Constitution. We have been holding Conclaves and writing Open Letters on matters of concern since we came together as the Constitutional Conduct Group in May 2017.

We write this letter to bring to the notice of the general public how the Solicitor General (SG) of India has sought to mislead the Honorable Supreme Court (SC) in the matter of Harsh Mander's speech at Jamia Millia Islamia on 16 December 2019. The background is that Harsh Mander, as a public-spirited citizen of India, had filed a petition before the Honourable Supreme Court in connection with the registering of FIRs against certain political leaders for using hate speech and inciting violence that resulted in the deaths of more than 50 people in Delhi. On 4 March , instead of responding to the contents of his petition, one of the highest law officers of the land alleged that Harsh Mander had made derogatory statements about

* Disclosure: Harsh Mander is a member of the group but has played no part in issue of this letter.

the Supreme Court. When this was denied by Mander's advocate, the SG was asked by the bench to file an affidavit.

It seems that after an affidavit was filed by the Deputy Commissioner of Police to the effect that Harsh Mander had not only instigated violence but also been seriously contemptuous of the SC, the SC decided not to hear Harsh Mander's case until the matter of his allegedly 'derogatory remarks' was looked into. A link was provided to the video in the affidavit and a prayer was made to dismiss his petition and file charges of contempt against him. We understand, however, that the full video of the speech was not presented before the Court.

We feel that had the full video been presented, it would have clearly brought out the falsehood of the allegations that he had incited violence in any manner or been contemptuous of the SC. It is apparent that the video-recording submitted by the SG and the police was an edited version comprising selectively chosen excerpts from the recording, which had been clipped in places so as to convey the impression that Harsh Mander had both instigated violence and committed contempt of the SC. We strongly feel that the speech has to be read in context, in sequence and in full to appreciate its message.

When the speech is so read, it becomes apparent that Harsh Mander meant that the fight would ultimately be decided in people's hearts and not in any other forum. The following paragraph makes it abundantly clear: 'What will be the future of this country—you all are the youth—what sort of country do you want to leave for your kids—where will this decision happen? One, it will happen on the streets, we have come out on the streets, but even beyond the streets, there is another place where this decision will take place. Which is the place in which this fight will eventually be decided? That is in our hearts, in my heart, in your heart, we have to give a response—if they want to fill our hearts with hate, if we respond with hate, hatred will become deeper'.

Harsh Mander further said: 'If someone is attempting to bring

darkness to the country, and we also do the same in order to fight, then the darkness will only become more severe. If there is darkness, then the only way that can be fought is by lighting a lamp. And if there is a huge storm, we will light a lamp against the darkness. The only answer we have to their hate is love. They will resort to violence, they will instigate us to indulge in violence but we will never carry out any violence. You must understand that it is their plan to instigate you towards violence so that when we commit 2 per cent violence, they respond with 100 per cent. We have learnt from Gandhiji how to respond to violence and injustice. We will fight with non-violence. Anyone who instigates you toward violence or hatred, they are not your friends.'

By what stretch of the imagination can such words be construed as being inciteful of violence when they refer to Mahatma Gandhi, father of the nation, who left us a priceless legacy of non-violence, truth-telling and compassion? By what inversion of meaning, by what distortion of facts and by what supreme disregard for the plain truth do the Solicitor General of India and the Deputy Commissioner of Police seek to mislead the Supreme Court of India?

In our considered and collective opinion, there is a good case for filing a suit for defamation against both worthy gentlemen but that is a decision for the person defamed to take.*

SATYAMEVA JAYATE

Yours sincerely,

Constitutional Conduct Group (95 signatories)

---

* 'Harsh Mander addressing students at Jamia Millia Islamia', *Karwan e Mohabbat*, 16 December 2019, YouTube (https://www.youtube.com/watch?v=yXS2MvqXNsM; Accessed March 2024). Chargesheet for the Ankit Sharma murder case (https://constitutionalconduct.files.wordpress.com/2020/06/charge-sheet-65.20-dayalpur-corrected.pdf; Accessed March 2024).

ANTI-BLASPHEMY LAWS IN PUNJAB: LETTERS TO CM, PUNJAB AND PRESIDENT, INDIAN NATIONAL CONGRESS

3 September 2018

To,
Capt. Amarinder Singh,
Hon'ble Chief Minister, Punjab,
Chandigarh
(
Copy also sent to Shri Rahul Gandhi, President, Indian National Congress)

Subject: Open letter in protest against reported plans to make sacrilege a major offence

Dear Mr Chief Minister,
It is with much anguish that we—a group of former civil servants anxious about the alarming decline recently, in secular, democratic and liberal values of the Constitution—write to you, confident that you will not allow political expediency to trump secular principles.

We write to express our alarm at recent reports of your government's plans to amend the Indian Penal Code (IPC) to make acts of sacrilege against religious books a major offence, punishable with life imprisonment. Our objections, echoing similar disagreements widely expressed in the press, are on several grounds. We hope your cabinet will reconsider this decision, that we consider is not wise or thought through, and will withdraw the amendment bill.

Our main arguments are:

- Blasphemy provisions, such as the one planned, go against the very grain of the secular character of our Constitution. Rather than reduce the role of religion from the matters of the state, expected of a secular polity, this move will further consolidate the hold of sectarianism, and strengthen the hands of religious extremists on all sides.
- Further, blasphemy laws are a direct threat to freedom of speech and expression, a fundamental right. Criminalising

sacrilege, and making it a major offence, will create a chilling effect on free speech, giving a handle to anyone claiming to be hurt, to pursue ill-founded prosecutions. This is exactly what is happening. Moreover, it will deter any one from even serious research and re-interpretation of religious texts, which will only encourage religious fundamentalism.

- Experience of the implementation of blasphemy laws the world over, point to their being particularly prone to misuse against minorities and weaker sections, to harass them, exact revenge and also to settle personal and professional quarrels, all matters entirely unrelated to blasphemy. (Pew Research Centre, 2016, US Commission on International Religious Freedoms, 2017). Making sacrilege a major offence, wherever it has been affected, has 'fostered an environment of intolerance and impunity, and led to violations of a broad range of human rights'. (Freedom House, 2010).
- Provisions already exist to deal with insults to religion. Any further amendments to the existing provisions are not merely unnecessary, but are a retrograde step. Laws that seek to restrict freedoms (speech, belief) have an insidious quality, in that they proliferate, also making space for more severe versions of the original, further restricting freedoms, and tend to gradually spin out of control.
- The proposed amendment is bad in law. It is poorly worded, offences are undefined and open-ended, speaking of 'sacrilege, and "hurt" caused to "people"'. It is also arbitrary—religious texts of only four major faiths are included, leaving others out (as far as Hinduism is considered it cites only one text, when there are a hundred other texts held sacred by different sections of Hinduism).
- By prescribing life imprisonment, the proposed amendment makes sacrilege a major offence. This is excessive and disproportionate. Supreme Court has, in its ruling on Sec. 295-A IPC (in *Ramjilal Modi v. State of UP, AIR 1957 SC 620*) already held that the said provision, that attracts a maximum

penalty of 4 years, punishes only the 'aggravated form of insult to religion'.

- We have seen that whenever a legislation has not been sufficiently thought through as to its ramifications, is imprecise in its definition of what constitutes an offence, e.g. 'sacrilege', and is capable of multiple interpretations, it lends itself to the gross abuse of power by vested political interests, particularly those that represent sectarian groups, and adds to the potential of increased police repression.

You will appreciate that we have already paid a heavy price for our past sins of pandering to extremist sentiments of various religions for short term political ends, whether it be the Shah Banu case, the Taslima Nasreen case, opening of the gates of Babri Masjid for pooja, banning of various books, paintings etc. This has brought us to a situation today where the very idea of an inclusive, pluralistic, and liberal India and Indian-ness is seriously threatened.

Our country has recently seen the development of a communally charged environment due to the empowerment of sectarian and illiberal ideas and ideologies, resulting in the targeting of minorities and a general increase in social disharmony. The need of the hour is for all responsible stakeholders to act to reduce the space provided to religious fundamentalists of all kind—not open up space further to them. Additionally, the proposed amendment has the potential to set off competitive mobilisation and copycat blasphemy and sacrilege legislations in other states too. It will only serve to underline divisions and encourage each community to look both over its shoulders as also over the shoulders of others to check what they are doing. It is not difficult to visualise a scenario where such a law can be brutally misused.

The Congress Party has had a chequered history of occasionally fishing in communal waters for short term political ends making it vulnerable to the charge of hypocrisy. In a situation where the need to uphold our secular values has become more critical than ever

before, we believe it is incumbent on you as an influential leader of that party to stand by those values and shun the temptation to score short term political points. We do hope your government will withdraw the Indian Penal Code (Punjab Amendment) bill, 2018 and Code of Criminal Procedure (Punjab Amendment) bill 2018.

Thank you and sincerely,
Constitutional Conduct Group (34 signatories)

OPEN LETTER: ARRESTS OF ACTIVISTS

30 August 2018

We are a group of retired civil servants who came together last year because of our concern over what we saw as an alarming decline in the secular, democratic, and liberal values enshrined in our Constitution. As citizens who have had a close association with issues of public policy and governance and the administering of our Constitution, we felt it was necessary to speak out against the rise in authoritarian and majoritarian tendencies, the abuse of political power and the increasing disregard of constitutional values. We have issued several Open Letters (sometimes in concert with a group of retired veterans of the Armed Forces) and have also together, with the veterans, organised Conclaves on several issues of public interest. As a group, we are resolutely committed to constitutional values and principles, and are non-political, whatever the political preferences of individual members might be.

We feel compelled to write an Open Letter once again—in what we perceive as the most brazen display yet of coercive authority by the State.

The arrests of Sudha Bharadwaj, Gautam Navlakha, Vernon Gonsalves, Varavara Rao and Arun Ferreira and the raids on the residences of Stan Swamy, Kranti Tekula, Naseem and Anand Teltumbde, all of whom have been in the forefront of the struggle for

justice for Adivasis, Dalits, Muslims, members of the working class and women and children (a struggle which has been a continuing one irrespective of which Government has been in power) have been the trigger. They have always used lawful and democratic means in their efforts, and this series of arrests shows how wilful and arbitrary the State is to intimidate and silence any signs of dissent and democratic resistance. Earlier Shoma Sen, Rona Wilson, Mahesh Raut, Surendra Gadling and Sudhir Dhawale were also arrested under the same charges for inciting violence in the context of Bhima Koregaon, and the same incident.

The use of draconian laws, which deny access and circumscribe the ability of those arrested to access protection of their fundamental rights is completely unjustified. The imposition of this law is a circumvention of the normal processes and allows the flimsiest of evidence to frame charges and arrest those who are politically inconvenient and may threaten powerful commercial interests complicit with the State. It is patently obvious that the objective is to create a climate of fear to deter those in civil society who are critical of the Government's treatment of Dalits, Adivasis and other marginalised and dispossessed groups and may be inclined to take up cudgels on their behalf.

The excuse for such action hinges on a fabricated tale of a 'terror' plot against a high functionary in which these allegedly 'urban Naxals' play a role. Incidents quoted refer to the Elgar Parishad held earlier in the year in Pune, of which the highly respected Justice P.B. Sawant (former Supreme Court Judge and Chairman of the Press Council) was a key organiser. The vagueness of the allegations, the manner and the timing of the arrests, the choice of the persons arrested (none of whom were a part of the Bhima Koregaon incident), the use of a law which has lower standards of evidence required for establishing a 'prima facie' case, all go to show the insidiousness of the intent. The evidence in the public domain against those arrested appears to be incredible. This is shameful.

The charges made against these respected human rights defenders and intellectuals—as broadcast by compliant sections

of the media—is that they are supporters of subversive violence, applying to them the newly minted tag of the 'urban Naxalite', alleged to be city based middle-class supporters of Maoist insurgents. That this tag has been applied to a group of persons who have always used lawful and democratic means in their efforts is an example of how wilful and arbitrary the State can be in quelling any signs of dissent and democratic resistance.

It is evident that these arrests follow a pattern designed by the current dispensation to tag any dissident or critical intellectual activity as anti-national or seditious or supportive of secession and terrorism. Ironically, while a 'Maoist sympathiser' is treated as a dangerous terrorist who needs to be incarcerated, a sympathiser of the Bajrang Dal or Sanatan Sanstha or Hindu Mahasabha, who flaunts the agenda of violence and hate, is seen as pursuing a worthwhile national cause. Coming from a political culture where ministers and legislators who fete and celebrate murder convicts and perpetrators of mob violence are given political support and patronage, this perversion of principles is sickening.

None of us is a supporter of Naxalism or the violent ideology it represents. In fact, as Ramachandra Guha, an eminent public intellectual, historian and a scholar of Gandhi, said in an interview to *NDTV*, the persons arrested have never preached violence and instead always upheld the rule of law as enshrined in the Constitution. Many of the activists arrested now and earlier in June this year are lawyers, who in representing Adivasis whose rights to natural resources and livelihoods stand expropriated or threatened, have bravely stood against the joint might of the State and its 'corporate cronies'. Their record is exemplary and their focus has been unwavering, whether the government was of the Congress or the BJP. For such persons to be charged as instigators of extremist violence is a deliberate official falsehood foisted to damage their reputations, and is truly bizarre and Kafkaesque.

Prime Minister, we know that this, our letter of protest and condemnation, will be given short shrift and we will be told, yet

again, that the law must be allowed to take its course. The question, Prime Minister, is of those who govern and misuse the law for promoting partisan politics at the cost of justice; and that must also stand the test of public accountability and the scrutiny of evidence. The refuge that law and order is a State subject, and that the Union has no role, is not convincing enough as the opinions that have led to these arrests have been built up deliberately by a series of statements in the public domain by the current establishment. Yet, Prime Minister, we know that you have the political authority to give suitable directions to a BJP Chief Minister to withdraw the cases and we also know that should it so choose, the Union Government has the constitutional authority to issue appropriate advisories and directives, which have been used many times in your period as PM for a variety of reasons. As the prime executive authority for administering the Constitution, we hope that you will not permit the brazen trampling of the Fundamental Rights of those who work to protect the rights of the poor and the dispossessed.

The Court of course will have to take a view on the legality and the legitimacy of the arrests. But the onus for the administration of the law vests with the Union and the state governments. These arrests could not have been made without their prior sanction. As the Head of the Government, we expect nothing less from you than an absolute commitment to upholding the core values of democracy and the principles of justice and fairness. It is time that your party and your government show their determination to stand by and protect our Constitution. Should you choose to ignore our letter, we will know how hollow that commitment is and demonstrate once again your willingness to crush public dissent, especially that which defends the rights of the country's disadvantaged castes and classes, with the misuse of state agencies and coercive laws.

SATYAMEVA JAYATE

Constitutional Conduct Group (48 signatories)

GOVERNANCE, PUBLIC POLICY AND ADMINISTRATION

Governance, Public Policy and Administration

E.A.S. SARMA

The way the present day rulers have weaponised the words, 'public policy', 'nationalism', 'national security', 'governance' and 'administration', to suppress dissent, reminds one of Humpty Dumpty's scornful words in Lewis Carroll's *Through the Looking Glass*—'When I use a word, it means just what I choose it to mean—neither more nor less.' It displays the rulers' contempt for the Constitution.

The Constitutional Conduct Group (CCG)'s 'open letters' reflect the anguish expressed at this by a diverse group of former civil servants belonging to different services that have played and continue to play a pivotal role in governance and administration in India. Such activism on the part of CCG will go a long way towards mobilising public opinion.

Public Policy:

Whether it is public policy, its administration or whether it relates to the governance of the country, its basis cannot be anything other than the Constitution, especially the democratic and the secular values enunciated in its Preamble, the citizen's fundamental rights and responsibilities listed in Parts II and III, the Directive Principles of State Policy stated in Part IV, the federal structure of the political system provided in Parts XI and XII, the special provisions that safeguard the interests of the disadvantaged sections of the society, the scheme of devolution of authority to elected local bodies as set out in Parts IX and IXA and the institutions that the Constitution has provided to enforce the Constitutional values.

The Constitution and its Basic Structure:

Though Article 368 empowers the Parliament to amend the Constitution, the apex court has reiterated time and again that its 'basic structure' represented by the provisions that define its democratic and federal character cannot be altered.

When political parties come to power with a brute majority, they are tempted to defy the statute to suit their own ideological whims and fancies and to appease corporate entities that fund them. This was exactly the fear expressed by Dr B.R. Ambedkar on 25 November 1949 in his address to the Constituent Assembly: 'There is danger of democracy giving place to dictatorship. It is quite possible for this newborn democracy to retain its form but give place to dictatorship in fact. If there is a landslide, the danger of the second possibility becoming actuality is much greater'. What is happening today in India seems to justify his apprehension beyond all expectations.

A Welfare State:

The Directive Principles of State Policy provide a welfare character to the Constitution, enunciating the principles that should govern public policy in India. Since 1991, when the so-called 'economic reforms' were initiated, successive governments diluted the role of the public sector at the cost of welfare, unmindful of the negative socio-economic consequences of such an approach. In one of its letters ('India's plummeting rank in key global indices'; 15 November 2021), the CCG expressed its concern at this.

The Directive Principles have unambiguously defined the two terms 'public policy' and 'governance'. Article 37 states, 'the provisions contained in this Part shall not be enforceable by any court, but the principles therein laid down are nevertheless fundamental in the governance of the country and it shall be the duty of the State to apply these principles in making laws'.

Article 38 mandates the State to promote people's 'welfare' by 'securing and protecting…a social order in which justice, social,

economic and political, shall inform all the institutions of the national life...The State shall, in particular, strive to minimise the inequalities in income, and endeavour to eliminate inequalities in status, facilities and opportunities, not only amongst individuals but also amongst groups of people residing in different areas or engaged in different vocations'.

Other important principles of State policy are stated in Article 39: 'The State shall, in particular, direct its policy towards securing that the citizens, men and women equally, have the right to an adequate means of livelihood; that the ownership and control of the material resources of the community are so distributed as best to subserve the common good; that the operation of the economic system does not result in the concentration of wealth and means of production to the common detriment'.

Article 46, (read with Articles 15&16) seeks to promote the educational and economic interests of Scheduled Castes, Scheduled Tribes and other weaker sections, in particular, to protect them from social injustice and exploitation.

Article 48A enjoins upon the State to conserve the environment.

Several initiatives taken by the present government and its predecessors run counter to the letter and the spirit of Articles 38, 39, 46, 48A and other provisions. They include the wholesale privatisation of public assets and services launched by the government in 2021[*]; Niti Ayog's idea of grooming a few corporate entities into 'global champions'[†], a euphemism for choking competition to suit the interests of a few corporate oligarchs; providing subsidies to the extent of Rs 2 lakhs under the so-called 'Production Linked Incentive' (PLI) scheme to profit-earning corporate entities in the guise of promoting self-reliance, tweaking policies to enable a few big business houses

---

* 'Speech of Nirmala Sitharaman, Minister of Finance', *Budget 2012-2022*, Government of India, 1 February 2021 (https://www.indiabudget.gov.in/budget2021-22/doc/Budget_Speech.pdf; Accessed March 2024).

† 'Battling Barrier Scale', NITI Ayog, 10 April 2021 (https://www.niti.gov.in/battling-barrier-scale; Accessed March 2024).

to secure monopoly control over the country's vital infrastructure facilities such as ports and airports, amending the environment and forest conservation laws to eliminate public consultation processes in the guise of promoting 'ease of doing business' for private project promoters and handing over valuable minerals to private companies, bypassing laws such as the Panchayats (Extension to the Scheduled Areas) Act [PESA] and the Forest Rights Act [FRA] that exist to safeguard the interests of adivasis, especially in areas notified under the Fifth Schedule to the Constitution.

Federalism under Threat:

The CCG, in one of its letters ('Statement on Simultaneous Elections to Parliament and State Assemblies', 8 December 2020) emphasised the need for the Centre to respect the federal character of our democracy. As Dr Ambedkar clarified in his address to the Constituent Assembly, 'the States under our Constitution are in no way dependent upon the Centre for their legislative or executive authority. The Centre and the States are co-equal in this matter'.

While Part XI of the Constitution defines the legislative powers of the Union and the states, Part XII provides a basis for allocating the Union's tax revenues between the Union and the states to enable them to discharge their respective Constitutional obligations. The Finance Commission set up under Article 280 examines the revenue-expenditure profiles of the Union and the states and recommends an equitable basis for such an allocation. Article 282, by way of exception, allows the Union to appropriate a portion of its tax revenues to take up special schemes to supplement the States' efforts in areas where they need it. In the past, successive governments at the Centre misused the provision under Article 282, somewhat reluctantly, to make undue intrusions into areas that legitimately belong to the states, by introducing several Centrally Sponsored Schemes (CSSs), which reduce the political space of the states and weaken the federal structure. Since 2014, when the NDA government came to power, the extent of misuse of Article 282 has

become far more deliberate, aggressive and alarming. The share of the Union's tax revenues allocated to the states under Article 282 has steeply increased from 7.5 per cent in 2014 to more than 45 per cent now, which has literally marginalised the role of the Finance Commission, replacing rule-based approach to allocation of revenues between the Union and the states with a scheme of allocation pattern unilaterally decided by the Central political leadership, unrelated to the states' respective development needs and without any consultation with them. Many newly introduced CSSs through which funds are transferred to the States under Article 282 force the states to fall in line with the Centre's ideas and ideology. The Centre's intrusive approach through Article 282 has the effect of shrinking the political space of the states. It poses a serious threat to federalism.

There are many other fronts on which the Centre has made attempts to impose its policies on the states. The unilateral decision of the Centre to impose three contentious farm laws on the states and a law to amend the 2003 Electricity Act without consulting the states, is an example of how the Centre has tried to cut at the root of federalism and progressively introduce a unitary form of government.

In a country like India with its diverse cultures, geographic and socio-economic features, any attempt on the part of the Centre to impose its policies on the states amounts to an unhealthy interference with the federal character of the Constitution, which, in the long run, will prove counter-productive.

Lack of Transparency in Governance:

The present government has displayed utter disregard for transparency in governance. The CCG specifically referred to the way the government refused to disclose the details of funds received by the PM CARES Fund ('Open Letter to the Prime Minister on the PM CARES Fund', 16 January 2021), though the Fund is run entirely by public functionaries, using public funds to a large extent.

The citizen's access to information is a fundamental right under Article 19. The citizens are entitled to be informed of the manner in which the government and the other public authorities function. The Right to Information (RTI) Act enacted in 2005 provides the necessary institutional mechanism for citizens to exercise that right. The Central and the State Information Commissions set up under the Act have fixed tenures and well-defined terms of service. They are expected to function independently of executive control. The Information Commissioners are empowered to order the public authorities to make *suo moto* public disclosure of all information of public interest, in addition to directing them to provide information whenever a citizen seeks it under the RTI Act.

The RTI Act, enacted during UPA rule, became a powerful instrument in the hands of the citizen to force the government to become accountable to the public. The present government is reluctant to submit itself to the RTI Act regime. In 2019, it went to the extent of amending the Act to dilute the independence of the Information Commissioners by introducing provisions that empower the executive to tinker with their tenures and service conditions.

Article 19, as interpreted by the apex court, requires political parties receiving donations from individuals and private companies to disclose details of their donors. Contrary to it, through the backdoor of the Finance Act of 2017, the present government introduced a regressive scheme of Electoral Bonds to enable political parties to receive donations from donors whose identities need not be disclosed to the public.

In Gandhiji's words, 'Truth never damages a cause that is just'. The citizens should worry when a government brazenly tries to hide the truth!

The Role of Institutions:

The CCG expressed its distress ('India's plummeting rank in key global indices', 15 November 2021) at the executive's attempts to

weaken Constitutional authorities to further its own interest. In his book, *Considerations on Representative Government* (1861), John Stuart Mill, a political economist, cautioned that in 'a fit of enthusiasm for an individual, they [the citizens] can be induced to lay their liberties at the feet even of a great man, or trust him with powers which enable him to subvert their institutions; in all these cases they are more or less unfit for liberty'.

Institutions like the judiciary, the Election Commission of India (ECI), the National Commission for the Scheduled Castes (NCSC), the National Commission for the Scheduled Tribes (NCST) ensure the executive's compliance with the requirements of the Constitution. When such institutions are subject to subversion, the structure of India's democracy will get weakened.

The present government has made attempts to erode the independence of the judiciary by interfering with appointments to the higher echelons of judiciary and dangling post-retirement assignments to induce members of the judiciary to be executive-friendly. A weakened judiciary results in the citizens arbitrarily deprived of their fundamental rights and the nation of its democratic values.

The ECI, set up under Article 324, is expected to function independently of the political executive to be able to conduct elections in a free and fair manner. Over the years, since it is the political executive that decides on the selection of candidates for appointment to the Commission, with a few outstanding exceptions, most incumbents of the office considered themselves to be a part of the government, obliged to please those in power, rather than remaining apolitical, subserving the public interest.

When the question of ECI's independence came up before the apex court recently, the court directed, by way of an interim measure pending a law to be enacted by the Parliament, that appointment of 'the Election Commissioners shall be made on the recommendations made by a three-member Committee comprising of the Prime Minister, Leader of the Opposition of the Lok Sabha and in case

no Leader of Opposition is available, the Leader of the largest opposition party in the Lok Sabha in terms of numerical strength, and the Chief Justice of India. It is desirable that the grounds of removal of the Election Commissioners shall be the same as that of the Chief Election Commissioner—that is on the like grounds as a Judge of the Supreme Court subject to the "recommendation of the Chief Election Commissioner" as provided under the second proviso to Article 324(5) of the Constitution of India. The conditions of service of the Election Commissioners shall not be varied to his disadvantage after appointment'.

The way the present government responded to the apex court's directions was extraordinary, to say the least. It introduced a Bill in the Parliament, proposing a committee chaired by the Prime Minister but without the Chief Justice of India in it and, instead, a Union Minister as its member, in addition to the Leader of the largest party in opposition, in brazen defiance of the idea put forward by the apex court to impart transparency and objectivity to the procedure of appointment of the Election Commissioners. The rest of the provisions of the Bill also run counter to the apex court's recommendation. If such a procedure becomes a reality, it will amount to nothing but outright subversion of the concept of an independent Election Commission and the idea of an independent electoral process. It is ironic that a political party that boasts of securing a convincing mandate to rule through a democratically conducted process of election should go all out to weaken that very same electoral process by proposing to reduce the Election Commission to an agency subservient to the ruling political establishment! It shows how undemocratic its mindset is and how myopic its vision.

The NCST is an authority set up under Article 338A to safeguard the interests of the tribals. Article 338A(9) stipulates that 'the Union and every State Government shall consult the Commission on all major policy matters affecting Scheduled Tribes'. The present government has chosen to ignore Article 338A(9) altogether in

several matters, defying the authority of the NCST. For example, it undertook large scale auction of mineral blocks in the Scheduled Areas to private miners, where mining will uproot thousands of tribals and disrupt their lives. In that matter, the concerned ministries bypassed the NCST altogether, apart from non-compliance with the PESA Act and the FRA. Without prior consultation with the NCST, it introduced far reaching policy changes in Lakshadweep and the Andaman and Nicobar Islands, without caring to appreciate the long-term adverse implications of such policy changes for the tribals.

Is democratic dissent 'anti-national'?

It is ironic that political leaders in India should get elected, taking advantage of the democratic processes put in place by the Constitution and later, subvert those very same processes to suppress dissent and opposition, to be able to tweak policies to suit the interests of big businesses who fund their elections. It is equally ironic that the political executive should harass thousands of NGOs and individuals on the flimsy ground that they committed procedural lapses under the Foreign Contributions Regulation Act (FCRA) and subject them to coercive action including arbitrary detention, merely because they questioned and exposed the political executive's authoritarian conduct, its undue concessions to big businesses and its complicity in human rights violations. At the same time, the same political executive showed no hesitation whatsoever when it came to amending that very same FCRA, through the Finance Act of 2016, to regularise its own serious lapses in receiving foreign donations and clear the way for it to receive larger amounts of political donations from questionable foreign sources.

In several of its letters (e.g. 'Government of India Must Replace UAPA with Legislation that Fights Terrorism while Safeguarding Personal Liberties', 16 August 2021), the CCG pointed out the desirability of reviewing regressive laws such as the Unlawful Activities (Prevention) Act (UAPA). Recently, inaugurating the new Parliament building, the Prime Minister proudly announced

to the world, 'India is not only a democratic nation but also the mother of democracy'. In addition to sovereignty of the people, the idea of a democracy also implies protection of the citizen's right to life and personal liberty. A truly democratic State should ensure compliance with the three cardinal principles of natural justice, 'no one will be subject to arbitrary arrest', 'the burden of proof always rests on the person who makes the accusation' and 'a person accused of a crime is considered innocent until proven guilty'. Contrary to it, lakhs of persons in India are detained in jails indefinitely, largely for petty offences, without trial. Among those detained are hundreds of persons, vaguely accused of 'offences against the State', subject to detention for years under the UAPA, the 'conspiracy' and 'sedition' provisions in Chapter VI of the IPC, the National Security Act etc. In all such cases, the investigating officers, who do not seem to be accountable to any authority, casually take years to bring the accused to trial, while those accused languish in jails, making a mockery of the idea of India being a 'mother of democracy'.

One may recall the unfortunate case of Stan Swamy, an octogenarian activist working on behalf of the tribals in central India, accused of involvement in 'terrorism' and detained under the UAPA in October 2020, who was forced to languish in a jail without any trial, till he tragically died of ill health in July 2021.

What next?

Addressing the University of Edinburgh's Law School in June, 2023, the Chief Justice of India, Justice D.Y. Chandrachud said, 'There is something wider, more profound and fundamental at play in the realisation of rights to citizens… In terms of columns, the structures of governance are extremely crucial. This includes the legislature, the executive, the courts, the whole decentralisation of power down to local bodies on one hand, to setting up of institutions to prevent centralisation of power [on the other]. But equally, the citizenry have a very vital role to play in the protection of rights.'

The CCG and others who form part of the 'citizenry', have rightly raised their voice against the political executive's authoritarianism, against erosion of citizen's rights and against the growing threat to Constitutional values. While elected representatives have an important role in running the government, they should remember that they cannot overstep the boundaries of the Constitution or disrespect the values that characterise it.

In Gandhiji's words, 'To forgive and accept injustice is cowardice'. Civil society should raise its voice against any kind of injustice. Defending the Constitution and its values is its legitimate right. It is in that context that one earnestly hopes that the CCG and others among the civil society will continue to play their role in representing the concerns of the people.

India and Democratic Backslinding

NEERA CHANDHOKE

The publication of open letters written to the Union and state governments, as well as the political public since 2017 by the Constitutional Conduct Group of distinguished (retired) civil servants, signifies an important intervention in contemporary politics. The letters address relevant authorities and the people on troublesome issues relating to elections, parliamentary procedures, communalism and intolerance, restrictions on the rights of serving and retired civil servants, free speech and dissent, targeting of individuals, repression of the media and civil society organisations, the NRC and CAA, development in the Andaman and Nicobar islands, judicial accountability, coercive laws, and the Central Vista Project, among other concerns. The wider message is that the cause of flawed laws, inept governance, and coercive administration is a structural crisis in Indian democracy.

In democracies the objectives of governance, public policy and administration are to expand and deepen the democratic project, through the making and implementation of policies that are sensitive to the needs of the people. By themselves, each of these concepts and associated practices do not possess any special meaning. The text depends on the context. Authoritarian governments can give people governance, enact public policy and deliver efficient administration. But they are not compelled to enhance popular participation, facilitate a free print and visual media, secure a prominent role for civil society, ensure accountability, uphold the rights of citizens, and limit the scope of power. All of these features are the hallmark of democracy.

The firmness, clarity and acuity of arguments of these letters, tell us of the long experience of the signatories with political leaders and the institutions and practices of democracy. The anxiety, the passion, and the lucidity of prose we find here, provides a powerful commentary on the rather dismal state of democracy in the country. These are in the nature of primary documents that chart out and engage with the multiple crises that bedevil the country, and that signify democratic regression. This essay draws upon these letters to sketch out the consequence of the crises of governance, public policy and administration that follow the decline of democracy in India. The consequence is best termed as 'democratic backsliding'.

The Contemporary Political Moment

Prominent academics and activists from across the world protested against the arrest of Prabir Purkayastha, the editor in chief of *NewsClick*, its head of human resources, Amit Chakravarty, and the raids conducted by Delhi police on the residences/offices of 46 journalists connected with the news portal on 3 October 2023. The protest statement condemned increasing restrictions on press freedom, and democratic backsliding in South Asia. 'Denying citizens the democratic space for critical questioning will drag South Asian countries into a new phase of authoritarian decay.'

The anxiety is legitimate. The print, visual and online media are an integral part of civil society: the space of social associations and organisations that keep watch on acts of omission and commission of the government. This is necessary, because all governments, howsoever democratic be their credentials, have a fatal tendency to accumulate and abuse power. 'The condition upon which God hath given liberty to man is vigilance', wrote John Curran (1750-1817), Irish statesman, lawyer and an acclaimed wit. Vigilance is the role civil society organisations—the media, civil liberty associations, and human rights defenders—play in in a democracy.

Where the media is intimidated and harassed, where it is taken over by corporate houses that benefit from government patronage,

and when journalists and editors are coerced into submission, democracy is in great danger. The surveillance state keeps watch on us, who is going to keep watch on a democratically elected government? Who will hold It accountable? A handful of leaders, we have seen, can hold the entire country to ransom by blocking dissent, which can reasonably be interpreted as constructive criticism. It is precisely the blocking of dissent that has occurred in India through the implementation of draconian laws, e.g., the Unlawful Activities (Prevention) Act. The Act was amended in 2019 to enable the Union Government to categorise a citizen as a terrorist without going through the judicial process. One of the letters in this collection expresses great concern about the inherently coercive law.

Ironically, muzzling of the media through the use of the UAPA does not pre-empt criticism of the government. As every newspaper reader knows, in the annual reports of global organisations that track the record of democracy across the world, the status of India has fallen every year. Another letter focuses on precisely the ranking of India or rather the lack thereof, in these reports. This is cause for concern since these widely respected organisations have developed rigorous indexes to rank democracies. Over the past few years, they have issued worrying reports on the erosion of democracy in India: frightening polarisation, institutional decay, violence on minorities, censorship, suppression of any research that casts doubt on electoral integrity, and rapidly closing space for dissent. Freedom House in its report 'Freedom in the World' (2023) held that India is a 'partly free nation'. The Varieties of Democracy (V-Dem) project (2023) termed India as an 'electoral autocracy' and ranked it below countries known for authoritarianism and suppression of human rights. The Economist Intelligence Unit in its 2023 report called India a 'flawed democracy'. India's rank in the 2023 World Press Freedom Index dropped from 151 to 161.

Our postcolonial leadership had institutionalised democracy despite the scepticism that the country lacked the basic preconditions of democracy—literacy, a middle class, wealth and civic virtue.

Millions of Indians who had fought shoulder to shoulder for independence did not deserve anything less than democracy. By the second decade of the twenty-first century, the scene changed in India and abroad. The generalised optimism because of the waves of protest that had transformed a number of countries into democracies in the 1980s—the democratic upsurge—has now been replaced with pessimism at democratic backsliding in the global south, in the former socialist world, Israel, and in countries of Europe where the populist right wing has acquired prominence in politics. The United States has been marked by deep political polarisation under the rule of former President Donald Trump. After the 2021 Presidential elections which Trump lost, he refused to accept the election results and his supporters stormed Capitol Hill.

In recent years, India has also been placed in the category of democratic backsliders. The concept is marked by the following characteristics: decline of institutional autonomy, truncation of freedom of expression, of the right to association, and of the right to dissent, shrinking of civic space for public discussion, debate and contestation, rise of intolerance that affects minorities, polarisation and a sharp decline in civic culture. Democratic backsliding is used to describe a process whereby established democracies become less democratic for a variety of reasons.[1]

Some of these factors are external—such as the interference of powerful countries, e.g., China and Russia in elections in other countries. The social media, it is held, has introduced into the political discourse vocabularies of abuse, unsubstantiated allegations, attacks on independent voices and fomented polarisation. Many commentators hold it responsible for hate speech and attacks on vulnerable minorities.

The main and the proximate cause of democratic decline has to do with domestic factors. In country after country, the backsliding of democracy is associated with the rise of right-wing populists and their open contempt for institutions of liberal democracy—constitutional limits on power, basic rights to liberty, and civility

in public speech, among others. This is accompanied by dismissal of other political leaders as elitist and attacks on minorities and immigrants.

The rise of authoritarian populism has introduced a new dimension to the debate on the crisis of democracy. Theorists have normally assumed a strong link between economic wellbeing and democracy. Low growth rates, unemployment, and accompanying illbeing has been interpreted as one of the main reasons for the rise of authoritarianism. In India, it is difficult to trace the rise of the quintessential right-wing populist, Narendra Modi, in 2014, to economic decline during the ten-year (2004-2014) rule of the United Progressive Alliance under the leadership of the Congress.

Economists record that though the economy slowed down in the last two years of the government (2012-2014), the first eight years of the UPA rule saw high levels of economic growth. Overall economic growth accelerated, saving and investment rates increased, poverty declined under the impact of social welfare policies, and statistics on nutrition levels, educational attainments, and life expectancy went up.[2] Oddly, economic growth and social welfare policies that institutionalised the right to food, the right to employment, the right to information, and the right to primary education, threw up completely unanticipated results. 'Growth can also unleash powerful expectations as well as frustration, and political parties who can tap into these emotions reap the benefits'.[3] This is precisely what the BJP accomplished. It exploited the rising discontent of the aspirational class, which the UPA had been unable to do, and dismissed the ten years of UPA rule as corrupt, inefficient and as non-performing.

Wider issues that were thrown up by Mr Modi during the 2014 election campaign fall within the repertoire of the quintessential populist leader. He attacked dynastic rule as elitist and corrupt, delegitimised political institutions because they failed to meet expectations, and highlighted corruption and the collapse of governance. What resonated with the electorate, it is generally held, was the attack on dynasty, mainly because he drew attention to his

own humble origins. He identified with the disadvantaged and the disadvantaged identified with him.

Above all, he appealed to the majority community in the name of hyper-nationalism. Nationalism is inherently exclusionary, it manufactures enemies. The ideology of the BJP has always identified the Muslim community as responsible for the misdeeds of the Mughal rulers in the remote past, and the partition of the country. The outcome could have been predicted. As several letters of the Constitutional Conduct Group point out, the rise of hate speech, violence against minorities and the consolidation of the Hindu vote was a logical outcome of majoritarian democracy.

Even as the religious right invoked history to Hinduise the country, Modi created a highly personalised relationship of social welfare. Democracy has always presumed the institutionalisation of social rights through policy and administration. Today we witness the marginalisation of the social rights discourse that marked the UPA government, and repression of civil society organisations that led to the demand for social goods. The democratic objective of redistribution of resources has been superseded by the handing over of a handful of grain, building of toilets, health insurance, construction of houses, free gas connections and a cutback in the price of gas cylinders during elections. No longer is the citizen the bearer of rights she can assert against the State; she is the grateful recipient of charity. In return she is expected to vote for the ruling party.

Yamini Aiyar has an interesting formulation on this aspect of welfarism. Since 2017, Modi has refashioned himself as the 'Vikas Purush' and proceeded to announce a slew of welfare schemes. The term 'labarthi' (beneficiary) has become a part of the political lexicon, and has benefited the BJP in elections. This as the economist Arvind Subramaniam argues is the 'new welfarism'. It prioritises subsidised public provisioning of private goods over public goods. At the same time, government expenditure on health and education as a percentage of the GDP has stagnated, and funds for the UPA-

sponsored Mahatma Gandhi National Rural Employment Guarantee Act (NREGA) have been drastically cut.[4]

The 2014 elections and the 2019 elections validated the success of a leader-centric, illiberal democracy. Eswaran Sridharan analysing the 2014 and 2019 elections suggests that unlike the first election the higher turnout of upper and middle classes with a strong pro-BJP preference influenced the magnitude of the 12 per cent pro-BJP swing. In 2019, the further 6 per cent swing was uniform across classes and within classes by age group, rural-urban location and caste-community disaggregation.[5] Another study reported that in the 2019 elections the party managed to increase support among most social groups—Dalits and OBCs and in rural as well as urban constituencies. 'The bedrock of the BJP's increased electoral dominance in the last few years is high support among economically weaker sections of the electorate'. Among the upper middle class and rich voter, the support for the BJP remains much higher.[6]

The delivery of social goods as personalised benefit, not as public goods that characterise the welfare state, the development of a major cult of personality, and demagoguery that seems to sway audiences, have been accompanied by the elimination of rights that protect citizens against the power of the State. The increased use of draconian laws to jail dissenters, institutional decline, and a submissive media have cast a pall of fear. This is democratic backsliding.

Liberal philosophers have been wary of two factors that can cripple democratic life—demagogues and brute majorities. In the Constituent Assembly on 25 November 1948, Dr Ambedkar warned his colleagues and the country thus: we can only maintain democracy when we observe the warning that the Liberal philosopher John Stuart Mill had issued to all who are interested in the maintenance of democracy. People should not 'lay their liberties at the feet of even a great man, or to trust him with powers which enable him to subvert their institutions. There is nothing wrong in being grateful to great men who have rendered life-long service to the country but there are limits to gratefulness.' The caution, continued Dr Ambedkar,

is even more necessary in India. 'For in India, Bhakti or what may be called the path of devotion or hero-worship, plays a part in its politics unequalled in magnitude by the part it plays in the politics of any other country in the world. Bhakti in religion may be a road to salvation of the soul. But in politics, Bhakti or hero-worship is a sure road to degradation and to eventual dictatorship.'[7]

Dr Ambedkar's warning was prescient, for Indians have revealed a troublesome propensity to hero-worship leaders they see as strong and decisive. This pre-empts citizen engagement with the government. But it is precisely citizen engagement with democracy that distinguishes this form of rule. When citizens resort to silence or withdraw into the private sphere for fear of toxic trolling, democracy falters and slides downwards. No longer is democracy dramatically captured by military regimes/ dictators in midnight coups. It erodes, surely and steadily as elected leaders proceed to erode the pillars of democracy.

NOTES

1. Christophe Jaffrelot, *Modi's India: Hindu Nationalism and the Rise of Ethnic Democracy*, Princeton University Press, Princeton: 2021.
2. Maitreesh Ghatak, Parikshat Ghosh and Ashok Kotwal, 'Growth in the Time of UPA' *Economic and Political Weekly* (vol. XLIX, no 16), 2014.
3. Ibid, p. 34.
4. Yamini Aiyar, 'From Citizen to labarthi? Interrogating the Welfare State', *Seminar*, January, 2023.
5. Eswaran Sridharan, 'Understanding Voting Patterns by Class in the 2019 Elections', *Indian Politics and Policy* (vol. 3, no. 1), 2020, pp. 50-65, p. 51.
6. Sanjay Kumar and Pranav Gupta, 'Where did the BJP get its votes from in 2019?', *Mint*, 3 June, 2019 (https://www.livemint.com/politics/news/where-did-the-bjp-get-its-votes-from-in-2019-1559547933995.html; Accessed March 2024).
7. Ibid.

Letters and Statements

OPEN STATEMENT—AMENDMENT TO ALL INDIA SERVICES RULES

25 July 2023

The Constitutional Conduct Group, a collective of former civil servants, has noted with concern the recent amendments by the Ministry of Personnel, Public Grievances and Pensioners, Government of India, to the All India Services (Death cum Retirement Benefits) Rules 1958 (hereinafter referred to as the Rules). Through a notification dated 6.7.2023, these amendments have, inter alia, sought to impose a complete ban on the right of retired civil servants to comment on public matters, by threatening them with the withdrawal of their pensions. This would be violative of Article 51A of the Constitution which enjoins upon all citizens to 'cherish and follow the noble ideals that inspired the national struggle for freedom.' The right to criticise the government in power is part of these ideals and cannot be termed as 'misconduct'.

The original Rules of 1958 (as amended from time to time) did contain a provision in Rule 3 that 'future good conduct shall be an implied condition of every grant of pension and its continuation' and that the pension could be withheld or withdrawn, in part or in full, if the pensioner is convicted of a serious crime or is held to be guilty of grave misconduct. However, such action could only be taken by the Union Government on a reference from the state government (the cadre to which the officer belonged). But now, Rule 3 has been amended to provide that such punitive action can be taken by the Union Government 'either on a reference from the

state government concerned or otherwise.' This, we feel, violates the principles of federalism and confers draconian powers of oversight and overrule on the Union Government, which is not in conformity with the duality of control envisaged in the All India Services structure. It will further expose officers in opposition-ruled states to intimidation by the party in power at the centre.

We note with apprehension that nowhere in the Rules has the term 'good conduct' or 'grave misconduct' been defined, other than in sub-rule 8 of Rule 3 which merely 'includes' disclosure of any information covered by the Official Secrets Act as a grave misconduct. Other than this, however, the Rules are completely silent on this issue, and everything is left to the decision or interpretation of the central government. Considering the severe penalties prescribed for misconduct, it is legally incumbent on the Union Government to have provided an exhaustive definition of the term. By leaving this deliberately vague, ambiguous and amorphous, the Union Government has armed itself with unlimited powers to harass and persecute any pensioner whose action is not to its liking, whether it be an article, an interview, participation in a protest march or seminar, or any form of criticism. In effect, this will totally muzzle and silence anyone who draws a pension from the state, which appears to be the intention behind these amendments.

The withdrawal/withholding of pension for any criminal conviction is equally pernicious and untenable in law as it amounts to double jeopardy, punishing a person twice for the same offence. The pension is something (s)he has already earned by dint of long service. If (s)he commits a crime, (s)he will suffer the consequences of that by the operation of that criminal law: (s)he cannot be penalised a second time for the same offence by withdrawing her/his pension. Furthermore, the law punishes the perpetrator of a crime, not her/his next of kin; by withdrawing/withholding her/his pension the government would be inflicting unjustified tribulations and misery on her/his family too.

Finally, both the original and the amended provision of Rule 3 (except the newly introduced sub-rule 6 about divulging secret and security related information) violate multiple rulings of the Supreme Court and various High Courts which have, over the last 65 years, constantly held that pension is an employee's right and a kind of deferred payment for service already rendered. It is not largesse or charity bestowed by the government and does not depend upon the discretion of the government (*State of Punjab and Another v. Iqbal Singh*). In *DS Nakara v. Union of India* (1983), the Supreme Court held that a law cannot discriminate between the same class of people, and that all statutes or laws must have some rational nexus with the object of the law. Rule 3, both the original and the amended versions, do not conform to these legal requirements. Pensioners are no longer government servants: they are free citizens of the country like any other citizen, with the same freedom of expression. By curbing this right under the specious guise of 'good conduct' the government is discriminating against them and, therefore, also violating Article 14 of the Constitution. Furthermore, what is the 'object' of this rule, if not to silence any form of criticism of the government? This cannot be held to be rational, reasonable or based on some valid principle, as is required in another judgment (*Ramana Dayaram Shetty v. The Airport Authority of India and Others*). Rule 3 has become obsolete: it is a legal anachronism which also militates against the right to freedom of speech and dissent. It makes pensioners bonded labourers for life, a separate and inferior-class of citizens who do not enjoy the freedom of expression. It further seeks to impose the Conduct Rules (which apply only to those in service of the government) on pensioners through the back door, which is abhorrent in law, as the latter are no longer in service. They are free citizens and there exists no employer-employee relationship between them and the government.

Rules governing conditions of service need to be dynamic and in sync with the changes in interpretation of laws, the evolution of jurisprudence on rights and freedoms, the development of the

concepts of democracy and an open society. Rule 3 fails to do so, is stuck in a time warp and needs to go.

The Constitutional Conduct Group urges the governments in the states and the Union Government to review this rule with a view to abolishing it, and not to further build upon it. In the interim we further request the Union Government to hold in abeyance these amendments in the interests of federalism, fair play, equality of citizens, freedom of expression and a vibrant democracy.

SATYAMEVA JAYATE

Constitutional Conduct Group (94 signatories)

OPEN LETTER TO THE HON'BLE PRESIDENT OF INDIA ON ATTEMPTS TO CHANGE THE CHARACTER OF CIVIL SERVICES

25 May 2023

Honourable Rashtrapatiji,

We are a group of former civil servants of the All India and Central Services who have worked with the Central and State Governments in the course of our careers. Both as individuals and as a group, we believe in impartiality, neutrality and commitment to the Constitution of India. We do not owe allegiance to any political party.

A systematic attempt is being made to change the character of the civil services, particularly the IAS and the IPS, which, in our constitutional scheme, were uniquely intended to be a protective ring around the Constitution, unaffected by political changes, having an All India perspective rather than a regional, parochial one and being secure enough to maintain an independent, nonpartisan outlook, without fear or favour. It is in this context that we seek to approach you on a matter which, of late, is causing much concern to us and which we are duty bound to bring to your notice.

The bedrock of all civil services in any democracy worth the name is their independence, neutrality, non-adherence to any

political ideology in the discharge of official duties, the freedom to articulate their views to the political executive and the security of knowing that they would not be subjected to arbitrary actions for adhering to these values.

These foundational characteristics had been forcefully expressed by Sardar Patel in his address to the Constituent Assembly in October 1947 in the following words:

> 'There is no alternative to this administrative system...The Union will go, you will not have a united India if you do not have a good All India Service which has the independence to speak out its mind, which has the sense of security that you will stand by your work...If you do not follow this course, then do not follow the present Constitution... Remove them and I see nothing but a picture of chaos all over the country.'

Contrary to the above exhortation, we fear that the government, of which you are the constitutional head, is now attempting to distort this basic framework and historical understanding.

Further, measures are being taken that threaten the unique federal design of the IAS and the IPS, which underlies Sardar Patel's vision of a permanent civil service that would both bind the country together and enable it to maintain a balance between the interests of the Union and the interests of the states. There are noticeable attempts to pressurise officers to show exclusive loyalty to the Union rather than to the 'parent' state cadre to which they are allotted. On occasion, arbitrary departmental actions have been taken against those who refuse to do so. Service Rules are sought to be amended to compel central deputations without the consent of either the officers concerned or their state governments, effectively undermining the authority and control of Chief Ministers over their officers. This has disturbed the federal balance and left civil servants torn between conflicting loyalties, thereby weakening their ability to be impartial.

In the past, governments have permitted lateral recruitment at senior levels and many such officers have distinguished themselves.

Lately, however, there has been opacity in the recruitment process at mid-levels and concerns that candidates are being chosen based on their ideological predilections. The consequences of this for the future of an independent civil service requires no comment.

The actions and words of some very senior functionaries of the central government increases our concern on the future of the civil service and the consequent danger to democracy in India. In this context we would like to mention that the National Security Advisor (NSA), while addressing IPS officers at their passing out function in 2021, had emphasised that they should treat civil society as the 'fourth generation of warfare, that can be subverted, suborned, divided and manipulated to hurt the interests of the nation'. Such sentiments are antithetical to any democratic dispensation and aim at placing civil society in a position of conflict with the state.

On the 21st of April this year, the Prime Minister addressed a gathering of civil service officers on Civil Services Day. The address was unremarkable and comprised largely of a litany of the achievements of the present government over the past nine years, with a proforma acknowledgement of the contributions of the civil services. What was disturbing was his exhortation to the officers to be firm in dealing with malfeasance of political parties while in power. Though couched neutrally, the intent and objective were unmistakable.

Our concern about the future of the civil services is heightened by the reaction of some civil servants. The Lal Bahadur Shastri National Academy of Administration, Mussoorie (LBSNAA) is the foundational training institute for All India Services and Central Services. In a recent op-ed, the Director of the LBSNAA wrote, 'The task of defining an Indian ethos for the civil servants began in the 75th year of India's independence, with Prime Minister Narendra Modi's address where he spelt out the country's vision…' Such unwarranted encomiums to the Prime Minister, by the Director of the premier academy for training future civil servants, are deeply disturbing.

We apprehend that moves are afoot to redact Sardar Patel's vision of an independent and apolitical civil service and replace it with

apparatchiks and foot soldiers whose loyalty shall be to the ruling party and not to the Constitution of India.

At a time when politics is leaning dangerously towards a centralised, authoritarian, national security state with a leadership seemingly amenable to abandoning, without demur, the fundamental principles on which our Constitution is based, it has become critical for citizens to ensure that institutions and systems like the civil services which can check this frightening erosion of constitutional values in the manner envisaged by the great Sardar are protected and strengthened. By virtue of their allegiance to the Constitution and not the government of the day, the All India Services, particularly the IAS and IPS, have a critical role to play. As the Constitutional Head of the Republic, we appeal to you to convey our concerns to the Union Government and caution them that this attempt to change the character of the civil services is fraught with extreme danger and, as Sardar Patel had warned many years ago, will spell the death of constitutional government in India.

SATYAMEVA JAYATE

With profound regards,

Constitutional Conduct Group (82 signatories)

STATEMENT—AMENDMENTS TO AIS CADRE RULES

27 January 2022

We are a group of former officers of the All India and Central Services who have worked with the Central and State Governments in the course of our careers. As members of the Constitutional Conduct Group, we believe in impartiality, neutrality and commitment to the Indian Constitution and in safeguarding its values.

In the federal structure of the Union of India, the Union and the states exist as distinct and separate entities, though they work in tandem to subserve common constitutional objectives. The All

India Services (AIS)—the Indian Administrative Service (IAS), the Indian Police Service (IPS) and the Indian Forest Service (IFoS)—constitute the administrative framework for this unique relationship between the two levels of government and give it stability and balance. Maintaining this balance is critical to good governance.

The proposed amendments to the cadre rules of all the three AIS seek to give unilateral powers to the Union to pick and choose any AIS officer(s) working in the states to be withdrawn from their services in the state of their allotment and brought to the Centre without the concurrence either of the officer concerned or of the state government that the officer is serving. While this change in the rules may appear to be a minor, technical one, it, in fact, hits at the very core of the constitutional scheme of Indian federalism.

It is important to remember that the conceptual design of the AIS is anchored on two features which make it unique among public services anywhere in the world.

One, that the creation of the AIS (initially the IAS and the IPS and, subsequently, the IFoS) was covenanted in the main body of the Constitution, making them creatures not of the Executive but of the Constitution itself. This is a feature unique to the AIS and distinguishes them from other Central Services created by the Centre as well as from services created by state governments. For Sardar Patel, this feature was critical to guaranteeing members of the AIS their independence and their ability to speak their mind. Their Constitutional status and independence would give them the security to function as a protective ring around the Constitution. It was not merely that Constitutional protection was available to members of the Service but that they were expected to be the ones protecting the Constitution from the vicissitudes of politics and centrifugal forces, thereby giving governance stability and endurance.

Two, the Constitution places the AIS squarely in the middle of a federal, dual polity so that there is a sense of shared ownership between the Union and the states. Whereas recruitment is done centrally by the Union Government on the recommendations of

the Union Public Service Commission and the AIS are a part of the subjects listed in the Union List, all members of the AIS are divided into state-based cadres, with the Union borrowing officers from the state cadres. Each member treats the cadre of his/her allotment as the 'parent' cadre to which he/she belongs.

The allotted state is not just a region where an officer spends a substantial part of his/her career, it is a 'parent' that nurtures and grooms his/her career. The primary career management role is performed by the state and it is to the state that each officer reverts after a spell of central posting. This is a unique relationship and establishes a strong connection between an officer and the parent state cadre. When the Union borrows an officer for posts in the Union, each officer brings to the assignment in the Union the perspective he/she has gained in the state. This gives the AIS their distinctive federal character and is central to the constitutional scheme of the AIS.

The proposed amendment to the Cadre Rules fundamentally alters this relationship and makes a mockery of the delicate federal balance that the AIS are designed to maintain. The whole idea of the Centre not having a 'cadre' of its own but having to 'borrow' the services of an officer for specific periods at key senior management levels is destroyed if the State as a 'lender' has no authority on what it lends and on what terms and conditions, but the borrower, on the other hand, exercises superior rights over the lender. This is turning the federal arrangement upside down.

An important factor which determined the unique conceptual design of the AIS was the need to ensure that certain 'strategic' posts (as Dr Ambedkar called them) throughout the country, both at the Centre and in the states, would be the exclusive preserve of the members of the AIS. While the states would be free to have Civil Services of their own, there would be a set of strategic 'cadre' posts in every state to which only members of the AIS could be appointed. The intent was twofold—one, to have officers recruited centrally through a rigorous and impartial selection process to maintain uniformly high administrative standards throughout the

country; and two, to act as a check against fissiparous tendencies without disturbing the autonomy of the states within their own allotted spheres. Whatever else may be said about the AIS, their contribution to this spirit of 'unity in diversity' in administration has been singular. The proposed amendments in the Rules will adversely impact this distinctive design feature.

It is abundantly evident that the proposed amendments have not been thought through and are being rushed through without adequate federal consultation in a manner which shows the present establishment's—by now familiar—penchant for arbitrary exercise of centralised power. It is not possible to anticipate, at this stage, all the long term consequences of such a major design alteration but the following implications are self-evident:

- The shifting of the balance disproportionately in favour of the Union in matters of cadre deployment and cadre management will effectively convert the three AIS into three more Central Services.
- It is possible that AIS officers may view the interests of the state as secondary and subordinate to the Centre and to the political regime in power there. AIS officers working in the state will be reluctant to take any decision or action against the wishes of the political party in power at the Centre for fear of being summarily transferred to the Centre and harassed there. This will undermine the ability of the state governments to implement their policies and stand up against any arbitrary diktats of the Centre.
- There is a likelihood that states will consider the State Civil Services as more amenable to them and may treat AIS officers with suspicion and distrust.
- States may choose to reduce 'cadre' posts meant exclusively for the AIS and open them up to the State Services, thereby seriously undermining Dr Ambedkar's intention of maintaining uniformly high administrative standards across the country, free of any regional biases.

- If the AIS begin to play a lesser role in the states, it will also affect the unifying role which they play in the context of federal diversity—social, economic, and cultural (including administrative culture).
- It will allow greater scope for abuse of power by the Union Government so that whenever it is unhappy with the state government it can target AIS officers occupying strategic posts (e.g., Chief Secretary, Home Secretary, Director General of Police, Principal Chief Conservator of Forests, District Magistrate, Superintendent of Police etc.), withdraw them from their posts and place them elsewhere, thereby effectively derailing the functioning of the state administrative apparatus.
- The introduction of an element of compulsion in cadre management and doing away with a robust and healthy system of federal consultation, consent/concurrence and coordination will severely impact the morale of the AIS. This will eventually make careers in the AIS unattractive.

We are, therefore, of the view that the proposed set of amendments to the cadre rules of the three AIS are arbitrary, unreasonable and unconstitutional. They interfere with the basic structure of the Constitution of India as a Union of States and can cause irreparable damage to the one institution which Sardar Patel held as being the most critical to the unity of the country. It is important to remind ourselves of what he said, 'The Union will go, you will not have a united India if you have not a good All India Service which has the independence to speak out its mind, which has a sense of security…' (Speech to the Constituent Assembly, 10 October 1949). Will a government which holds the Sardar in higher esteem than any other figure in the history of the freedom movement pay heed to his words and drop the proposal to change the AIS Cadre Rules?

SATYAMEVA JAYATE
Constitutional Conduct Group (109 signatories)

OPEN STATEMENT ON INDIA'S PLUMMETING RANK IN KEY GLOBAL INDICES

15 November 2021

We are a group of former civil servants of the All India and Central Services who have worked with the Central and State Governments in the course of our careers. As a group, we have no affiliation with any political party but believe in impartiality, neutrality and commitment to the Constitution of India.

India's rank in the list of countries in the world across different indices has been slipping and that is a matter of enormous concern. Not only because the rankings, when taken cumulatively, show that the socio-economic situation in India has been steadily deteriorating, but also because the very things that make India an important democracy are slowly getting extinguished. Sadly, the Government of India (GoI), instead of expressing concern at such a decline and attempting to stop the deterioration, has been more concerned with attacking the reports and surveys and stating that they are wrong or deliberately misleading.

The latest such report showing a fall in India's ranking among countries is the Global Hunger Index, 2021. The Global Hunger Index (GHI) is prepared by European NGOs—Concern Worldwide and Welthungerhilfe—and measures and compares hunger in different countries of the world. According to earlier reports of the GHI, India had ranked 55 in 2015, but slipped to 94 in 2020 with Pakistan, Bangladesh and Nepal, all doing better than us. Even worse is the fact that, in 2021, in the course of a year, we have gone from rank 94 to rank 101, with only 15 countries ranking lower. The GHI measures hunger through four indicators, viz. undernourishment (i.e. the share of population whose caloric intake is insufficient), the percentage of wasting of children under 5 (i.e. children who have low weight for their height), the percentage of stunting for children (i.e. those children whose height is low for their age) as also the mortality rate for children under 5 years of age. While the

index may have some limitations, the argument by the GoI that it is 'devoid of ground reality' and is based on 'unscientific methodology' is misplaced. Government's own data from the National Family Health Survey, the Centre for Monitoring Indian Economy and from academic studies broadly confirm the statistics which are contested by the GoI.

Several other reports which rank the different countries of the world also do not show India in a very happy light. The Human Development Report of the UNDP measures three basic scales of human development: education, life expectancy and per capita income and ranks countries on that basis. The Human Development Index of 2020 shows India at rank 131 out of 189 countries, having slipped two spots from 2018. In fact, there has been practically no improvement since 2014, when, too, India ranked at 131.

As regards the status of women, the 2021 Global Gender Gap Report placed India at the dismal rank of 140, a drop of 28 spots, much below the 65th rank that Bangladesh is at. Moreover, the child sex ratio has fallen from 983 girls per 1000 boys in 1951 to 899 per 1000 in 2018, underlining the strong and pervasive male child preference in Indian society.

The World Happiness Report which is brought out by the UN Sustainable Development Solutions Network measures subjective wellbeing by relying on life evaluations, positive emotions and negative emotions. The World Happiness Report of 2020 also places India very low. It ranks India at 139 out of 149 countries. As per this report Pakistan is a happier country than India standing at rank 105. The ten countries behind India in 2020 are Burundi, Yemen, Tanzania, Haiti, Malawi, Lesotho, Botswana, Rwanda, Zimbabwe and Afghanistan.

The March, 2020, 'Democracy Report' of the widely respected V-Dem Institute in Sweden noted the increasing challenges for the media, civil society and the opposition to function freely under the current regime and observed that 'India has continued on a path of steep decline, to the extent it has almost lost its status as a democracy.'

In an unflattering grouping of India with Hungary, Poland and Brazil, the report argues that the 'first steps of autocratisation involve eliminating media freedom and curtailing civil society.' The report could not have been more explicit when it says: '…the dive in press freedom along with increasing repression of civil society in India [is] associated with the current Hindu-nationalist regime of Prime Minister Narendra Modi'.

V-Dem Institute is not alone in its assessment. The Democracy Index of the Economist Intelligence Unit noted a precipitous decline in India's position, which fell by 26 places from rank 27 out of 167 countries in 2014 to rank 53 in 2020. The United States Commission for International Religious Freedom flagged India as one of 15 'countries of particular concern' for the treatment of its minorities and has continued that label for this year as well. Finally, in the judgement of Freedom House—an NGO based in the US—India was described as 'partly free', downgraded from an earlier characterisation as 'free' and more specifically, Jammu and Kashmir was downgraded from being 'partly free' to 'not free'. The GoI sidestepped a discussion in Parliament on the Democracy Index's findings on the grounds that the issue was both trivial and also too sensitive. It dismissed the allegations of the US Commission for International Religious Freedom as 'biased and untrue', and brushed aside Freedom House's political judgements as 'inaccurate and distorted'.

India has become known internationally for criminalizing dissent and using laws relating to sedition and terrorism against those activists, media persons and opposition politicians who stand up against the ruling dispensation. Human rights violations continue apace and constitutional institutions like the Election Commission and the judiciary are undermined and eviscerated by all manner of means including the lure of post-retirement sinecures, intimidation and threats.

India has not done well with respect to levels of education, life expectancy, the status of girls/women and per capita income. Hunger

and malnutrition stalk the land. Moreover, democracy, freedom of speech, the right to protest and secularism, all basic features of the Indian Constitution, are in grave danger. There has to be a vigorous push back. These challenges have to be met head on by a vigilant civil society, the media, political opposition, people's movements and revitalized Constitutional institutions like the Election Commission and the judiciary. What is at stake is no less than the life and liberty of the poor and the disadvantaged and the hard won rights of the people of India under the Constitution.

SATYAMEVA JAYATE

Constitutional Conduct Group (83 signatories)

OPEN LETTER TO THE PRIME MINISTER—AMENDMENT TO CENTRAL CIVIL SERVICES PENSION RULES CURTAILS FREEDOM OF EXPRESSION OF RETIRED OFFICIALS

17 July 2021

Dear Prime Minister,

We are former officers of the All India and Central Services who have worked with the Central and State Governments in the course of our careers.

We have no political affiliation but have come together as the Constitutional Conduct Group because we believe in impartiality and neutrality and in safeguarding the values of the Indian Constitution. We were surprised, and deeply disturbed, by the recent amendment to the Central Pension Rules notified by the Ministry of Personnel, Public Grievances and Pensions on 31 May 2021. By this amendment, retired government servants who have worked in any intelligence or security related organisation included in the Second Schedule of the Right to Information Act 2005 have to take the clearance of the head of the organisation if they wish to make any publication after retirement, if such publication relates to and includes:

(i) domain of the organisation, including any reference or information about any personnel and his designation, and expertise or knowledge gained by virtue of working in that organisation;

(ii) sensitive information, the disclosure of which would prejudicially affect the sovereignty and integrity of India, the security, strategic, scientific or economic interests of the State, or relation with a foreign State or which would lead to incitement of an offence (publication here would, presumably, be an inclusive term encompassing verbal communication, though that is not very clear).

We are unable to understand why there is a need for such an amendment to the Central Pension Rules, when there already exists an Official Secrets Act 1923 and the State can, under it, prosecute officials and former officials who reveal information prejudicial to the State.

Pension is a right that accrues to every government servant for the service put in while in the government. It is subject only to future good conduct and cannot be taken away except for conviction for serious crime or grave misconduct. If writing about certain matters amounts to grave misconduct, the government can certainly take action, as per law, to deprive the former official of his or her pension.

The practice of retired bureaucrats writing their memoirs or articles on different aspects of the work done by them during their working years or commenting on current affairs using their 'domain' knowledge is universal and is appreciated the world over. Only those who have been involved in security related matters, internal or external, can speak with authority and credibility. Other domain experts, scholars and even interested members of the public look forward to such words of wisdom based on personal experience. It helps current practitioners to perform better.

It is true of India, as of any other country, that the government version of events, either current or past, is seen as the point of

view of the party in power and is not, necessarily, reflective of the whole truth. It is because of this that the views and memoirs of past practitioners, unencumbered by the constraints of office, have value.

The recent amendment to the Pension Rules attempts to impose a silence that will seriously affect scholarship and be a permanent impediment to an understanding of the imperatives of our security concerns. Officers who have spent a lifetime in security related matters are unlikely to be irresponsible and reveal sensitive secrets. The laudable objective of ensuring that retirees do not divulge any sensitive material to the detriment of the nation's security is best achieved by reiteration of the Official Secrets Act and stern action thereunder in case of infraction. And if the government is anxious to protect national security in keeping with the times and the Constitution of India, they should also carry out wide ranging consultations with political and civil society as well as the legal fraternity to find a replacement for the Official Secrets Act, which is itself in conflict with Article 19 of the Constitution.

We believe the framers of the new rules have not thought through the consequences of the order. It would mean that before publishing any article or speaking at any seminar or interview, the retired officers concerned would have to obtain prior permission. The reported assurance from the establishment that the order, in fact, makes it easier for the officers to contact their former employer to seek clarifications before they speak, is too fatuous to even merit comment. If strictly enforced, it could also mean, in effect, that no retiree from the specified services can participate in seminars or discussions, let alone engage in Track II dialogues, even if this is, possibly, not the intention.

In 2008, the UPA government tried to introduce such an order for officers who had served in the IB and RAW. The order was widely criticized and eventually withdrawn. The well-known lawyer A.G. Noorani had pointed out at that time that 'the fundamental right to freedom of speech, which includes the right to know, is not absolute. But the state can impose only "reasonable restrictions" on

the right, on grounds specified in Article 19 and only by "law" and not by an executive fiat'.

With the current order, the government has gone beyond the 2008 order of the UPA government. With this order, India also acquires the dubious distinction of being, possibly, the only major democratic country in the world today which effectively bars its employees from expressing their views after retirement. Curiously, this is being made to apply to all officers who have retired, even those who have retired decades ago. This is not merely a restraint on free speech, which it is, but an effort to entomb all relevant information and knowledge in the coffin of untrammelled state power. In 2008, the UPA government, perhaps persuaded of the wrongness of the order, did not finally bring the amendment into being. We hope that the present government would display similar sagacity.

SATYAMEVA JAYATE

Yours sincerely,

Constitutional Conduct Group (109 signatories)

OPEN LETTER TO THE PRIME MINISTER: INDIA NEEDS ACTION NOW

20 May 2021

Dear Prime Minister,

We, a group of former civil servants from the All India and Central Services, with a deep commitment to the Constitution of India and with no political affiliations, have written to you as well as other constitutional authorities on a number of occasions in the past, whenever we felt that executive actions violated the provisions of the Constitution. Today, in the midst of the COVID pandemic and the suffering that has engulfed the people of our country, we write to you in anguish as well as in anger. We are aware that this pandemic threatens the entire world and is not going to leave the citizens of

India untouched. And yet, what numbs our senses daily is not just the cries of the citizenry for medical assistance and the death toll in its thousands but the manifestly casual attitude of your government to the magnitude of the crisis and its implications for the mental and physical health of the community of Indians.

The steady erosion of the Cabinet system of governance, the worsening of federal relationships with the states, especially those governed by parties opposed to the party ruling at the Centre, the lack of informed consultation with experts and Parliamentary committees, the failure to take the timely advice of expert committees and the absence of effective coordination with state governments have had disastrous consequences for the poor and disadvantaged and now for the better off sections of society as well. Despite warnings from the international community and our own scientists, the breathing space between the first and the second waves was not used to augment critical resources such as medical staff, hospital beds, oxygen supplies, ventilators and drugs and other medical supplies. Even more inexcusably, no advance planning was done to secure adequate stocks of vaccines, despite India being one of the major vaccine suppliers to the world. The complacency displayed by you and your ministerial colleagues at various forums not only diverted attention from the looming threat but probably also contributed to both state governments and citizens letting down their guard at a crucial juncture. As a result, your Atmanirbhar Bharat is today compelled to seek the help of the outside world to lessen the agony inflicted on its own people by your government.

Right from the outset of the pandemic in March 2020, your government has never systematically assessed the funds that state governments would need to tackle the pandemic. The PM-CARES fund was set up when there was already a Prime Minister National Relief Fund in place. No disclosures have been made regarding the funds collected and the expenditures on various items. This fund attracted to itself moneys which would otherwise have gone from

corporates and the public to the various CM Relief Funds and to NGOs. Your government has not been prompt in paying outstanding GST dues to the states, which could have helped them defray COVID care expenses. At the same time, your government has incurred unnecessary expenditure on the Central Vista redevelopment project; these funds could well have been more gainfully used to tackle the crisis. On top of this, the harsh restrictions imposed on NGOs, especially those obtaining foreign contributions, have hampered their efforts in providing relief during the pandemic.

While the holding of elections to the legislative assemblies of four states and one union territory may have been unavoidable, you, Mr Prime Minister, and your party functionaries threw all caution to the winds by conducting huge public rallies in different states, when a restrained campaign by your party would have served as a salutary example to other political parties. The Kumbh Mela at Haridwar was conducted with scant regard for COVID safety regulations. With two such 'super spreader' events taking place just when the second surge of the virus was becoming a major threat, we are now witnessing the horrifying spectacle of the rampant spread of the COVID virus across the rural hinterland of the country.

Your government seems to be more concerned with managing the narrative of 'efficient' management of the COVID crisis rather than addressing the crucial issues at stake. Even authentic data on the testing carried out in different states, the number of positive cases, the number of persons hospitalised and mortality figures have not been publicly disseminated. This has had serious implications for the adequate provision of necessary medical facilities in different states as well as for devising appropriate measures in different states to control the spread of the pandemic.

We urge the Government of India to take the following actions immediately:

- Provide for free, universal vaccination to all citizens of India. Government of India must centralize the procurement of

vaccines from all available sources and supply them to state governments and all other implementing agencies.

- Coordinate effectively with state governments to ensure the adequacy of oxygen facilities, essential lifesaving drugs and equipment and hospital beds in all States of the country.
- Greatly ramp up RT-PCR testing in both rural and urban areas.
- Make adequate funds available to the States for provision of medical facilities and stop expenditures on non-essential items like the Central Vista redevelopment project.
- Draw on the existing surplus foodgrain stocks to provide free rations to the families of the marginalised and deprived sections of society as well as unorganised labour who have lost their employment opportunities until the ferocity of the pandemic and the hunger and livelihood crisis abates.
- Fully provide, in consultation with state governments, for existing nutrition schemes for school going children and supplementary nutrition for mothers and children in the pre-school age groups. .
- Provide a monthly income support for the current financial year to the needy sections of society to enable them to meet contingent expenses and unforeseen emergencies. Economists have recommended Rs 7,000 per month per household, equivalent to minimum wages.
- Immediately remove the FCRA restrictions imposed on NGOs so that they can avail of funds provided by foreign governments and charities for Covid management and other related activities.
- Place all data in the public domain and ensure that evidence-based policy measures are implemented.

Constitute an all-party committee at the central level to advise on and review all government decisions and monitor the control of the pandemic in different areas of the country.

While the above constitute actions to be taken at the politico-administrative level, the most important action relates to building up the confidence and morale of a population hard hit by the loss of their near and dear ones. Compassion and caring have to be the cornerstones of government policy. History will judge our society, your government and, above all, you personally, on how effectively we handle this crisis.

SATYAMEVA JAYATE

Yours sincerely,

Constitutional Conduct Group (116 signatories)

OPEN STATEMENT—GOVERNMENT OF NATIONAL CAPITAL TERRITORY OF DELHI (AMENDMENT) ACT, 2021

9 April 2021

We are a group of former civil servants of the All India Services and Central Services who have worked for decades with the Central and State Governments. As a group, we have no affiliation with any political party but are committed to the values and principles enshrined in the Constitution of India.

In India's democracy, we have adopted a republican structure and the Westminster model, in which the Governor is a titular head, acting on the aid and advice of the Council of Ministers. This constitutionally mandated structure has been repeatedly upheld and endorsed by the Honourable Supreme Court. That the legislature is supreme within its functional powers is a cardinal federal principle. Elected representatives link the will of the people with that of the Government, regardless of whether citizens live in a State or a Union Territory.

The demand for full Statehood for Delhi has been consistently championed by all political parties, even though it is a National Capital Territory that may necessitate differential treatment. That

led to the insertion of Article 239 AA into the Constitution of India, establishing an elected legislature for Delhi. Ambiguities in the interpretation of Article 239 AA have been clarified by the Honourable Supreme Court in its Constitution Bench judgment of 4th July 2018 (*Govt Of NCT of Delhi v. Union of India*)

The opening lines of Article 239 AA states, 'The Council of Ministers shall be collectively responsible to the Legislative Assembly.' Interpreting the scope of this provision, the Honourable Supreme Court ruled that 'the Lieutenant Governor has not been entrusted with any independent decision making power. He has to either act on the "aid and advice" of the Council of Ministers or he is bound to implement the decision taken by the President on a reference being made by him' (Para 277).

However, the recently enacted GNCTD (Amendment) Act 2021, strikes at the root of these principles and renders null the democratic right of the citizens of Delhi.

The Statements and Objectives of the Act states; 'It further seeks to ensure that the Lieutenant Governor is necessarily granted an opportunity to exercise the power entrusted to him under proviso to clause (4) of article 239AA of the Constitution, in select category of cases and also to make rules in matters which incidentally encroach upon matters falling outside the purview of the Legislative Assembly.'

First, a new sub-section has been added to Section 21 of the GNCTD Act, changing the definition of the 'Government' to mean the 'Lieutenant Governor.' This provision appears to have turned parliamentary democracy on its head.

Second, Section 33 of the act, which relates to 'conduct of its business' states that the State legislature can enact rules 'which shall not be inconsistent with the Rules of Procedure and Conduct of Business in the House of the People'. All state legislatures have the right to frame their own rules; indeed, the rules of the Delhi Assembly are nearly identical with those of the UP Assembly. Even the Lok Sabha and Rajya Sabha Rules are not identical.

Third, Section 44 of the Act now states that before taking any executive action, the elected government shall have to take prior permission of the Lieutenant Governor, even in matters in which the Assembly has the right to make laws. This is in direct contravention of the Supreme Court's judgment, where it stated; 'A conjoint reading of clauses (3)(a) and (4) of Article 239AA, divulges that the executive power of the Government of NCTD is co-extensive with the legislative power of the Delhi Legislative Assembly and accordingly, the executive power of the Council of Ministers of Delhi spans over all subjects in the Concurrent list and all, but three excluded subjects, in the State List.' (para 277(XV)).

By curtailing the powers of the Delhi Assembly and subordinating the executive power of the elected government to the Lieutenant Governor, Parliament has negated the provisions of Article 239 AA of the Constitution without amending the Constitution, but merely through amendments to the GNCTD Act. This is an unfortunate move and bad in law. It deprives Delhi's citizens of the right to govern themselves in matters such as health, education, water, power, electric supply and roads. There is no justification to concentrate all powers of governance in the Union Government merely because Delhi is the country's capital. This move will not only paralyse governance in Delhi, much to the detriment of public interest, but also have grave repercussions on how federal governance is carried out in India.

We are deeply concerned that Parliament should pass a law which appears to make a mockery of constitutional provisions and their interpretation by the Supreme Court. We recognise that the same strategy of ramming through changes in law, with no consultation with the legislature or discussion with other political parties, was gone through when Article 370 was abrogated with respect to Jammu and Kashmir. We fear that a pattern is being established by which similar strategies could be adopted to destroy the federal principles on the basis of which India's governance has been structured. The dangers of unilateral decision-making to establish a culture of

unitary politics will put federal democracy in danger. This would violate the basic structure of the Constitution.

We sincerely hope that the Honourable Supreme Court, taking note of the fact that this law violates their own order, will declare it unconstitutional and restore the status quo ante.

SATYAMEVA JAYATE

Constitutional Conduct Group (76 signatories)

LETTER TO THE CHIEF MINISTER OF PUNJAB REGARDING THE FARMERS' MOVEMENT AND THE NEWLY ENACTED FARM LAWS

19 March 2021

To
Capt. Amarinder Singh
Hon'ble Chief Minister of Punjab,
Chandigarh

Dear Shri Amarinder Singhji,

The farmers' movement has entered the fourth month now and despite attempts on the part of the ruling establishment at the Centre to show that it is losing steam, ground reports show otherwise. The Centre's continued intransigence and its refusal to yield any ground to the demand for the repeal of the three laws appears to be calculated to wait out the protests until such time as the movement dissipates itself. This is a dangerous strategy and as you have been rightly pointing out in your public expressions, it is fraught with security risks especially in a sensitive border state like Punjab.

Irrespective of the merits or otherwise of the three laws pushed through by the Government in unseemly haste, one thing is very clear—the enactments are in complete violation of the federal structure of the Constitution of India and have given short shrift

to democratic processes of consultation and consensus building. While the erosion of the federal system has been going on for several decades now, the systematic assault on it since 2014 has been far more pronounced. The enactment of the three laws was just the latest example of the contempt the Centre has for our federal architecture.

We, the signatories to this letter, annex a detailed note (Annexure 1) on this alarming trend and also highlight how the institutional mechanisms for federal policy coordination, such as the Inter State Council (hereinafter referred to as 'the Council'), which should have been central to the decision making process were disregarded in the case of the enactment of the three farm laws (as they have been for long in most matters requiring federal coordination). The absence of federal consultation, coordination and consensus building is at the root of the current crisis and no resolution is possible unless the centrality of federal policy coordination is restored. This can happen only if the states assert themselves and demand a bigger role in policy making at the national level.

Annexure 1 speaks for itself and we urge you to give it your detailed consideration. Our earnest plea is for you and the Chief Ministers of states most affected by the crisis to take the initiative to seek the following:

- An urgent meeting of the Council to discuss the complete range of issues relating to the current crisis;
- The constitution of a Committee of selected Chief Ministers (on the lines of the Empowered Committee of Finance Ministers for the introduction of GST) under the aegis of the Council that, in turn, will undertake an extensive and comprehensive process of stakeholder consultation;
- Make the issue of the repeal of the three laws a subset of the larger issues of agricultural reform to be gone into by the proposed Committee to avoid it becoming a binary conflict.

The disputed laws should be kept in abeyance till such time that the proposed Committee completes its task and a consensus emerges

on the prospective legislative framework and strategy required to bring about agricultural reforms.

Except in the initial years of its constitution, the Council has rarely been used for the purposes for which it was set up. Should you agree to lead this initiative for its revival, it will mark a new beginning towards restoring federal processes of governance and policy making. The current crisis can be turned into an opportunity for doing that.

As past experience of making use of the Council for inter-state and centre-state policy coordination has been very limited, most people carry many misconceptions about its status and its usefulness. In this context we would like to stress the following:

- It is necessary to dispel the impression that the Council is an appendage of the Ministry of Home Affairs and under its control. It is not. It is an independent institution under Article 263 of the Constitution and was established not under the Rules of Business of the Central Government but by a separate Presidential Order under Article 263 (Annexure 2). It derives its authority from the Constitution and has its own independent rules and procedures.
- As a Chief Minister you occupy a position of equality in this forum. A reference made by you has to be taken up albeit with the approval of the Chairman for its inclusion in the agenda of the Council.
- The Council is mandated to meet thrice a year and the word used is 'shall'. It is a pity that this mandatory requirement has never been met; yet, because the provision exists, a request for a meeting from you cannot be turned down, especially if there are other Chief Ministers also backing the proposal.
- The proposal to have the Council constitute a Chief Ministers' Committee to investigate the issues further, in accordance with the remit of the Council, should also find acceptance as it avoids a politically confrontationist approach and makes

mediation politic and expedient. It should also find broad acceptance with the Kisan Unions because a Chief Ministers' Committee will be seen as independent and impartial and carry greater credibility than the Committee appointed by the Supreme Court, which, in any case, has been a nonstarter because of its rejection by the Kisan Unions.

- The meetings of the Council are held 'in camera' and therefore it will be possible to avoid the temptation to strike political postures and take hardened, polarised positions for public consumption. That should make it easier to find a way out of the current impasse.

For the reasons given above, we think this is the right time to take such an initiative. Even if it yields no immediate results, it will signal the importance that needs to be attached to make the states active participants in federal policy making processes. If the Council is used by the Chief Ministers of states to reassert their position, it will have set a very healthy precedent.

As the Chief Minister of the state with which the farmers' movement is popularly identified, we believe that the lead in taking this initiative should come from you. More so, your stature as a senior political leader at the national level, with an extraordinary degree of public acceptability, will give the initiative the gravitas and the importance it deserves.

The laid down procedure for the conduct of the business of the Council (Annexure 3) requires the Government of a state to make a formal reference to the Secretary of the Council with a self-contained note setting out the issues involved and the reasons for making the reference. This is then examined by the Council Secretariat and submitted to the Chairman (the Prime Minister) for obtaining his/her orders for inclusion in the Council meeting agenda. We hope that this can be done by the state government under your direction and that you can, in parallel, write to the Prime Minister as the Council Chairperson and seek his personal attention to give the reference a

high priority. Simultaneously, you may consider speaking to some other Chief Ministers to also write to the Prime Minister endorsing your proposal. We leave that to your judgment and, should you agree, we can forward them copies of our communication for a better appreciation of the proposal, but only if you think that to be appropriate.

We are writing to you as members of the Constitutional Conduct Group—a group of former civil servants of the All India and Central Civil Services who have come together because of our shared concern over the erosion of constitutional values and principles in public policy and governance and the need to make efforts to arrest this decline. We hold no allegiance to any political party or association.

We do hope that you will give our letter your most earnest consideration.

SATYAMEVA JAYATE

Yours faithfully,

Constitutional Conduct Group (90 signatories, as below)

ANNEXURE 1

Detailed Note on the Inter State Council and Its Relevance

Despite attempts by the ruling political establishment to malign the farmers' protests and the stray episode of a disruption in public order on 26 January during the protest rally/parade organised by the Sanyukta Kisan Morcha, it remains one of the most remarkable, peaceful, non-violent people's movements of our times. Its extraordinary energy, purposefulness and inspirational quality needs to be harnessed to focus on the restoration of those constitutional values which were substantially eroded with the enactment of the three purported farm 'reform' laws.

One of the most significant aspects of the farmers' movement has been that it has foregrounded not merely the specific threats to the

agrarian ecosystem posed by the move to disrupt existing institutions like the APMC* that make it easier for conglomerate private capital to dominate the food supply chain and eventually gain control of the production and marketing of agricultural produce, but the larger threat to democracy and the federal architecture of governance. Under the pretext of exercising jurisdiction in relation to 'trade in foodstuffs' as a part of the Concurrent List in the Constitution, the Centre surreptitiously usurped legislative powers which belong exclusively to the states—a domain of legislation from which the Centre is explicitly excluded.

Typical of its modus operandi in recent times, however, the Centre paid no heed to these constitutional checks and proceeded to push through a set of legislative measures which damage the foundations of our federal architecture. The pandemic was the pretext to bring in these laws via the ordinance route, without consultation and without any attempt at consensus building among multiple stakeholders. Brute majority was used as a means to pass the laws in the Lok Sabha and, when there were doubts about being able to secure a majority in the Rajya Sabha, the laws were passed by a voice vote without conducting an actual count of the votes through a 'division'.

It is a pity that, over the years, despite repeated assaults on federal and democratic processes, the states (even those ruled by Opposition parties) as well as the principal opposition political parties have been quiescent. The erosion of the federal structure by successive Central Governments, whether of the UPA or the NDA, has never been projected as a major political issue. No electoral battles have been fought on it and federalism does not feature as an important item in any party election manifesto.

---

* Agricultural Produce Market Committees (APMC) is the marketing board established by the state governments in order to eliminate the exploitation incidences of the farmers by the intermediaries, where they are forced to sell their produce at extremely low prices.

In this context, it is remarkable that the farmers' movement has stepped in to give the federal dimension a sharp political focus. The insistence on total repeal of laws rather than on a compromise settlement reflects the farmers' rejection of the Central Government's unitarian approach. They know better than so many so-called 'experts' that agriculture is a sector in which policies have to be specific to a state and its unique agro-climatic and ecological conditions and that centralised and autocratic decision making has to be steadfastly opposed. Only by creating conditions in which a more federalist, a more participatory and democratic way of decision making is established can there be any resolution of the challenges facing Indian agriculture.

While many members of the urban intelligentsia find the farmers' insistence on repeal of laws an unnecessarily maximalist position, the fact is that it is the Government's intransigence and its refusal to give up its centralising, authoritarian ways of taking decisions which is 'maximalist'. On their part the farmers have maintained from day one that the Centre had no business to legislate on a matter which was clearly the domain of the states and that they object to a 'reform' measure being imposed on them unilaterally, especially when they themselves never asked for it. The supreme irony is that the Government which created a problem which never existed is not held accountable but the farmers who oppose its arbitrariness are expected to be reasonable. That the farmers have remained steadfast and unyielding is the strength of this movement and this needs to be respected.

Under the circumstances it appears extremely difficult that the current stalemate can end anytime soon. A continued confrontation, however, is fraught with dangerous consequences, especially if the anger spills over and turns violent. A Government at war with its own people threatens democracy fundamentally, especially when there is a Government which has no qualms about using fierce repression and brutality to quell any kind of democratic resistance.

It is encouraging that, while in terms of optics, the movement may have suffered a temporary setback by the events of 26 January, in actuality it has gained momentum and strength both across the caste, class and gender divide as well as across regions. It is no longer possible to dismiss it as a Punjab-centric protest of limited electoral significance. Publicly, the Central Government may continue to be in denial about the impact of the movement, but it shows that they are under pressure. Each Maha Panchayat, each rally is now attended by thousands and the increasing participation of women from traditionally patriarchal societies is a sign that the movement has touched a chord with the rural population and that this can upset the electoral calculations of the party in power.

In many ways, it is the right time to press for a resolution which is not an attempt at an unsatisfactory compromise, but becomes an opportunity to achieve the following:

- Enabling the states to come together to reclaim the legislative space usurped by the Centre at least in those matters which are their exclusive domain under the Constitution;
- Emboldening the states to find ways to reaffirm the federal principles underlying the Constitution, reject unitarian decisions imposed on them and find ways in which they can join up on matters of common interest (e.g. agriculture) to evolve a framework, set of norms, standards and guidelines within which each state frames its own laws, policies, programmes and strategies.
- Ensuring that stakeholder participation, consultation, and consensus building is inbuilt in the policy making process—before the policies are made, not after.

The Constitution provides a perfect platform/institutional mechanism for achieving these objectives in a manner which is completely federal. That institutional mechanism is the Inter State Council, established by a Presidential Order in May 1990, under Article 263 of the Constitution. The remit of the Council, of which

the Prime Minister is the Chairperson and all the Chief Ministers its members, is the following:

1. Investigating and discussing such subjects in which some or all of the states or the Union and one or more of the states have a common interest, as may be brought up before it;
2. Making recommendations upon any such subject and, in particular, recommendations for the better coordination of policy and action with respect to that subject; and
3. Deliberating upon such other matters of general interest to the states as may be referred by the Chairman to the Council.

The Council has some unique features which make it different from other institutions like the NITI Aayog or the erstwhile Planning Commission:

- It is the only inter-governmental platform specifically dedicated to policy coordination which derives its authority from the Constitution.
- Its architecture is built on an equality of relationship between the Prime Minister and the Chief Ministers.
- It has a flexible, open ended remit which does not restrict its sphere of activity.
- It is required to 'investigate' and research into issues before taking them up for deliberation.
- Stakeholder consultation is inbuilt into its procedures.
- By virtue of its Constitutional position it is equidistant from the Centre as well as the states.
- The prescribed procedure for the Council functioning requires the discussions/deliberations to be 'in camera' so that the tendency to strike postures for public consumption or to seek popularity are curbed and the discussions can be candid, held in a collegial environment and be free of rancour.
- It has a permanent secretariat, headed by an officer who in terms of the original scheme was meant to be of the same

rank and seniority as the Cabinet Secretary reporting directly to the Prime Minister (as the Chairperson of the Council) and have the powers to call for papers from any Department of the Union Government or the State Governments.

- It can devote unstinted attention to long term policy issues unencumbered as it is from having to deliver short term outcomes or deal with crisis management.

There is an impression that the Inter State Council is an appendage of the Ministry of Home Affairs and whether by intent or by default nothing has been done to dispel this impression. The Centre is so used to unitarian and unilateral thinking that it avoids making use of an institution which would give the states a bigger role in policy making. It has therefore seen to it that, in practice, the status of the Council is reduced to that of a subordinate office. The states themselves have never taken ownership of the Council to insist that all policy matters which impact on the states should be deliberated on by the Council before any decision is taken. Had this been done, the crisis caused by abandoning federalist approaches to decision making would not have taken place.

Whatever be the reasons for the dormancy of the Council, the current crisis offers a perfect opportunity to revive it and bring the states together to have an agreed framework (including framework legislation) within which each state devises its own policies and programmes. It is vital that the initiative for this is led by the states and not by the Centre for four reasons. One, that the Constitutional scheme regarding division of roles between the Centre and the states remains sacrosanct. Two, that the states take complete ownership of the recommendations that are made. Three, that a precedent gets established for the states to come together for an experiment in 'joined up' governance which is capable of being achieved without dominant Central control and direction. Four, that federalist practices get embedded in processes of governance and keep a check on forces of centralism and authoritarianism.

To give effect to the suggestions made above, it is proposed that a group of Chief Ministers be requested to make a formal reference to the Prime Minister as the Chairperson of the Council to demand that a meeting of the Council be convened to discuss the full range of issues arising out of the farmer's movement. It is the prerogative of every member to have an issue brought up before the Council albeit the Chairman has to approve such a reference. In the last two decades there is no precedent of a meeting being sought by any of the members but it is most unlikely that if such a reference is made it will be turned down.

The proposal before the Council in such a meeting should be to establish a Committee of Chief Ministers to investigate and make recommendations, inter alia, on the following:

- Alternative legislation in lieu of the three contested Central Laws to be undertaken by the States to reform the functioning of agricultural markets (whether by enacting new laws or by amending existing laws) so as to remove restrictions, if any, on free trade in agricultural commodities; to incentivise investment in post-harvest infrastructure for better price realisation for the farmer and for ensuring complete transparency in buyer/ seller transactions;
- Ways of guaranteeing off take at prices which are stable and remunerative and ensuring that the system of having a Minimum Support Price for all crops is made effective throughout the country.
- Ways in which farmers can be protected against manipulative and restrictive trade practices and unforeseen market failures.
- An agreed enabling framework/template within which State specific laws can operate.
- Policy interventions to support new ways of pooling of resources for agricultural production, harvesting and marketing especially through cooperatives and/or producer companies to improve farm incomes and productivity.

- Incentives for adopting ecologically and environmentally sustainable practices, reducing energy and material intensity, conserving water, maintaining soil health and disincentives for wasteful use of resources.
- Ways of strengthening S&T capacity at the grassroots to enable the use of advanced technologies (including GIS based decision support systems and modelling tools) for making location specific choices on what, when and how to grow factoring in the need for combating impact of climate change, increasing incomes and productivity, and meeting the needs of changing markets.
- Finding ways in which financial assistance can be provided to the States through the Finance Commission for relevant infrastructure creation specific to each State/District/Block/ Village Panchayat.

The suggested Committee of Chief Ministers on Agricultural Reforms should be assisted by a multidisciplinary team of eminent experts. A provision exists in the Inter State Council working procedure for engaging such persons/ institutions to carry out research and provide inputs to the Council or any of its Committees. The Chief Minister's Committee should have the freedom to engage/ associate experts of their choice to ensure that they are bipartisan and ideologically neutral.

Many Task Forces, Commissions, Expert Committees etc. have gone into these issues in considerable depth at several times and made very important recommendations. As is usual with most such efforts, however, the failure to follow a carefully structured process of stakeholder participation and consultation at every stage of the deliberations has meant that no one, especially the states which are expected to implement the recommendations, have ever owned them up. This is primarily a failure of process design. Ideally, if the process of problem identification and definition at the very first stage, i.e. before undertaking the investigation, follows a participatory process

and the research is also participatory, it is possible to achieve a consensus even in the most contentious of issues. It would be important for the proposed Chief Minister's Committee as well as the group of experts to follow a process design which is meticulously structured so as to be continuously consultative and participative. Care would have to be taken to avoid the tyranny of experts and allow for farmers' groups to be involved at every stage of the process. Process design is critical.

The proposed Committee of Chief Ministers should be chaired by one of them—ideally from the states most affected by the farmers' movement, say Punjab—and while the Centre may be represented through the Agriculture Minister, the Centre should not be seen as a dominant actor. The Committee should use the window offered by the Centre to keep the contested laws in abeyance to complete their task, at the end of which the Central Laws should be capable of being replaced by State Laws following an accepted framework design.

The above proposals offer a way out of the current impasse and if successful will:

- Restore the sanctity of the federal division of powers and responsibilities.
- Use the energy and the spirit of this extraordinary farmers' movement to a constructive and creative end.
- Set an example for processes of governance to become democratic, consultative and participative.
- Revive institutions intended to conserve and promote the federal core of the Constitution.

ANNEXURE 2

The Gazette of India

असाधारण

EXTRAORDINARY

भाग II—खण्ड 3—उप-खण्ड (i)

PART II—Section 3—Sub-section (i)

प्राधिकार से प्रकाशित

PUBLISHED BY AUTHORITY

सं. 200] नई दिल्ली, सोमवार, मई 28, 1990/ज्येष्ठ 7, 1912

No. 200] NEW DELHI, MONDAY, MAY 28, 1990/JYAISTHA 7, 1912

इस भाग में भिन्न पृष्ठ संख्या दी जाती है जिससे कि यह अलग संकलन के रूप में रखा जा सके

Separate Paging is given to this Part in order that it may be filed as a separate compilation

गृह मंत्रालय

आदेश

नई दिल्ली, 28 मई, 1990

सा. का. नि. 512 (अ).—राष्ट्रपति द्वारा जारी किया गया निम्नलिखित आदेश सर्वसाधारण के सूचनार्थ प्रकाशित किया जा रहा है :

यतः राष्ट्रपति को ऐसा प्रतीत होता है कि अंतर-राज्य परिषद् के गठन से लोकहित की रक्षा होगी;

अतः, अब, संविधान के अनुच्छेद 263 द्वारा प्रदत्त शक्तियों का प्रयोग करते हुए, राष्ट्रपति एतद्द्वारा निम्नलिखित आदेश करते हैं, अर्थात् :—

1. संक्षिप्त नाम और प्रारम्भ—(1) इस आदेश को अन्तर-राज्य परिषद आदेश, 1990 कहा जायेगा। (2) यह आदेश तत्काल लागू होगा

2. परिषद् की संरचना—एक अंतर-राज्य परिषद् (जिसे इसमें इसके बाद परिषद् कहा जाएगा) गठित की जायेगी जिसमें निम्नलिखित शामिल होंगे ;

(क) प्रधान मंत्री;

(ख) सभी राज्यों के मुख्य मंत्री;

(ग) विधान सभा वाले संघ-राज्य क्षेत्रों के मुख्य मंत्री तथा विधान सभा बगैर संघ-राज्य क्षेत्रों के प्रशासक;

(घ) प्रधान मंत्री द्वारा नामजद किए जाने वाले केन्द्रीय मंत्री परिषद् के केबिनेट स्तर के छह मंत्रीगण।

(नोट : केन्द्र सरकार के अन्य मंत्रियों तथा स्वतंत्र प्रभार वाले राज्य मंत्रियों को उस स्थिति में आमंत्रित किया जा सकता है जब उनके द्वारा देखे जा रहे विषय से संबंधित किसी मद पर विचार किया जाना हो)।

(1)

1379GI/90

3. परिषद के अध्यक्ष—प्रधान मंत्री इस परिषद् के अध्यक्ष होंगे तथा वह परिषद की बैठकों की अध्यक्षता करेंगे :

बशर्ते कि अगर किसी बैठक की अध्यक्षता करने में प्रधान-मंत्री असमर्थ हों तो वह बैठक की अध्यक्षता करने के लिए कैबिनेट स्तर के किसी अन्य केन्द्रीय मंत्री को नामज़द कर सकते हैं।

4. परिषद् कर्तव्य—परिषद् सिफारिश करने वाली निकाय होगी तथा, इस क्षमता में, यह निम्नलिखित कर्तव्यों का निष्पादन करेगी, अर्थात् :—

(क) ऐसे विषयों का अन्वेषण तथा उन पर विचार करना जिनमें कुछ या सभी राज्यों या संघ और एक या एक से अधिक राज्यों का समान हित निहित हो; तथा जिसे इस परिषद् के सामने लाया जाये;

(ख) ऐसे किसी विषय पर सिफारिश करना तथा विशेष-कर उस विषय के संदर्भ में नीति तथा कार्रवाई के बेहतर समन्वय हेतु सिफारिश करना; तथा

(ग) राज्यों के हितों से संबंधित ऐसे मामलों पर विचार करना जिन्हें अध्यक्ष महोदय द्वारा परिषद् के सामने रखा जाय।

5. परिषद् की कार्य-विधि—परिषद् अपने कार्य के संचालन में निम्नलिखित प्रक्रिया का अनुपालन करेगी, अर्थात् :—

(क) परिषद् अपने समक्ष लाए जाने वाले मुद्दों का पता लगाने तथा उनका चयन करने हेतु दिशा-निर्देश अपनाएगी।

(ख) परिषद् प्रत्येक वर्ष ऐसे समय और स्थान पर कम-से-कम अपनी तीन बैठकें करेगी जैसाकि इस निमित्त अध्यक्ष द्वारा नियत किया जाएगा;

(ग) परिषद् की बैठकें गुप्त रूप से होंगी;

(घ) परिषद् की बैठक के लिए 10 सदस्यों (अध्यक्ष सहित) का कोरम होगा;

(ङ) बैठक में परिषद् के विचारार्थ आने वाले सभी प्रश्नों पर सर्वसम्मति से निर्णय लिया जाएगा और सर्व-सम्मति के बारे में अध्यक्ष का निर्णय अंतिम होगा; और

(च) परिषद् अपने कार्य के संचालन के लिए ऐसी अन्य कार्य-विधि अपनाएगी जिसे वह केन्द्रीय सरकार के अनुमोदन से समय-समय पर निर्धारित करे।

6. परिषद् का सचिवालय—परिषद् का अपना सचिवालय होगा जिसमें ऐसे अधिकारी तथा स्टाफ होगा जिन्हें अध्यक्ष नियुक्त करना उचित समझें।

आर. वेंकटरामन, राष्ट्रपति

कैम्प शिमला,

दिनांक : 25 मई, 1990

[एफ सं. IV-11017/3/90-सी.एस.आर.]

MINISTRY OF HOME AFFAIRS

ORDER

New Delhi, the 28th May, 1990

G.S.R. 512(E).—The following Order by the President is published for general information.

Whereas it appears to the President that the public interest would be served by the establishment of an Inter-State Council;

Now, therefore, in exercise of the powers conferred by Article 263 of the Constitution, the President hereby makes the following order, namely :—

1. Short title and commencement.—(1) This order may be called the Inter-State Council Order, 1990.

(2) It shall come into force at once.

2. Composition of the Council.—There shall be an Inter-State Council (hereinafter referred to as the Council) consisting of the;

(a) Prime Minister;

(b) Chief Ministers of all States ;

(c) Chief Ministers of Union territories having a Legislative Assembly and Administrators of Union territories not having a Legislative Assembly;

(d) Six Ministers of Cabinet rank in the Union Council of Ministers to be nominated by the Prime Minister.

(Note : Other Ministers and Ministers of State having independent charge in the Union Government may be invited as and when any item relating to a subject under their charge is to be discussed).

3. Chairman of the Council.—The Prime Minister shall be the Chairman of the Council and shall preside over the meetings of the Council :

Provided that when the Prime Minister is unable to preside over any meeting, he may nominate by Union Minister of Cabinet rank to preside over the meeting.

4. Duties of the Council.—The Council shall be a recommendatory body and in that capacity, shall perform the following duties, namely:—

(a) investigating and discussing such subjects, in which some or all of the States or the Union and one or more of the States have a common interest, as may be brought up before it ;

(b) making recommendations upon any such subject and in particular recommendations for the better coordination of policy and action with respect to that subject; and

(c) deliberating upon such other matters of general interest to the States as may be referred by the Chairman to the Council.

5. Procedure of the Council.—The Council shall, in the conduct of its business, observe the following procedure, namely :—

(a) the Council shall adopt guidelines for identifying and selecting issues to be brought up before it;

(b) the Council shall meet at least thrice in every year and at such time and place as the Chairman may appoint in this behalf;

(c) the meetings of the Council shall be held in camera;

(d) ten members (including the Chairman) shall form the quorum for a meeting of the Council;

(e) all questions which may come up for consideration of the Council at a meeting shall be decided by consensus and the decision the Chairman as to consensus shall be final; and

(f) the Council shall, in the conduct of its business, observe such other procedure as it may, with the approval of the Central Government, lay down from time to time.

6. Secretariat of the Council.—The Council shall have a Secretariat comprising of such officers and staff as the Chairman may think fit to appoint.

R. VENKATARAMAN,
President

Camp Shimla,
Dated, the 25th May, 1990.

[F. No. IV/11017/3/90-CSR]
NARESH CHANDRA, Home Secy.

ANNEXURE 3

Procedure for Conduct of Business of the Inter-State Council

In pursuance of clause (f) of paragraph 5 of the Inter-State Council Order, 1990, the Council hereby lays down, with the approval of the Central Government, the following other procedure to be observed by it in the conduct of its business, namely:

1. Reference to the Council: If any matter is sought up before the Council by the Central Government or by the Government of any State or Union territory, a formal reference shall be made to the Council, addressed to the Secretary of the Council, with a self-contained note setting out—the issue or issues involved and the reasons for making the reference, together with supporting documents, if any; and the constitutional and legal implications of the said issue or issues.

2. Examination of reference: (a) On receipt of the reference, the Secretariat of the Council shall examine it in all its aspects, inter-alia, with reference to the guidelines adopted by the Council and other relevant material; (b) After reference has been examined, the Secretary of the Council shall submit the case to the Chairman with his recommendation for obtaining the orders of the Chairman as to whether the issue or issues raised therein should be included in the Agenda for the meeting of the Council.
3. Inclusion of matters of general interest in the Agenda: It shall be open to the Secretariat to take up any proposal relating to a matter of general interest as referred to in clause (c) of paragraph 4 of the aforesaid Order and submit the same to the Chairman, for his orders as to its inclusion in the Agenda. If the Chairman approves such inclusion, the procedure in relation to such matter will be the same as for references received under paragraph 1 above.
4. Brief for the Meeting: If, under the orders of the Chairman, a matter is included in the Agenda for a meeting of the Council, the Secretariat shall proceed to prepare a comprehensive Brief for the meeting which should include a note explaining the issues involved in the matter under reference, the historical or other background, the constitutional and legal implications, the views of various authorities, institutions and other consulted by the Secretary on the said matter.
5. Meetings: The meetings of the Council shall be held in Delhi or any other convenient place determined by the Chairman.
6. Notice of meetings: Notice of every meeting shall be given to the Members at least ten days before the date of such meeting and such notice shall be accompanied by a copy of the Agenda and other papers required by the Chairman to be circulated.
7. Attendance at Meetings: The meetings of the Council shall be attended by its members. Others, including officials, may

attend the Council's meeting only with the prior approval of the Chairman.

8. Agenda: (a) The items of business to be transacted at any meeting of the Council shall be listed in an Agenda prepared with the approval of the Chairman; (b) As far as possible the items of business shall be taken up for discussion in the order in which they are set out in the Agenda. No business, not included in the Agenda, shall be taken up at the meeting without the leave of the Chairman.
9. Discussion: (a) When any item in the agenda is taken up for discussion, the Chairman may initiate the discussion explaining the points involved or may request any Member concerned to do so and the Chairman may fix time to the Members for presenting their views; (b) The discussion on any matter before the Council should be confined to the specific issue involved and reading prepared speeches may be avoided.
10. Report on proceedings: (a) The Secretary shall cause to be prepared a report of the proceedings of the Council at each of its meetings in such form and manner as the Chairman may, from time to time, direct; (b) A copy of the report of the proceedings shall be forwarded as soon as possible to the Central Government, the Governments of the States and Union territories together with a copy of the formal recommendations, if any, made by the Council.
11. Record: The record to be maintained by the Secretariat shall consist of—(a) the reference and all papers received under paragraph 1 for consideration of the matter; (b) all papers considered by the Council, including minutes of meetings held by the Secretary with officers and other authorities referred to in clause (a) of paragraph 15; (c) the final decision of the Council; (d) reports, if any, regarding action on the recommendations of the Council.
12. Press Briefing: At the conclusion of a meeting, if the Chairman

so directs, an appropriate press note may be released to the press on the proceedings of the Council.

13. Follow-up action: The Secretary shall evolve a system of monitoring the action taken on the recommendations of the Council by the Central Government, the Government of any State or the Union territory concerned. He shall, at appropriate stages, cause information in this regard to be made available to the Council.
14. Residuary: All matters not provided for in this procedure and all questions relating to the conduct of the proceedings in the Council shall be regulated in such manner as the Chairman may, from time to time, direct.

Powers of the Secretary: For facilitating the work of the Council, including the preparation of papers for it, the Secretary of the Council shall have the power to—(a) Call for information or papers from, or hold discussions with the officers of the Central Government or, as the case may be, of any State Government or Union territory Administration or any other authorities or sources; (b) Issue instructions from time to time as to the manner of preparing the references to or the brief for the consideration of the Council and for the proper functioning of the Secretariat of the council; (c) Engage the services of institutions, experts or consultants on contract on such terms as may be approved by the Chairman.

OPEN STATEMENT IN SUPPORT OF FARMERS

5 February 2021

We are a group of former civil servants of the All India and Central Services who have worked with the Central and State Governments in the course of our careers. As a group, we have no affiliation with any political party but believe in impartiality, neutrality and

commitment to the Constitution of India. We, the Constitutional Conduct Group (CCG), would like to reassert and reiterate our support for the farmers who are agitating for repeal of the three farm laws. We are particularly concerned about the developments that took place on 26 January 2021, Republic Day, the efforts to lay the blame on the farmers for the disruption of law and order on that day and the events that have followed.

We note the following with grave concern:

The approach of the Government of India (GoI) towards the farmers' protest has been an adversarial and confrontationist one from the very beginning, treating the apolitical farmers like an irresponsible opposition to be derided, demonised and defeated. The repeated, albeit unsuccessful, attempts to polarise the agitation along regional, communal and other lines are also reprehensible. Such an approach can never lead to a solution.

- Regarding the incidents that happened on Republic Day:
  1. The GoI has still not responded to the farmers' assertion that the Delhi Police erected barricades on the route agreed upon by both the farmers and the Delhi Police for the tractor rally due to which a few of the farmers were forced to take another route.
  2. When one section of farmers hoisted their flag below the National Flag at the Red Fort, why were the police doing literally nothing to prevent this occurrence? What action has the GoI initiated against those in the Delhi Police, Ministry of Home Affairs and Ministry of Defence for dereliction of duty?
  3. Why is it that this particular action by a few unruly elements was shown repeatedly by the government-controlled and other media? What happened in the remaining places? Why was the peaceful tractor parade in other places, with citizens welcoming the farmers with flowers and food, not shown?

- Post Republic Day:
  1. How is it that in Singhu, where there were barricades clearly dividing the farmers sitting in demonstration, a few hooligans were able to break the barricades and attack the farmers in the presence of police? Why did the police intervene much after the attack took place? We have seen TV visuals where one unruly person had even snatched a lathi from a policeman and attacked one of the farmers.
  2. Why is it that essential services to the agitating farmers such as water, electricity and the internet have been blocked, putting the thousands of people gathered there to unspeakable difficulties?
  3. Why have barricades with concrete barriers, concertina wire, nails and spikes been raised on the borders of Delhi to prevent the agitating farmers from entering? Such barricades are not even erected on the borders of India with its neighbouring countries! Are the agitating farmers being seen as enemies of the country?
     a) Why are sedition charges made out against certain journalists and a Member of Parliament of an opposition party on flimsy grounds, solely for certain tweets posted by them when the factual position was not clear? The registration of the same case with very similar First Information Reports in various states run by the BJP smacks of vindictiveness and seems to be aimed at muzzling legitimate, democratic protests against the policies of the GoI.
     b) Holding or presenting a view against the GoI or reporting different versions given by different people about an incident can, under no law, be held as an act against the nation. It bears repetition to say that a protest against a policy or action of the Government is not an act of sedition against the nation.

c) Withdrawal of cases against the farmers and tweeters, including the journalists, withdrawal of cases against all except miscreants who engaged in unlawful activities and stopping the vicious and sickening propaganda of calling the farmers Khalistanis are the minimum requirement for a conducive atmosphere for resumption of talks.

4. If the GoI is indeed interested in an amicable solution, instead of proposing half-hearted steps such as putting the laws on hold for eighteen months, it can withdraw the three laws and think of other possible solutions, given the basic Constitutional position that the subject of agriculture is in the States' list in the Constitution of India.
5. We in the CCG have, on 11 December 2020, issued a statement supporting the stand of the farmers. All that has happened since has made us feel even more strongly that great injustice has been done and continues to be done to the farmers. Therefore, we urge the GoI to take remedial action on an issue which has caused so much turmoil in the country over the past several months.
6. We reassert and reiterate our support to the agitating farmers while expecting the GoI to provide a healing touch and to solve the issue to the satisfaction of the stakeholders.

SATYAMEVA JAYATE

Constitutional Conduct Group (75 signatories)

OPEN LETTER TO THE PRIME MINISTER ON THE PM CARES FUND

16 January 2021

Dear Prime Minister,

We are a group of former civil servants of the All India and Central Services who have worked for decades with the Central and State Governments. As a group, we have no affiliation with any political party but are committed to the Constitution of India.

We have been keenly following the ongoing debate about the 'Citizen Assistance and Relief in Emergency Situations', or 'PM CARES'—a fund created for the benefit of people affected by the COVID pandemic. Both the purpose for which it has been created as well as the way it has been administered have left a number of questions unanswered.

The speed with which the fund was set up was breathtaking. It was registered on 27 March 2020, within three days of the first nationwide lockdown. As per information available on the website of the fund, in less than a week, the fund had received Rs 3,076.62 crores. The actual amount received to date is yet to be disclosed.

The immediate cause of this letter is the refusal of the Government of India on 24 December 2020, to divulge details under the Right to Information (RTI) Act on the grounds that the PM CARES Fund is not a Public Authority under the ambit of Section 2(h) of the RTI Act, 2005. If it is not a public authority, how have the Prime Minister, Home Minister, Defence Minister and Finance Minister, as members of the government, lent their designations and official positions to it? Why are they Trustees in their official capacity and not as private citizens?

If the PM CARES is a private Trust, should donations to it be eligible as Corporate Social Responsibility (CSR) expenditure? Schedule VII (ix) under Section 135 of the Companies Act allows CSR exemptions for only certain types of funds established by the Government, including for socio-economic and relief work.

On 28 March 2020, the Ministry of Corporate Affairs issued a circular stating 'Item no. (viii) of Schedule VII of the Companies Act, 2013, which enumerates activities that may be undertaken by companies in discharge of their CSR obligations, inter alia provides that contribution to any fund set up by the Central Government for socio-economic development and relief qualifies as CSR expenditure. The PM-CARES Fund has been set up to provide relief to those affected by any kind of emergency or distress situation. Accordingly, it is clarified that any contribution made to the PM-CARES Fund shall qualify as CSR expenditure under the Companies Act 2013.' Clearly, contributions to the fund could not have been legitimate CSR expenditure had the fund not been 'set up by the Central Government'.

The question that then arises is whether the circular of 28 March 2020 is legally deficient, more particularly when the Ministry of Corporate Affairs issues a gazette notification on 26 May 2020 to include this fund in Schedule VII under Section 135 of the Companies Act as eligible to receive CSR funds with retrospective effect from 28 March 2020. The new entry of the PM CARES to the list at item (viii) in Schedule VII comes after the entry 'Prime Minister's National Relief Fund (PMNRF)'. Why was the new fund necessary when the nation already had a fund for national relief?

The Trust deed of the PM CARES fund states in point 5.3 that 'this trust is neither intended to be or is in fact owned, controlled or substantially financed by any government or any instrumentality of the government. There is no control of either the central government or any state governments, either direct or indirect, in the functioning of the trust in any manner whatsoever.' Then how is it that such large deposits have come from the public sector? If the Fund is not a public authority, why are our Embassies seeking funds from abroad? The MEA's press release of 30 March 2020 states that in a video conference you had with our Ambassadors on that day, you had explicitly 'advised Heads of Mission to suitably publicize the newly-established PM-CARES Fund to mobilize donations from

abroad.' Most certainly, the fact that you and other senior Ministers of Government handling sensitive portfolios are Trustees would ensure a substantial flow of funds. Also, contributions are being solicited by government officials from private citizens. The then Secretary, Ministry of Corporate Affairs, appealed to the Institute of Chartered Accountants (ICAI) to donate to the Fund and the ICAI complied. Can the Secretary seek donations from an organisation he has official dealings with?

Though the PM CARES Fund is not being accepted as a public authority, under the RTI Act, in 2019, the Supreme Court held that trusts, societies and non-government organisations, both private and public, which enjoy 'substantial government financing', should be treated as 'public authorities' under the RTI Act. The substantial government funding in the case of PM CARES is evident from the wages and other moneys received directly or indirectly from the Consolidated Fund. As per a *Times of India* report on 19 May 2020, out of over Rs 10,600 crores in the fund, over Rs 3,200 crores was from public companies and nearly Rs 1,200 crores from public sector employees—apparently from out of salaries and wages of members of the defence forces, and other government and semi-government organisations.

There is a clear absence of transparency in every aspect of the PM CARES. Neither details of donors and amounts received, nor details of expenditures incurred are in the public domain. This opacity is disturbing as the State governments handling the COVID-19 challenge were, and continue to be, sorely in need of financial assistance.

Public memory is short, Mr Prime Minister. The young people of our country may not have even heard of A.R. Antulay, who in 1980, as the Chief Minister of Maharashtra, created a number of funds, including one called the Indira Gandhi Pratibha Pratishthan. In that case, the fund was apparently a private fund but couched as if it were the Government's. Ultimately, Antulay was charged by BJP functionaries in court and had to resign.

It is necessary that, for reasons of probity and adherence to standards of public accountability, the financial details of receipts and expenditures be made available in order to avoid doubts of wrongdoing. In the well-known 1975 Raj Narain case, Justice Mathew observed that 'the people of this country have a right to know every public act, everything that is done in a public way by their public functionaries.' It is essential that the position and stature of the Prime Minister is kept intact by ensuring total transparency in all dealings the Prime Minister is associated with.

SATYAMEVA JAYATE

Constitutional Conduct Group (100 signatories)

OPEN LETTER REGARDING THE FARMERS' AGITATION

11 December 2020

We are a group of former civil servants belonging to the All India and Central Services who have worked with the Central Government as well as different State Governments of India. As a group, we have no affiliation with any political party but believe in being neutral, impartial and committed to the Constitution of India.

A huge farmers' agitation—primarily in Punjab, Haryana, UP and Rajasthan—to repeal three new laws has been under way for many months and has been supported by many other sectors like trade unions, student organizations, university teachers' associations, a range of political parties and others. A Bharat Bandh was called for 8 December after several rounds of talks between farmers' unions, and yet the Government of India failed to yield results. We do not wish to discuss here the merits and demerits of these laws but focus on the violation of Constitutional provisions and the breakdown of democratic processes in this saga.

In keeping with the federal structure of the Constitution and the range and diversity of State-specific needs, 'agriculture' is at

Entry 14 in List-II in the Seventh Schedule to the Constitution. The subjects in this List are within the exclusive legislative jurisdiction of the States and it has been argued convincingly that the laws passed are, therefore, unconstitutional. Unconstitutionality apart, they represent an assault upon the federal character of the Constitution: some legal experts have argued that they violate 'the basic structure of the Constitution.' The passing of these laws appears to be a case of legislative legerdemain and they have been challenged in court.

There were no consultations with farmers' representatives before the legal process. To start with, ordinances were issued during a colossal pandemic which deserved undiluted attention. When the Bills were introduced in Parliament in September 2020, the demand to send them to Parliamentary Committees was denied. It is pertinent to point out that according to a newspaper report of September 2020, in recent times, the percentage of Bills scrutinised by Parliamentary Select Committees rose from 60 per cent during UPA I (14th Lok Sabha) to a high of 71 per cent during UPA II (15th Lok Sabha) but fell to 25 per cent in NDA I (16th Lok Sabha). In the current Lok Sabha, very few Bills have been sent to Parliamentary Committees.

Time was not given to debate the Bills and they were railroaded through Parliament; the demand for a division in the Rajya Sabha was not accepted and a voice vote was held amid tumult and confusion, leading to suspicions about the procedure employed. At the same time, some labour laws were passed during a walk-out by the Opposition. The question has been raised pointedly: was this done in the belief that during a pandemic, and with restrictions on public gatherings, organised protest would not be possible?

The undermining of democratic processes and the total disregard for public consultation and convenience has been evident in the ways in which Article 370 was repealed, demonetisation was implemented without warning or preparation, the Citizenship Amendment Act was brought in and a lockdown ordered with hardly any notice, resulting in untold suffering for millions of migrant workers. What

is noteworthy and common to all these actions was a refusal to consult the people affected beforehand and a determination to not hold a dialogue afterwards. The facile option of labelling all those who disagree with one or other of the actions of the government as 'anti-national', 'pro-Pakistani,' 'award-vapasi gang', 'urban Naxals' and 'Khan Market gang' is chosen to avoid substantive discussion and debate, the very heart of the democratic process, and to vilify and criminalise dissent.

It is a measure of their discontent that farmers in lakhs are braving the winter cold as also the risks of COVID-19. The farmers' agitation has been peaceful and in exercise of their Constitutional and democratic right to protest. Yet, they were greeted by teargas and water cannons as they tried to reach Delhi and highways in Haryana were dug up to impede their onward march. It is difficult to label these protests as instigated by political parties or Khalistanis when the farmers explicitly keep political parties at bay and a senior SAD leader, once a part of the ruling alliance of NDA, returns his Padma Vibhushan award.

The protests have spread across many states and are being supported by several other groups even though a largely complicit media refuses to report their true magnitude and reach. In our capacity as former civil servants who stand up for Constitutional freedoms, we would like to emphasise our support for the democratic and Constitutional right of peaceful protest being exercised by farmers and others. It is time that the ruling dispensation listens carefully to the demands being made and demonstrates its respect for democratic traditions, procedures and practices by engaging in dialogue inside and outside Parliament.

SATYAMEVA JAYATE

Constitutional Conduct Group (78 signatories)

AN OPEN LETTER ON THE CENTRAL VISTA PROJECT

17 May 2020

Honourable Prime Minister of India, Shri Narendra Modi
Honourable Housing and Urban Affairs Minister of India,
Shri Hardeep Singh Puri

We are a group of retired civil servants belonging to the All India and Central Services from all over India. As a group, we do not subscribe to any particular political ideology but focus upon issues that have a bearing upon the Indian Constitution and issues of democracy.

We are writing this letter to express our grave concerns about the Central Vista Redevelopment Project currently planned in the most iconic heritage precinct of New Delhi. The preliminaries for the execution of the first building among many in this area, viz. the new Parliament building have already been obtained as seen in the national news. This, despite widespread, and very relevant opposition from the public and innumerable flaws in the selection procedure.

India and its capital Delhi are the proud possessors of this remarkable, historical precinct, known as the Central Vista, built during the British Raj, but nurtured, savoured and celebrated largely in the post-Independence era. Any interventions to change this area would need to be mindful of this history. The Central Vista area has been accorded Grade 1 heritage status under the extant Unified Building Bye Laws of Delhi. Construction and redesign on the scale planned in the redevelopment project will significantly affect the heritage nature of this precinct, and destroy it irrevocably.

The redevelopment planned will, moreover cause severe environmental damage. This precinct is at the core of the congested capital of Delhi, and acts as the lungs of the city, with its dense mature tree canopies serving as a repository of biodiversity and the vast lawns of the Vista as a watershed for the city between the Ridge and the Yamuna. Constructing a large number of multi-storeyed office

buildings, with basements, in this open area will create congestion and irreversibly change and damage the environment. Delhi already suffers from enormous environmental pollution. To plan something which will increase this pollution many, many times, not merely during the construction phase but also subsequently, is clearly a thoughtless and irresponsible act.

A third purpose that the Central Vista serves at present is as a recreational space for the whole city. Families throng the area on summer nights to sit around in the open air and enjoy the occasional ice cream—innocent and inexpensive pleasures which they will be deprived of once the Vista's character undergoes a change. One must realise that open spaces which are gated or surrounded by government office buildings are not the same as public open spaces where citizens are free to carry out routine activities of recreation and celebration or even of peaceful protest. Governments hold public land in a fiduciary capacity and large scale changes based on flawed perceptions should not have place in a democratic country.

There is a great deal wrong with the conceptualisation of the project. Rather than establishing the necessity of the project with sound prior studies on environmental and technical parameters, this project began, if reports are to be believed, because of a superstitious belief that the present Parliament building is 'unlucky', as well as with the thought of leaving a particular government and its leader's impress on the architecture of Delhi. There was no Parliamentary debate or discussion that preceded the decisions taken. Moreover, the redevelopment plans were not substantiated by any public consultation or expert review. Instead, a hastily drafted and inappropriate tender was rushed through in record time to select an architectural firm in what was an extremely flawed process. The selected architectural firm appears to have been given carte blanche to make whatever changes it wishes, with all government departments seemingly mandated to do whatever is required to enable the firm's actions. The selection of the firm and the processes employed to do so leave a lot of questions unanswered. It is also pertinent to note

that there has been no accessible explicit exhibition of the scheme drawings, data or preceding studies for domain experts or common citizens to understand what exactly is planned in this very important public space. This goes against all democratic norms.

One of the premises on which the proposal is founded is the construction of an all new Parliament adjoining the iconic old Parliament in anticipation of the delimitation, stating as a reason the supposedly antiquated nature of its present premises, which need renovation and updating. A larger parliament building to accommodate a larger number of MPs (in view of the increase in population) is itself questionable because the population is projected to decrease post 2061 as borne out by the Economic Survey, indicating declining fertility rates in several states. Moreover, constructing a second Parliament building in close proximity to the existing one would diminish the existing Parliament building and might even endanger its foundations. The land use of the area on which the new Parliament building is proposed to be constructed was changed by the DDA after conducting a perfunctory hearing into a very large number of objections made by the public. Preliminary studies have shown that the existing Parliament can be repurposed to meet the requirement of expansion and modernisation. Indeed, this is the norm for all heritage structures including Parliament buildings all over the world. Surely our Parliament deserves the same respect. No Heritage Assessment Analysis has been done for any of the valuable buildings proposed to be either demolished or re-purposed.

A premise on which the redevelopment of Central Vista is based, appears to be the necessity to concentrate offices of the Central Government in one place. This is against the basic tenets of the Master Plan of Delhi, which stipulates that no new offices should be built in New Delhi and that efforts should be made to decongest it. It is also out of sync with the maxim of 'less government, more governance', which the present government had in its manifesto.

Though much of the plan is shrouded in secrecy, it is learnt that the proposal also calls for the demolition of four Bhawans built in

the 1960s, the iconic National Museum, Vigyan Bhawan, the fairly recently built IGNCA, and the very new and expensive Ministry of External Affairs buildings. Other than the value, both monetary and symbolic, embedded in these buildings, this flies in the face of the principles of conservation and the basic tenets of sustainability. Some of these buildings, moreover, and the National Archives to which additions impermissible as per extant rules are planned, are repositories of artefactual and documentary cultural heritage which would be gravely endangered in the large scale project so casually proposed.

Eminent professional bodies like the Council of Architecture (COA), the Indian Institute of Architects (IIA), the Indian National Trust for Art and Cultural Heritage (INTACH), the Institute of Urban Designers India (IUDI), and the Indian Society of Landscape Architects (ISOLA) have written numerous letters with sound and detailed advice on various aspects of the redesign plan to the Minister of Housing and Urban Affairs. Unfortunately, these letters have been ignored and even replies to these letters have not been forthcoming. If the institutions meant to safeguard the rights and wellbeing of people in a democratic country can be so arbitrarily ignored, can India still claim to be a democracy?

It is sad to note that approvals of empowered supervisory bodies like the Environmental Assessment Committee of the Ministry of Environment and the Central Vista Committee have been pushed through in great haste at meetings convened at short notice while the country is in lockdown due to the COVID-19 epidemic, and despite the absence of private members who expressed their inability to attend and advised waiting till the nation returned to normalcy. The clearances are being given despite the matters being sub judice. These bodies have, unfortunately, been reduced to mere rubber stamps with notes of dissent not even recorded.

Finally, in the post COVID-19 scenario, when enormous funds are required for strengthening the public health system, to provide sustenance to people and to rebuild the economy, taking up a proposal

to redesign the entire Central Vista at a cost of at least Rs 20,000 crores, a figure likely to escalate significantly, seems particularly irresponsible. It seems like Nero fiddling while Rome burns.

We strongly believe that this project needs to be stopped forthwith for the multiple and complex reasons we have mentioned above. We appeal to the government to see the fallacy in going ahead with this project and to issue the necessary notifications forthwith to stop the work from going ahead.

SATYAMEVA JAYATE

Constitutional Conduct Group (60 signatures)

LETTER TO CHIEF MINISTERS OF STATES AND LT GOVERNORS OF UNION TERRITORIES—MAINTAINING SOCIAL HARMONY AND JUSTICE DURING THE CORONAVIRUS CHALLENGE

23 April 2020

To

Chief Ministers of all States of India

Lt Governors of all Union Territories of India

Copied to: Prime Minister of India

Dear Chief Minister/Lt Governor,

We are a group of former civil servants belonging to the All India and Central Services, from all over India. As a group, we do not subscribe to any particular political ideology but rather focus on issues that have a bearing upon the Indian Constitution. We have been holding Conclaves and writing Open Letters on matters of concern since we came together as the Constitutional Conduct Group in June 2017.

It is with much anguish that we bring to your attention reports of harassment of Muslims in some parts of the country, particularly following the meeting of the Tablighi Jamaat in March in the Nizamuddin area of New Delhi. The Jamaat was criticised

for ignoring the principles of social distancing when cases of COVID-19 had started emerging in the country. Although this was hardly the only incident of such gatherings, both political and religious, sections of the media hastened to give a communal colour to COVID-19, including attributing motives to the Tablighi Jamaat in spreading the virus to different parts of the country. The action of the Jamaat in organising such an event, ignoring the Delhi Government's advisories was, without question, misguided and condemnable. However, the action of the media in communalising it and extending it to the Muslim community as a whole is utterly irresponsible and reprehensible.

Such coverage has fuelled hostility towards the Muslim community in parts of the country. Fake video clips have been doing the rounds showing Muslim vendors spitting on the fruits and vegetables that they have for sale—purportedly to spread the COVID-19 disease. Cases have been reported of vegetable vendors being asked their religion, even being assaulted when they mention Muslim names. Video recordings of such incidents are circulating through social media at this time. The fear and insecurity generated by the pandemic is sought to be channelled into the 'othering' of the Muslim community in different places to keep them out of public spaces, purportedly to protect the rest of the population!

There are reports from Hoshiarpur that Muslim Gujjars who traditionally migrate from Punjab to Himachal Pradesh with their cattle were denied entry at the border by the police due to apprehension of tension created by mobs on the other side to prevent their entry. Photographs of men, women and children forced to take shelter on the banks of the Swan river, where hundreds of litres of milk had to be dumped following this blockade, have appeared. Photos from a market in Biharsharif, Nalanda district, Bihar, show pictures of flags being affixed to the carts of non-Muslim vendors with exhortations that buyers should only purchase produce from such carts. These seemingly isolated incidents appear to be building up to an ostracism of Muslims.

More disturbingly, reports of discrimination are also coming in from various places about Muslims being turned away from hospitals and health facilities. It is reported that on 8 April, Fauzia Shaheen, a weaver from the Muslim-dominated area of Madanpura in Varanasi, who was experiencing labour pains, was repeatedly turned away from clinics and hospitals including from the Sir Sunderlal Hospital at the Banaras Hindu University, even after she delivered a baby outside the hospital. Following an outcry in the social media, police registered a case against the management of a cancer hospital in Meerut that had put out an advertisement saying that it would treat Muslims only when they produce a report showing that they have tested negative for coronavirus. In Ahmedabad, we learn that separate wards have been designated for Muslim patients of Coronavirus.

In addition, there are reports of the special entitlements of rations and cash that governments have sanctioned at this time being denied to Muslim families.

The entire country is going through unprecedented trauma. We can endure, survive and overcome the challenges that this pandemic has imposed on us only by remaining united and helping each other. We laud those Chief Ministers who have been resolutely secular in their approach both in general and, in particular, in relation to this pandemic.

We should remember that traditionally India has maintained good relations with Muslim nations and has been seen as their friend. Millions of our fellow citizens live and work in these countries. There has been serious concern expressed in these countries about the recent developments. We should ensure, through our non-discriminatory action and relief measures, that the minorities have nothing to fear in India. This will help assuage the misgivings of these countries and avoid any consequential detriment to the prospects of the sizable Indian diaspora there.

We call upon you to reassure all the people in your state that by following the instructions for social distancing and the practices

regarding using face covering and hand washing, they can keep safe from COVID-19. It needs to be emphasised that there is no truth whatsoever in the rumours that any particular group has more infections than others in our country.

Incidents like the one in Karnataka, where three Hindu youth created panic at a police check post in Mandya district on 8 April by posing as Muslims with Coronavirus infection, need to be dealt with firmly, as was done in this case by the Karnataka police.

We request you to instruct all public functionaries to be particularly vigilant to prevent social boycott of any community in the State and to ensure that all the entitlements including medical and hospital care, rations and financial assistance are available equally to all those in need.

At this time of grave national and international crisis, we count on your leadership in bringing the people of India together rather than allowing the deepening of fissures in our country.

SATYAMEVA JAYATE

Yours faithfully,

Constitutional Conduct Group (101 signatories)

AN OPEN LETTER TO THE PRESIDENT OF INDIA: DELHI VIOLENCE AND ITS AFTERMATH—RECOMMENDATIONS OF A FACT-FINDING MISSION

18 March 2020

Hon'ble President of India, Rashtrapati Bhavan, New Delhi

Respected Rashtrapatiji,

It is with deep anguish and concern that we, the members of the Constitutional Conduct Group ('CCG') comprising former civil servants, write this letter to place before you some major issues in the aftermath of the widespread violence in Northeast Delhi, which began on 23 February 2020 and continued till 26 February 2020.

On 12 March 2020, eleven members of the CCG visited violence-affected areas of Northeast Delhi including Shiv Vihar, Brijpuri and Mustafabad. It is distressing that, even more than two weeks after the violence, the group did not see much evidence of any serious outreach by political parties to provide mental or physical support to victims of violence. There is no serious effort to re-establish much needed confidence building measures between communities.

The observations of the group which visited the affected areas are summarised below:

1. In Aulia Masjid of Shiv Vihar, almost the entire building was found burnt and charred. A local resident pointed out that several cooking gas cylinders were thrown into the Masjid and set alight to ensure its total destruction. The building was saved by the fire brigade which responded to frantic distress calls from a member of the Hindu community. The group was informed that the miscreants were continuously shouting slogans like *'Jai Shri Ram; Azadi dilate hain; Andar ki baat hai, police hamare saath hain'*. We were also informed that the electricity lines were deliberately cut and electricity meters were burnt, throwing the entire area into darkness and forcing the members of the Muslim community to run for survival in the ensuing violence, pandemonium and panic.
2. In Brijpuri, the group visited Arun Public School owned by Mr Bhisham Sharma, an ex-MLA, who claimed to have suffered a loss of Rs 1.5 to 2.0 crores, with the school library burnt and most classrooms damaged. All the school records maintained over thirty years were also destroyed in the fire. The school has been quickly repaired and was being painted. There were children writing their examinations. We learnt that the fire brigade responded after a period of twelve hours and repeated calls to the police control room met with no response.
3. The group visited Rajdhani Public Senior Secondary School, Shiv Vihar, but could not go inside as the gate was locked.

From the outside, it looked as if the school was badly damaged and several classrooms were burnt. The owner of the school, Mr Faisal Farooq, has recently been arrested by the police.

4. The group also visited the Eidgah Relief Camp set up by Delhi Waqf Board. It has given refuge to approximately 1,200 displaced Muslims, including women and children, who fled their homes after the violence. There was no medical facility provided by the Delhi Government. An NGO, Doctors Unity Welfare Association (a private NGO), has set up a stall which was manned by four MBBS doctors. It was well stocked with medicines for treatment of common ailments like fever, diarrhoea, hypertension, diabetes, wounds, schizophrenia etc.
5. Two severely disabled women met members of the group and pointed out that they did not have access to a toilet, both of them being unable to walk. However, the Eidgah authorities and officials of the Delhi Waqf Board said that toilets cannot be provided within the premises of the Eidgah, as it is a place of worship. This highlights both the ignorance and complete lack of sensitivity of the members of the Delhi Waqf Board and the Eidgah towards the women and the disabled from amongst those affected.
6. The group met several displaced families from Karawal Nagar whose houses were looted or burnt. They informed that they were rescued by paramilitary forces on 26th February 2020. Some of them showed handwritten complaints given to the police which bore the daily diary entry number from the police station. Some others mentioned that online FIRs filed by them are not being accepted for payment of compensation. Some of these people, who are tenants, informed that they would like to go back to their villages/towns in UP etc. while others, who own houses, informed that they would like to go back to their houses, provided they are assured of their security and are given assistance to rebuild their damaged properties.

7. There was a police camp at Eidgah where two police constables, including a lady constable, were helping those who wanted to lodge their complaints. There was a camp set up by the District Legal Services Authority, where legal help was being offered. However, we consistently found that people were too scared to name the persons who may have indulged in violence.
8. It was heartening to visit the stall set up by the Delhi Commission for Protection of Child Rights. Several young children, 4-10 years old, were being read stories by volunteers.
9. The group visited the car garage belonging to Mr. Virender Singh. There were some 40 vehicles lying completely burnt. It was pointed out that the garage was used by both Muslims and Hindus to park their cars on payment basis.
10. The group visited Madina Masjid located in a bye-lane in Shiv Vihar. The Masjid was badly damaged and burnt. One LPG cylinder was still lying on the ground floor of the building. Several twisted ceiling fans showed the extent of destruction and the precision of the violence.
11. In some houses near the Madina Masjid, there were several motorcycles, dragged inside by rioters and burnt. Several houses were completely destroyed and burnt beyond repair with fallen girders. The residents informed that they had run away from their homes.
12. The group learnt that there were several instances of Hindus protecting and sheltering their Muslim neighbours, some for several days. Similarly, Muslims have stood guard to protect the temples and Hindu neighbours of the area. There is no instance of damage to a single Hindu temple. However, we were told that in some cases, the neighbours facilitated identification of Muslim houses and properties.
13. The visit revealed that though there were some properties owned by Hindus which were damaged and burnt as well, there were a much larger number of properties and houses

owned by Muslims which were looted, burnt and badly damaged. The group did not see any camp for Hindus displaced from their homes.

The general impression the group gathered was that on 23 February 2020, miscreants and rioters from both Muslim and Hindu communities fought pitched battles and damaged properties of the other community. On 24 and 25 February 2020, however, the rioting seemed to have become well organised with rioters seen wearing helmets and bearing sharp weapons, targeting the homes and businesses of Muslims.

The group is appalled that the Police Commissioner, Delhi failed to mobilise adequate force and did not impose curfew and issue shoot at sight orders. Much of the arson, damage and deaths could have been prevented had the Police Commissioner exercised his duty to maintain law and order on the very first day of violence on 23 February. He could have imposed curfew and ordered firing on any mob indulging in violence and arson. We hope that he was not waiting for instructions from anyone as he had all the powers under the Criminal Procedure Code to bring the situation under control. It was due to this failure that so many lives were lost and the incident is being referred to as a pogrom.

Recommendations:

1. If such violence has to be prevented from erupting in other places, the Government must come down with a heavy hand on hate speech. Several politicians and the electronic and social media have been spreading hatred amongst communities but the Government has taken hardly any action to check this. The dissemination of such acts through print and electronic media also needs to be checked to prevent inter-communal hatred. In future, the failure to check hate speeches will be the cause of any communal violence. If the idea of India has to be saved, hate speech has to be stopped forthwith.

2. In the past, in several incidents of communal violence, senior officers responsible for law and order have got away scot free and very junior officers were punished. We request the setting up of a Judicial Commission of Enquiry headed by a serving or retired judge of the Supreme Court to enquire into the present incidents. The Commission should be specifically authorised to look into the failures of the administrative leadership of the Lieutenant Governor and Police Commissioner of Delhi. It should also be mandated to inquire into the role of hate speech by political leaders and electronic and social media in dividing communities, spreading hatred and setting them against each other. The other Terms of Reference of the Commission should include fixing responsibility on politicians who incited violence and police officers who failed to perform their duty in checking the same. The guilty must be expeditiously punished so that it acts as a deterrent for the future.
3. The attitude and conduct of the Delhi Police during the build-up of tension over the CAA-NPR-NRC protests and the outbreak of violence in Northeast Delhi has once again underscored the urgency of correcting the institutional bias of the force. Even after the violence ended, the Delhi Police is not seen as neutral. In the immediate term, a programme of retraining of police personnel at all levels should be designed to rid them of their deep-seated prejudices against the minorities and other disadvantaged sections of society, and to develop empathy and compassion towards human suffering. In the medium term, concerted efforts need to be made to rectify the skewed representation of Muslims, women and other poorly represented demographies in the police force through special recruitment drives. A diverse and pluralist police force is necessary to ensure an effective and humane response to communal tension and violence.
4. The Delhi government is distributing relief to families affected by violence. There are several NGOs who are keen

to help the victims in relief and rehabilitation but there is no coordination and supervision of their activities. We suggest that the Delhi government should set up a well-staffed committee for relief and rehabilitation, headed by a Secretary level officer and including officers from the departments of revenue, relief, women and child welfare, waqf board and education to coordinate relief measures. Officers having experience in cyclone and flood relief could also be drafted to contribute to this effort.

5. We had thought that after repeated instances of violence over the past four decades, there would be no repetition of targeted violence, complicity of the police and lack of empathy of the state in relief and rehabilitation of victims. Unfortunately, history is repeating itself in 2020, that too in the capital of the country. It must be ensured by the Union and State Governments that strong preventive and deterrent action is taken in the first few hours of any such violence. Police Training Institutes must impress on their officers that they do not need any direction from their political masters for doing everything possible to prevent violence.
6. Several Commissions of Enquiry have investigated various communal riots since independence. The entire police force, from the constabulary to the IPS officers, must be made fully conversant with the findings of these reports as they highlight the failings of local administration. In such training programmes, success stories of police in preventing such violence must also be highlighted, as several conscientious officers have, in the past, successfully prevented violence in their jurisdictions even while other areas experienced huge loss of life and property.
7. The Government of India and the Delhi Government must take all measures necessary to mitigate the sufferings of the population of Northeast Delhi. In particular, the Government of India should expedite the enquiry into the incidents and

fix responsibility and take action against those personnel of the Delhi Police guilty of inaction, instigation of and/or participation in the violence.

SATYAMEVA JAYATE

Yours sincerely,

Constitutional Conduct Group (89 signatories)

AN OPEN LETTER TO THE CITIZENS OF INDIA: INDIA DOES NOT NEED THE CAA-NPR-NRIC

9 January 2020

Dear Fellow Citizens of India,

Over the past few weeks, many of you have been understandably agitated over the enactment of the Citizenship Amendment Act, 2019 ('CAA'). Your fears have been compounded by the contradictory and confusing statements made by spokespersons of the Government of India on the implementation of the National Register of Indian Citizens ('NRIC'). Though that government now seeks to delink the National Population Register ('NPR') from the NRIC, we, the Constitutional Conduct Group, comprising former civil servants from the All India and Central Services committed to the Constitution of India, consider it our duty to inform you that the three issues are linked, acquaint you with the facts regarding the NPR, NRIC and the CAA and emphasise why these measures need to be resolutely opposed. For easy comprehension, we are listing the issues pointwise:

- There is no need for the NPR and NRIC

Both the NPR and NRIC exercises flow out of the amendments in 2003 to the Citizenship Act, 1955 ('1955 Act') and the Citizenship (Registration of Citizens and Issue of National Identity Cards) Rules, 2003 ('2003 Rules') framed by the then NDA government in

2003. The NPR has nothing to do with the Census of India, which is conducted every ten years and is next due in 2021. While the Census collects information about all residents of India without listing their names, the NPR is a list of names of all those who have lived in India for over six months, regardless of their nationality. A Population Register will contain the list of persons usually residing within a specified local area (village/town/ward/demarcated area). The NRIC will effectively be a subset of the Population Registers for the entire country.

The 2003 Rules provide for verification of the details in the Population Register by the Local Registrar (normally a taluka or town functionary) who will separate out cases of doubtful citizenship and conduct further enquiries. After carrying out enquiries in respect of residents whose citizenship status is suspect, the Local Registrar will prepare a draft Local Register of Indian Citizens, which would exclude those not able to establish, through documentary proof, their claim to be citizens of India.

It is at this stage that the experience of the citizens of Assam can cause apprehensions in the minds of those who are required to establish their citizenship, whether or not they profess any religion. The NPR 2020, unlike the NPR 2010, asks not only for the names of the parents of the resident, but also seeks to also record their dates and places of birth. A person who is not able to furnish these details for his/her parents or, for that matter, for himself/herself, could well be classified a 'doubtful citizen'.

The 2003 amendments to the 1955 Act (vide Sections 3(b), 3(c) and 14A) and the consequent introduction of the 2003 Rules seem to indicate an undue obsession about illegal migrants, without any factual basis. We fail to understand the need for a nationwide identification of 'illegal migrants', which is what the NRIC in effect amounts to, when census statistics over the past seven decades do not show any major demographic shifts, except in certain pockets in some areas of North-Eastern and Eastern India adjoining our neighbouring countries.

We are apprehensive that the vast powers to include or exclude a person from the Local Register of Indian Citizens that is going to be vested in the bureaucracy at a fairly junior level has the scope to be employed in an arbitrary and discriminatory manner, subject to local pressures and to meet specific political objectives, not to mention the unbridled scope for large-scale corruption. Added to this is the provision for objections to the draft Local Register from any person. The Assam NRC exercise has thrown up the dangers of such a large-scale exercise: lakhs of citizens have been made to spend their life's savings running from pillar to post to establish their citizenship credentials. Worrying reports are already coming in of people in different parts of India rushing in panic to obtain the necessary birth documents. The problem is magnified in a country where the maintenance of birth records is poor, coupled with highly inefficient birth registration systems. Errors of inclusion and exclusion have been a feature of all large-scale surveys in India, the Below Poverty Line survey and the Socio-Economic Caste Census being prime examples. The recently completed NRC exercise in Assam has been equally error-ridden and has led to major discontent.

Indeed the State Government itself, with the BJP in power, has rejected its own NRC data, an extremely ludicrous scenario.

The provisions of the CAA, coupled with rather aggressive statements over the past few years from the highest levels of this government, rightly cause deep unease in India's Muslim community, which has already faced discrimination and attacks on issues ranging from allegations of love jihad to cattle smuggling and beef consumption. That the Muslim community has had to face the brunt of police action in recent days only in those states where the local police is controlled by the party in power at the centre only adds credence to the widespread feeling that the NPR-NRIC exercise could be used for selective targeting of specific communities and individuals.

Added to the inconvenience that the NPR would put the common person through, is the unnecessary expenditure on the NPR

exercise, when data which is now to be gathered is already available through the Aadhaar system: these include name, address, date of birth, father/husband's name and gender. Most Indian citizens are already covered by Aadhaar. The purpose of gathering a lot of the additional data (over and above the Aadhaar details) is unclear and will only give rise to the reasonable apprehension that the bona fide citizen could be enmeshed in an interminable, costly bureaucratic exercise if his/her citizenship status comes under doubt.

Our group of former civil servants, with many years of service in the public sphere, is firmly of the view that both the NPR and the NRIC are unnecessary and wasteful exercises, which will cause hardship to the public at large and will also entail public expenditure that is better spent on schemes benefiting the poor and disadvantaged sections of society. They also constitute an invasion of the citizens' right to privacy, since a lot of information, including Aadhaar, mobile numbers and voter IDs will be listed in a document, with scope for misuse.

- Why authorise widespread setting up of Foreigners' Tribunals and detention camps?:

The Foreigners (Tribunals) Amendment Order, 2019 (issued on 30 May 2019) has unnecessarily stoked fears that Foreigners' Tribunals can now be set up on the orders of any District Magistrate in India and is the precursor to a widespread exercise to identify 'illegal migrants'. While the central government may contend that there is no such intention, it was surely impolitic, given the prevailing atmosphere in Assam and elsewhere, to issue such blanket orders delegating powers for constituting Foreigners' Tribunals. The experience with Foreigners' Tribunals in Assam has been, to put it bluntly, traumatic for those at the receiving end. After running the gamut of gathering documents and answering objections to their citizenship claims, 'doubtful citizens' have also had to contend with these Tribunals, the composition and functioning of which were highly discretionary and arbitrary.

Consequently, a number of citizens lost their lives in the quest for affirming citizenship or have had to suffer the indignity of incarceration in detention camps.

There have also been media reports, not denied by the Government of India, that orders for setting up detention camps have been given to all state governments. We are frankly bemused by the Prime Minister's recent statement that no such camps are in existence, when reports have documented the construction of such camps in states as far apart as Goalpara in Assam and Nelamangala in Karnataka and the intention to construct a detention centre in Navi Mumbai in Maharashtra. The Government of India has not come out with any statistics to show that the 'illegal migrants' problem in India is so severe that it requires the large-scale construction of detention camps all over the country.

- The constitutional and moral untenability of the CAA:

We have our grave reservations about the constitutional validity of the CAA provisions, which we also consider to be morally indefensible. We would like to emphasise that a statute that consciously excludes the Muslim religion from its purview is bound to give rise to apprehensions in what is a very large segment of India's population. A formulation that focused on those suffering persecution (religious, political, social) in any country in the world would not only have calmed local apprehensions but would also have been appreciated by the international community. In its current formulation, the CAA does not even mention the word 'persecuted', probably because using this word in the context of Afghanistan and Bangladesh would have marred India's relations with these countries.

Given that the Government of India has powers to grant citizenship after a migrant has completed eleven years in India, it would be instructive to know whether the Government of India has cleared all pending cases of 'illegal migrants' till end-2008. Since the discretion to grant citizenship and to exempt

individuals/groups from the purview of the Passport Act, 1920 and the Foreigners Act, 1946 lies entirely with the Government of India, this discretion could have been exercised on a case by case basis by the Government of India without any need to go through the exercise of the CAA and mentioning specific communities from specific countries.

What has given rise to grave apprehensions about the intentions of the Government of India has been the rash of statements by Ministers of the Government of India in recent times, linking the NRIC and the CAA. The Prime Minister's statement at a public meeting in Delhi on 22 December that the CAA and the NRIC are not linked contradicts the averments of his Home Minister on repeated occasions in various fora. In such a welter of conflicting and confusing utterances, it is hardly surprising that the ordinary citizen is left bewildered and is overcome by unknown fears, more so when government has not entered into any dialogue on this issue. At a time when the economic situation in the country warrants the closest attention of the government, India can ill afford a situation where the citizenry and the government enter into confrontation on the roads. Nor is it desirable to have a situation where the majority of State Governments are not inclined to implement the NPR/NRIC, leading to an impasse in centre-state relations, so crucial in a federal set up like India. Above all, we see a situation developing where India is in danger of losing international goodwill and alienating its immediate neighbours, with adverse consequences for the security set-up in the sub-continent. India also stands to lose its position as a moral beacon guiding many other countries on the path to liberal democracy.

We, therefore, urge our fellow citizens to insist, as we do, that the Government of India pay heed to the voice of the citizens of India and take the following steps at the earliest:

- Repeal Sections 14A and 18 (2) (ia) of the Citizenship Act, 1955, pertaining to the issue of national identity cards and its

procedures and the Citizenship (Registration of Citizens and Issue of National Identity Cards) Rules, 2003 in its entirety.

- Withdraw the Foreigners (Tribunals) Amendment Order, 2019 and withdraw all instructions for construction of detention camps.
- Repeal the Citizenship Amendment Act, 2019.

SATYAMEVA JAYATE

Constitutional Conduct Group (106 signatories)

OPEN LETTER TO THE PRIME MINISTER OF INDIA: VICTIMISATION OF HONEST CIVIL SERVANTS

4 October 2019

Dear Sir,

We write to you to express the deep concern of our group of former civil servants at the selective targeting of retired and serving officers, apparently for gaining narrow political advantages.

Having served government all our working lives, it is our duty to point out the very dangerous repercussions that the latest move to prosecute four former officers of the Ministry of Finance—Smt. Sindhushree Khullar, Shri Anup Pujari, Shri Prabodh Saxena and Shri Rabindra Prasad—in the INX Media case are bound to have on serving officers.

Government had made an effort to avoid policy paralysis by amending the provisions of the Prevention of Corruption Act last year and making it mandatory to obtain the prior sanction of government before prosecuting retired and serving officers. This latest move will serve as a severe dampener to this effort. It will only seem to confirm the worst apprehensions of civil servants, namely, that they will be afforded no protection for bona fide acts in the performance of their official duties. Henceforth, it will not be surprising if civil servants procrastinate before processing and examining every proposal

of importance, as they have no guarantee that they would not be implicated in criminal proceedings many years later.

It is most unfortunate that officers, especially those no longer in service, are made to bear the brunt of criminal proceedings that originate from settling of political scores. All regimes, irrespective of their political affiliations, at both central and state levels, have been guilty of this transgression. Serving officials will naturally be demotivated if diligent and honest officers are selectively targeted for punishment for no fault of theirs other than that they were implementing the policy decisions of the government of the day.

We are of the firm view that Rules must be framed to make the legal principle of estoppel apply on reopening decisions based on information provided at the time the decision was taken. If files are allowed to be exhumed and dissected on the basis of hindsight and that too with no bar on the time that has elapsed, no decisions will be made at all in government. There should be a reasonable period after which files should not be reopened. Officers, particularly after retirement, need that reassurance to lead a peaceful post-government life.

It is indeed a travesty when governance systems spare no effort in ensuring that political elements charged with or prosecuted for very serious offences are given latitude while officers who have faithfully served the nation for over three decades are arraigned on the flimsiest of technical grounds. In the interests of justice, we earnestly urge that there be an early resolution of this issue.

Yours faithfully,

Constitutional Conduct Group (71 signatories)

LETTER TO CHIEF MINISTER, BIHAR—CUSTODIAL DEATHS IN SITAMARHI DISTRICT

15 March 2019

To,
Shri Nitish Kumar
Hon'ble Chief Minister, Bihar,
Patna, Bihar
Email: cmbihar@nic.in

Subject: Torture and death of two men in police custody (Dumra PS, Sitamarhi district)

Dear Chief Minister,
It is with much anguish that we, members of Constitutional Conduct—a group of former civil servants that takes up, from time to time, matters of exceptional national interest—write to you, to express our alarm at the reported case of custodial torture leading to death of two men in police custody in Sitamarhi district on 7 March 2019. We urge you to take immediate action to conduct independent enquiry; follow set guidelines of the National Human Rights Commission (NHRC) and the Supreme Court in custodial torture and death cases; prosecute those found responsible, ensuring the severest punishment; and provide the families adequate compensation, besides protection where need be, and legal aid.

Media reports of the incident reveal grave violations by the police. These include the alleged torture to death of the men picked up in a case of robbery and murder. Families have shared photos and a video clip of the victims' bodies showing marks of nails hammered into them. The police did not allow the families to see the bodies when they first informed them of the deaths, the bodies themselves having been handed over to the families only after 24 hours. And while the Director General of Bihar Police

has confirmed the custodial death and called it 'unacceptable', it is being reported that the FIR registered does not mention the appropriate sections, viz. Section 302, IPC for murder, nor does it name the police personnel involved. These lacunae already raise serious suspicion about the police's intent to probe this case lawfully.

You would agree, Mr Chief Minister, that this is a very serious case of violation of right to life and due judicial process of the victims. In an environment of communal polarisation, concerns are being raised about this being, besides a case of police excess, also one that might be motivated by bias against a particular community. Given the circumstance, we urge you to ensure immediate action so as to restore trust in your administration.

We specifically demand the following actions:

1. Immediate arrest and prosecution of the absconding police officers under Sec. 302 IPC;
2. Follow in full, NHRC's guidelines on custodial torture and death, including instructions on conducting post mortem, video-filming, and magisterial enquiry;
3. Ensure that the investigation is conducted by police from outside the district, preferably by an SIT comprising of senior officers with impeccable integrity;
4. A time-bound and independent inquiry under Section 176(1-A) CrPC be conducted immediately by a Judicial Magistrate, and her report acted upon, besides sharing the report with the NHRC as required under law;
5. State government award compensation to the families for reparation of the loss;
6. State government ensure victim/witness protection, and provision of legal aid to the families, seeing to it that the State Legal Services Authority appoint a senior lawyer to assist the family from this stage.

We thank you for your consideration and look forward to speedy action against the perpetrators of the custodial crime.

Yours sincerely,
Constitutional Conduct Group (38 signatories)

Full list of signatories available at: https://constitutionalconduct.com/2019/03/23/letter-to-chief-minister-bihar-custodial-deaths-in-sitamarhi-district/

OPEN LETTER ON THE PROPER IMPLEMENTATION OF VVPAT-BASED AUDIT OF EVMS

24 February 2019

We are a group of former civil servants of the All India and Central Services who have worked for decades with the Central and State Governments during our careers. We wish to make it clear that, as a group, we have no affiliation with any political party but believe in impartiality, neutrality and commitment to the Constitution of India. With our collective experience of conducting and supervising elections from the local body to the parliamentary level, we wish to suggest what needs to be done to make the actual process of voting and counting as free as possible from suspicions of Electronic Voting Machine (EVM) malfunction and manipulation.

It is common knowledge that EVMs are 'black boxes' in which it is impossible for voters to verify whether their votes have been recorded and counted correctly, and in which miscounts due to EVM malfunction or manipulation are undetectable and unchallengeable. Hence, there is an imperative need for an additional verifiable physical record of every vote cast, in the form of 'voter verified paper audit trail' (VVPAT). It allows for a partial or total recount independent of the EVM's electronic count and helps detect counting mistakes and frauds that would otherwise go undetected.

In 2013, the Supreme Court passed an order mandating the use of EVMs with VVPAT units, and the Election Commission of India (ECI) has been deploying VVPAT units in Assembly Elections from 2017 onwards.

If VVPAT is to have any real security or accuracy value, it should form the basis of a proper audit plan. This entails tallying the electronic count as per the EVMs with the manual count as per the VVPAT slips for a 'statistically significant' sample size of EVMs chosen at random from a suitably defined 'population' of EVMs. Equally important is a clear 'decision rule' about what should be done in the event of a 'defective EVM' turning up in the sample. A 'defective EVM' is one in which the EVM count does not tally with the VVPAT count due to either EVM malfunction or manipulation. But the audit plan that the ECI has followed in recent elections suffers from the following serious shortcomings:

First, the ECI has prescribed a statistically incorrect sample size of just 'one polling station [i.e. 1 EVM] per Assembly Constituency' uniformly for all Assembly Constituencies and all states. It has not taken into account the fact that the number of EVMs in an Assembly Constituency varies widely across states from about 20 to about 300, and in a state from 589 (for Sikkim) to 23,672 (for Chhattisgarh which is the median state) to nearly 1,50,000 (for Uttar Pradesh). We are of the view that a uniform sample size for widely varying finite population sizes does not conform to fundamental principles of statistical sampling theory.

Second, the ECI has not made public as to how it arrived at its sample size nor has it specified the population to which this sample size relates. The latter is important because the sample size is dependent upon how the population is defined. If we assume that one percent of the EVMs are defective, the probability that the ECI's present sample size will fail to detect at least one defective EVM is 99 per cent if 'EVMs deployed in an Assembly Constituency' are defined as the population; 94 per cent if 'EVMs deployed in a Parliamentary Constituency' are defined as the population; and varies from about 2

per cent (UP) to 40 per cent (Chhattisgarh) to 71 per cent (Sikkim) if 'EVMs deployed in a state as a whole' are defined as the population. Such high margins of error are unacceptable in a democracy.

Third, the ECI has been vague about its 'decision rule' in the event of one or more defective EVMs turning up in the chosen sample.

Fourth, the ECI has not been transparent about the results of its VVPAT-based audit of EVMs for the various Assembly Elections held in 2017 and 2018 and the details are not available on its website.

In short, the ECI's audit plan is unable to detect outcome-altering miscounts due to EVM malfunction or manipulation, which defeats the very purpose of introducing VVPATs. Spending hundreds of crores of rupees on procurement of VVPAT units makes little sense if their utilisation for audit purposes is reduced to an exercise in tokenism.

Our group has been engaged over the past nine months in discussions with the ECI on issues relating to the proper VVPAT-based audit of EVMs. In our letter dated 10 December 2018 to the Chief Election Commissioner, we had sought clarifications from the ECI about certain pointed queries regarding the sample size and the decision rules. We had requested that in the interest of ensuring public confidence and the cooperation of political parties, it would be in the fitness of things if the clear reasons for adoption of a particular sample size and the decision rule for counting of VVPAT paper ballots are placed in the public domain, including on the ECI website. But there has been no action on this front.

The lack of transparency in VVPAT-based audit of EVMs has fuelled various conspiracy theories about 'mass rigging of EVMs'. There have been unacceptable demands for reversion to paper ballots. But the real issue today is not about 'EVMs versus Paper Ballots'; rather it is about 'EVMs with perfunctory VVPAT audit versus EVMs with proper VVPAT audit'.

Any electronic equipment is inherently subject to random malfunction. By its own admission, the ECI keeps about 20-25 per cent of EVMs and VVPAT units in reserve to replace those

which malfunction on the polling day within a few hours of the commencement of the poll. There is every likelihood that a certain percentage of EVMs may again malfunction randomly during the long interval of 15-30 days between the date of polling and the date of counting. Perhaps this explains the occasionally noticed random discrepancies between the polling station-wise figures of voter turnout and the votes as counted in EVMs. The argument that some Presiding Officers 'forgot' to initialise the EVM count to zero at the end of the mock poll demonstration before the regular polling commences does not explain why there are positive as well as negative discrepancies.

As regards EVM manipulation, we wish to state that though it is highly improbable, this low probability can increase significantly with insider collusion. While the ECI has put in place a security protocol and various administrative safeguards that look impressive on paper, vulnerabilities do exist. Large-scale rigging of EVMs may not be possible or necessary because potential attackers need to target only select EVMs to tip the balance in a few marginal, closely fought constituencies. What is worrisome is that without a credible VVPAT-based audit of EVMs, the fraud may be undetectable and may be carried on with impunity.

We, therefore, appeal to the ECI to go in for a statistically correct sample size that can detect at least one defective EVM with 99.9 per cent reliability, in a suitably defined population, by adopting the hypergeometric probability distribution model. In something as important as ensuring the integrity of the election process—a process which in any case takes about 2-3 months from the date of announcement to the date of counting—a delay of a few hours or even a day in the manual counting of VVPAT slips of a larger (statistically correct) sample size of EVMs should not matter at all.

We also appeal to the ECI to adopt the following 'decision rules'. Full manual counting of VVPAT slips should be done (1) for all the remaining EVMs of the defined population if the sample throws up one or more defective EVMs, (2) for closely contested constituencies

where the margin of victory is below 2 per cent of the votes cast or 1000 votes, whichever is less, even if no defective EVM turns up in the sample, and (3) for those polling stations where the discrepancy between the votes polled in EVMs and votes as counted in EVMs is more than 2 per cent.

We request the ECI to implement these suggestions in the Lok Sabha elections due in April-May 2019. Though the counting process may take a little longer, the confidence of the voters and political parties in the electoral process will be reinforced. The ECI has a long and honourable record of holding free and fair elections. It is in the spirit of supporting it in maintaining these high standards that we write this open letter.

SATYAMEV JAYATE

Constitutional Conduct Group (73 signatories)

OPEN LETTER TO CITIZENS OF INDIA—ASSAM NRC EXERCISE AND CITIZENSHIP

4 February 2019

Our group of former civil servants of the All India and Central Services has, over the last twenty months, issued a number of letters expressing our concern at the erosion of constitutional values in the country and the weakening of institutions entrusted with ensuring the functioning of a healthy democracy. As in our earlier letters, we reiterate our allegiance to the Constitution of India and clarify that we neither have a political agenda nor are we linked to any political party.

The complete draft of the National Register of Citizens (NRC) in Assam was published on 30 July 2018, leaving over 40 lakh persons ineligible, making up some 12 per cent of the total applicants. There is a real fear among those excluded—overwhelmingly from minority groups, both Muslims and Hindus of Bengali descent,

besides Nepali and Hindi-speaking persons, among them a large percentage of women, children and daily wage workers, constituting the poorest of the poor—that they might be rendered stateless.

Although the NRC process is being monitored by the Supreme Court (SC), we believe there has been little informed debate in the country on the NRC updation that affects the lives of lakhs of persons; there is also no clarity on what the legal status and fate of those excluded from the final NRC will be, at the end of this court-monitored process. The large exclusion of names from the draft NRC is the outcome of a mix of procedural and capacity weaknesses of the NRC State Coordinator and has been much reported about. The shortcomings include poor record management, technical glitches and arbitrary physical verifications, among others. Central to the exclusion from the NRC, disproportionately, of linguistic, religious and gender minorities, however, is also the in-built discrimination in rules and procedures, segregating populations into 'original' and 'non-original' inhabitants and the use of differential standards to verify claims and supporting documents for the two categories. The SC has endorsed this segregation of applicants into so-called 'original' and 'non-original' inhabitants and has also approved automatic inclusion of 'original' inhabitants in the draft NRC while, on the other hand, decreeing a two-step process of 'exhaustive' and 'thorough' verification for applicants deemed 'non-original'. Without any definition or directions to determine who the 'original' inhabitants of Assam were, 'non-original' applicants, in practice, have been taken to mean mostly Bengali and Nepali-speaking persons and other minorities.

Those aggrieved by their non-inclusion in the draft NRC had the right to file Claims and Objections (C&O) till 31 December 2018. But this does not seem to provide redress against the already built-in discriminations, exacerbated by the rather liberal provisions for filing objections against wrongful inclusion, which include removing the bar on the number of objections, doing away with the requirement of the objector being a local resident and removing

the penalty against false and frivolous objections. Not surprisingly, media reports appear to indicate that, in the final hours of receipt of C&O, the number of objections against inclusion in the final NRC jumped from a mere 6,000 to 3 lakhs.

Those not satisfied with the NRC C&O results have the option to appeal to Foreigners Tribunals (FTs), based on whose decisions, the final inclusion in NRC will be decided. FTs use the Foreigners Act, 1946 to test claims to citizenship, wherein the burden of proof is on those proceeded against. These are heavily weighted against so-called 'suspected foreigners' without providing them any statutory rights. In practice, by shifting the burden of proof on those proceeded against, they set the bar too high, with likely severe consequences, as those affected by the NRC exclusion are mostly poor and illiterate, and government record keeping is neither efficient nor accessible.

Those excluded from the final NRC will face the risk of being declared foreigners and locked up in detention centres. With Bangladesh or any other country not recognising those excluded from the NRC as their citizens, nor there being any repatriation treaty between India and Bangladesh, these detentions will potentially be indefinite. The six detention centres in Assam currently house, between them, over a thousand persons declared as foreigners. Providing an early warning of the shape of things to come, a recent enquiry by the National Human Rights Commission (NHRC) into these detention centres provides a chilling account. It speaks of the absence of a legal regime governing rights of the detainees, indefinite incarcerations and accompanying vulnerabilities suffered by detainees, the lack of any legal redress whatsoever and the sheer hopelessness of the detainees' condition.

Even while the exercise to finalise the NRC is going on, the ill-advised decision of the Government of India to push a flawed Citizenship (Amendment) Bill through Parliament has added fuel to an already simmering fire. This has already led to a storm of protest in the Northeastern states and will further vitiate the NRC process. Not only will this proposed legislation exacerbate local tensions

the issues confronting us today. We appeal to all citizens concerned with the development of a healthy democracy to debate the issues raised by us in the hope that we are able to evolve workable solutions in the near future.

SATYAMEVA JAYATE

Constitutional Conduct Group (48 signatories)

PUBLIC LETTER TO COMPTROLLER AND AUDITOR GENERAL (CAG) FROM FORMER CIVIL SERVANTS SEEKING THE EARLY SUBMISSION OF AUDIT REPORTS BY THE CAG ON THE RAFALE DEAL AND DEMONETISATION

12 November 2018

We are a group of former civil servants of the All India and Central Services, who have worked for decades with the Central and State Governments during our careers. We wish to make it clear that, as a group, we have no affiliation with any political party but believe in impartiality, neutrality and commitment to the Constitution of India. We are committed to protecting, preserving and promoting the independence and integrity of the various Constitutional and statutory institutions in India.

During the debates in the Constituent Assembly, Dr B.R. Ambedkar had described the Comptroller and Auditor General (CAG) as the most important functionary in the Constitution, more important than even the Judiciary. Rightly so, because the CAG functions as a watchdog of the public purse, and it is his duty to ensure that every financial transaction is as per rule, sanction, provision and propriety, and guided by the principles of economy, efficiency and effectiveness. Articles 148-151 of the Constitution of India read with the CAG's (Duties, Powers and Conditions of Service) Act, 1971, ensure his complete independence from the Executive.

We wish to bring to the CAG's notice our concern about what seems to be unconscionable and unwarranted delay in bringing out the audit reports on Demonetisation (November 2016) and the Rafale deal (April 2015). A news item in *The Hindu* dated 3 March 2017, titled 'CAG to undertake audit of demonetisation fallout' quoted the previous CAG as saying that the CAG was well within its rights to seek audit of the fiscal impact of demonetisation, especially its impact on tax revenues. He had pointed out that the audit would also cover the expenditure on printing of notes, RBI's dividend to the Consolidated Fund of India, the huge amount of data generated by banks, and the effectiveness of the follow-up action taken by the Income Tax Department in identifying potential tax evaders and pursuing action against them, and so on. It is more than 20 months since the previous CAG made the above statement but there is no sight of the promised audit report on Demonetisation.

Equally conspicuous is the delay in presenting the CAG's audit report on the Rafale deal, even though 42 months have elapsed since the deal was announced in April 2015. A news item in *The Times of India* dated 24 July 2018 titled 'Rs. 59000 crore Rafale deal: CAG's audit report misses deadline' stated that the report was still in the draft stage and 'may be finalised not before the Winter session in December'. Another news item in *The Indian Express* dated 19 September 2018 titled 'Rafale deal: Congress delegation meets CAG, demands report on "irregularities"' stated that the CAG had assured the delegation that he was 'already examining all aspects of the deal'. But another news item published in *Business Today* dated 23 September 2018 titled 'No question of scrapping Rafale deal, will wait for CAG report, says Arun Jaitley' quoted the Finance Minister as saying that it was for the CAG to examine whether the planes were bought at a higher price or not and that 'all these facts and figures will be placed before CAG for consideration'. It would appear from his statement that as late as September 2018, the related files were yet to be scrutinised by the CAG. The precise stage of the audit is therefore unclear.

The CAG's audit reports on the 2G scam, Coal scam, Adarsh scam, Commonwealth Games scam, etc., which influenced public perception of the then government's actions, had invited appreciation from various quarters. But an impression is gaining ground that the CAG is deliberately delaying its audit reports on Demonetisation and the Rafale deal till after the May 2019 elections so as not to embarrass the present government. The CAG's failure to present the audit reports on Demonetisation and the Rafale deal in time may be seen as a partisan action and may create a crisis of credibility for this important institution. Due to the cacophony of claims and counterclaims, accusations and mudslinging in the media and elsewhere, the citizens do not know what the reality is. We believe that citizens have a right to insist upon the timely submission of audit reports by the CAG so that they can make an informed choice while voting.

In the past, the CAG has been criticised for nit-picking and focusing on trivial issues on the one hand, and for audit over-reach on the other. But there was never any occasion to accuse the CAG of being influenced by the Government of India or having to remind it about the timely performance of its Constitutional duties. While we are confident that the CAG will continue the tradition set by the past incumbents of this office, we urge it to complete the audit of both Demonetisation and the Rafale deal and submit the audit reports without any further delay so that they can be tabled by the Government of India in the Winter session of Parliament in December 2018.

(A copy of this letter is also being sent to the President of India)

SATYAMEVA JAYATE

Constitutional Conduct Group (60 signatories)

PUBLIC STATEMENT AND APPEAL BY RETIRED CIVIL SERVANTS AND DIPLOMATS ON THE COMMENTS VIOLATIVE OF THE CONSTITUTION MADE BY THE PRESIDENT OF THE MAIN RULING PARTY IN HIS PUBLIC SPEECH AT KANNUR, KERALA

5 November 2018

We are a group of former civil servants of the All India and Central Services, who have worked for decades with the Central and State Governments during our careers. We wish to make it clear that, as a group, we have no affiliation with any political party but believe in impartiality, neutrality and commitment to the Indian Constitution. We continue to uphold the oath of allegiance to our Constitution we took when we entered service.

Addressing a public meeting at Kannur, Kerala, on Saturday, 27 October 2018, the President of the main ruling party at the Centre made two interrelated comments: That the Supreme Court ought to have issued implementable orders; and, that the State Government in Kerala would be brought down for its temerity to enforce the Supreme Court orders regarding the entry of women from a certain age group into the Sabrimala temple by arresting and suppressing 'Ayyappa devotees.' Taken together, these two comments make for a scary reading that the President of the main ruling party at the Centre is casting aspersions upon and questioning the lawful authority of the highest court of the land, asking the State government to refrain from implementing the Court's orders, and is explicitly threatening to bring it down by vigilante action of political workers in the streets by fuelling their religious sentiments. There is also an implicit threat of the dismissal of the State Government by the Union Government.

Under the Election Symbols (Reservation and Allotment) Order, 1968, framed by the Election Commission India (ECI) under the plenary powers vested in it by Article 324 of the Constitution, the Commission has codified the provisions relating to the functioning of political parties. This Order provides for the registration of

political parties and its general bases by the ECI. It also provides for their recognition on the basis of their poll performance in the general elections. In 1989, the Parliament inserted a new section 29A in the Representation of the People Act, 1951, which provides that the registration of political parties by the Election Commission India (ECI) would involve an additional condition: every political party must include in its constitution/by-laws an undertaking that it 'shall bear true faith allegiance to the Constitution of India as by law established, and to the principles of socialism, secularism and democracy, and would uphold the sovereignty, unity and integrity of India'. The main ruling party at the Centre too has made the necessary insertion of this additional condition in its Constitution. Further, the ECI has the power to suspend or withdraw the recognition of a recognised political party for its failure to observe the Model Code of Conduct or to follow lawful directions and instructions of the Commission.

It is well within the rights of any individual to critically opine upon a judicial decision without casting aspersions on the juridical intent. Indeed, judicial decisions do vary between one juridical level and another, and also from one bench to the other in the High and Supreme Courts. There is a due process in place to seek redressal from a decision that has caused one to feel aggrieved; this even applies, in some cases, to the decisions taken by a particular bench of the Supreme Court. There have also been instances of legislative interventions in the Parliament by the executive to countermand an inconvenient judicial decision within the parameters set out in the Constitution. It is not open to any individual, group, or a political party to subvert the due constitutional process by threatening street action or adverse political action by the Union executive.

The cited public speech of the President of the ruling party at the Centre amounts to a gross Constitutional misconduct. It is likely to have far-reaching adverse implications for our national polity if it passes unnoticed. The Hon'ble Prime Minister has been a great votary of strengthening federalism during his long innings as the

Chief Minister of one of India's frontline states. As a Prime Minister, he has enthusiastically spoken of the cooperative federalism among the Union and the states. Therefore, the cited content of the public speech of the powerful President of the ruling party is as worrying as it is inexplicable even in the present times when political discourse touches a new low every day.

We respectfully ask:

1. The ECI to take cognisance of the cited public speech by the President of the main ruling party at the Centre, to seek necessary explanations from the political party concerned, and to initiate thereafter such steps as deemed fit for defending the sanctity of the Constitution and of the laws made thereunder;
2. The Head of the Government, the Hon'ble PM, to counsel his party President as appropriate and to categorically delink the executive's support of his cited public speech.
3. The Hon'ble Supreme Court to take suo motu cognisance of its contempt in such a blatant manner at a public forum, and to proceed forthwith with necessary legal action.
4. The Head of the State, The Hon'ble President of India, to give his sage counsel to all concerned to maintain constitutional decorum and to enforce the corrective executive action to rectify its breach.

SATYAMEVA JAYATE

Constitutional Conduct Group (49 signatories)

OPEN LETTER TO THE PRESIDENT OF INDIA REGARDING CONTINUATION OF SHRI M.J. AKBAR IN THE UNION COUNCIL OF MINISTERS

17 October 2018

To
The Honourable President of India,
New Delhi

Copied to: The Honourable Prime Minister of India, New Delhi)

Honourable Rashtrapatiji,
We are a group of former civil servants of the All India and Central Services, who have worked for decades with the Central and State Governments in the course of our careers. We wish to make it clear that, as a group, we have no affiliation with any political party but believe in the credo of impartiality, neutrality and commitment to the Indian Constitution. We continue to uphold the oath of allegiance to our Constitution we took when we entered service.

We write this letter to express our deep disappointment and outrage at the conspicuous lack of action by the Government of India in responding to the statements by twenty women regarding the sexual harassment faced by them from a person who is today a member of the Union Council of Ministers. In clear and explicit terms, these women have detailed the behaviour of the present Minister of State for External Affairs, Shri M.J. Akbar, over a period of almost three decades from about the mid-1980s to the end of the first decade of this century, when he was in a position of power and responsibility in some of the major news organisations of this country. A number of instances of such harassment by men in positions of power and authority in the fields of journalism, advertising and films have come to light since the first week of October 2018 through social, print and electronic media. While many of these organisations have initiated action to enquire into the allegations by the affected women and have either removed

the persons involved from their employment or distanced those under investigation from participation in the day to day affairs of their organisations, it comes as a rude shock to us that no action whatsoever has been forthcoming from the institution primarily charged with upholding the rule of law, namely, the Government of India, against one of its senior members.

As former civil servants, we are fully aware of the need to follow the due process of law. At the same time, constitutional propriety and morality dictate that the functionary concerned should resign from his office pending an enquiry and must not be reappointed to a high constitutional post till he is cleared of all the charges against him. The Vishakha Guidelines issued by the Honourable Supreme Court in 1997 and the Sexual Harassment of Women at Workplace (Prevention, Prohibition and Redressal) Act, 2013 ('POSH Act') have clearly laid down the steps to be taken to protect women at their workplaces. While it is true that the instances referred to where the Minister was allegedly involved refer to the period before the POSH Act came into effect, it is also a fact that the Vishakha Guidelines were in force when at least three (and possibly more) of these incidents are said to have taken place. It is a sad commentary on our respect for the rule of law that the newspaper organisations concerned had not put in place mechanisms to implement the Vishakha Guidelines, which would have provided an avenue for redressal to women who felt they were the victims of sexual harassment.

While the facts will come out in a full-fledged impartial enquiry, which we hope will be entrusted to a committee comprising eminent citizens, it behoves the Government of India to act in a manner which gives the public confidence that the government is responsibly discharging its constitutional duties. As reported in the media, Shri Akbar is attempting to involve the complainants in time-consuming and costly litigation to avoid answering the allegations which have been levelled against him. We look forward to you, Honourable Rashtrapatiji, to uphold the dignity of the many women who have put their reputations at stake in making these allegations.

We earnestly request you, as the first citizen of our country, to advise the Government of India to seek the resignation of Shri Akbar, failing which it should recommend his removal from the Union Council of Ministers. We also request you to issue directions to the Government of India and the State Governments to put in place robust mechanisms to ensure that women can engage in gainful employment free of the fear of sexual harassment and to ensure that all organisations (in the public and private sectors) follow the provisions of the POSH Act in both letter and spirit.

Yours faithfully,
Constitutional Conduct Group (72 signatories)

LAW AND THE JUDICIAL SYSTEM

Some are More Equal Than Others

REBECCA MAMMEN JOHN

The letters of the Constitutional Conduct Group (CCG) archive the ways in which constitutional values have been imperiled in recent times. Spanning six years, the letters document various forms of communal violence—societal, political, and institutional—that the country has seen in the last few years. For instance, the letter dated 28 January 2018 details multiple instances of Muslims being targeted and killed by violent mobs. Each of these instances has at least three constitutive elements: the first is a communal fault-line that has gained political mileage in recent years, such as cow vigilantism or the 'love jihad' narrative. This offers the opportunity or pretext to exacerbate underlying historical tensions, mobilise the majority community, and produce the minority individual as the object of violence. This dual process—mobilisation of the majority and the dehumanisation of the minority so as to produce them as disposable, abject and ultimately 'deserving' of violence—is a result of the two additional elements: political support and institutional impunity. Political support, active and tacit, is found in the poisoning of public discourse with hate speech as well as in legislative developments that weaponise the law to foster and institutionalise discrimination and violence. Finally, there is institutional impunity for such acts of violence, be it in police inaction or in courts abdicating their constitutional duties.

Arguably, it is this third element of institutional impunity that makes the state of affairs unprecedented. India, like any other democratic polity, has been no stranger to the existence of structural discrimination and violence along lines of religion, caste, and class.

However, in the last few years, we have borne witness to the complicity of several institutions in deepening these fault-lines in the polity and perpetrating the consequent violent fallouts. The legislature has proactively introduced legislations that arguably discriminate against minorities in violation of constitutional standards, without adequate or even any democratic deliberation. The Parliament has enacted laws like the Citizenship (Amendment) Act[1] which along with the National Register of Citizens has the potential of keeping vulnerable sections of society, especially Muslims, on the margins; introduced identification regimes for transgender persons[2] despite strong opposition from the community;[3] made reservation for economically weaker sections,[4] that was held by Justice Ravindra Bhat of the Supreme Court to be discriminatory against Scheduled Caste and Scheduled Tribe persons;[5] and the Digital Personal Data Protection Act,[6] that gives an impoverished version of data privacy rights.[7] Various state legislatures[8] have enacted laws against religious conversion and inter-faith marriages.[9] The letters written by the CCG also document instances of the Election Commission selectively enforcing the Model Code of Conduct against certain politicians and not against others.

Further, there are reports on the partisan and dubious role of investigating agencies. For instance, the Delhi Minorities Commission[10] and the Citizens' Committee appointed by the CCG,[11] in their respective fact-finding reports on the North-east Delhi Riots, have documented the complicity of the police in the terrible violence that broke out between two communities in February 2020. A petition by fourteen opposition parties, although ultimately dismissed, was also filed before the Supreme Court, arguing that special investigating agencies like the Directorate of Enforcement and Central Bureau of Investigation disproportionately target opposition leaders and thereby violate their right to dissent.[12]

These institutional tendencies must be read alongside the persistence of a public discourse that has normalised and perpetrated anti-minority violence. A Member of Parliament belonging to the

Ruling Party used communal slurs against a Muslim Member of Parliament belonging to an Opposition Party, on the floor of the Lok Sabha,[13] without facing any repercussions in Parliament. The Chief Minister of Assam made a similarly vile campaign speech against a Muslim minister in the Chhattisgarh government, with complete impunity.[14] The CCG letter dated 7 January 2023 calls for action against a ruling party MP who openly called for genocidal violence against Muslims.[15] This kind of political speech has had a tangible effect in the form of an upsurge of communal violence against Muslims and Christians, amongst other religious minorities.[16]

Given this institutional complicity that thrives in a sociopolitical ecosystem of anti-minority violence, the courts inevitably become the last bastion of democratic values for citizens. Quite apart from the fact that the judiciary has repeatedly affirmed its own role as the final guardian of the Constitution, courts remain the last resort for individuals to seek justice in the context of a shrinking democratic space in the political sphere. Courts, therefore, must be held especially accountable for their response to the circumstances in which we find ourselves today.

It is in this regard that one finds a worrying trend of courts treating similarly placed litigants differentially. Take for instance, the Delhi High Court's dismissal of a petition seeking registration of an FIR against Anurag Thakur and Parvesh Verma for hate speech.[17] In early 2020, prior to the riots in North-east Delhi, Anurag Thakur had raised the slogan, '*Desh ke gaddaro ko, goli maaro saalon ko*' (Shoot the traitors of the nation). During the hearings, a single judge of the Delhi High Court observed: 'In the election speech, so many things are said by the politicians to politicians and that is also a wrong thing. But I have to see the criminality of the act. If you're saying something with a smile then there is no criminality, if you're saying something offensive then definitely.'[18]

This distinction between speech during elections and otherwise did not, however, come to the rescue of opposition MP Rahul Gandhi. Gandhi, in reference to Nirav Modi and Lalit Modi, two

persons wanted for criminal cases in India, had rhetorically asked, 'Why do all thieves have the same surname?' He was convicted for defamation against the entire Modi community and sentenced to two years' imprisonment, and subsequently disqualified from his membership in the Lok Sabha. The Sessions Court in Ahmedabad, while admitting his appeal, refused to stay his conviction and this order was then endorsed by the Gujarat High Court.[19] It is worth scrutinising the discursive moves that the court, as an institution, deploys to reach opposite conclusions. In Anurag Thakur's case, the single judge of the Delhi High Court had observed that the impugned speech did not have any communal intent since it referred to '*ye log*' (these people) and not to a specific community.[20] Thus, the court refused to consider the sociopolitical context of the speeches that made the identity of the targeted '*log*' (people) obvious to both the speaker and the audience. However, Rahul Gandhi's comment about two specific individuals is considered to be a defamatory remark against a vague, nebulous community of individuals bearing the 'Modi' surname.

In *Alok Kumar v. Harsh Mander*,[21] the Delhi High Court held that where a speaker engages in communal hate speech at a meeting arranged by the Vishwa Hindu Parishad (VHP), the VHP President cannot be held criminally liable for the same. This legal reasoning did not, however, extend to the accused persons in the Elgar Parishad cases,[22] largely based on a set of electronic communications, not originating from most of the charged accused. Similarly, consider the Bombay High Court order where criminal proceedings against a cartoonist were quashed.[23] Here, the impugned speech was a graphic of 'Piggy Bank' with a sketch of a pig and the words 'Allah Rasool Muhammad', in connection with an article on the funding sources of a terrorist organisation. In contrast, the Allahabad High Court refused to grant anticipatory bail to a studio executive on the ground that a web series titled *Tandav* was promoting communal disharmony by naming its characters after Hindu gods.[24]

This pattern of the court reaching different conclusions in comparable facts involving identical offences cannot be dismissed as coincidental or inconsequential. On the one hand, courts are willing and quick to grant relief to some sections of society. On the other hand, in cases involving litigants from minority communities or from the political opposition, they often obfuscate the analysis to deny relief, and the relief when finally granted is the result of the apex court's intervention after the trial courts and the High Courts have ruled against such litigants. Thus, hate speech and speech inciting violence against minorities is allowed to proliferate, and judicial pronouncements validating them protect future instances of such speech. On the other hand, any form of dissent or aberration is considered unacceptable and subjected to prosecution. Further, since speech from minority individuals is anti-majoritarian by design, it is almost always considered suspect and subjected to censorship.

There are two key consequences of this approach of courts. Firstly, the judicial process is being increasingly weaponised to target minorities and political opponents. Even when courts eventually intervene in favour of the latter, the process itself becomes the punishment. Consider the previous example of Rahul Gandhi, where the Supreme Court stayed his conviction pending the final disposal of the appeal.[25] This stay only came after his membership from Parliament was suspended precisely because of the failure of the Sessions Court and the High Court to grant relief. It is important to remember that the stay is only an interim relief, and Gandhi's appeal against his conviction is still pending for final disposal before the Sessions Court. However, civil liberties and key fundamental rights are often crucially staked in interim orders, much more often than in final orders.

Similarly, examine the prolonged incarceration of political prisoners like Umar Khalid[26] and those in custody following the 2020 Delhi riots: this extended incarceration is largely due to repeated, apathetic adjournments in bail hearings. Members of

the ruling political party who openly incited violence were never investigated or charge-sheeted. Contrast this with the overnight listing and immediate hearing of the petition by television anchor Arnab Goswami pursuant to his arrest by the Maharashtra police.[27] Sidhique Kappan, on the other hand, a journalist who was arrested in October 2020 on charges under the draconian Unlawful Activities (Prevention) Act, while reporting the gang rape and murder of a Dalit girl in Hathras, did not receive timely relief despite the tenuous nature of the allegations against him and was granted bail by the Supreme Court only in September 2022,[28] after both the Trial Court and High Court rejected his plea for release. He continued to remain incarcerated even after the Supreme Court's order, due to proceedings initiated against him under the Prevention of Money Laundering Act and was eventually released from custody only in January 2023.[29] In sharp contrast, television anchor Amish Devgan, who had referred to a Sufi saint as a terrorist and robber who forcefully converted people, in a televised programme aired on 15 June 2020, approached the Supreme Court when multiple FIRs were registered against him and the apex court stayed the investigations and protected him from any coercive action on 26 June 2020, a mere ten days after the FIRs were registered.[30] Where there are majoritarian and anti-democratic interests targeting minorities, courts are required to be especially vigilant, otherwise the judicial process itself becomes punitive notwithstanding the final outcome.

Secondly, this pattern of differential treatment by courts shuts out crucial institutional remedies to minorities and political opponents. This must be considered, especially in light of the jurisprudence that has consistently viewed the judiciary as a sentinel for the rights of the most marginalised and vulnerable sections. The Supreme Court's legacy and the faith placed in institutional solutions by citizens stems from the apex court's assumed responsibility of protecting minority rights. Therefore, the above-described pattern of differential treatment comes across as an abdication of this constitutional duty of the court.

The consequence of this kind of institutional impunity is a severe shrinking of democratic space. One can see various instances of this growing intolerance. The discourse in purportedly premier higher educational institutions now harbours bigotry and hate speech. Contemplate the remarks made by the Director of IIT Mandi that landslides and cloudbursts in Himachal Pradesh are attributable to the consumption of meat,[31] or IIT Bombay imposing a fine of Rs 10,000 on a student for eating meat at a 'vegetarian' table.[32] Another example is the days-long event in National Law University, Bhopal where hate speech against Muslims, Christians and gender minorities was made with impunity.[33] It is a widely known fact that large sections of the Indian media are rife with anti-minority editorial positions. There is a documented spike in hate speech during elections.[34] As far as incidents of violence are concerned, there have been 3,399 cases of communal rioting between 2016 and 2020 as per data provided by the Ministry of Home Affairs in Parliament.[35] There are multiple news reports around the violence spurred by the 'love jihad' discourse, which was notably initiated by an order of the Kerala High Court.[36] In Assam, out of 3,141 people arrested in February 2023 under the pretext of curbing child marriage, 62.24 per cent were Muslims.[37] In the Parliament, the share of Muslim Members of Parliament has declined to 5 per cent or less; and there are many states with a Muslim population higher than the national proportion, that have no Muslim MPs.[38]

Law is a means of securing justice in a liberal democratic state, yet it is a mere technical instrument to secure the ends of power in an authoritarian state. In polities like India, there is a constant threat of the law slipping from its liberal function to its authoritarian one. While various factors determine the occurrence or prevention of such slippage, institutions like the court play a major, decisive role. Guarantees of democracy and protection of minorities from majoritarian discrimination and violence remain empty platitudes of constitutional jurisprudence unless courts give effect to such guarantees in practice. This requires judges to remain discerning and

vigilant, and not allow the court to be weaponised and/or become complicit in violence (be it social, political or institutional). In her introduction to an anthology of K.G. Kannabiran's writings titled *The Speaking Constitution*, Kalpana Kannabiran writes, of her father's work, 'Kannabiran was clear that courts needed to take insurgent positions in terms of the social and political contexts within which constitutional jurisprudence must be located. Anything less would only be "jurisprudential dissociation" at best, at its worst, "judicial pusillanimity"...'[39] In the present moment, this must be considered a clarion call.

NOTES

1. Citizenship (Amendment) Act, No. 47 of 2019.
2. Transgender Persons (Protection of Rights) Act, No. 40 of 2019.
3. G. Ram Mohan, 'Halt Implementation of the Trans Act 2019: Activists', *The Wire* (https://thewire.in/lgbtqia/trans-act-2019-rules-feedback-activists; Accessed March 2024).
4. The Constitution (One Hundred and Third Amendment) Act, 2019.
5. See Bhat J.'s dissenting opinion in *Janhit Abhiyan v. Union of India*, 2022 SCC OnLine SC 1540.
6. Digital Personal Data Protection Act, No. 22 of 2023.
7. Anushka Jain and Prateek Waghre, 'IFF's first read of the draft Digital Personal Data Protection Bill, 2023', Internet Freedom Foundation, 3 August 2023 (https://internetfreedom.in/iffs-first-read-of-the-draft-digital-personal-data-protection-bill-2023/; Accessed March 2024).
8. Till date, the following states have enacted such laws—Orissa, Madhya Pradesh, Chhattisgarh, Gujarat, Himachal Pradesh, Arunachal Pradesh, Jharkhand, Uttarakhand, Uttar Pradesh, Haryana and Karnataka.
9. Rohan Venkataramakrishnan, '"Love Jihad": As pandemic rages, BJP states turn focus to laws based on Hindutva conspiracy theory', *Scroll.in*, 21 November, 2020 (https://scroll.in/article/979015/love-jihad-as-pandemic-rages-bjp-states-turn-focus-to-laws-based-on-hindutva-conspiracy-theory; Accessed March 2024).

10. *Report of the DMC Fact-Finding Committee on North-East Delhi Riots of February 2020*, Delhi Minorities Commission, Govt. of NCT of Delhi, New Delhi: July 2020, p.68. (https://dn790009.ca.archive.org/0/items/dmc-delhi-riot-fact-report-2020/-Delhi-riots-Fact-Finding-2020.pdf; Accessed March 2024).
11. Constitutional Conduct Group, *Uncertain Justice: A Citizens Committee Report on the North East Delhi Violence 2020*, October 2022 (https://constitutionalconduct.files.wordpress.com/2022/10/uncertain-justice-citizens-committee-report-on-north-east-delhi-violence-2020.pdf; Accessed March 2024).
12. Padmakshi Sharma, '95 Per Cent Of Political Leaders Investigated By CBI & ED Are Opposition Leaders: Non-BJP Parties Tell Supreme Court', *LiveLaw*, 24 March 2023 (https://www.livelaw.in/top-stories/95-of-political-leaders-investigated-by-cbi-ed-are-opposition-leaders-non-bjp-parties-tell-supreme-court-224653; Accessed March 2024).
13. '"Mullah Terrorist": BJP MP Ramesh Bidhuri Uses Slurs Against BSP MP Danish Ali in Lok Sabha', *The Wire*, 22 September 2023 (https://thewire.in/communalism/ramesh-bidhuri-danish-ali-lok-sabha-hate-speech; Accessed March 2024).
14. Shubhomoy Shikdar, 'Assam CM attacks Chhattisgarh's lone Muslim Minister', *The Hindu*, 18 October 2023 (https://www.thehindu.com/elections/chhattisgarh-assembly/assam-cm-makes-communal-tirade-against-chhattisgarhs-lone-muslim-minister/article67435205.ece; Accessed March 2024).
15. See CCG Open Letter – Demand for Action on Hate Speech by Lok Sabha MP Pragya Thakur, 07th January 2023.
16. See *2022 Report on International Religious Freedom: India, Office of International Religious Freedom*, U.S. Department of State. (https://www.state.gov/wp-content/uploads/2023/05/441219-INDIA-2022-INTERNATIONAL-RELIGIOUS-FREEDOM-REPORT.pdf; Accessed March 2024).
17. *Brinda Karat v. State of NCT of Delhi*, 2022 SCC OnLine Del 1775.
18. Nupur Thapliyal, 'Delhi High Court Dismisses Brinda Karat's Plea Seeking FIR Against Anurag Thakur & Parvesh Verma For Alleged Hate Speeches', *LiveLaw*, 13 June, 2022 (https://www.livelaw.in/news-updates/delhi-high-court-anurag-thakur-hate-speech-fir-

dismiss-brinda-karat-appeal-201469?infinitescroll=1; Accessed March 2024).

19. *Rahul Gandhi v. Purnesh Ishwarbhai Modi*, Cri. Rev. Application No. 521/2023, order dated 07.07.2023 (Gujarat High Court, 2023).
20. Op cit, 'Delhi High Court Dismisses Brinda Karat's Plea Seeking FIR Against Anurag Thakur & Parvesh Verma For Alleged Hate Speeches'.
21. Crl. M.C. No. 1463/2020, judgment dated 21.07.2023 (Delhi High Court, 2023).
22. *Sudha Bharadwaj v. State of Maharashtra*, Criminal Bail Application No. 428/2019 (Bombay High Court); *Arun v State of Maharashtra*, Criminal Bail App. No. 3006/2018 (Bombay High Court); *Vernon v. State of Maharashtra*, Criminal Bail Application 3007/2018 (Bombay High Court); *Anand Teltumbde v. State of Maharashtra*, Criminal Anticipatory Bail Application 314/2019 (Bombay High Court); *Gautam P Navlakha v. State of Maharashtra*, WP 4425/2018 (Bombay High Court); *Gautam Navlakha v. NIA*, Cr. Appeal 1707/2020 (Bombay High Court).
23. *Pawan Kamalakar Deshpande v. State of Maharashtra*, Crl. App. No. 6323/2017 (Bombay High Court).
24. *Aparna Purohit v. State of UP*, Crl. Misc. Anticipatory Bail Application No. 2640/2021, order dt. 25.02.2021 (All HC, 2021).
25. *Rahul Gandhi v. Purnesh Ishwarbhai Modi & Ors.*, SLP (Crl.) No. 8644/2023, order dt. 04.08.2023 (Supreme Court, 2023).
26. Sheryl Sebastian, 'Umar Khalid Bail: "Can Demonstrate In 20 Mins That There's No Case", Sibal Says; Supreme Court Adjourns Hearing Citing Paucity Of Time', *LiveLaw*, 12 October 2023 (https://www.livelaw.in/top-stories/supreme-court-umar-khalid-delhi-riots-larger-conspiracy-bail-239980; Accessed March 2024).
27. 'Bombay High Court To Pronounce Order On Arnab Goswami's Interim Bail Application Tomorrow', *LiveLaw*, 8 November 2020 (https://www.livelaw.in/top-stories/bombay-high-court-to-pronounce-order-on-arnab-goswamis-interim-bail-application-tomorrow-165640; Accessed March 2024).
28. *Sidhique Kappan v. State of UP*, SLP(Crl.) No. 7844/2022, order dt. 09.09.2022 (Supreme Court, 2022).
29. Sparsh Upadhyay, 'Siddique Kappan Walks Out Of Jail On Bail After Over Two Years Of Incarceration', *LiveLaw* 2 February, 2023 (https://

www.livelaw.in/top-stories/siddique-kappan-walks-out-jail-after-over-two-years-jail-220486; Accessed March 2024).

30. *Amish Devgan v. Union of India & Ors.*, W.P.(Crl.) No. 160/2020, order dt. 26.06.2020 (Supreme Court, 2020).
31. Anwesha Mitra, '"Landslides, cloudbursts happen in Himachal Pradesh as people eat meat...": IIT Mandi director makes shocking claim', *Mint*, 8 September 2023 (https://www.livemint.com/news/india/landslides-cloudbursts-happen-in-himachal-pradesh-as-people-eat-meat-iit-mandi-director-makes-shocking-claim-11694097827367.html; Accessed March 2024).
32. Purva Chitnis, 'IIT Bombay faces flak after "imposing Rs 10k fine on student for eating meat at vegetarian table"', *The Print*, 4 October 2023 (https://theprint.in/india/education/iit-bombay-faces-flak-after-imposing-rs-10k-fine-on-student-for-eating-meat-at-vegetarian-table/1790191/; Accessed March 2024).
33. Betwa Sharma, 'Islamophobia, Literature Hostile To Minorities At Event Launched By Union Minister At National Law School In Bhopal', *Article 14*, 2 October 2023 (https://article-14.com/post/islamophobia-literature-hostile-to-minorities-at-event-launched-by-union-minister-at-national-law-school-in-bhopal-651a3f8e6f82b; Accessed March 2024).
34. Raqib Hameed Naik et al., *2023 Half-Yearly Report: Anti-Muslim Hate Speech Events in India*, Hindutva Watch, September, 2023 (https://hindutvawatch.org/hate-speech-events-india/; Accessed March 2024).
35. 'India Witnessed 3,399 Cases of Communal or Religious Rioting Between 2016 and 2020', *The Wire*, 29 March 2022 (https://thewire.in/government/india-commuanl-religious-riots-2016-2020; Accessed March 2024).
36. 'Kerala HC asks govt to frame laws to stop "love jihad"', *The Economic Times*, 10 December 2009 (https://economictimes.indiatimes.com/news/politics-and-nation/kerala-hc-asks-govt-to-frame-laws-to-stop-love-jihad/articleshow/5320856.cms; Accessed March 2024).
37. Sukrita Baruah, 'Overnight crackdown, tip-offs from sources: Behind the 916 child marriage arrests in Assam', *The Indian Express*, 4 October, 2023 (https://indianexpress.com/article/india/assam-child-marriage-crackdown-arrest-8966223/; Accessed March 2024).
38. Anushka Kataruka and Vignesh Radhakrishnan, 'Data | Zero Muslim

MPs in many States with over 10 per cent Muslim population', *The Hindu*, 6 June, 2023 (https://www.thehindu.com/data/data-zero-muslim-mps-in-many-states-with-over-ten-per-cent-muslim-population/article67048120.ece; Accessed March 2024).

39. Kalpana Kannabiran, 'Introduction: Speaking the Constitution' in K.G. Kannabiran, *The Speaking Constitution: A Sisyphean Life in Law*, HarperCollins India, New Delhi: 2022, p.xxii

Letters and Statements

OPEN LETTER TO THE UNION MINISTER OF LAW AND JUSTICE OF INDIA—INCONSISTENT STATEMENTS ON THE COLLEGIUM SYSTEM

30 March 2023

Honourable Minister Shri Kiren Rijiju,

We are a group of former civil servants of the All India and Central Services who have worked in the Central and State Governments during our careers. As a group, we have no affiliation with any political party but believe in impartiality, neutrality and share a commitment to the Constitution of India.

We write to you today in response to comments you made on various occasions and very recently at the India Today Conclave on March 18, 2023. Your statements that day are the latest in what is emerging as a concerted attack by the government on the collegium system of appointments, the Supreme Court of India and, ultimately, on judicial independence. We unequivocally condemn this onslaught.

We are puzzled by your repeated criticisms of the Supreme Court collegium while simultaneously stating that there was no confrontation between the government and the Supreme Court. To the average Indian, there does, indeed, seem to be a confrontation. In the appointment of judges to the High Courts and Supreme Court it appears that it is the government that is stonewalling appointments. Names forwarded by the collegium are left pending for years, only to be finally returned without approval. Candidates with distinguished careers marked by their commitment to due process and to

constitutional norms are turned down by the government. Rather than engage constructively with the Supreme Court and collegium, high offices of the executive such as yours, and that of the Vice President, have responded with venomous barbs. The government's continued refusal to accept some candidates can only give rise to the suspicion that the underlying intention is to create a pliant judiciary.

It is no surprise that retired judges, senior lawyers, and experts have been expressing serious concern in the public domain on the urgent need to safeguard judicial independence. The process of determining judicial appointments goes to the heart of this independence. It is a testament to their commitment to the institution that retired judges of the Supreme Court and High Courts are not mute spectators to abrasive attacks on the judiciary. These are individuals with distinguished careers of public service and unimpeachable integrity. Yet you have not hesitated to call them anti-Indian and have stated that a few retired judges are working in tandem with activists, groupings you described as 'anti-India gangs' and attempting to influence the judiciary to 'play the role of an Opposition party'. When asked if any action would be taken against this so-called 'anti-India gang', you replied that 'actions will be taken', that 'nobody will escape' and that 'those who have worked against the country will have to pay a price'.

It seems to us that you are confusing the government with the country, construing criticism of the government as disloyalty to the country. You seem to believe that if a person disagrees with the views of the government, that is enough to permanently label him or her as 'anti-national'. Using that label, the government then initiates all manner of punitive action, and attempts to suppress dissent of any kind. Have you considered the implications of what you said in terms of the right to free speech under the Indian Constitution? You need to urgently explain the legal basis of your open threat in a public forum.

As the Law Minister, if you have concerns about opinions being expressed or discussions taking place in public fora, you can avail

of multiple platforms and ways to respond, beginning with inviting dialogue. To label public-spirited citizens as an 'anti-India gang' and threaten them with action which will exact 'a price' rings sharply of authoritarianism, particularly in the absence of any attempt to dialogue or engage. These are abrasive statements unbecoming of your high post.

We recognise that there is need for continued deliberations on ways to improve the current system of judicial appointments, to deepen transparency and the rigour of the process as also diversity amongst appointees. However, preserving the independence of the judiciary is non-negotiable, and any sign of executive overreach cannot be accepted in a democracy. We conclude by reminding you of a simple but cardinal truth: all organs of the State are bound by the Constitution of India and a government, simply because it is in a majority, cannot ride roughshod over Constitutional provisions regarding the separation of powers amongst the executive, the legislature and the judiciary. By doing so, you breach your own oath of office.

SATYAMEVA JAYATE

Yours sincerely,

Constitutional Conduct Group (90 signatories)

OPEN STATEMENT ON THE SEDITION PROVISION IN THE INDIAN PENAL CODE

12 June 2022

We are a group of former civil servants of the All India and Central Services who have worked with the Central and State Governments in the course of our careers. Our group has no affiliation with any political party, and we, as its members, believe in impartiality, neutrality and commitment to the Constitution of India.

On May 11, 2022, a chorus of appreciation greeted the Supreme

Court's interim orders on a batch of cases which had challenged the constitutionality of the sedition provision contained in Section 124A of the Indian Penal Code (IPC). The Supreme Court's order was an interim one, viz. to keep in abeyance this section and all related pending trials, appeals and proceedings until further orders. While we would, like others, wish to applaud this decision of the Supreme Court, we feel that, at present, it deserves only a muted cheer.

The Supreme Court's order, inasmuch as it results in immediate relief against arrest, investigation or under-trial detention under Section 124A, is certainly laudable (provided it does not adversely affect the persons already charged). Not so laudable is the impression it gives that the suspension is a response to the union government's statement that it is reviewing Section 124A and considering its revision and reform. Review and revision by the executive cannot be a substitute for judicial determination of the constitutional limits of the power of the executive to restrict freedom of speech and expression. It is important for the Supreme Court not to get sidetracked by the executive and instead to answer the fundamental issue raised by the petitioners, viz. is Section 124A of the IPC constitutionally valid?

Section 124A of the IPC is certainly a strange provision to have in a democracy. It criminalises the feelings of dislike, contempt and disaffection towards 'the government established by law in India', even where such feelings are not linked to any violent, illegal or criminal act. Disaffection and contempt for the government of the day are feelings through which democratic republics are born. Such feelings are considered criminal only in autocracies. Where the government of the day can be, and is, changed through the electoral process, it can surely not be a criminal offence for any citizen to merely harbour and express feelings of disaffection, etc. towards the government. In the words of Mahatma Gandhi: 'Affection cannot be manufactured or regulated by law. If one has no affection for a person or system, one should be free to give the fullest expression to his disaffection, so long as he does not contemplate, promote, or

incite to violence.' Yet this disaffection is what Section 124A treats as criminal. Sixty years ago, in *Kedar Nath Singh v. State of Bihar*, a five-judge bench of the Supreme Court upheld Section 124A IPC, but qualified their decision as follows: '...we propose to limit [the] operation [of Section 124A] only to such activities...involving incitement to violence or intention or tendency to create public disorder or cause disturbance of public peace.'

This limiting of Section 124A to activities which involve incitement to violence or public disorder has, however, been by and large ignored in practice by the police and by the courts. As against the thousands of cases charged by the police under Section 124A and similar draconian provisions/laws, the low rate of conviction casts serious doubt about the genuineness of claims made during investigation and prosecution. It shows that the real purpose of such laws is to provide autocratic rulers a powerful weapon to suppress their rivals and control public opinion.

However, whether or not Section 124A is finally deleted or altered, it will make little difference to the common citizen insofar as freedom of speech and expression as spelt out in Article 19(1) of the Constitution is concerned. This is because, apart from Section 124A of the IPC, there are several other provisions in the IPC and other Acts which shackle this fundamental right of citizens and leave them open to arbitrary arrest and prosecution by the government. The only way that the citizen's right to freedom of speech and expression can be protected is if the Supreme Court examines Article 19 under the 'basic structure of the Constitution' principle with reference to all existing laws and provisions that put curbs on this freedom.

The armoury of arbitrary weapons used to suppress dissent and opposition and control the free formation of public opinion has expanded over the years to include a number of offences similar to those under Section 124A. Prominent amongst these offences are Section 153A of the IPC (promoting enmity between different groups on ground of religion, race, place of birth, etc.), Section 153B (imputations, assertions prejudicial to national integration), Section

505 (statements conducive to public mischief) and Section 505(2) (statements creating or promoting enmity, hatred or ill-will between classes). These provisions are today widely and routinely misused by the police and their political masters with the same objective as in the case of Section 124A.

Over the years, slowly and surreptitiously, the substance of the offence of sedition has been 'snuck' into the Unlawful Activities (Prevention) Act, 1967 (UAPA), defined more elaborately, and with more draconian consequences, than in Section 124A. Significantly, no political party is blameless in this regard and governments of all political complexions have been trampling upon human rights and the freedom of expression Section 13(1) of the UAPA states that 'Whoever: (a) takes part in or commits, or (b) advocates, abets, advises or incites the commission of, any unlawful activity...' shall be punishable with imprisonment for a term which may extend to seven years. 'Unlawful activity' as defined under Section 2(1)(o)(iii) of the UAPA is very similar to the definition of sedition contained in Section 124A IPC.

If Section 124A of the IPC is held by the court to be unconstitutional, because speech and expression that merely create disaffection are protected (and not prohibited) under Article 19(1), Section 2(1)(o)(iii) of the UAPA will also need to be amended to delete elements imported from Section 124A, viz. the criminalisation of speech and expression which is not an integral part of any violent, illegal, criminal act. Deletion of one, while retaining the other, would be irrational.

Deleting Section 124A from the IPC, while retaining criminalisation of 'unlawful activities' under the UAPA, will give substantial political advantage to the Union Government and the party in power at the national level. Currently, state governments are free to prosecute persons for offences under the IPC, including for sedition under Section 124A. No permission of the union government is required. States ruled by political parties other than that at the national level sometimes use Section 124A to prosecute

supporters of the national ruling party for sedition (as recently happened in Maharashtra). The ruling party at the union level is powerless to prevent such prosecution. The UAPA, on the other hand, vests no powers with the state governments. It provides that no court shall take cognisance of any offence of unlawful activity without the previous sanction of the Central Government. Deleting Section 124A of the IPC will mean that the power to prosecute those who promote unfavourable opinions against the government will rest solely with the Union Government. This provides a major incentive for the Union Government to delete Section 124A under the pretext of protecting human rights while in reality strengthening its ability to suppress liberty in an even more draconian manner.

Given that no democracy can exist without freedom of speech and expression, including the right to promote opinions unfavourable to the government, the Supreme Court should use this opportunity to declare an overarching 'basic structure principle' of the Constitution protecting freedom of speech and expression including the reasonable restrictions mentioned in Article 19(2), so that government interference with individual freedom of speech and expression can be prevented. In doing so, the Court should hew to the principle that any permissible restriction on speech and expression must be only against speech or expression that is likely to result in imminent violence or restricts the freedom of speech and expression of others.

SATYAMEVA JAYATE

Constitutional Conduct Group (108 signatories)

OPEN LETTER TO THE MINISTER OF LAW AND JUSTICE, GOVERNMENT OF INDIA NOTIFICATION OF S. 3 OF THE CONSTITUTION (FORTY FOURTH AMENDMENT) ACT, 1978 TO PROVIDE FOR IMPARTIAL AND INDEPENDENT ADVISORY BOARD TO EXAMINE THE JUSTIFICATION FOR PREVENTIVE DETENTION

16 October 2021

To
Shri Kiren Rijiju,
Hon. Minister of Law and Justice, Government of India

Dear Shri Rijiju,
We are a group of former civil servants of the All India and Central Services who have worked with the Central and State Governments in the course of our careers. As a group, we have no affiliation with any political party but believe in impartiality, neutrality and commitment to the Constitution of India.

You would be aware that Art. 22(4) of the Constitution of India was amended by the Constitution (Forty Fourth Amendment) Act, 1978. S. 3 of this Amendment Act provides that the Advisory Board, to be constituted for examining the justification for preventive detention under this Article, is to be appointed in accordance with the recommendation of the Chief Justice of the High Court; it is to be headed by a sitting judge of that High Court and have at least two serving/former judges of any High Court as members of the Board. The said S. 3 also deleted Art 22(7)(a) of the Constitution, thereby deleting the provision authorizing preventive detention without obtaining the opinion of an Advisory Board.

These amendments were meant to curtail the arbitrary power of governments to appoint on the Advisory Board any person qualified to be a judge of a High Court, and to ensure that no preventive detentions could be made, or continued, without obtaining the opinion of the Advisory Board within two months of the detention. These provisions have yet to come into force since a notification

to give effect to S. 3 of the 44th Constitutional Amendment has not been issued.

At present, any advocate who is qualified to be a judge of a High Court, can be appointed to the Advisory Board. In effect, any advocate with ten years or more of practice can sit on an Advisory Board. This provision is, thus, vulnerable to abuse by governments which, instead of appointing neutral, independent members to the Board, may appoint persons of their choice, including those owing allegiance to the political party in power.

A look at the Objects and Reasons of the Constitution (Forty Fourth Amendment) Act, 1978 explains why Parliament, soon after the experience of the Emergency of 1975-77, considered it necessary to check arbitrary preventive detentions. Para 1 of the Objects and Reasons is cited below:

> 'Recent experience has shown that the fundamental rights, including those of life and liberty, granted to citizens by the Constitution are capable of being taken away by a transient majority. It is, therefore, necessary to provide adequate safeguards against the recurrence of such a contingency in the future and to ensure to the people themselves an effective voice in determining the form of government under which they are to live. This is one of the primary objects of this Bill.'

Successive Union Governments have, however, failed to notify any date for the coming into force of this Constitutional Amendment that was passed by Parliament as far back as 1978. It is not open to the Government of India to sit in judgment over the wisdom of Parliament, which was convinced of the necessity of amending Clause (4)(a) and deleting Clause (7)(a) of Article 22 through the Constitution (Forty Fourth Amendment) Act, 1978.

The provision empowering the Government of India to notify the dates for the coming into force of different provisions of the Constitution (Forty Fourth Amendment) Act was intended to give the government some flexibility in this regard. It will be a travesty

if this provision is conveniently used by the government to negate the legislative intent by refusing to notify the date of coming into effect of the Constitution (Forty Fourth Amendment) Act. The unconscionable delay of 43 years in the issue of this notification has resulted in a brazen abuse of preventive detention laws in gross violation of human rights and a progressive erosion of our cherished democratic values.

We, therefore, urge the Government of India to forthwith notify a date for the coming into force of S. 3 of the Constitution (Forty Fourth Amendment) Act, 1978.

SATYAMEVA JAYATE

Yours sincerely,

Constitutional Conduct Group (100 signatories)

STATEMENT: PERVERSION OF CRIMINAL JUSTICE

5 March 2021

We are a group of former civil servants of the All India and Central Services who have worked for decades with the Central and State Governments. As a group, we have no affiliation with any political party but are committed to the values and principles enshrined in the Constitution of India.

Justice is the most fundamental of constitutional principles and criminal justice is the foundation of law and order in a civilized society. Fair and impartial investigation of crimes is at the root of criminal justice. The reports that the police and other investigative agencies may have violated constitutional guarantees and judicial pronouncements in the practices adopted in search and seizure operations, as well as the possibility that they may have been party to planting incriminating material in personal digital devices and harvesting evidence therefrom, have caused us grave concern.

Recent reports of false evidence being planted remotely in the

personal computer of one of the accused in a long-dragging sedition case are alarming. It is entirely possible that a similar situation is prevalent with regard to the evidence being used in many other UAPA cases. Such blatantly illegal practices could sound the death knell of the criminal justice system in the country. Hence the need for issuing this statement.

There are several examples that cause deep disquiet about the handling of digital evidence, particularly evidence to be found in personal digital devices. If justice is to prevail, the awesome capabilities that present-day surveillance and spyware technology offers investigative agencies must be circumscribed by strict, meaningful and enforceable statutory safeguards.

There are also persistent concerns about investigative agencies seizing, confiscating or searching through the entire contents of personal digital devices such as mobile phones and laptops of not only accused persons but even those called for investigation or questioning.

We wish to state that the extant generic search and seizure provisions in the Code of Criminal Procedure do not address the issues that arise in the context of search, seizure and handling of modern day personal devices.

It is therefore imperative that urgent legislative changes are put in place to guide the investigative agencies with due regard to and adherence to the following principles:

i) Right to privacy
   The landmark judgment of the nine-judge bench of the Supreme Court in Puttaswamy's case makes privacy a fundamental right. This judgment prohibits the investigative agencies seeking transcripts of communications—including Call recordings, WhatsApp/Telegram/Skype/Messenger Chat logs and similar communication records in a wholesale manner without due regard to having to demonstrate necessity and proportionality and respect for privacy of correspondence.

ii) Right against self-incrimination
The right against self-incrimination is expressly protected under Article 20(3) of the Constitution and has also received statutory reinforcement under Section 132 of the Evidence Act and Section 161(2) of the Criminal Procedure Code. It is applicable at the stage of investigation and applies equally to witnesses as well as to the accused. Thus, the practice of investigative agencies acquiring passwords to unlock the personal devices or accounts is violative of the right against self-incrimination.

iii) Protection of Privileged Communication
Indiscriminate access to personal information, particularly personal communication, also involves the question of the right of protection of privileged communications, such as communication with one's spouse, doctor, lawyer etc. At the time of investigation, safeguards must be in place to ensure that there is specific application of mind in respect of each unit of information searched for or seized to ascertain whether such communication has a reasonable likelihood of being privileged.

iv) Integrity of Electronic Evidence
Another important issue is the minimum standards to be adhered to in order to establish the integrity of the electronic material or device that has been taken into custody by the investigative agency. Forensic processes adopted by the investigation agencies also must look for and rule out both pre-seizure and post-seizure tampering of such digital devices.

v) Maintaining Transparency
Finally, there is need for full transparency with regard to the technical capabilities that the investigative agencies have either developed and/or acquired for the purposes of either surveillance or processing of digital evidence. The capabilities of our investigative agencies and the methods and processes

they employ in relation to surveillance, digital data recovery, replication, storage and destruction must be proactively disclosed.

We are of the considered view that whenever the prosecution relies on such electronic/digital evidence, these should be taken cognizance of only after authentication by a Statutory Expert Body set up for the purpose. The law should also provide that if the Statutory Expert Body comes to the conclusion that there has been mala fide planting or manipulation of such evidence, then it must result in prosecution of the perpetrators under the relevant provisions of Chapter XI of the Indian Penal Code.

We, therefore, urge the Government of India to make necessary legislative changes on the above lines to prevent planting of incriminating material and false evidence in personal digital devices and lay down the overall practice and procedure of handling electronic evidence in a manner that will protect privacy, privileged communications, the right against self-incrimination and the integrity of the evidence and ensure complete transparency in order to ensure the constitutional guarantees of rendering justice to all.

SATYAMEVA JAYATE

Constitutional Conduct Group (92 signatories)

OPEN LETTER TO HONOURABLE MEMBERS OF PARLIAMENT ON THE RECENT POLICE ENCOUNTER IN HYDERABAD

13 December 2019

Dear Honourable Members of Parliament,

We, a group of retired civil servants deeply committed to the values and guarantees of the Constitution of India, are appalled by the recent incident of the gunning down by the police of four men accused of raping, killing and burning a young veterinary doctor in Hyderabad. While the crimes of rape and murder were truly horrific, and we

condemn them in the strongest terms, we were equally aghast by the widespread clamour among the public, and calls from the media and responsible persons to castrate, publicly execute, hang or lynch the persons responsible for the offence. Even some Members of Parliament demanded instant and kangaroo justice.

It is quite possible that the response of the Hyderabad police to kill the four accused in an early morning 'encounter' on 6 December was a result of this clamour. Criticised for poor policing and pressured to show quick results, they could have decided to take the easy way out. The actions of the police, prima facie, do not inspire confidence. How was it possible for a team of ten armed police officers to be overpowered by four men who had been in the police lock-up for several hours and without weapons? Why could not the accused have been handcuffed? Why could they not have been shot at to wound but not to kill when they tried to escape? Several retired police officers have gone on record stating that the police version of the encounter is not believable. And at least one Minister of the Telangana government is reported to have said that the orders for the extra-judicial killing came from the very top!

Article 21 of the Constitution says no person can be deprived of his or her life without due process of law being followed. Due process is essential not only to ascertain that the persons arrested are actually guilty and if so, to what degree, but also to know whether or not the persons arrested are the real criminals and not some persons rounded up by the police to satisfy the outburst of public anger. The fundamental premise of our jurisprudence is that a person is innocent until proved guilty.

A kind of blood lust seems to have swamped India in recent years. Lynching of persons accused of cattle smuggling, of thieving, of child lifting, of witchcraft, in fact of any kind of crime at all, is becoming increasingly common and the Indian public does not turn a hair when such incidents are reported. Shockingly, many of these gory incidents of lynching are even video-recorded and widely distributed. More and more people in India seem to be in

favour of this crude and instant justice. Unfortunately, this is getting encouragement from the statements made and actions taken by some of the MPs both within and outside Parliament. But, as the Chief Justice of India has said, 'justice loses its character if it becomes revenge'.

The public offering garlands and sweets to the policemen responsible for the encounter killings in Hyderabad is of a piece with this. When MPs and MLAs demand summary justice, the common man will believe that that is what is desirable and will have no difficulty in seeing killings by policemen as laudable. It will not cross their minds that perhaps those men were not the real culprits, or perhaps all of them were not equally guilty. Everything gets drowned in the chorus of 'Kill! Kill! Kill!' But to quote Barry Eisler, 'Beware that, when fighting monsters, you do not become a monster yourself.'

It is not as if it is impossible to deliver justice speedily. Swifter investigation by the police and quicker and continuous trials in the courts are the key. Without this, the police and the people could be tempted to take the law into their own hands and act as judge and executioner. As MPs, you can ensure these changes are brought about. You can stop calling for lynching and summary executions; you can also prevail upon your parties not to give tickets to people who are accused of rape and murder. Without such actions, your speeches will be seen as hypocritical. We hope to see you work to bring about the meaningful changes necessary to curb such crimes in the future.

Yours faithfully,
Constitutional Conduct Group (65 signatories)

JUDGE LOYA'S DEATH—LETTER TO SUPREMECOURT/ BOMBAY HIGH COURT

2 December 2017

The Honourable Chief Justice of India
The Honourable Chief Justice of the Bombay High Court

Honourable Chief Justices,
Please find attached a report about the request made by Admiral (Retd) L. Ramdas to yourselves that a high-level judicial enquiry be initiated into the controversial circumstances of the death of Judge Brijgopal Harkishan Loya. Justice (Retd) B.H. Marlapalle, former judge of the Bombay High Court, and Justice (Retd) A.P. Shah, former Chief Justice of the Delhi High Court, have also expressed the opinion that a probe or enquiry is needed.

We, the undersigned retired civil servants, would like to place on record our support for the request made by Admiral (Retd.) L. Ramdas to institute a 'high level judicial inquiry' into this matter and urge you to take appropriate action for all the reasons mentioned in his representation.

Yours faithfully,
Constitutional Conduct Group (32 signatories)

~

Regarding Admiral (Retd) L. Ramdas' request

Former Navy Chief Admiral L. Ramdas has requested that a 'high level judicial inquiry' into 'mysterious circumstances' of the death of Brijgopal Harkishan Loya, the Special CBI Judge presiding over the trial of BJP President Amit Shah and several Gujarat Police Officers in the Sohrabuddin fake encounter case. In a letter addressed to the Chief Justice of India Dipak Misra, Admiral L. Ramdas has requested that a 'high level judicial inquiry' be immediately initiated. Former Bombay High Court Judge, Justice (Retd.) B.H. Marlapalle, has also

sought an SIT probe into the Judge's death. Former Chief Justice of Delhi High Court, Justice A.P. Shah had also recently spoken out about the allegations, opining that not enquiring into the allegations made by the family 'would send a very wrong signal to the judiciary, particularly the lower cadre'. He had also expressed concerns over allegations of corruption, as Judge Loya was allegedly offered a bribe of Rs 100 crore.

~

Full text of Admiral L. Ramdas's letter*:

Subject: Need for a special judicial enquiry to investigate into the sudden death of Justice Loya

Dear Hon Chief Justice of India,

All Democracies exist and survive on three main pillars—namely the Executive, Legislature and the Judiciary. Freedom from British rule, was won after a prolonged struggle and The Indian Constitution was evolved after nearly two and a half years of debate in the Constituent Assembly, and passed on 29 November 1949 and India became a Republic on 26 January 1950. Our Constitution became effective. This one and only holy book which matters, subscribes to the above concept of our Democracy, wherein all our citizens are considered to be equal in the eyes of the law.

This is all the more important when a CBI judge, Justice Loya, specially appointed by the CJI of the Mumbai High Court to investigate the murder of Sohrabbudin, dies under mysterious circumstances while on a visit to Nagpur. The silence of the two judges who apparently persuaded the late Judge Loya to travel to Nagpur, and accompanied him, is disturbing to say the least. The

---

* 'Admiral Ramdas Requests Judicial Enquiry Into Judge Loya's Mysterious Death', *Countercurrents.org*, 28 November 2017 (https://countercurrents.org/2017/11/admiral-ramdas-requests-judicial-enquiry-into-judge-loyas-mysterious-death/; Accessed March 2024)

inaction of the judiciary about this sequence of events thus far is indeed surprising. This is all the more puzzling in the context of the recent revelations by family members of the late Justice Loya, who have raised certain questions, apprehending foul play in the circumstances leading to his sudden death.

A judicial probe at this point, at least to respond to the queries raised by the family, and to uphold the image of the judiciary in the eyes of the people of India, is absolutely necessary. As a former Chief of the Indian Navy, I feel strongly that it is critically important to clear any doubts about this entire incident. Therefore, in the larger interests of the nation and its people, and above all in upholding the Constitution of India and the image of our entire legal system, a high level judicial enquiry be initiated immediately.

CONSERVATION AND THE RIGHTS OF TRIBAL COMMUNITIES

Thinking Adivasi: The Rights and the Wrongs*

G.N. DEVY

Jaipalsingh Munda and Devendranath Samanta were the only two representatives of the Adivsis in the Constituent Assembly. In the debate on 24 January 1947, responding to the Resolution based on the report of the sub-committee for partially excluded areas, Jaipal Singh had said:

> 'I rise to speak on behalf of millions of unknown hordes—yet very important—of unrecognised warriors of freedom, the original people of India who have variously been known as backward tribes, primitive tribes, criminal tribes and everything else... On behalf of more than 30 millions of the *Adibasis*, I support it not merely because it may have been sponsored by a leader of the Indian National Congress. I support it because it is a resolution which gives expression to sentiments that throb in every heart in this country. Sir, if there is any group of Indian people that has been shabbily treated it is my people. They have been disgracefully treated, neglected for the last 6,000 years. The history of the Indus Valley civilization, a child of which I am, shows quite clearly that it is the new comers—most of you here—are intruders as far as I am concerned—it is the new comers who have driven away my people from the Indus Valley to the jungle fastnesses. This Resolution is not going to teach *Adibasis* democracy. You cannot teach democracy to the tribal people; you have to learn democratic ways from them. They are the most democratic people on earth.'

---

* This article is a modified and extended version of G.N. Devy's 'Introduction' to *Being Adivasi* (edited by Abhay Xax and G. N. Devy, Pengiun India, 2021)

The thoughtfulness, wisdom and pain with which Jaipalsingh Munda spoke have been all but forgotten by India during the last seven decades; and the Scheduled Tribes (ST) have come to be seen as another Scheduled Caste (SC), forgetting that the caste society and the tribal society need to be understood differently, in terms of their history and cultural distinctiveness. For several decades following Independence, 'Adivasi' was an anthropomorphic 'type' cast in sentiment and piety, or else dismissed as historical baggage worth leaving behind in India's march to modernity and nationhood. Though the complexities of the Adivasi society received attention in scholarship related to the theme, the popular attitude to Adivasis was severely restricted by the acronym 'ST'. Excessive pity and excessive contempt are both equally patent instruments of 'othering' people.

Census data over several decades shows that their population normally amounts to 8 or 9 per cent of India's overall population. One does not have to go any further to identify the main reason for the political ineffectiveness of Adivasis in India. To be indigenous is, in our time, to be severely marginalised in economy, politics, institutionalised knowledge and institutionalised religion. The space for the indigenous is rapidly shrinking. One can illustrate this: The semi-official definition of 'Adivasi' in India is that they are 'shy'. They live in remote areas. They have their belief systems and their own languages. The year 2019 was declared by UNESCO as the Year of the Indigenous Languages. There were official celebrations and academic conferences to 'celebrate' the year. However, it is a fact that several hundreds of the languages of the Adivasis still kept alive by the communities are close to extinction. A comprehensive survey of languages that I had conducted of the 780 living languages in India in 2010 showed that nearly 300 languages, mainly spoken by the indigenous peoples, may disappear in the next few decades. The UPA-1 government passed a law in 2008 requiring land ownership of the tribal communities to be returned to them. However, nearly half of the claims have yet to be settled. The Supreme Court of India

has already asked that the families—whose land title claims have not been accepted—be evacuated. Despite legal provisions aimed at safeguarding communities and their cultures, they are diminishing and suffering an undeserving obsolescence in a world that has been vandalising the natural resources of the earth as never before.

Several decades ago, I started working with the Adivasis in Gujarat. Soon, I noticed how the rapid depletion of their forest resources had become a major cause of their pauperisation. It is not as if there were not enough laws to protect their interests; but all of the laws came to them as an alien system of thought and practice. The struggle to understand this alien sense of justice has taken the Adivasis such a long time that by now they are almost at the fag-end of their losing battle and left with a few broken English words as their only consolation. In that sense, the forest with which they had a symbiotic and intimate relation and which they lost is now alienated. Now speaks English!

The debate on the genesis of the social category called Adivasi in India is not yet a settled one. Different views exist on this question. One strong contender is that colonial rule in India resulted in the designation of Adivasis as a distinct ethnic and social group. It is true that European colonialism applied 'indigenous' as an anthropological tag to numerous local communities in North and South America, Australia and the Pacific, Africa and Asia. However, while the idea could be applied with a much greater clarity in North America and Australia, in South America, Africa and Asia, the communities encountered by the colonial powers were far too complex to be covered under the simple 'indigenous' tag. The rise of terms such as 'aboriginal', 'Indians', 'indigenous' and 'tribes' in different continents too indicates that the process of imagining 'the other' during the extended history of colonialism was not without complexities and grey areas. It cannot, however, be denied that the current discourse related to the Adivasis in India owes a great deal to its colonial history.

There is another theory on this question which likes to view

Adivasis as a social legacy inherited by us from pre-colonial times. There are ample descriptions of forest dwellers in epics, plays, myths and folktales, giving evidence of communities distinct from the urban and rural Indian society in existence since pre-historic times. These forest people appear in those narratives and descriptions as being outside the pale of the law, social customs, traditions and belief systems prevailing in different historical epochs in India's history. The question of whether all of these forest-dwelling communities got designated during the colonial times as 'tribals' is difficult to answer in a simple affirmation or negation. The process could not avoid demographic mix-ups. For instance, the people of Manipur and Tripura appear in the epics as the 'main people'. During colonial times, many of them are found to be relegated to the category 'tribe'. On the other hand, many subsets of the population in Rajasthan would be placed in the category of 'out of the pale' in pre-colonial India; but they find place in non-tribal, caste-bound Indian society from the fifteenth century onwards. Given this, who exactly is 'tribal', 'Adivasi' or 'janajati', as a post-Independence bureaucrat may describe them, is a question quite difficult to answer.

Ever since the Schedule of Tribes was conceptualised after Independence, the question has become even more difficult. Over the last seven decades, the demand for a given community's inclusion in the Schedule has come up far too frequently and such inclusions have been made not too infrequently. Given this uncertainty related to the exact genesis of Adivasis, their ethnic characteristics and their social standing, the use of terms such as 'Adivasis' or 'Tribes' has to be understood entirely with reference to the context in which these terms get used. What is common to all, or most, of the tribes in India is their endangered identity, environment, language, and notions of gender, belief-systems, performance-traditions and human rights. The local features of these struggles may vary from community to community and from state to state. However, the general narrative is fairly common. Quintessentially, this narrative refers to a colonial experience that hammered a break in the long-standing traditions of

the indigenous; yet they kept close to their traditions and close also to Nature, losing in the process their control over natural resources, land, rivers and forests and continued to clash with a radically different framework of justice, ethics and spirituality.

For the indigenous, invariably, there are two points in time marking their emergence: one that is traced back to a mythological time enshrined in their collective memory and expressed in their community's 'story of origin', the other that is synchronous with a colonial forest officer or beat guard setting foot on the land that was once their dominion. It is true that no established research or theory in archaeology, anthropology, genetics, cultural geography, historical linguistics, agriculture and forestry goes to show that all or any of the indigenous people have been inhabitants of the very same land where they were when colonialism made its presence felt. Probably, a very small portion of them have been associated with their present habitat since the time Homo sapiens inhabited the subcontinent. Yet, notwithstanding the pre-historic migrations, it is true that indigenous communities have been associated with their habitats for a considerably long time. The European colonial quest, the territorial and cultural invasion associated with it and the interference of alien political, ecological and belief-system-related paradigms brought a threat to the traditions that the indigenous had developed. The absence of desire on their part to accept the new paradigms and to internalise them made them stand out, be marked as 'others' interpreted as 'primitive' and represented as 'indigenous' not just for the colonial rulers but also for other sections of Indian society.

Despite inadequacy in the knowledge that the non-Adivasi society has about them, it is clear that their existence, environment, cultural ethos, lifestyles and values have been under a relentless assault by the practices, culture and value of the rest of the world. In recognition of the threat to Indigenous cultures and knowledge systems, to their land and environment, languages, livelihood and law, the United Nations came out with a *Declaration on the Rights*

of Indigenous People, accepted by the UN General Assembly in September 2007. However, the UN framework has been only a normative framework and produced little impact on the situation of the indigenous.

If the awareness of Adivasis and their concerns is scant among the non-Adivasi population of India, knowledge about communities described as 'Denotified Tribes' is almost absent. Lest the term be misunderstood as 'some kind of Adivasis' or 'officially non-recognised Adivasis'—which is not unusual among even those who know something about Adivasis—I would like to offer the following brief description of the Denotified Tribes. During the nineteenth century, after the British had more or less secured authority over all princely states in India, they found it necessary to disarm the disbanded soldiers of the vanquished armies of Indian princes. The British also wanted to ensure safe travels in Indian states for commercial purposes. In order to accomplish the two objectives, they appointed William Henry Sleeman to detect every unauthorised use of arms by individuals. Sleeman made copious notes and listed instances of armed clashes on highways in central India. In the process, he gave rise to the idea of the 'Thugee'. The idea attracted readers of his books back in England. The list of persons and their communities came to be associated with the idea of thugee or communities that make looting and crime their profession. The 1871 Criminal Tribes Act was based on this notion. It listed communities as 'criminal communities', implying that being born in any of those communities made one automatically criminal in tendency. The CTA provided for 'reformatory settlement', a euphemism for labour camps turned into prisons. The listed communities were interned in these settlements, with severe restrictions placed on their free movement. Sleeman's list had many flaws in it. Most of the communities had been traditionally nomadic in habit, an age-old social phenomenon in India. Members of the interned communities were put to hard labour, in most instances, unpaid labour. It is difficult to estimate as to how many perished due to the stress of labour.

Members of these communities continued to live in the settlements for several generations spread over eight decades. In 1952, two years after India adopted the Constitution, the 'notified' communities were 'denotified'. They continued to be described as Denotified and Nomadic Tribes (DNT), while very few of them found a place in the official lists of *janjatis*, the Adivasis. The stigma of criminality continued to stick to them despite the slight change in the nomenclature. Not being included in the lists of STs and SCs, barring a few exceptions, they continued to languish without land, livelihood or access to schools and healthcare. Not having fixed addresses, their minimum rights as citizens too were not safeguarded. The stigma around their name often causes harassment from villagers and the urban population. There has been a widespread incidence of mob lynching of members of the DNT communities.

Successive governments have been generally indifferent to the plight of the DNTs as they do not form even any significant minority, though their total population in the country is by no means insignificant. At present, the number may have gone up and may be close to ten crore. The Census of India has never carried out any clear count of the DNTs. And since the numbers are not officially ascertained, and as locations of these communities are not properly documented and any systematic thought has been given to their livelihood requirements and human rights; they continue to remain in India's imagination as the invisible nowhere-people. The only time a ray of hope was seen by the DNTs of India was when Dr Manmohan Singh constituted a DNT National Commission in 2007 and a Technical advisory Group soon after. The TAG report and the Commission report have useful recommendations for improving the life of the DNTs; but those reports have not been implemented so far. It is the same fate that the report of the Xaxa Committee appointed for reviewing the status of Adivasis in India. Apart from various development issues, there are stringent anti-conversion laws which are being used as a tool to divide the Adivasi

communities on religious lines. The communal agenda of religion-fanatic organisations has gradually created a fear among people who don't subscribe to the idea of assimilating the Adivasis in the Hindu fold. As a result, communal violence has become common in Adivasi areas.

India's Ecocide—A grim picture

PRERNA SINGH BINDRA

In July 2023, over 100 people were killed across Himachal Pradesh, Uttar Pradesh, and Delhi due to intense, prolonged rain and flooding. Thousands were evacuated, crops lands were flooded, wasted, cattle and livelihoods lost, houses demolished, entire villages washed away.

For much of north India, June and July were also months of intense heat—over 100 were killed in Bihar and UP due to extreme heatwaves. In neighbouring Uttarakhand, the picturesque, holy town of Joshimath was sinking under the weight of mindless over-construction, large hydel projects and the severe denudation of once verdant hills.

Meanwhile, Maharashtra and Karnataka—which faced floods over past four years, withered with scant rainfall in 2023.

Floods. Landslides. Cyclones. Heat. Drought. Land subsidence.

India had 314 days of erratic weather in 2022 causing over 3,000 deaths as per a report by the Delhi-based Centre of Science and Environment. Such tragedies triggered by the Climate Crisis and rampant deforestation are unfolding with alarming frequency, and severity. They are not mirages in the distant future.

The Climate Crisis is here to stay.

The United Nations recognises forests and biodiversity as one of the most effective defence to mitigate Climate Change impacts. Old growth, natural forests are the biggest terrestrial carbon sink. Since 1750, forests and other ecosystems like grasslands, mangroves, peatlands have sequestered about half of the carbon emissions from the atmosphere—the rest is absorbed by the oceans. Conversely, the clearing of such forests—deforestation contributes 12 to 20 per cent of global greenhouse gas emissions.

Which is why a central pledge of the CoP26 Climate Summit in Glasgow was to end deforestation by 2030. Incidentally, India was not among the 100 signatory countries. Without going into the politics of the issue or undermining the colonial history of climate injustice, *conserving forests is in the country's own self-interest.* India is one of the most vulnerable countries to Climate Change, and the poorest of the poor bear the brunt of extreme weather and other impacts.

Yet, despite the mounting crisis, India has steadily diluted and eroded environmental safeguards leaving cities choking with severe air pollution, poisoning our rivers and soil, and destroying India's glorious natural heritage—its forests and endangered wildlife.

Worse, what the government is engaging in is subterfuge—best explained by the Forest (Conservation) Amendment Act, 1980 notified on 4 August 2023, which positions itself as an enabler to 'achieve national targets of Net Zero Emission by 2070 and to maintain or enhance forest carbon stock through sustainable development.' But couched in the language of carbon neutrality, it allows, indeed facilitates the corporate takeover of natural forests by encouraging commercial plantations.

The original FCA had a clear objective—and a system of checks and balances—to prevent deforestation by regulating and restricting diversion of forest land for industrial, infrastructure and other purposes. The 2023 amendment negates these safeguards. It redefines forests to only include notified and officially recorded forests, thereby removing large tracts of forest from legal protection through its various—and deliberately—ambiguous, ill-defined clauses, making each and every patch of forest vulnerable to commercial interests.

The devastation that this Act will unleash cannot be overstated, a matter raised by members of civil society—including by the Constitutional Conduct Group that forms part of this compendium. What is equally worrying is the insidious manner in which this amendment undermines the Constitution, striking at India's founding principles of democracy, equality and justice.

The proposed Forest Conservation Bill was referred in March 2023 to a Joint Committee of Parliament (JCP), itself an anomaly as procedurally it ought to have been scrutinised by the Parliamentary Committee on Science, Technology, Environment and Forests. That bias apart, the JCP received over 1,300 representations from serving forest officers, civil servants, scientists, domain experts, community groups and even state governments. For instance, Kerala categorically asked for the original FCA to be retained as it had, 'proved to be a single solid barrier in preventing massive deforestation in the country.' Nagaland too opposed the amendments—on the grounds that they 'came into direct conflict with the constitutional safeguards guaranteed to the state on land and its resources.' Besides, Nagaland, Mizoram and other Northeastern states worried that the amended FCA 'will make precious forest land more vulnerable to damage and destruction.' This, as not only does the 2023 amendments strip unrecorded forests from legal safeguards, but also allows diversion of forests for construction of roads, railway lines or strategic linear projects within 100 km of India's international borders—without any environment assessment or scrutiny—effectively removing forests in entire states from protective legal cover.

Yet, not one of the concerns: of the people, of the states or even dissent from members within the JCP itself was considered or taken on board; there was no attempt at consensus building or addressing genuine apprehensions. The amended FCA passed through the Lok Sabha and the Rajya Sabha without a single change, making a mockery of democratic processes.

The 2023 FCA, or the 'Van (Sanrakshan Evam Samvardhan) Adhiniyam, 1980' as it is now titled is non-inclusive in other ways as well, alienating non-Hindi speaking states like Kerala, Tamil Nadu and those in the Northeast. It's another matter altogether that the law has no provision for either '*Sanrakshan*' (Conservation) or '*Samvardhan*' (fostering, regeneration) of forests as claimed in the title.

The amended Act also takes further the Centre's steady encroachment into the domain of states. It confers sweeping powers on the Central government, to decide which and on what terms and to whom a forest area can be diverted especially in 'security related activities' or 'public utilities'—both undefined, further widening the scope of misuse. Moreover, land is a state subject and such concentration of authority will only further disrupt the delicate consensus between India's states and the Union.

The new Act is a betrayal of justice to our people, especially marginalised rural populations and indigenous tribes who depend on our forests for sustenance and livelihood, besides having deep cultural connections to forests. Equally, it is a betrayal of future generations as it denies our children the right to a liveable, viable environment, leaving them an impoverished planet—and future.

I dwell extensively on the amended FCA as it signifies a dangerous turn in the governance of forests. Environmental historians like Ramchandra Guha mark the advent of the British railways as a watershed moment in the history of Indian forestry, as it ushered in state control of forests for massive timber exploitation. Post-independence, in the late 1960s through the 1980s, in response to our deteriorating environment, the focus shifted to check rampant deforestation and the decline of wildlife. A legal and policy framework was established to safeguard the environment and to protect forests and wildlife. Project Tiger, the largest conservation initiative of its kind globally was launched in 1973.

The notification of the amended FCA is another retrograde landmark in forest governance as the state derelicts its constitutional duty of protecting the forest, wildlife and environment. It signals a shift from an ecology centric approach to one focusing on the economic exploitation of forests; the handing over of a public resource to private hands. Beyond the destruction it will unleash, the amendments signify a hubristic mindset which lays emphasis on the 'creation' rather than conservation of existing forests, even though plantations can never replace the complex web of organisms

and ecosystems of natural forests. Besides, plantations are poor at provisioning of ecosystem services such as containing soil erosion, harbouring wildlife, water retention. As per a study published in *Nature*, the carbon sequestration potential of natural forests is 40 times greater as compared to plantations. The amended FCA also glorifies safaris and zoos even as they destroy the natural habitats—forests and mangroves, mountains and wetlands—of wildlife.

It is evident that the FCA is a culmination of a series of reengineering the legal and policy framework to suit the 'ease of doing business'. Put another way, laws and policies—the bedrock of forest and wildlife conservation—are being rewritten at the behest of powerful business houses, destroying pristine forests and the life and livelihoods of communities dependent on them.

One striking example is how the energy giant Vedanta lobbied, with the then environment minister Prakash Javadekar, to weaken environmental regulations to suit its mining and oil interests, even as the country was gripped by the COVID-19 pandemic. The 'Organized Crime and Corruption Reporting Project', a global network of investigative journalists, reports how Vedanta pushed for mining companies to expand production by 50 per cent without the 'hassle' of needing environment approvals or public hearings, which are considered by business houses as a major irritant in the environment and social regulatory process. A year later in early 2022, the government obliged. As per the same report, Cairn India—Vedanta's oil business—also pushed for scrapping public hearings for exploratory drilling in oil blocks. Again, successfully. It's worth noting that the amended FCA also accommodates this by removing legal scrutiny for exploratory and prospecting activities in forest lands.

Forests previously marked as 'no-go' areas by the Ministry of Environment Forests and Climate Change (MoEFCC) for their high biodiversity value, density, contiguity and water reserves are also fair game. An expose by *The Reporters Collective* shows how the Association of Power Producers exploited a rumoured coal

shortage in October 2021 to lobby with the coal ministry to open up two coal blocks nestled in India's densest forests. One of these blocks is in Chhattisgarh's ecologically sensitive Hasdeo Arand, a prime elephant habitat. It is also home to the Gonds—among other indigenous people—who hold the land sacred and have been agitating against the mining. Most depend on farming or forest produce for a livelihood, which the mining will usurp, and destroy. A friend who is associated with the struggle says mining is 'death'. A cancer that kills forests, and the rivers that flow through and the fields they sustain. In Hasdeo Arand, it will obliterate the wildlife and a way of life in tune with the rhythms of nature.

But, in New India none of this matters. Not the people, not the environment, not the wildlife; only conglomerates do. So, again, the government obliged, and coal blocks were allocated to the Adani Group.

If environment laws are onerous, they are simply ignored or circumvented. Take the case of the contentious 900 km Char Dham highway expansion project in Uttarakhand, broken into 53 segments of less than 100 km to bypass the Environmental Impact Assessment (EIA) that is mandatory for road projects over 100 km in length. Earlier touted as a tourism initiative that would connect four pilgrim centres, the highway expansion was repackaged as one of strategic importance to allow for easier passage. Despite concerns raised by local citizens, who also petitioned the court, the project bulldozed ahead. Mountains were blasted, slashed, tunnelled, muck dumped into rivers, about 900 hectares of pristine oak and Deodhar forests, cleared. Consequently, slopes have destabilised, the soil is eroding, and perennial mountain springs drying up. The wildlife—musk deer, black bears, leopards, monal pheasants—have diminished. Like the native people, they are being eroded from their own land.

This is just one among the many wounds inflicted on the mountains. Bumper to bumper dam projects have been planned in Himalayan rivers. For instance, there are 53 hydropower projects in the upper reaches of Satluj basin in just Kinnaur district in Himachal

Pradesh. No less than 90 per cent of forest land has been diverted here for hydropower projects and transmission lines. The eastern Himalayas have not been spared either. Arunachal Pradesh is another hub for hydel projects—169 at last count, the largest Dibang will submerge pristine rainforests, felling no less than 3 lakh trees.

In an interview with *NewsClick*, seismo-tectonics expert Dr CP Rajendran warns that such massive and unscientific mega construction projects and tourism infrastructure on the Himalayas are catastrophic. The resilience of this fragile, seismically active mountain range is threatened leading to frequent and severe disasters like flash floods, landslides and earthquakes.

Nothing is sacred in India's growth cult. Even our Protected Areas are unprotected and diverted for various development activities. India's 981 PAs are critical to conserve its increasingly endangered wildlife and cover about 5 per cent of its terrestrial surface, just about half of the world average of 9.3 per cent. Yet, nearly all projects, 99.8 per cent to be precise, considered between 2014-2019, were cleared by the National Board for Wildlife (NBWL), a body tasked with the protection of wildlife.

Among the projects approved is a road through the Kutch Wildlife Sanctuary (Gujarat) that will destroy the only known nesting site of flamingos in India, the expansion of a highway and railway line through a national park—and global biodiversity hotspot in Goa and the Ken-Betwa river-linking project that would affect about a third of Panna Tiger reserve's (Madhya Pradesh) core area, drowning breeding sites of critically endangered vultures and tigers. Yes, tigers. Our national animal. The same we profess to conserve.

Such loss of habitat has grave impacts, and even led to local extinctions. The Hirpora Wildlife Sanctuary was one of two strongholds of the Kashmir Markhor, of which there are only about 300 in India. The construction of the Mughal Road—with the allied disturbance and development—proved to be fatal for this endangered spiral-horned mountain goat. A recent estimation

exercise showed no signs of the Markhor. It is functionally, locally extinct from an area deemed to be its sanctuary.

Entire sanctuaries have been de-notified, erased off the map of India. One among these is the Galathea Bay sanctuary, an important nesting site of leatherback sea turtles, the world's largest turtles. This was done to make way for 'development' plans for the Great Nicobar Island which include a mega port, airport, township and a power plant in a Special Economic Zone. Leatherbacks are migratory, swimming over 10,000 miles a year between foraging and nesting grounds. With their nesting beach up for destruction for a port where would the turtles go? The project will also compromise the isolated Shompen tribe, a particularly vulnerable tribal Group that inhabit the island. They live in the unique, primal rainforests of the island, also up for destruction. Drawing the attention of the President, and the National Commission for Scheduled Tribes, the CCG write how the planned development will 'virtually destroy the unique ecology of this island, and the habitat of vulnerable tribal groups', who, as the letter explains, were deceived in signing off their lands. They write, poignantly of the Shompen*, considered one of the most isolated tribes on earth, who 'continue to live, cultivate and collect food resources from the forests, little aware that some of their forests would soon be taken away.'

Our natural heritage is being sold for a song, bulldozing the fundamental rights of the most vulnerable, and marginalised of our people.

Ramchandra Guha aptly calls India an 'an environmental basket-case.' Our rivers—our lifelines and once a symbol of purity—are sewers, choking on our filth. Most of are biologically dead. Our aquifers are depleting and soils, contaminated. We are eating, drinking, inhaling poison. Delhi ranks as amongst the most polluted cities in the world—and four others make it to the global top 10.

---

* Believed to be the first inhabitants of the Nicobar islands. Only about 100-400 of the Shompen survive.

No surprises then that India has tanked to the bottom of the 180 countries evaluated in the 2022 Environment Performance Index, on various indices by the Yale Center for Environmental Law and Policy and the Columbia University Center for International Earth Science Information Network.

The doctrine of development at all costs that India has adopted has led to an ecological holocaust. We need to appreciate that environment safeguards are not about saving a few animals; they are not hurdles in the race for 'development', nor a luxury but an existential necessity, vital for our economy and health. Millions in India directly depend on rain-fed farming and forests for sustenance. India's GDP is still subject to the whims of the monsoon; good rains can boost growth, while a deficit may lead to a slump. Air pollution costs us dear, resulting in 1.67 million premature deaths in 2019, and $36.8 billion in economic loss—or 1.7 per cent of the GDP. Pollution has been linked to rising incidences of cancers, strokes, heart disease, obesity and diabetes among other ailments. A friend's six-year-old child struggled to breathe; her lung was impaired, not working to capacity. She was breathing Delhi's foul air, the doctor said she had the lungs of a chain smoker.

We have barely recovered from the ravages caused by the SARS-CoV-2 pandemic, whose origin is linked to deforestation. Multiple studies support a link between global deforestation and outbreaks of zoonotic and vector borne diseases—about 60 per cent of emerging infectious diseases in humans are zoonotic.

India's ecocide needs to stop.

Tragically, voices of dissent: be it to defend our forests, or fight for the rights of the marginalised—for instance, the tribals, the farmers, or to retain the secular fabric of the country are being silenced. As the breadth of the letters in this compendium show, the Constitutional Conduct Group has spoken stridently to defend our freedoms and to uphold the sanctity of our constitution. And while it is all-too-easy to give in to cynicism, dissent has shaped our history as historian Romila Thapar explains in her book *Voices of Dissent*, it has shaped

civilisations, for knowledge evolves by questioning the world we live in. It shapes history. Gandhiji's Satyagraha movement was an act of—non-violent—dissent. Margaret Mead's famous quote bears repeating: 'Never doubt that a small group of thoughtful, committed citizens can change the world; indeed, it's the only thing that ever has.'

I am aware this makes for a bleak read; it is, but, a reflection of our times—the age of Climate Crisis and the Sixth Extinction. Most writings on environment, be they work of fiction or non-fiction tend to be dystopian. While speaking on Climate Change at an event in New Delhi, writer Amitav Ghosh apologised for the 'the really grim picture.' Ghosh struggles to be optimistic, 'Once you start looking into Climate Change you realise the impacts are really frightening and there's no way to make this look positive.'

Ghosh is right, yet...we must hold on to hope, and take action.

We stand today at another watershed moment in India's environmental history. Even as we suffer the consequences of the environment crisis; we are, chillingly, faced with a governance paradigm that hurtle us towards further ecological collapse. As citizens, we need to ask crucial questions from our policy makers, and hold them accountable. We need to question the current model of mindless, unplanned, non-inclusive development; not treat it as a holy cow, in whose name our forest wealth and natural heritage is being decimated. We must question why our legislations are being moulded to favour corporate greed instead of public well-being.

Healthy ecosystems are crucial for our ecological and financial security, economic growth is a mere subset of the environment. But looking beyond hard numbers; our country's culture is rooted in nature, we worship mountains and rivers, revere elephants, even snakes. We hold life sacred; the Mahatma taught us, and the world, Ahimsa. Our forests and wildlife are part of the fabric of the country. Our constitution guarantees us a fundamental right to a clean environment while imposing on citizens a duty to protect our forests and wildlife.

As we must, if we are to save the idea of India.

Letters and Statements

OPEN LETTER TO MEMBERS OF PARLIAMENT ON THE FOREST CONSERVATION (AMENDMENT) BILL 2023

12 July 2023

Honourable MPs of the Lok Sabha, Honourable MPs of the Rajya Sabha,

We are a group of former civil servants of the All India and Central Services who have worked with the Central and State Governments in the course of our careers. As a group, we have no affiliation with any political party but believe in impartiality, neutrality and commitment to the Constitution of India.

We are deeply perturbed by the Forest Conservation (Amendment) Bill, 2023, which was introduced in Parliament in March 2023 and is slated to be passed in the coming monsoon session. Our concerns are both about the content of the Bill as well as the procedure by which the Bill is being examined and passed.

Procedurally, the Bill should have been referred to the Parliamentary Committee on science, technology, environment and forests, instead of being referred to a Select Committee, all the members of which, except one, belong to the ruling party, making the examination partisan and unsatisfactory.

The historical reason for the passing of the Forest Conservation Act (FCA) in 1980, viz. to prevent deforestation, needs to be appreciated, before we discuss the present Bill. In the thirty years prior to 1980, about 4.2 million hectares of forest land were lost, being diverted for non-forestry purposes. In over forty years since the enactment of the FCA, 1980, only about 1.5 million hectares have

been diverted. Even though the adverse impacts of climate change were not obvious in 1980, it is a testament to the sagacity of our lawmakers that they considered it critical to regulate the diversion of forest lands through the enactment of the FCA, 1980.

Unfortunately, in the last few years, despite the adverse impacts of climate change becoming increasingly obvious—the floods now sweeping north India are a glaring example—the diversion of forest lands has gathered pace. Between 2018-19 and 2022-23, almost 90,000 hectares of forest land have been diverted for non-forest use. The institutions of the Forest Advisory Committee and the Regional Empowered Committees, which are meant to regulate and minimise this diversion, have been ineffective. Hardly any proposal for diversion of forest land seems to be rejected! In 2020, alone, of the 367 proposals received for diversion of 14,855 hectares of forest land, only three proposals amounting to about 11 hectares were rejected!

This tendency of liberally giving away forest land for non-forest purposes, is now sought to be further strengthened through the FCA Amendment Bill. This Bill allows forest land, other than in protected areas, to be used for several non-forest purposes, viz. (i) defence-related purposes within 100 kms of the border of India; (ii) stretches of land alongside railway lines and highways; (iii) zoos and safaris owned by the government or any authority; (iv) ecotourism facilities; (v) silvi-cultural operations (to enhance forest growth); and, most worryingly, (vi) any other purpose specified by the central government. The Bill also specifies that reconnaissance and prospecting surveys, among other surveying activities, may be undertaken, under conditions to be specified by the central government. One wonders what is the purpose of prospecting surveys? Does it mean that if any important minerals are found in dense forests, mining will be allowed? A recent print article mentions that diamond mining is proposed to be undertaken in the dense natural forests of Buxwaha, in Madhya Pradesh, even though this will endanger water availability in the region, and contribute to local as

well as global warming. Permission for this mining project has been given even under the existing, stricter, Act. What will happen once the Act is amended, and permissions are granted freely? The preamble of the Bill mentions that as a result of this Bill, forest and tree cover will be increased to create a carbon sink of an additional 2.5 to 3.0 billion tonnes of CO2 equivalent, by 2030. It puts its faith, apparently, in compensatory afforestation. Such an expectation is unrealistic given the fact that large tracts of existing natural forests will be diverted for non-forest use. There are ample studies which suggest that natural forests are forty times more efficient as carbon sinks than newly planted forests. Moreover, the results of compensatory afforestation, as of today, have not been rosy. Between 2008 and 2019, an area equal to only 72 per cent of the diverted forest area was brought under compensatory afforestation; moreover, 24 per cent of this was on existing, but degraded, forest land.

It is important to remember that natural forests are important not only as carbon sinks but also because they harbour immensely precious flora and fauna. India is one of only seventeen megadiverse countries in the world with more than 5,000 endemic species of plants and animals. This myopic Bill threatens all of this biodiversity.

Besides the fact that the Bill seeks to overturn the praiseworthy Supreme Court judgment of 1996 in the Godavarman case (which, inter alia, defined forests as any piece of land that resembles the dictionary meaning of forest), one of its most damaging provisions is to allow forest lands within 100 kms of the country's borders to be used for 'strategic linear projects of national importance and concerning national security'. This 100 km stretch would cover all the north-eastern States and would include Sikkim and Uttarakhand—states which have the highest forest cover in the country and are also biodiversity hotspots.

The preamble of the Bill also mentions that it will 'enhance forest based economic, social and environmental benefits, including improvement of livelihoods of forest dependent communities'. One of the main Acts which supports forest-dependent communities is

the Forest Rights Act (FRA) 2006. The current Bill does not contain any provision to protect the rights granted under the FRA; nor does it mention whether the provisions of the Bill are in conflict or conformity with the provisions of the FRA. For example, what happens if the lands, on which one or more forest communities depend, are leased out for ecotourism or safari parks or used for defence installations? This conflict was observed by Mr Harsh Chauhan, until recently the Chairman of the National Commission on Scheduled Tribes; he resigned, reportedly, because his request that the Bill be deferred was not accepted by the government. It is apparent that far from protecting forest-dependent communities, the Bill may actually threaten their livelihoods and their lives.

Article 48A of the Constitution says that 'the State shall endeavour to protect and improve the environment and to safeguard the forests and wildlife of the country'. It is apparent that the FCA Amendment Bill will do just the opposite.

The Amendment Bill is replete with flaws and is totally misleading. We urge you not to pass it in its present form as it will nullify the very Act it seeks to amend, and will prove to be the last nail in the coffin for the existing forest resources of the country.

SATYAMEVA JAYATE

Constitutional Conduct Group (105 signatories)

OPEN LETTER TO THE NATIONAL COMMISSION FOR SCHEDULED TRIBES—EFFECTS OF THE GREAT NICOBAR PROJECTS ON TRIBAL GROUPS

02 May 2023

Dear Chairperson and Members of the National Commission for Scheduled Tribes,

We are a group of former civil servants of the All India and Central Services who have worked with the Central and State Governments

in the course of our careers. Both as individuals and as a group, we believe in impartiality, neutrality and commitment to the Constitution of India. We do not owe allegiance to any political party.

On 27 January 2023, we had written an open letter to the President of India on the proposed port and container terminal on the island of Great Nicobar that will virtually destroy the unique ecology of this island and the habitat of vulnerable tribal groups. But neither our letter, nor the very many others written by other individuals and groups, about the flaws in the environment and forest clearances, seem to have had any effect in making the Government of India re-examine the project. It is only very recently that the National Green Tribunal has ordered a closer look at some of the environmental issues raised.

We write today, not about the environmental and ecological destruction that the project is likely to wreak, but about the fate of the two groups of tribal people that the island of Great Nicobar harbours, viz., the Shompen, a Particularly Vulnerable Tribal Group who stand to lose much of their traditional forest foraging grounds, and the southern Great Nicobarese, a Scheduled Tribe, who have already been badly affected by the tsunami of 2004, having had to move out from their ancestral villages and be resettled closer to the administrative hub of the island. The project will be extremely detrimental to both these groups: hence, this letter to you.

According to the timeline of events as learnt by us, on 12 August 2021, the Directorate of Tribal Welfare, A & N islands, a body meant to protect the rights of the tribal communities and to ensure that the various regulations and policies are implemented, issued an undertaking that any exemptions from the regulations, laws and policies required for the project would be obtained by it, thereby violating the very objective of the Directorate. A year later, on 12 August 2022, a special Gram Sabha meeting was held in which it was decided that part of the tribal reserve land within the boundaries of the island would be diverted for the 'holistic development of Great

Nicobar' and another portion of land, outside the current tribal reserve, and on a different part of the island, would be added to the tribal reserve. We are unaware of any provision in the law which allows such a switch to be done; and all this without the willingness of the tribal groups concerned. Four days later, on 16 August, the NOC for the diversion of tribal reserve land was signed by the BDO, the Pramukh, Andaman Adim Janjati Vikas Samiti representative (AAJVS) (for the Shompen), and the Chairman of the Tribal Council (for the Nicobarese). On 25 August 2022 the Nicobarese, having become aware that the land that was agreed to be diverted was their own former ancestral home lands, wrote to the Lieutenant Governor requesting for relocation to their pre-tsunami villages of Chingenh and Pulo Babhi (this area was now the proposed site for the port and the airport of the project). On 23 September 2022, a meeting chaired by the DC Nicobar was held with the Tribal Council to discuss the matter of their relocation. The officers again tried to persuade the Nicobarese not to insist on going back, with the promise of making available all facilities at their current resettlement sites. But the Tribal Council stuck to their stand. Therefore, another meeting was proposed to be held by the officers. This meeting was, however, never held.

Despite the Nicobarese's insistence on returning to their ancestral settlements, both forest clearance and environment clearance were given to the Great Nicobar Holistic Development Project on 27 October and 11 November 2022 respectively. The lands involved covered the original home lands of the Nicobarese. Shortly thereafter, on 22 November 2022, the Tribal Council sent a letter withdrawing their NOC for diversion of their lands, mentioning that they had not been informed earlier that the land being earmarked for development included areas where the group lived prior to the tsunami. They stated that they were completely dependent on forests in their original homes and they wanted to go back to foraging and tending to plantations on their lands, and rearing domestic animals, rather than working as manual labour in

menial jobs, as they do at present. They said that losing access to their lands would be damaging both to their future generations and to their 'Shompen brothers'.

It will thus be seen that the Nicobarese have consistently been unwilling to give their consent to the diversion of their ancestral homelands, which they had used until the tsunami of 2004. They have also been asking to be sent back to their pre-tsunami settlement areas since 2007. That they agreed at one point of time to the diversion of tribal reserve land can be ascribed to their lack of knowledge of the areas proposed to be used for the project, their lack of awareness of their rights, and the insistence of the administrative authorities. Even so, the Tribal Council (of the Nicobarese) withdrew the consent they had given earlier for diversion of their tribal reserve land as soon as they could.

The Shompen, meanwhile continue to live, cultivate and collect food resources from the forests, little aware that some of their forests would soon be taken away.

Several people have written to the government objecting to the use of tribal reserve land for the project, among them the anthropologists of the Indian Anthropological Association. They wrote to the Andaman Nicobar Pollution Control Committee ahead of the public hearing, stressing the need to take great care when clearing the project, particularly where it concerned the lands of the Shompen and the Great Nicobarese. They emphasised the damage that would occur if the project came too close to the dwellings or foraging grounds of the Shompen. They too mentioned that the Nicobarese were anxious to return to their pre-tsunami settlements. Yet all these calls for caution have gone unheeded and the project has been cleared despite the damage it will cause to these defenceless tribal people.

As the National Commission for Scheduled Tribes (NCST), you are mandated under Article 338 of the Constitution to oversee the implementation of the safeguards provided to the Scheduled Tribes under the Constitution or under any other law for the time being in

force. For the tribes of the islands this would mean, the Andaman and Nicobar (Protection of Aboriginal Tribes) Regulation, 1956. This Regulation governs the statutory safeguards applicable to the tribes in these islands and overrides any law, agreement, court decree or order inconsistent with it. All Acts, including the Forest (Conservation) Act, 1980 and the Environment (Protection) Act, 1986, would, in our opinion, be subordinate to this regulation.

Under Art 338A (9) of the Constitution, the Union and every State Government is meant to consult the NCST on all major policy matters affecting Scheduled Tribes. We are aware that in this major matter of a mega project coming up in Great Nicobar, displacing the vulnerable tribes from their traditional forest and tribal reserve areas, this consultation has not been done. We are happy that on learning of this, a notice has been sent on 20 April 2023 by your Commission to the Andaman and Nicobar Administration asking them to explain the facts of the matter within fifteen days. This letter was sent on a complaint made by Dr EAS Sarma, a former Secretary in the Union Finance Ministry, and an expert on tribal matters.

We would like to add our voice to that of Dr Sarma and of the many others who have expressed their concern about the many flaws in the clearances given and the damage that the displacement will cause to the tribal groups. We hope you will look into this matter thoroughly and ensure that a project meant for the holistic development of Great Nicobar does not result in the immiseration and ultimate extinction of these highly vulnerable tribal communities, whose original and only home the island is.

SATYAMEVA JAYATE

Yours sincerely,

Constitutional Conduct Group (70 signatories)

OPEN LETTER TO HON'BLE PRESIDENT OF INDIA—UNDESIRABLE DEVELOPMENT OF GREAT NICOBAR ISLAND

22 January 2023

Hon'ble Rashtrapatiji, Smt. Droupadi Murmu,
We are a group of former civil servants of the All India and Central Services who have worked with the Central and State Governments in the course of our careers. As a group, we have no affiliation with any political party but believe in impartiality, neutrality and commitment to the Constitution of India.

We are heartened by your recent words at the Human Rights Day celebrations on 10 December 2022, wherein you stated that the concept of justice should be expanded to include the environment. You said 'just as the concept of human rights exhorts us to consider every human being as no different from ourselves, we should treat the whole living world and its habitat with respect'.

However, even as you say this, the Government of India is all set to destroy one of the most pristine habitats in the country, one which is home to various rare and endemic species, as well as to an extremely vulnerable tribe, the Shompens of Great Nicobar.

The plans for a massive development project on the island of Great Nicobar consist of an international container transhipment terminal, a large green field international airport, a township, and a solar and gas-based power plant, to be set up over 16,610 hectares. Considering that the entire island of Great Nicobar covers 1,03,870 hectares, almost 16 per cent of the island will be given over to the project. Of the total area of the island, 75,100 hectares have been statutorily notified as a Tribal Reserve for the Shompen tribe, a Particularly Vulnerable Tribal Group (PVTG). These shy and isolated tribal people, who are almost on the brink of extinction, need to be handled with extreme care and sensitivity, not carelessly removed from their existing home territory and resettled elsewhere on the island to make room for the 'development project'. The Shompens have, from time to time, experienced serious incursions by outsiders

into their area. The National Commission for Scheduled Tribes is aware of this matter and has instructed the government to prevent such intrusions. Instead of taking heed of this, the government itself is now all set to make a major intrusion.

Apart from the human dimensions, there is no denying the immense adverse impact that the project will have on the ecology of the island. Great Nicobar covers a variety of unique and threatened eco systems—tropical, wet evergreen forests, mountain ranges reaching 642 metres above sea level and coastal plains. It is home to myriad species of angiosperms, gymnosperms, ferns and bryophytes, as well as to hundreds of species of fauna, many of which are rare and threatened species, not found anywhere else in the world. These include endemic or endangered species such as the crab eating macaque, the Nicobar tree shrew, the dugong, the Nicobar megapode, the salt water crocodile, the Nicobar cricket frog and several others. All these are seriously threatened and will quite possibly be rendered extinct by the enormous 'development project' proposed to be taken up.

Although an Environment Impact Assessment (EIA) was carried out for the project, it is clear from the published reports that the scope of the analysis was limited. The persons involved with the environmental appraisal were reportedly advised that the project was a 'given' and were asked to try and minimise the impact. The airfield, being a defence project, was not even part of the mandate. No one was authorised to check if alternative arrangements and/or relocation of the project were feasible. The entire exercise seemed to presume that the project would be good for the islands and the country and lead to rapid development. We strongly believe that this presumption may not be valid.

We are pained to learn that the Ministry of Environment, Forests and Climate Change has not only granted environmental and coastal regulation zone (CRZ) clearance with certain conditions, it has also given an 'in principle' clearance for diversion of 13,075 hectares of forest land, with compensatory afforestation to be carried out in the

State of Haryana. The idea of replacing the virgin forests of Great Nicobar with planted forests in Haryana would be laughable if it weren't so tragic: 13,075 acres of rich, evergreen, rain forests teeming with extraordinary flora and fauna species to be compensated with newly planted trees in the dry Aravalli hills of Haryana!

Several recent occurrences should have discouraged the government from undertaking such a major environment-destroying project. The first is the decision taken on 19 December 2022 at the Conference of Parties for the Convention for Biological Diversity, at which it was agreed, among other things, to halt and reverse biodiversity loss by 2030; also, specifically, to protect 30 per cent of the world's lands, inland waters, coastal areas and oceans with emphasis on areas of particular importance for biodiversity and ecosystem functioning and services. This decision which was ratified by nearly 200 countries, including India, specifically mentions 'reducing to near zero the loss of areas of high biodiversity importance, including ecosystems of high ecological integrity'. Considering such a commitment, it is baffling how India can even consider the loss of such an enormously ecologically important area like Great Nicobar.

The all too palpable change in the climate of India—unbelievably hot temperatures in summer, erratic rainfall, repeated cyclones, mild winters in most of the country but sharp falls in temperature in the north, should also have sent alarm signals to the government. The changes in climate throughout the country and all over the world have made it apparent to even the casual observer that a warmer world is here to stay; and that urgent measures need to be taken by the government and the people to keep the increase in temperatures to a minimum. Stopping the denudation of existing forests, especially rich, virgin rainforests and adding to the existing forest cover are obviously the major steps needed.

The subsidence of land in Joshimath is a glaring indication of the damage that unthinking development can do to the country. Destroying the forests and the ecology of Great Nicobar to set up

container terminals and airports would be a mistake of the same order. The frequent prevalence of undersea quakes that occur in the oceans of that region and the resultant subsidence of land in the islands is also a major risk.

Our opposition to the proposed development in Great Nicobar should not be construed as opposition to development or technology in general. It is because of the particular vulnerability of Great Nicobar that we are concerned. Experience has shown that what starts out as a small 'development project' in a vulnerable locality keeps expanding inexorably, leading to a total destruction of the environment in which it is situated. The ecology and tribal people of Great Nicobar are far too precious to India and the world at large to be sacrificed on the altar of 'development'.

The Andaman and Nicobar archipelago is a group of rare volcanic islands with among the very few surviving rainforests in the world. Its preservation, and the conservation of some of the rarest surviving pristine tribal communities anywhere in the world, has earned for our country and our government a standing as champions of the environment in an ecologically threatened world. This carefully nurtured reputation will be totally lost in one fell swoop if this project goes forward

Having assumed the leadership of the G-20 group of nations this year, India should surely demonstrate that economic development does not, and should not, have to be at the expense of the environment, and that protecting the environment is the wisest of economic decisions.

We earnestly request you to advise your government to immediately stop the commencement of destructive projects in Great Nicobar.

SATYAMEVA JAYATE

Yours faithfully,

Constitutional Conduct Group (87 signatories)

LETTER TO THE PRIME MINISTER ON DISTURBING DEVELOPMENTS IN LAKSHADWEEP

5 June 2021

The Hon'ble Prime Minister of India
Cc: The Hon'ble Minister for Home Affairs, Govt. of India
Cc: The Hon'ble Minister for Environment & Forests, Govt. of India

Dear Prime Minister,
We are a group of former civil servants of the All India and Central Services who have worked with the Central and State Governments in the course of our careers. As a group, we have no affiliation with any political party but believe in impartiality, neutrality and commitment to the Constitution of India. We write to you today to register our deep concern over disturbing developments taking place in the pristine Union Territory (UT) of Lakshadweep in the name of 'development'.

Lakshadweep occupies a unique place in India's geographic and cultural diversity. It is an ecologically sensitive coral archipelago located off the Malabar coast consisting of 36 islands (of which 10 are inhabited and one developed as a tourist resort) spread out over 32 sq. km in the Indian Ocean, with a Muslim majority population of around 65,000 that is matrilineal, largely egalitarian, and ethnically close to Kerala, from where it was ruled through much of its history. According to the Scheduled Castes and Scheduled Tribes list (modification orders), 1956, the inhabitants of Lakshadweep are treated as Scheduled Tribes.

Mindful of the intimate and symbiotic bonds between the land, climate, culture and livelihoods of the local population, the Central government has, over the decades, tried to pursue an environmentally sound and people-centric development policy towards the islands through a centrally appointed Administrator guided by a specially constituted Island Development Authority for the island territories of India, chaired by the Prime Minister.

In 1988, the Authority approved a framework for development of India's island territories that concluded that: 'An environmentally sound strategy for both island groups hinges on better exploitation of marine resources coupled with much greater care in the use of land resources.'

Since then, scientists and climate experts have been documenting the threats to the coral atolls protecting the islands, from increasing human activity, climate change and rising sea levels, and warning that the coral reefs around some of the islands such as Kavaratti are declining beyond their power of regeneration and threatening their very existence. The need to pursue environment and climate sensitive policies in fragile ecologies becomes even more relevant with the Prime Minister himself reaffirming India's commitment to climate change and the upcoming COP 26 meeting in the UK.

Although there have been pressures for more aggressive development over the years at the cost of the islanders, and the administration of the islands, staffed at higher levels by officers from the AGMUT cadre, is open to the charge of paternalism, this island sensitive pattern of development has held so far. The assumption of additional charge of Administrator of Lakshadweep by Shri P.K. Patel, Administrator of Dadra and Nagar Haveli, Daman and Diu in December 2020 threatens to undo this paradigm entirely. Since taking charge, he has introduced drafts of three regulations—the Lakshadweep Development Authority Regulation (LDAR), the Lakshadweep Prevention of Anti-Social Activities Regulation (commonly known as PASA or the Goonda Act elsewhere), and the Lakshadweep Animal Preservation Regulation (LAPR)—as well as an amendment to the Lakshadweep Panchayat Regulations that have generated widespread anxiety in Lakshadweep and the nation at large. These drafts have been introduced without local consultation and are presently with the Ministry of Home Affairs, Government of India for necessary approvals.

It is clear that each of these draft regulations is part of a larger agenda that is against the ethos and interests of the islands

and islanders. Claiming that there has been no development in Lakshadweep for the past seventy years, the LDAR reflects a model of land and tourism development which includes resorts, hotels and beachfronts on the 'Maldives model' unmindful of the differences between the two island groups in size, population, number of islands and their spread. Draft provisions that permit 'building, engineering, mining, quarrying or other operations in, on, over or under land, the cutting of a hill or any portion thereof or the making of any material change in any building or land or in the use of any building including sub-division of any land' for highways etc. in small islands that barely exceed 3-4 km in length, constitute a serious threat to the fragile ecosystem of Lakshadweep.

Besides ignoring the unique geography of the UT and its community life, the LADR also vests arbitrary and draconian powers in the Administrator to acquire, alter, and transfer properties and/or remove or relocate islanders from their property, for town planning or any developmental activity that he decides is necessary, threatening the islanders' rights to possess and retain their property. The administration has already razed beach huts, storing boats, nets and other fishing equipment of local fishermen, presumably to clear beaches for tourism development, alleging that they had encroached onto government land and citing violations of the Coastal Regulation Zone rules and the Coast Guard Act, even though the fishermen were exempt from Coastal Regulation Zone rules.

Concerns over dispossession of land, predatory corporate development and destruction of the environment have been compounded by the draft PASA, a preventive detention regulation that enables the Administrator to detain any person for up to a year for common crimes (like anti-social behaviour, smuggling contraband drugs and liquor, involvement in immoral traffic, land grabbing, cyber-crimes, sexual offences or damaging the environment). National security concerns in a sensitive maritime area, including infiltration of terrorists and arms, have also been cited in support of the Regulation. In a territory where, according

to the National Crime Records Bureau, crime rates are very low compared to the rest of India, it has generated fears that the real purpose of the Regulation is to smother dissent or protests against the policies and actions of the Administrator or on any other issue.

Other regulations proposed by the Administrator target food and dietary habits and religious injunctions of the local islanders, 96.5 per cent of whom are Muslims. The LAPR will, if passed into law, effectively ban the killing of bovine animals and prohibit the consumption, storage, transport or sale of cattle meat in an island environment where there are inherent limits to livestock development. No such prohibitions apply to several states in the Northeast and even the state of Kerala next door. Inexplicably, a government run dairy farm producing milk for the islanders has been shut down by the Administrator. Stringent conditions for fitness certificates for animals to be slaughtered will make the slaughtering of any animal very difficult.

In addition, in an island territory where fruits, vegetables, cereals and pulses have to be supplied and distributed from the mainland by sea and are frequently not fresh, where fishing is risky during the monsoon months, and meat is part of their daily diet, non-vegetarian food has been arbitrarily removed from mid-day school meals. A ban on the sale and consumption of alcohol in keeping with the religious sensitivities of the overwhelmingly Muslim population has been lifted, once again ostensibly to promote tourism, giving both the beef ban and lifting of prohibition on alcohol an avoidable communal colour in a sensitive maritime region where communal disharmony could harm national security.

The changes being proposed by the Lakshadweep Panchayat Regulation, 2021 for elections to gram panchayats that will disqualify candidates with more than two children from contesting seats for the gram panchayat too have been proposed without any local consultation or taking into account local sensitivities. Other arbitrary actions like the shutting down of schools in the islands 'to reduce public expenditure' and terminating employment of youth working

in different departments before the completion of their tenure, have added to the unhappiness of the islanders with the Administrator. Another inexplicable recent modification excludes Beypore port (Kozhikode) from the three ports connecting Lakshadweep to the mainland (Kochi and Mangaluru being the others), compounding the perennial problem of connectivity of the dispersed north-south island chain with the mainland.

The District Dweep Panchayat led by the 'President cum Chief Counsellor' is the only elected local body in Lakshadweep in an archipelago already perceived to be ruled by remote central administrators, with whom there exists a linguistic barrier. Rather than undermining its status and sanctity, the Dweep Panchayat is the obvious forum for consultation for new legislation, particularly those as disruptive as the LDAR, PASA and LAPR. It could be empowered instead of being ridden rough shod over. Without such consultations with local bodies, the Lakshadweep Development Authority and the powers vested in it, will be seen as just grabbing land for real estate and tourism interests.

The arrival of the Administrator has also aggravated problems relating to COVID. Until his appointment in December 2020, Lakshadweep did not report a single case of COVID-19. With his arrival and occasional visits, mandatory quarantine guidelines and SOPs for those arriving from the mainland (taking into account its small island character, density of population and rudimentary health facilities) have been relaxed, leading to the first reported case of COVID-19 on 18 January 2021, the first COVID death on 24 February 2021, 8,479 cumulative cases and 35 deaths as of date, leading to a total lockdown situation until recently.

Each of these measures smacks not of development but of alien and arbitrary policy making, in violation of established practices that respect the environment and society of Lakshadweep. Taken together, the actions and far-reaching proposals of the Administrator, without due consultation with the islanders, constitute an onslaught on the very fabric of Lakshadweep society, economy and landscape

as if the islands were just a piece of real estate for tourists and tourism investors from the outside world. They threaten to deprive the local population of their lands and livelihoods for an alien and exploitative model of development for the benefit of others in which they may at best occupy the lowest rung of service providers, that will disrupt traditional lifestyles, food, customs, society and social harmony and impose alien lifestyles, seriously and irreversibly damage the island's fragile egology and threaten the peace and tranquillity of the island. There have already been protests against these policies by the islanders as well as political figures from the island, neighbouring Kerala and political parties.

The present Administrator's various measures, including the introduction of the three new Regulations and the modification of an existing Regulation, seem entirely misconceived, opening the islands to predatory development and threatening to disrupt and displace a peaceful island community and change their lives for the worse. We urge that these measures be withdrawn forthwith, the UT be provided with a full-time, people-sensitive and responsive Administrator, and that an appropriate development model that emphasises access to safe and secure healthcare, education, just governance, food security and livelihood options linked to the ecosystem, in consultation with islanders, be put in place, building on the achievements thus far. Such a model of sustainable development of the coral atolls will highlight our commitment to environmental conservation while also improving the living standards of the people of Lakshadweep. That our letter to you is sent on World Environment Day is an affirmation of our unshakeable conviction that human life is firmly tied to the earth.

SATYAMEVA JAYATE

Yours sincerely.

Constitutional Conduct Group (93 signatories)

AFTERWORDS

A Beacon for Democracy

India is today hurtling deeper and deeper into a place of darkness. In many ways, this is democracy's most difficult hour in the journey so far of the Indian republic.

Every democratic institution is today under grave attack, and each have crumbled to varying degrees. The Parliament barely functions. The judiciary is not consistent in its defence of both human rights and religious freedoms. The Election Commission is no longer trusted to be non-partisan. The collapse of the civil services has been abject. India's vibrant and assertive media has been transformed into cheerleaders of the ruling regime, or worse into purveyors of hate and defenders of crony capital.

Democratic freedoms are in tatters. Fear dominates all spaces of public articulation: politics, the media, social media, academia, culture and civil society. Dissent comes with such a high cost that more and more people are choosing silence.

What makes this period even more ominous is that the gargantuan power of an authoritarian state is ranged against three of its paramount ideological enemies: India's Muslim (and sometimes Christian) minorities; the frighteningly shrinking band of liberal left-leaning dissenters; and—as was displayed in the response of the Indian government to the COVID-19 pandemic—to the informal working poor.

At the heart of the bitter contestation underway in India's public life is the Constitution itself, and most of all of its pledge of equal citizenship to people of every faith, caste, gender, language and ethnicity. It is this contestation that makes the role of the Constitutional Conduct Group (CCG) so significant. This band of

retired civil servants—diplomats, administrators, policepersons, public accountants and others—have not only occupied a range of high offices, but even more significantly include many women and men who have earned formidable reputations for their integrity, competence and public services.

This voluntary, loose and highly democratic collective stands in vigil for public acts that threaten India's constitutional pledges, and its secular democratic credentials. This work is formidable. Barely a week passes without some news pouring in of grave assaults on freedoms and fraternity, of lynching and hate attacks, of runaway hate speech by people in high public office, of evidence of elite capture, of questionable benefits to big business, of perilous compromises with environmental protection, and of charging journalists, intellectuals and activists of grave crimes, and often their incarceration, at times for years without bail, but with no opportunity for them to prove their innocence.

The members of the CCG debate are alert to each such potential attack on India's secular democratic constitutional arrangements, and frequently propose public statements calling out these public acts and seeking their reversal or redress. These proposals are vigorously debated among the members. There are often differences between them of evaluation and the proposed actions, even the language of each public statement. The quality of these debates that daily crowd my mailbox never fail to invigorate me.

I take immense heart that these former public servants of impeccable reputations—some of them in their eighties and even in their nineties—care so deeply that their country is swerving away from the pathways of justice, liberty, equality and fraternity that were imagined in the freedom struggle and promised in the Constitution. In times that seem so dark that even my usually robust optimism begins to slip, the conviction and courage of my colleagues of the CCG help restore my sense of hope that we will overcome.

The CCG has also been a precious source of personal strength to me. Almost every investigating federal agency is today charging

or investigating me and the organisations I am associated with, with many of the country's gravest crimes. The agencies include the police, the Home Ministry, the Central Bureau of Investigation, the Enforcement Directorate (charged with investigating money-laundering and high financial crime) and the Income Tax Department. The charges include hate-mongering and aiding in terror conspiracies, money-laundering, grave financial misdemeanours, and more recently writing articles against the sovereignty of the nation. The punishment so far remains mainly of process. The social media is filled with innuendo and defamation. Most of the staff has left, partly because of the sustained witch-hunt, partly because there is almost no money to pay their salaries. Responding to the summons requiring regular mountains of paper becomes increasingly more challenging because not more than a handful of staff remain, mainly driven by loyalty. Pro bono lawyers stand for us in court, but the cases deliberately barely move, while the sword of possible incarceration always hangs over your head.

My resolve through all of this is that nothing the government does should allow the silencing of my public voice, and our work. Most important for me in these times is the 'Karwan e Mohabbat' or 'Caravan of Love'. We continue to travel and speak out in every corner of the country that is set alit by hate violence—most recently Manipur, Assam, Haryana, Bihar, and Uttarakhand. We continue to help fight a few hundred cases for justice and compensation for the survivors of hate violence. We continue to file criminal complaints against hate speeches, by senior leaders and in the media. We continue to offer pensions to widows and school support to the families, totalling around a hundred, of those killed in hate violence. We still make short films reporting hate speech and violence and also stories of humanity. I have not allowed my office to be shut, paying part of the rent from my pocket.

How has all of this been possible? After all, the government has leaned on the very few Indian foundations left that were brave enough to still fund me, and every one of them has withdrawn. But

our efforts continue mainly with regular small donations from many friends and supporters. Prominent among these are many members of the CCG, who send regular contributions, often monthly, from their pensions. It is these contributions that translate into regular pensions for widows and parents who lost their loved ones to hate violence, to pay modestly for lawyers who fight for justice and compensation and against hate.

But even more precious than these contributions is the steady, shining solidarity that they represent. It means a lot to me when some CCG members publicly express unconditional faith in and support for my work and me, despite all the official charges that have been mounted against me. These remind me that I am not alone in the battles that I have chosen in defence of the Constitution, of equal rights, of justice, freedom and kindness.

When these times are behind us, as they must one day, the role of the CCG in standing firmly and publicly in defence of the morality of the Constitution, for peace, justice and human rights, for solidarity, for humanism and love, will be acknowledged for its iridescence.

—Harsh Mander

'In times of universal deceit—telling the truth is a revolutionary act'—George Orwell

The Orwell quotation manages to draw our attention to the shift in public discourse and the devaluation of human values. There was faith that the democratic system would protect peoples' lives and justice would prevail. But peoples' sensibilities have been taken over by the deliberate exploitation of religious prejudice and incitement to violence. The simple task of asking a question, of speaking the truth, requires courage and commitment in the climate of fear that is now the new normal.

I am an amphibian, a former civil servant who resigned to become a social activist.

The inclusion of some of us—former resigned civil servants turned civil society activists as members of the Constitutional Conduct Group (CCG)—has been graceful and equal. The collective belief in the CCG, that constitutional values are seminal to keep the integrity of the nation, has bonded us to walk the path resolutely.

The trajectory of my work led me from the civil service to an NGO, and finally to a peoples' political organisation. I have had an interesting dialectical relationship with the civil service. I resigned looking for more freedom and fewer rules to dictate my action. I went through disturbing encounters with the petty bureaucracy and even some senior district officers. Nevertheless, what it did establish was that you can step out of the civil service, but not out of governance.

In the campaign and struggle of the Mazdoor Kisan Shakti Sagathan (MKSS) for the Right to Information Act (RTI), Mahatma

Gandhi National Rural Employment Guarantee Act (MGNREGA) and other rights-based legislations, we learnt that we had to engage with the government and look for support amongst civil servants with integrity and commitment to Constitutional values. Mr S.R. Sankaran, a legendary civil servant is remembered by his fellow officers and the people, for his courage and probity while in service and afterwards. He gave critical support to public action, which fell within the constitutional frame at all times. The campaigns for the RTI and other rights-based campaigns in the early 2000s engaged in conversations across roles and sectors, and the discourse benefitted.

When Pehlu Khan was lynched in Alwar in 2017, the IAS68 Google group, of which I too was a member, wrote to Vasundhara Raje, then Chief Minister of Rajasthan, asking for justice. It made an impact on the decisions of the government. The CCG's many letters written subsequently at various points in time have similarly had an impact on government and public opinion. The members have used their freedom from the 'civil service conduct rules', and the hierarchy of political control, to speak for constitutional justice. In identifying with 'We, the people of India', the organised voices of former civil servants, underscore the basic guarantee of life and liberty, violated with impunity by the current dispensation.

People who are victims of the misuse of power, have increasingly realised the value of the Constitution. It plays a normative role of custodian and keeper of the values we gave ourselves in the Preamble. It is an ethical, cultural and political document that bonds a multi-sectoral and multi-cultural nation. For the oppressed, the Preamble of the Constitution reads like a democratic prayer and the Constitution itself is the '*Granth*' (text) for ethical public action. The collective voice of former civil servants has lent credibility to struggles otherwise dismissed as untrue, biased and even seditious. The CCG has shown courage at critical times, to magnify voices, to draw public attention to human rights violations and constitutional norms, with rational arguments.

With the open and flagrant violation of Constitutional equality and secularism, and the political demand of a 'Hindu Rashtra', struggles for rights have become even more basic. These fears can no longer be dismissed as unreal, as we receive reports that a new theocratic Hindu constitution is being drafted to replace the Constitution. The biggest assault in contemporary India has been on equality and secularism.

The articulation and protests of burgeoning civil society movements were gagged by restrictions on free speech and expression, for promoting economic and social integrity and struggling for rights. The ruthless incarceration of those who advocate these values or dissent has led to a culture of fear. Free speech has been the biggest casualty in the aftermath of hate speeches and violence, fostering a fear psychosis. The CCG has avoided getting embroiled in countering criticism, but instead resolutely carried on speaking truth to power.

The image of the CCG has grown from its tentative beginnings. Its considered voice has afforded a degree of support and courage to civil society campaigns that continue to wage their Constitutional battles against hunger, incarceration and violence. The Group retains its distinct identity, as separate from activists' positions, speaking for justice in measured tones. The CCG has also used other platforms where issues have been examined with logic, rigorous scrutiny and evidence, to demand the protection and implementation of Constitutional rights. I would like to mention in particular, the committee set up to look at the riots in northeast Delhi. It was remarkable, for its conception and courage, which validated the plight of many members of the minority community in a hostile environment.

It has also been able in part, to speak to the elite, and those in power who are often the most entrenched in the status quo, and averse to listening to the voices of the marginalised. It has strengthened the fragile hope that reason will still work in making justice and equality the basis for the future of governance and democracy in India.

Activists are always looking for platforms from where they can elicit support from different groups. The CCG has been an ethically comfortable and reassuring one. It has given me added moral support and psychological wellbeing, in these critical times. I would like to personally acknowledge and thank the pioneering group that quietly, and without fanfare set about the task of bringing us all together. This is no mean chore, given the fact that keeping any group of individuals with strong opinions together is always a huge challenge.

The unwavering and systematic voice of the CCG has vindicated the promise of its formation, to speak truth to power.

—Aruna Roy

Being a Part of the CCG

Why did I join the Constitution Conduct Group (CCG)? How did I hear of it? Who was the initiator who got me involved? And, lastly, why do I intend to be a part of this noble band till I finally close my eyes forever?

'They also serve who only stand and wait', wrote the poet whose name I am unable to recollect now, at this advanced age of 94.* I have never hesitated to stand up to what I felt was an injustice. In fact, that has been the one defining principle of my entire career of 36 years in the Indian Police Service. How could a set of malcontents, demanding a separate State of Khalistan, go about killing innocent citizens with the sole purpose of creating fear and terror? That was the question that troubled me in 1986 when I accepted the assignment that other officers, junior to me, had turned down.

A more subtle form of terror has gripped our country since 2014, when a majoritarian right-wing government was voted to power. A minority community is being targeted and terrorised on suspicion of slaughtering cows and their progeny or possessing the meat for consumption. Many were lynched to death! Cattle traders were routinely targeted, rendering them jobless.

The harassment also was extended to those young men of the community who dared to fall in love with girls of the majority community. They were accused of converting those love-lorn girls to Islam. That was termed as 'Love Jihad', fit to be fought by the

---

* The author here is referring to John Milton's sonnet 'When I consider how my light is spent'.

newly minted warriors of the majority, who went around scouring for such lads to teach them a lesson.

Some attempts to deprive members of the community of livelihood were also reported. Muslim butchers, cattle traders and meat sellers had already been rendered jobless. The goons then turned their attention to prevent Muslim street vendors from entering Hindu localities to sell fruits, vegetables or other wares. Lowly paid occupations like drivers, hired by middle-class car owners, were also picked on. The car owner would be advised on phone to discontinue the services of the poor man!

This was the scenario that was prevalent when a former IPS colleague approached me on behalf of one of the prime movers of the CCG. I met one of the members of the group, a former IAS officer of the Maharashtra cadre, who explained the concept of the CCG. What he told me about this group of retired civil servants convinced me that my days of merely standing and staring could be put behind. I could become more useful to my countrymen and women by speaking up against the injustices, which were coursing along merrily in the body politic.

My idea of India, where my ancestors have lived for thousands of years, was diametrically opposed to that of Mr Modi and the Sangh Parivar. As a member of a tiny minority community, and one who had a voice that would be heard, I decided that I would join this committed group of IAS, IFS and IPS officers who were ready to speak 'Truth to Power'. That was a task for the media to perform, but it was apparent, even at that stage when I first met members of the CCG, that Power had systematically eroded the willingness of a large chunk of the media to perform its traditional, democratically ordained role.

The CCG had partially filled this vacuum. Since the Modi-led version of the BJP is poles apart from the previous Vajpayee-led version, it will be criminally negligent on the part of liberal-minded citizens to become part of a herd that is being led by the nose. We have to speak up when instances of injustice confront us. At the

CCG's promptings I took up the case against the Delhi police when it so brazenly let off the BJP leaders responsible for rousing passions and feelings of hate against the Muslims who were peacefully protesting against the CAA. I wrote an open letter to the then Police Commissioner of Delhi which provoked *The Times of India* to pen an editorial in its newspaper the next day. Even Justice Murlidhar of the Delhi High Court had asked the Delhi Police the same questions that I had posed to its Chief. The poor Judge was transferred that very night. Fortunately, I was not in the government's service!

Now for question three: Why have I decided to be part of this group, called the CCG, which now boasts of nearly 200 like-minded members?

Well, for one, they are old civil servants who share with me the values that I have always cherished. They are all wedded to truth and justice, not to forget compassion, like I was. I dare say that many of my new friends in the CCG are left-oriented. I do not belong to that tribe, but I see no problem in consorting with them. The moot question is 'Do they pursue Truth and Justice?' I have not an iota of doubt that they do and, hence, I am comfortable and happy in their company.

Of all the thematic categories that CCG's published letters deal with, the 'Politics of Communal Hate and Violence' is the one which interests me the most. When I returned to my city—Mumbai—from Romania in December 1993, I got involved in the 'Mohalla Committee Movement', which sought to address the alienation felt by our Muslim brothers and sisters and the suspicions of Hindu and Muslim slum-dwellers about each other. Our work helped the police to avert many a difficult situation of the communally charged variety. Successive Police Commissioners had acknowledged our contribution to peace in the city.

In our latest general meeting of the Mohalla Committee Movement Trust that mentors a host of committed grassroots workers, the feedback was disturbing. Subtle attempts to disturb the understanding that dictates the interaction between the two major

communities and the police that is the bedrock of our measures to assure peace in the various mohallas, have become evident. We hope for saner counsels to prevail, just as the CCG waits for its voice to be heard in order that a more compassionate Bharat emerges.

—*Julio Ribeiro*

My Engagement with the Constitutional Conduct Group

Only a few would have imagined that Indian democracy would be so fragile.

Of course, there are occasional voices of concern and protest at the deteriorating situation, mostly from diehard liberals, some journalists, especially women, and only sometimes, from mainstream political parties.

One such voice of dissent is the Constitutional Conduct Group—a small, informal group of retired civil servants, mostly in their 70s, voicing their deep concern over the slow decline of constitutional values. At present, it has 176 members. The number is surprisingly low. And I keep thinking why so few of my former colleagues are unconcerned about the state of our polity and the direction we have been made to take.

It cannot be ignorance or lack of commitment to the values, which they would have cherished during their career in civil services. Even the events of Manipur do not seem to bother them. 'Whataboutery' is a common refrain.

I keep wondering if it is fear? Or if it is the commitment to a new ideology? It cannot be that the mainstream TV channels have influenced such a well-informed and successful group of citizens. Some friends call it an awakening from a long slumber.

In this rather gloomy scenario, the Constitutional Conduct Group provides succor and hope—that there are some who care about the right direction and the future of the nation; about the true idea of India, a highly diverse nation where diverse people have

lived and can live together in peace. It could be a unique Indian contribution to multi-culturalism.

This idea has lately been under threat.

The first letter written by the CCG on 10 June 2017 was about the growing climate of religious intolerance. We have traveled a long distance since then, regrettably in the wrong direction. Hate speech has become so common that now even the liberal media does not find it newsworthy. It is to the credit of the common masses that they have not been entirely taken in by hate speech notwithstanding several instances of mob violence against hapless victims where the perpetrators were welcomed. And occasionally garlanded too.

The CCG has been highlighting the need to check this violence before it takes the form of mass violence. Even though the Group's calls have only occasionally been heeded, I get the satisfaction in knowing that so many of my former seniors and colleagues have not hesitated in coming forward to draw attention to such gross violation of constitutional provisions.

Another area of concern to the CCG has been the integrity of elections. Letters have been addressed to the Election Commission of India to ensure the impartiality and integrity of elections. Many members of the CCG have firsthand experience of conducting elections. So, we do reasonably expect the Commission to address the various issues raised by the CCG relating not only to the day of voting but also the entire process leading to an impartial and free election. The biggest challenge before the eighteenth Lok Sabha elections in April-May 2024 will be hate news. We can only hope that the Election Commission will be cognizant of the CCG's anxieties and will take remedial action.

The next few years may be very challenging for those who respect the Constitution and hold its values dear. It is well known that there have been efforts to frame a new Constitution. Senior functionaries of the Government have publicly mentioned such a need, though this is an old dream.

As early as February 2000, the Vajpayee Government had set up a National Commission to Review the Working of the Constitution (NCRWC) under the chairmanship of Justice Venkatachaliah. The Commission did not suggest an entirely new Constitution though it recommended several amendments. Successive governments have however not accepted its recommendations.

If there are renewed efforts to frame one now, Ambedkar's Constitution may not survive in its current spirit and form. It means that the CCG may have its hands full as several constitutional values cherished over the years, from federalism to secularism, to reservations in legislatures, may not find a place in it. In fact, it may also take India in the direction of a Presidential form of Government. As a sign of current times, such changes are unlikely to be challenged in mainstream media and judicial scrutiny may take long years to even hear the challenge, even if it is mounted.

It is my earnest hope and desire that the CCG endures its vigil and continues to offer a platform for those who share the vision of a truly democratic, federal and inclusive India.

—Siraj Hussain

About the Contributors

Aakar Patel is an author, activist and columnist who has edited English and Gujarati newspapers. His translation of Saadat Hasan Manto's Urdu non-fiction, *Why I Write*, was published in 2014. His study of majoritarianism in India, *Our Hindu Rashtra: What It Is. How We Got Here*, was published in 2020. And his analysis of India's performance under Prime Minister Narendra Modi, *Price of the Modi Years*, was published in 2021. He is the chair of Amnesty International India.

Anjana Prakash is a senior advocate at the Supreme Court, and a former judge of the Patna High Court, where she rose to be among the ranks of the topmost criminal lawyers in the country. She was among the first women to be elevated to the position of senior advocate at the Patna High Court. She is interested in child rights and civil liberties, and has acted as *amicus curiae* in multiple cases.

Anjali Bhardwaj is an Indian social activist working on issues of transparency and accountability. She is a co-convenor of the National Campaign for People's Right to Information (NCPRI) and a founding member of the Satark Nagrik Sangathan. She works on issues related to right to information, Lokpal, whistleblower protection, grievance redress, and right to food.

Apoorvanand is a professor at the Hindi Department, Faculty of Arts, University of Delhi. His critical essays have appeared in all major Hindi journals. Apart from his academic and literary writings, he is a regular columnist at *The Indian Express* and *The Wire*, and also frequently writes on other platforms such as *Scroll.in*,

Satya Hindi, Al Jazeera, and *The Kochi Post*. Apoorvanand has also appeared on Indian television as a panelist on issues concerning Higher Education, language and communalism.

Aruna Roy is an Indian social activist, professor, union organiser and former civil servant. She is the president of the National Federation of Indian Women and the founder of the Mazdoor Kisan Shakti Sangathan. Roy was awarded the Times Fellowships Award in 1991 for her work for rural workers' rights to social justice and creative development. In 2000, she received the Ramon Magsaysay Award for Community Leadership and in 2010, she received the Lal Bahadur Shastri National Award for Excellence in Public Administration, Academia and Management.

Dr E.A.S. Sarma was a member of the Indian Administrative Service from 1965-2000, and has held senior positions in the Government of Andhra Pradesh and was Secretary to the Government of India in the Ministries of Power and Finance. He was earlier Principal Adviser (Energy) in the National Planning Commission, and was closely associated in setting up independent statutory regulatory bodies in the electricity, telecommunications and insurance sectors in India. After retirement from the IAS, he headed the Administrative Staff College of India, Hyderabad.

G.N. Devy is an Indian cultural activist, literary critic and former professor of English. He is known for the People's Linguistic Survey of India and the Adivasi Academy. He is credited with starting the Bhaashaa Research and Publication Centre. He writes in three languages—Marathi, Gujarati and English—and has written and edited close to ninety books in areas including Literary Criticism, Anthropology, Education, Linguistics and Philosophy. His first full-length book in English, *After Amnesia* (1992), was awarded the Sahitya Akademi Award in 1993. Devy has also received the SAARC Writers' Foundation Award (2001) for his work with denotified tribals and was awarded the Padma Shri in 2014.

Harsh Mander is one of India's most trusted and courageous social justice and human rights activists. He is the director of the Centre for Equity Studies, a research organisation based in New Delhi, and has also served as a special monitor for the National Human Rights Commission to the detention centres for 'declared foreigners' in Assam. He is also the author of several acclaimed books including *Looking Away: Inequality, Prejudice and Indifference in New India; Ash in the Belly: India's Unfinished Battle Against Hunger; Locking Down the Poor: The Pandemic and India's Moral Centre; Burning Pyres, Mass Graves: India's COVID Tragedy;* and *Fatal Accidents at Birth: Stories of Oppression and Struggle.*

Julio Ribeiro is a former IPS officer. Ribeiro served as Director General of the Punjab Police during the worst years of terrorism in Punjab. He was also the Special Secretary to the Government of India in the Ministry of Home Affairs, an Adviser to the Governor of Punjab, and the Indian Ambassador to Romania. In 1987, he was awarded the Padma Bhushan. Ribeiro's autobiography, *Bullet for Bullet: My Life as a Police Officer* was published in 1998.

Madan Lokur is an Indian jurist and the judge of the Supreme Court of Fiji. He is former judge of the Supreme Court of India, a former chief justice of the Andhra Pradesh High Court and Gauhati High Court and a judge of the Delhi High Court.

Neera Chandhoke is a Distinguished Fellow at the Centre for Equity Studies, New Delhi. She was formerly the Professor of Political Science and the Director of the Developing Countries Research Centre at the University of Delhi. She has held several fellowships abroad and has authored many research papers and books. Some of her recent books include *We, the People, and Our Constitution* (2023), *Violence in Our Bones* (2021), *Rethinking Pluralism, Secularism, Tolerance: Anxieties of Co-Existence* (2019), *Democracy and Revolutionary Politics* (2015) and *Contested Secessions* (2012). She is a frequent contributor to print and online publications such as *The Hindu, The Wire, The Indian Express* and *The Tribune.*

Pamela Philipose is an Indian journalist and researcher, who is a senior fellow at the Indian Council of Social Science Research. She began her journalism career with *The Times of India* and has been a senior associate editor for *The Indian Express*, the director and editor-in-chief of *Women's Feature Service*, and a public editor for *The Wire*. She was the recipient of the Chameli Devi Jain Award for Outstanding Women Mediapersons in 1999 and has served as an advisor to the Media Task Force of the high level committee of the Government of India.

Prerna Singh Bindra is one of India's leading environmental journalists and travel writers, who has worked at daily newspapers like *The Asian Age, The Pioneer,* and *The Times of India* and has authored more than 1,500 articles on nature and wildlife in mainstream media. She is the editor of *Tigerlink*, a journal which collates and analyses information about tigers from across their range countries. She is also a visiting faculty member at the National Centre for Biological Sciences and has received the Carl Zeiss Wildlife Conservation Award.

Siraj Hussain joined the Indian Administrative Service in 1979 and has served both the Government of Uttar Pradesh and the Government of India in various capacities. He was posted as Union Secretary in the Ministries of Food Processing Industries and Agriculture, and several schemes of the first Modi government were formulated under his supervision as Secretary, Agriculture. Since his superannuation in January 2016, he has been working with the Indian Council for Research on International Economic Relations (ICRIER) as Visiting Senior Fellow. Hussain has authored several research papers on agriculture and rural economy and his columns have been published in several newspapers and online portals.